EARLY DOWNHOME
BLUES

EARLY DOWNHOME

BLUES

A Musical and Cultural Analysis

JEFF TODD TITON

S E C O N D   E D I T I O N

With a New Foreword by Alan Trachtenberg and a New Afterword by the Author

The University of North Carolina Press   Chapel Hill & London

Library of Congress Cataloging-in-Publication Data

Titon, Jeff Todd, 1943–

Early downhome blues : a musical and cultural analysis / by Jeff Todd
Titon ; with a new foreword by Alan Trachtenberg and a new afterword
by the author.

    p. cm. – (Cultural studies of the United States)

Originally published: Urbana : University of Illinois Press, c1977,
in series: Music in American life.

Includes bibliographical references and index.

ISBN 0-8078-2170-5 (cloth : alk. paper)

ISBN 0-8078-4482-9 (pbk. : alk. paper)

1. Blues (Music) – History and criticism. I. Title. II. Series.

ML3521.T58 1994

781.643'09 – dc20   94-6953

CIP

MN

Second edition © 1994
The University of North
Carolina Press
First edition © 1977
Board of Trustees of the
University of Illinois
Originally published by the
University of Illinois Press
Original publication of
this work was supported
in part by a grant from the
Andrew W. Mellon
Foundation.

The paper in this book meets the guidelines for permanence and
durability of the Committee on Production Guidelines for Book
Longevity of the Council on Library Resources.

98 97 96 95 94   5 4 3 2 1

FOR LAZY BILL LUCAS

CONTENTS

TRANSCRIPTIONS

FOREWORD by Alan Trachtenberg

      Already a classic of its kind, *Early Downhome Blues* now reappears with a new timeliness and relevance. A product of the folk revival of the 1960s, the book re-emerges now in the midst of another revival, another round of awakened interest in what many consider to be one of the nation's most compelling and seminal musical forms, African American blues. Jeff Titon's pioneering study of early country blues returns for a second life just when it can provide a major resource not only for scholars but also for an expanding public eager to know more about the blues yet still mired in ignorance and misunderstanding. As scholarship and analysis, and as an account of the author's own experiences of both research and musical participation, the book offers a feast of knowledge about the many facets of the subject: the origins of the blues in the experiences of country folk early in the twentieth century, the amazingly intricate and sophisticated musical forms that make up the blues, the industrial production of recorded blues as a cultural commodity, and the complex and contradictory amalgam of folk and commerce, country and city, black and white, which has developed into a modern culture of the blues. Blues names a realm or dimension within the entirety of American life, flooding beyond the boundaries of song into the worlds of dance, of dress, of romance and passion, of performance as such, a cultural presence near the heart (it perhaps *is* the heart) of what is distinctively national in the first place, the definition of "race" that suffuses all things American.

Readers today will find in the book's modest honesty, unpretentiousness, and integrity a source of wisdom regarding the issues that entangle us, whoever we are, as soon as the blues enters our minds as something to be thought about as well as something to entertain us. For blues names not just an autochthonous cultural form but also a realm of autochthonous American conflict and struggle. In regard to the study of the early blues and the struggle to comprehend or to produce its meanings today, the racial issues that are never far from the beat of the early songs are transposed into a new space of contest and challenge. What does the blues mean today, as historical heritage, as performative experience, as cultural event? By whom is this meaning determined? And who deserves the authority to say so? To whom does this heritage belong? How are heritages formed? How do they live in the continuing processes of culture, processes that are increasingly recognized as paradoxical and challenging, made up of overlapping and still conflicting cultural interests?

Blues are far from innocent; in themselves the songs are among the most worldly and sophisticated of inheritances from the American past for negotiating our lives as Americans. Neither can the blues as scholarly subject be innocent. In the study, the appreciation, and simply the experience of blues, we find ourselves caught up in questions of definition, authority, identity, nationality. In cultural origin, the blues may be black (even that is questionable as an absolute condition, for black life is unimaginable in total isolation from white life, and vice versa), but surely in its diffusion, the blues addresses and implicates white and black, however differently. For whites, the experience of the music is a nexus between white and black, a relationship, a form of interaction, and thus a challenge to one of the larger culture's constitutive premises – that white and black are inherently separate. For whites to feel and so to claim the blues as part of their own inheritance means to recognize what they share with blacks, to confront not only the part inequality and injustice play within a cultural inheritance but also the continuing presence of race-definition and the inequalities it projects in the making and remaking of a common culture.

The blues names an occasion, then, for all Americans to *feel* (as rhythm, as text, as innuendo) and to learn their common paradoxical condition: the interchangeability of race and culture within the national identity. *Early Downhome Blues,* the work of a white scholar who understands these matters, reappears at a time when its insights speak eloquently to contemporary issues. As interpretive scholarship, the book enlarges the context of discussion of the blues both as performance and as cultural expression.

"Downhome," Titon writes, is "a place in time and a state of mind"; he proceeds to show the link between place and mind, between social geography and cultural ecology. The book comes out of a conjunction of ethnomusicology and American studies, between a discipline of close textual analysis and an embracing perspective of cultural history. When it first appeared in 1977, the book represented something new in American studies, a cross-disciplinary academic study of the music in relation to culture; by combining transcription and analysis of music with the social history of performers and, in a brilliant chapter, an interpretation of "the cultural significance of race record advertisements," the book offered an early "cultural studies" model for popular music, one that returned the musical text to the life and experience of the performer, taking the performer's ideas and stated intentions into significant account. Although the author now feels, as he puts it in his new illuminating Afterword, that the book's synthesis of music and culture falls short of an ideal integration, his current view that "the proper object of our study is people making music rather than music 'in' culture or music 'as' culture" is exactly the view cultivated by the book as a whole. The discussion in the Afterword of blues as embodying an African American "approach to the world," a product of the tradition of "signifying," points a way toward making the integration of musical form and cultural practice even more potent.

The book also comes out of the author's "love of blues music," as he confesses. He reveals this not for the sake of adding to his credentials but to indicate a source of no small significance to the form and manner of the study itself, the respect and sympathy for the music and the musicians everywhere evident in the book. Himself an accomplished folk and blues musician, skilled instrumentalist and singer, Jeff Titon in a sense gives back in this book something of what he has gained from his several mentors among black artists. The narrative elements in the book link the study – the scholarship and the technical musical analysis – to the author's personal experience, his participation in his subject in the several roles of musician, interviewer, and interpreter (and, not incidentally, of picture-maker). He writes from both inside and outside the subject; as musician he shares, or at least sympathetically appreciates, the perspective of performers, the intricacies of the music, and the subtleties of the lyrics. An integrated cultural study, the book mingles close textual analysis with a cogent social portrait of the region of its origin; it places in a single focus the experience of performers, of their immediate audience, of the white entrepreneurs who in the 1920s recorded the music and marketed it as "race records," and of himself, as scholar, analyst, musician, and photographer. In its argument, *Early Downhome Blues* speaks vividly and wisely about early blues and how we might understand it as a product of place and mind. In its self-awareness and outgoingness, the book also gives us a mode of cultural studies rich with possibilities.

PREFACE

Downhome blues is folk music, but its earliest reliable documents are mass-culture artifacts: commercial phonograph records from the 1920s. Two kinds of blues songs were recorded in that decade: downhome and vaudeville. An easily audible but not always reliable distinction is that women sang vaudeville blues, accompanied by a pianist or a small group of jazz musicians, whereas men sang downhome blues, accompanying themselves on guitar. Put on "race records" – as the industry's segregated offerings for black Americans came to be known – blues songs were very successful; in the middle of the decade, for example, about as many race records were sold each year as there were black people living in the United States.[1]

Since 1959, when Samuel Charters surveyed the field,[2] most writers have used the adjective *country* to describe the blues I prefer to call *downhome*. (Black Americans employ both terms.) *Country* refers to a physical place: a rural landscape with a low population density, or, in the better words of Jo Jo Williams, where a town "ain't nothin' but a wide space in the highway." *Downhome* refers not to a place but to a spirit, a *sense* of place evoked in singer and listener by a style of music. The term *country* is troublesome because downhome blues songs were performed regularly in towns and cities and by people who grew up there. More important, since a structural definition of style is a description of something immediately and unconsciously recognized by native performers and listeners, the term *downhome* comes closer than does *country* to naming that feeling evoked by the recognition of the style. Most blues singers, asked "What is the blues?," do not respond with a structural definition; instead, they usually reply that blues is "a feeling." Leonard "Baby Doo" Caston expressed it eloquently: "Blues is a sound. It's not all the time the thing that rhyme; it's a feeling that a sound would put you into."[3] In the phrase *downhome blues,* the word *blues* indicates both a musical style based on particular sounds and a feeling associated with it; the juxtaposed *downhome* locates the feeling as a place in the mental landscape of black America.

As my subtitle indicates, *Early Downhome Blues* takes up music and culture; for music is, of course, a part of man's learned heritage. But there is good reason to suppose that a people's traditional music and the way they behave when performing it are symbolic expressions of broad cultural pattern and social organization.[4] Part I, therefore, considers the place of downhome blues within black American culture in the first quarter of this century, and the attitudes of the singers toward their music over a somewhat longer period. Part II subjects a representative sample of early recorded downhome blues songs to musical and textual analysis, and develops a description of downhome blues music sound which is at once an enumeration of melodic elements and a set of directions for their use: a productive system. This productive system is a model which may or may not correspond directly to the workings of the creative apparatus inside the blues singer's mind, but it serves the same purpose: it produces blues songs. It is, by analogy, like the system of molecular models which represents the chemical structure of compounds in such a way that their interactions are obvious and predictable under given conditions.[5]

When downhome blues songs were preserved and circulated on commercial recordings, they began to move, inevitably, into the larger American culture. Part III considers the early response of a representative group of urban white Americans – the record industry – to downhome blues and black culture during the Jazz Age. Scrutiny of the industry's use of plantation stereotype cartoons and urban jive talk in the advertisements for blues records placed in the black press reveals considerable anxiety toward the increasingly visible urban black. It also reveals the curious strategy the industry chose for dealing – or, rather, not dealing – with him. Turning its energy toward promoting downhome blues as the music of a folk group, the industry tried to befriend him, yet keep him safely in his place: on the farm, or newly arrived and in wonder at the city.

Before proceeding, I should like to make the distinction between the two kinds of early blues songs, vaudeville and downhome, more precise. Early vaudeville singers, such as Mamie Smith, Edith Wilson, Ma Rainey, Bessie Smith, Ida Cox, Ethel Waters, and Alberta Hunter, were black women with backgrounds in vaudeville and musical shows; versatile professionals, they took pride in their ability to deliver any kind of song. Billed as "queens" of the blues – advertisements pictured them with crowns – they dressed and acted the part, perhaps burlesquing the opera prima donna. By contrast, most of the men who sang downhome blues songs were farmers (or drifting seasonal laborers) entertaining their neighbors. Some had backgrounds in carnivals, minstrel shows, and medicine shows, where they had worn distinctive outfits and sung from a stage. But most downhome blues singing was more intimate, taking place at Saturday night parties in crowded juke joints, or outdoors, where listeners and dancers clustered around the singers. Despite the informal atmosphere of the downhome party, the singers considered themselves at least semiprofessional, for they asked for food, whiskey, and a little money in exchange for their services.

Vaudeville blues was popular music, not folk music. Its lyrics ordinarily were composed by a Tin Pan Alley of professional black tunesmiths who wrote sophisticated songs and skits for stage revues. The New York success of shows like *Shuffle Along* (1921) increased their prestige and made the singers even more anxious for their lyrics. Not surprisingly, most vaudeville blues songs from the 1920s remind today's listeners of musical comedies. Influenced by genteel white taste, the singers – with a few notable exceptions – strove for a sweet, mild vocal timbre and enunciated their words precisely, some even trilling their *r*'s; their delivery was intentionally dramatic. Downhome blues singers, on the other hand, obtained their lyrics by borrowing and trying to memorize traditional stanzas from other singers, which they mixed with idiosyncratic and improvised stanzas in most of their performances. Downhome blues timbre often was noisy and raspy; and the singers slurred their consonants, occasionally making it difficult for listeners to understand the words.

The women who sang vaudeville blues ordinarily did not accompany themselves on a musical instrument. If they sang in front of a small jazz group, the piano marked the beat, and the horns, "commenting" antiphonally, filled in the spaces left by pauses in the vocal, often with improvised lines. If a pianist was the sole accompanist, his stride bass usually marked the beat while his left hand played riffling fills in an elegant style far removed from the rough insistence of the blues and boogie heard in the Black Belt barrelhouses. Like the singers, the accompanists were music hall professionals, veterans of countless tours on the black stage circuit, or talented youngsters (such as Louis Armstrong). Downhome blues singers, on the other hand, almost always accompanied themselves, usually on guitar. Sometimes other singers and accompanists with portable instruments joined in. At a party in a tavern, someone was certain to sit down at the piano, if there was one on the premises. The instruments marked the beat and repeated riffs. Improvised responses were infrequent; instead, the accompaniments, like the tunes, were structural molds well set in advance to accommodate a variety of lyrics.

Downhome blues lyrics usually fell directly into three-line, AAB stanzas; that is, the second line repeated (sometimes with slight variation) the words in the first, and the third line completed the thought, with a rhyme at the close. Downhome blues lyrics, like vaudeville, took relations between lovers for a subject; but the downhome frame of reference was rural. Vaudeville blues lyrics, available in sheet music as well as on records, ordinarily began with a sung introduction, variable in form, in which the singer explained why she was blue. A blues section, frequently marked "tempo di blues," followed the introduction; usually it employed the three-line, AAB stanza. The structure of vaudeville blues owed a great debt to W. C. Handy, whose songs (e.g., "Memphis Blues," "St. Louis Blues") published a decade earlier had been responsible for a brief national blues craze. But what was only a fad among whites achieved a prominent place in black popular music, so that when blacks recorded vaudeville blues at the beginning of the 1920s, the industry was able to take advantage of an existing market.

When downhome blues was recorded later in the decade – it did not appear in quantity until 1926 – black Americans thought it somewhat old-fashioned, for downhome blues had been well established across the South before World War I. (In fact, Handy had drawn upon it for his compositions.) And, even though its form had proven malleable enough to change with the times, the musical situation which the records captured – male singers accompanying themselves on guitars – was sure to remind listeners of entertainment down home. Downhome blues songs do not sound like show tunes; nor, in most instances, do they sound like the folksongs of singers like Leadbelly, much of whose music was of an older generation (though he himself was not). Yet because the singers passed the songs on orally, because they relied on traditional lyrics, and because the songs show considerable, even deliberate, variation over space and time, early downhome blues is best regarded as folk music, despite the fact that many songs enjoyed additional circulation on commercial phonograph records, and despite the dangers of the implication that if downhome blues is folk music, then downhome black Americans must constitute a folk group.

Hearing downhome blues for the first time – especially the kernel Mississippi Delta style – many listeners today use adjectives such as "odd" or "strange" to describe it. (Even in 1926 it sounded weird to Paramount, who used that very word to advertise recordings of Blind Lemon Jefferson's songs.) The soundsheet accompanying this book will provide an introduction to the sound of early recorded downhome blues. Most of the music has been reissued on LP. Letters to the reissuing record companies, whose addresses are furnished in the Bibliography, will yield names and addresses of local or mail-order stores from which the albums may be obtained. If this information is outdated, one may write to the Archive of Folk Song, Library of Congress, Washington, D.C. 20540, requesting current addresses. A good purchase for the beginning listener is Origin Jazz Library OJL-2, *Really! The Country Blues.*

I take for my primary source in this book downhome blues records in their period of peak sales before World War II, 1926–30. (The record industry cut back sharply on blues records in the early years of the Depression.) Additionally, I have drawn on the recollections of singers and audience, as well as of workers in the record industry, and I have examined the advertisements which the predominantly white industry placed in the black press. Although the transcriptions and analysis of the music and many of the interviews are my own, I could not have proceeded without the findings of several other researchers; my debt to them is apparent in the text and the Bibliography. In cases where my interviews produced facts similar to those reported by others elsewhere, I generally used my own results in order to increase the richness of available data. Doubtless some of the hearsay will prove incorrect. Inevitably, factual errors will occur in a book such as this; one hopes they will be few. Yet the assumptions and the theoretical framework, and major and minor assertions, are, I believe, essentially correct. In any case, I willingly take responsibility for it all. I shall, of course, be glad to hear from researchers who hold opposite opinions or who wish to bring additional material to my attention.

ACKNOWLEDGMENTS

Much of the research for *Early Downhome Blues* was completed between 1967 and 1970, in preparation for my 1971 doctoral dissertation in American studies at the University of Minnesota. The present book is largely the result of theoretical revisions and additional research undertaken between 1971 and 1973, with the exception of the actual demonstration of the song-producing model (see chap. 4), which came to me late in January, 1974. Since projects like this are not usually completed without substantial help, I want to thank those who have provided it. I am grateful for travel grants from the Graduate School and the Macmillan Fund of the University of Minnesota, and for a summer fellowship from the Tufts University Faculty Awards Committee. For their good advice and kind encouragement I am indebted to Mojo Buford, Don Burke, Norm and Anne Cohen, Dan Dennett, John Fahey, Archie Green, Joe Grosz, Rod Gruver, Ken Irby, Alan Kagan, Alan Lomax, Lazy Bill Lucas, Simon Napier, Cameron Nickels, Johannes Riedel, Allen Spear, Mary Turpie, and Jo Jo Williams. The great teachers I have been fortunate enough to learn from – Frank Smith, Clyde Taylor, Bill Coles, Jack Levenson, Leo Marx, Robert Berkhofer – have, I hope, left some imprint on my mind and its methods. T. J. Anderson, Charles Archer, David Evans, Arthur Geffen, Albert Lord, and Judith McCulloh read this manuscript in various stages of its preparation and suggested valuable improvements. I also want to thank my colleagues and students at Tufts, who, sometimes knowingly and sometimes not, helped me clarify my ideas and contributed theirs to this endeavor. Finally, for help with the new Afterword and this edition of *Early Downhome Blues* I am grateful to Rosemary Cullen, David Evans, William Ferris, Jr., Tom Rankin, and Alan Trachtenberg. The illustrations in the Afterword were kindly supplied by the John Hay Library, Brown University.

PART 1 | THE MUSIC IN THE CULTURE

 **DOWN HOME**

Late in the 1960s, when I was playing guitar in Lazy Bill Lucas's blues band, I asked him what the phrase *down home* meant. "Down home, that mean down South, on the farm," he said. His friend and contemporary Jo Jo Williams, a blues singer in his fifties who, like Bill, was brought up in the rural South, explained that "the word *down home,* it mean back to the root, which mean where it all start at, this music, the blues and the church music, and so far as I can understand, it came from the country, the fields and the shacks and the towns that weren't but wide spaces in the highway."[1]

In the 1920s, when black American singers first made commercial blues phonograph records, *down home* meant the same thing. The great migration from southern farms to northern and western cities was not, in retrospect, the journey to the promised land; and although living conditions were better in Detroit or Chicago than on plantations outside Clarksdale or West Helena, many of the migrants thought back to family, friends, and old times down home. It is impossible for a people to leave a culture behind. The land of Jim Crow and lynch law was also the land of fish fries and barbecues, good music and getting religion, long talks and deep loves, the feel and the smell of soil and farm. Those women who had been "mistreated" by their lovers in the cold northern cities, Ethel Waters suggested in her 1921 recording "The Down Home Blues" (Black Swan 2021), should become "Dixie bound."[2] Equally popular was the best-selling "Arkansas Blues." It was described in a *Chicago Defender* advertisement as "a downhome chant," but in it nostalgia was shown up for sentimentality, for few black listeners could miss the biting irony of the lyrics.[3] Although the migrants wanted to transfer the best of downhome culture to the ghettos, few returned south.

Despite the large northern migration and the news it made, most black Americans stayed down home.[4] More black Americans could be found working on southern tenant farms than in all occupations in the North. The 1930 census statistics (see fig. 1) may be low; it is likely that several thousand black families were overlooked.[5] Yet as late as 1930 the largest single section of black American families comprised farmers who did not own the land they worked, who were living down home in a social and cultural system of broad uniformity – the plantation system. Judged by sheer weight of numbers, the black experience remained tied to the land and the downhome way of life it nurtured.

The plantation had not disappeared after the Civil War. The word remained in southern vernacular to identify any large farm which supported several tenant families. The 1910 census defined a plantation as "a continuous tract of land of considerable area under the general supervision or control of a single individual or firm, all or a part of such tract being divided into at least three smaller tracts, which are leased to tenants."[6] Even today a visitor to the Deep South can see signs by the roadside giving the name of the property owner, followed by the word *plantation*.

As might be expected, plantations were located where soil, climate, and topography were most suited for large-scale cotton farming. In figure 2, the dark areas indicate the high tenant-farm density in plantation regions of the South.

Depression-era ethnographies and sociological monographs emphasized continuities in southern farm life before and after Emancipation. The contemporary plantation owner was the counterpart of the slaveowner, the sharecropper the counterpart of the slave. Writing of Indianola, Mississippi, and its vicinity, Hortense Powdermaker developed the antebellum analogy:

> The plantation system in our community stems directly from the plantation of the old South. Before the Civil War the landlord had complete responsibility for

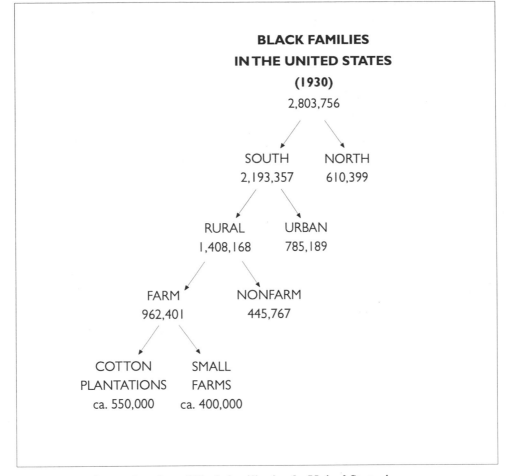

**BLACK FAMILIES
IN THE UNITED STATES
(1930)**
2,803,756

SOUTH
2,193,357

NORTH
610,399

RURAL
1,408,168

URBAN
785,189

FARM
962,401

NONFARM
445,767

COTTON
PLANTATIONS
ca. 550,000

SMALL
FARMS
ca. 400,000

FIGURE 1. *Census location of black families in the United States in 1930.
Adapted from Charles S. Johnson,* Growing Up in the Black Belt, *pp. xxii, 49.*

the welfare of the slave who provided the labor. He, or his agents, gave them their clothing, their food, their houses, selected the seeds for them to plant, told them where and how to work. Their first duty was to obey orders. They in turn worked during the season "from sun-up to sun-down" with the assurance of food and shelter as their reward. They had no control over their labor, and no direct share in its profits. Money played no part in the dealings between master and workers.

"After freedom" there was still the cotton to be planted, cultivated, and picked. There were still the plantations. And there was a set of *mores* so strongly entrenched that not even a war could dislodge them. The Negro was still the worker. The white man, much poorer than before, still made the decisions. Landlords who had sufficient wealth after the Civil War to continue as planters, translated the responsibility for slaves to responsibility for tenants. Sometimes a man's tenants were

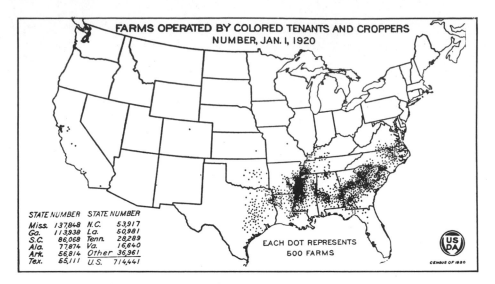

FIGURE 2. *The Black Belt. From* Agriculture Yearbook 1923, *p. 517. White tenant farmers lived in agricultural regions throughout the United States; most were located in the South and Midwest. According to the 1920 census, there were 714,441 "colored" tenant farms (including a scattering of farms worked by Orientals) and 1,740,363 "white" tenant farms.*

the same Negroes who had formerly been his slaves. Many slaves merely transferred their dependence from master to landlord. Money still played only a small part in their dealings. Nevertheless, the Negro was free. He had acquired the right to move, even though he has not always been free to exercise that right.[7]

Powdermaker and the other sociologists were right to stress that the plantation system remained similar from the Civil War to the Great Depression. But they overlooked the changes in black people's attitudes toward that system's hold over their lives. In the twentieth century, black tenant families frequently moved from one farm to the next, looking for better living conditions, hoping to save money so that they could own their land. A small but significant percentage did become landowners. Internal migration patterns comprised a general movement from the poorer hilly sections into the plantation areas (although some families went back after a few years) and then from one plantation to the next. Many families gradually worked their way to cities, and some went west or north.[8] Charley Patton expressed a common sentiment in his 1929 recording "Down the Dirt Road Blues" (Paramount 12854) (note that the larger spaces indicate vocal pauses):[9]

> Every day   seem like murder here
> Every day   seem like murder here
> I'm gonna leave tomorrow   I know you don't bid' my care.

Patton lived for many years on Will Dockery's plantation near Drew, Mississippi, in the heart of the Delta. Dockery's son described his father's plantation in a letter to Stephen Calt:

> In reference to this property: it had its own Post Office for 40–50 years. Issued its own paper script and also coins and was the center of an agricultural empire of about 15–18,000 acres in Mississippi and Arkansas. My father came to the Delta as a young man directly out of Ole Miss[10] with hardly any means but good credit from an uncle in Memphis. My father developed all this land himself and he later commuted between various plantations and our home in Memphis where he eventually took over his uncle's cotton factoring business.[11] I have heard that at one time there were between 400 and 500 negro families on all his properties. One year to my knowledge he made 7500 bales of cotton. He was a great philanthropist and contributed heavily to many causes.[12]

Ultimately, the antebellum analogy is misleading. Appealing initially because of its shocking irony, it emphasizes (in the words of black sociologist Charles S. Johnson) that "patterns of life, social codes, as well as social attitudes, were set in the economy of slavery."[13] Nonetheless, it overlooks important legal, geographical, and cultural changes. The post-Civil War black American was a free man, not a slave. If he became a debtor to a plantation owner, he usually extricated himself simply by moving to another farm. The Mississippi Delta, where rich soil produced the finest cotton in the nation, had been a swampy, fever-infested floodplain until it was developed into fertile fields in the 1880s.[14] Most important, black families were strengthened by their dream of becoming landowners. If the outward manifestations of their culture showed antebellum characteristics, the practical possibility of improving their living conditions had altered their ideas of themselves and their attitudes toward their lives.

Black families worked the land as owners, as hired laborers, or in one of the forms of tenant farming: sharecropping, share renting, or cash renting. The landowning family almost always worked its own land. Usually, landowners were wealthier than tenant farmers, but a few bad crop years could leave them in debt to whites in the community who lent them capital.[15] The hired laborer worked for a daily or weekly wage; he paid a monthly fee to a landlord in exchange for a shack and small plot of surrounding land.[16] Commonly the sharecropper worked "on the halvers," furnishing half his crop and the labor to produce it to the landlord in exchange for a shack, tools, seed, work animals and feed, fuel wood, and half the fertilizer he used. The share renter gave from one-fourth to one-third of his crop and labor to the landlord in exchange for a shack and fuel wood. Unlike the cropper, the share renter supplied his own tools, seed, work animals and feed, and a percentage of the fertilizer equal to his share of the crop. The cash renter paid a set price per acre of land which he worked; in exchange he received a shack and fuel wood. Like the share renter, he supplied tools, seed, work animals and feed, and (unlike the share renter) all the fertilizer.[17] Farm families tried to advance from share-cropping to share renting to cash renting and then to landowning. Unattached single men supported themselves as seasonal laborers, drifting from one place to the next.

Across the South, the proportion of farm families that took on each type of economic arrangement varied; in general, the better the soil, the higher was the tenant percentage. A 1916 investigation of the rich Yazoo-Mississippi Delta area found that 94.5 percent of the black farm families were tenants, while 5.5 percent were owners. Of the tenants, 50.7 percent were sharecroppers, 15.9 percent were share renters, and 33.4 percent were cash renters. Evidently hired laborers were not included.[18] Powdermaker's 1930 figures from the Indianola region revealed 98.9 percent tenants and 1.1 percent owners. Of the tenants, 77 percent were sharecroppers and 23 percent were share renters or cash renters. Again, hired laborers were not included.[19] A higher percentage of black families owned their farms in the less fertile areas. Smaller units, poorer soil, and mixed crops (cotton, tobacco, corn) characterized these farms outside the plantation areas. Here the supply of labor was not so plentiful; here fewer tenants found themselves in debt at year's end. In Macon County, Alabama, 1930 figures show that 10.1 percent of the black farm families owned the land they worked, while 17.1 percent were hired laborers and 72.8 percent were tenants.[20] A survey taken between 1927 and 1934 in Macon and Greene counties, Georgia, revealed that 10 percent owned their land, 22.5 percent were hired for their labor, and 67.5 percent were tenants.[21]

Farming methods, using hoe, plow, and draft animals, had not changed much from the Civil War until World War I. In the spring the ground had to be cleared, fences mended, ditches dug, cotton and other crops planted. From April through August, farm families worked in the fields during the daylight hours, "chopping" cotton: weeding, cultivating, picking joint grass. Chopping eased in August, when the yearly religious revivals were held.[22] The earliest harvest began at the end of the month; in September and October extra hands often were hired and relatives came from town, all to help gather in the crops. Winter was a slack season; tenants were entitled to live in their shacks on the farms year round, but many of them tried their luck living and working in town during the colder months, seeing to it that the children went to the town schools. Those who lived in towns and cities the whole year frequently "farmed out" their youngsters to relatives in the country during the growing season.

Children were an economic advantage, for they increased a farm family's labor force. But few children enjoyed farm work. Leonard "Baby Doo" Caston, who became a musician because he detested farming, described working on his mother's uncle's farm in 1931, when he was thirteen:

This was kind of a hard thing for me, I mean, getting up at five o'clock in the morning, and you had to go and eat your breakfast and hook up the mule and go up to the fields; when the sun come up you'd be plowing, you see. School was something I very seldom got to, I mean, because after we left the town where I was born at we was 'way back out in the country. . . .

This was quite a job. We'd be out in the fields and it'd be 110 to 115 degrees – you get used to it – and when you get wet with sweat then you start cooling off. There wasn't no such thing as ice; there was a spring. . . .

Now here was an animal – a mule – I mean he could work right up until 11:30 (and back in the country they had a great big bell that they would ring, you know, they call them dinner bells – one of these great big bells sound like a church bell) and this mule, if he's in the middle of the field, he would go to the other end of the row and this is where he would stop; and if you didn't unhook him and let him go on to the barn for dinner he would take you, plow, and all, wouldn't care nothing about what you would say. So you jump on him and he'd ride you right. He knowed the way to go, and you take him to the barn and you feed him and he would stop by the water pond and get his water, and he'd go right back to where he just left from; and he would do that until the sun goes down. But he would walk you to death, you know.[23]

From planting time to harvest, the weekly work fell into a pattern familiar for centuries to subsistence farmers in the Western world. On weekdays the family worked the fields during the daylight hours. The men worked more or less continuously, except for a lunch break, and took on the tasks which called for more strength when these needed to be done; the women took time out to cook, clean, wash, mend, tend the farmyard animals if the family had any, work the vegetable garden, and look after the littlest children. On rainy days there was always something to do around the farmhouse. Only men worked in the fields Saturday mornings, and on Saturday afternoons the black families went to town to shop and talk with their friends, while the head of the household drew the family rations for the week to supplement what was available at home: cornmeal, salt pork ("fatback"), sugar, coffee, molasses, and chewing tobacco. Saturday evening was party time; barbecues, fish fries, picnics, and other family gatherings, some sponsored by local churches, provided fellowship and recreation. Parties of a rougher sort, in houses, "juke" joints, or simply outdoors in a cleared area back in the country, provided a setting where members of the community could listen to music, drink, dance, gamble, and make love.[24] Sunday school classes for children and adults met weekly, whereas Sunday services usually were held every other week, since one minister often pastored several churches. Children rehearsed for the church choir on weekday evenings;

FIGURE 3. *Abandoned tenant shack, Roosevelt, Louisiana, August 21, 1970. Photograph by the author.*

and for the women who could afford the time, the church ladies' clubs met weekday afternoons.[25]

A visitor to the Black Belt countryside in the 1920s would have seen crop-growing fields alternating with patches of sandy and wooded areas. Tenant homes were located with the agricultural units, one cabin or a small group of cabins at the edge of each field. Johnson noticed that "the very large plantations have close set rows of cabins on the edges of vast stretches of cotton land. . . . Traveling throughout the country, one may observe, standing stark and alone at the crossroads, a church or store, with no dwelling in sight."[26]

The cabins were as confining as the fields were vast. The tenant "shack" (its common name) may still be observed from east Texas to South Carolina (fig. 3). Set on rocks or blocks, between road and field, it was a wooden dwelling, usually containing two, sometimes three, rooms. The leaky roof was made of split pine shingles or, later, galvanized iron, which turned a rusty brown after years of service. The tiny windows had board shutters or, later, sash and glass. The front door invariably opened onto a porch; here the family gathered "in the evening" (i.e., about 4:30 P.M.) to escape the heat of the house and await the fieldworkers' homecoming. In the larger plantations which had

FIGURE 4. *Showpiece farm bedroom. From Dorothy Dickins,* A Nutrition Investigation of Negro Tenants in the Yazoo-Mississippi Delta, *p. 10. The caption notes that "the phonograph [visible at right] is often found here for negroes are music lovers as well as musical."*

shacks in clusters, the neighbors gathered to exchange gossip and pleasantries at this time of day. The back door of the shack overlooked a small yard where vegetables were grown and livestock (chickens, a pig, perhaps a milk cow) were kept. The well and the privy also were in the back yard, the latter usually open, the former rarely boxed to prevent rainwater from carrying farmyard mud into the drinking water. If grandparents lived on the farm, they usually planted flowers around the front and sides of the shack. People, pets, livestock, insects, and the elements seemed to move in and out of the shack at will.

Two hundred square feet of floor space made up the average interior. The frame of the shack, often papered with newsprint, served as the wall. Most landlords furnished the shacks with beds or pallets, chairs, and a stove for cooking and heating. There was, of course, no electricity. The family put mementos on shelves or hung them in a collage on the wall (fig. 4). In these close quarters, physical privacy was difficult.

If the interdependence of the household in the close quarters of the shack worked against privacy, it encouraged interaction, communication, and love. Depression-era ethnographies emphasized promiscuity, common-law marriages, and the separation of the nuclear family.[27] Yet children were well cared for by relatives: stepparents, aunts, uncles, grandparents. Outside the protective shell of the nuclear family, the black child developed independence, and he defined himself in relation to a variety of adults. The black farm household was close and strong.[28]

The tenant farmers' food and clothing, like their shelter, placed them among the rural poor. The men wore overalls during the work week, putting old pants under them for warmth in wintertime. A woman was well off if she had more than one everyday dress. Children sometimes wore modified salt or feed sacks and went barefoot around the plantation. But families provided suitable Sunday attire for churchgoing, while many young men and women prized their store-bought fashions for the Saturday journey to town, for courting, and for other special occasions. The farm family ate a diet dependent on cornmeal fixings, molasses, and fatback. Most families could not depend on their cows for milk or their hens for eggs. Occasionally, when company came, a chicken was killed for Sunday dinner. Fish were eaten when and where they could be caught; vegetable greens were commonly grown, but superstition prevented consumption of certain varieties.[29] The food and clothing of the tenant farm families contributed inevitably to disease and early death.

In her nutritional investigation, Dorothy Dickins concluded that the farmers ate poorly not because they were poor, but because they did not know any better. The black family must be trained, she wrote, to raise more vegetables, increase the yield of hens, take advantage of wild fruit, and prepare food in a wholesome manner, because "the trained negro lives in better homes, wears better clothes, eats better food, does more efficient work, creates more wealth, rears his children more decently, makes a more decent citizen, and in time of race friction is always to be found on the side of law and order."[30] In contrast to this revealing argument, Johnson merely observed that "the people die, and with good reason."[31]

Under plantation conditions, for reasons of black self-preservation, tenant farmers' behavior which whites were permitted to see simply reassured the white stereotype of the Afro-American. In a behavior circle as closed as the economic system, and analogous to it, childlike black behavior could only reinforce belief in inferiority, while dignified or rebellious behavior was "uppity" and part of the "bad nigger" stereotype. In "Traits of My Plantation Negroes," an essay as unintentionally revealing as Dickins's, Howard Snyder described what he took to be their prominent characteristics: fighting, sexual promiscuity, "bedding" arrangements in lieu of marriage, gullibility, dishonesty, spendthrift prodigality, undependability in business transactions, and fear of the unknown.[32] Snyder admired the "robust" and "muscular" black woman who worked beside her family in the fields, yet found time to cook, wash, bear children, and "walk about" after supper to pass time with neighbors. "Again and again one sees the sad spectacle of a wife or 'woman' and perhaps five or six children deserted and left penniless in early winter," he wrote, observing that "it is now that she needs her landlord, and it is now that he furnishes her with cabin, mule, land, provisions, and all the necessaries for making a crop. She goes on with her farming just as her man did."[33]

Snyder concluded that his black tenants were at the mercy of their impulses. They rarely seemed able to reason and make decisions in light of their past experience; they lived in the present. So the behavior he observed served only to reinforce the plantation stereotype. A black farmer who violated decorum risked punishment and, in a larger sense, only moved into the "bad nigger" side of the stereotype. On the highways, for example, black drivers had to be very cautious, for in most accidents they would be charged with fault. Son House, a blues singer who was also a tenant farmer, had drunk enough whiskey one Saturday night during the Depression to make his driving reckless; when he refused to let a Greyhound bus pass him, a Mississippi sheriff arrested him and placed him in jail.[34] The arrangement for his release a few days later was typical, in that his landlord pretended to pay a fine, only to add the amount to House's indebtedness:

> Come and get me out of jail – they come put me in jail . . . and then the other man [the landlord] he come down there and tell talk to that judge or whosomever he be – least I know all he had to do was just tell me he wouldn't fool with me – he just –
>
> [Whispers to House, playing landlord's part:] "Let's go, House."
>
> [Whispers to sheriff, playing landlord's part:] "Let the little old nigger go, man, I need him Monday morning. He's too good with that old tractor. I need him. You let him out of there."
>
> [Takes sheriff's part:] "Well, all right then, you can come down and get him Monday morning."
>
> That's all there was to it. He wasn't fooling me. Course he was making out like he had to pay so many hundreds of dollars, and he ain't paid nothing but a good conversation. . . . See, they stepped in with each other that way. That's the way they worked together. And if you had something that I needed, well, I talk to you a little bit.
>
> [Whispers, playing sheriff's part:] "Well, go on, take him, make him think it's so and so and so."
>
> [Takes landlord's part:] "Well, all right, I'll tell him I had to pay this, that, and the other, and all that."
>
> Yeah, I know the score. Well, you couldn't say nothing, see?[35]

Under these legal practices Snyder's observations take on ominous meaning. "One of the best things about my field negroes," he wrote, "is that they harbor little revenge, though this applies, for the most part, to their relations with the whites. There is not a planter but who can give many cases in point. A field negro's memory seems to lose its grip on injury and favor alike." Snyder notes that "an indefinite, hazy fear is ever in the back of their minds." He does not know what it is, and apparently neither do they. "Often they do not seem to know what they are afraid of: it is an intangible, sinister something." But they knew perfectly well what they feared: the power of the white community. "If one of them has stolen some little article about the place," Snyder advises a would-be plantation owner, "never mind; just wait patiently until several are laughing and talking, then spring the matter of the stolen article. If one of them has done it, it is nine to one that he will take a sheepish attitude and sneak off. You have only to corner him and heighten his fear. Presently he will confess to the theft."[36] Cornered, accused, his fear "heightened," knowing he had neither legal nor other recourse, would anyone not confess to stealing "some little article" whether or not he had in fact done so? Snyder simply is disingenuous.

Shortly after harvest time, the landlord told the tenant whether he had made money, broken even, or fallen into debt. Normally no written records were given to the tenant proving his accumulated indebtedness or the value of his crop when sold. Powdermaker calculated that 17 to 18 percent of the Indianola-region tenant farmers made a profit in 1932; the rest broke even or went into debt.[37] In 1930, 9.4 percent of the black farmers in Macon County, Alabama, came out ahead; 61.7 percent broke even, and 26 percent went into debt.[38] Outside the plantation areas, where the labor supply was smaller, a lesser percentage of farmers found themselves in debt at year's end.[39] Because black people could not qualify to vote, hold office, or sit on juries, they had no effective legal challenge to landlords who cheated them. (Powdermaker estimated that at least 70 percent of the tenant families were cheated.)[40] And they knew it; a widely reported folk couplet went:

> Ought's a ought, figger's a figger;
> All for the white and none for the nigger.[41]

A piece of plantation humor I heard over and over again when interviewing ex-sharecroppers was the saying "The only way to get out of debt is to walk out." Walk out they did, if only to the next plantation. With an honest landlord and a good crop year, a family might clear $400, enough to buy a shack. But even with an honest landlord, success was rendered uncertain by weather conditions, insect pests, and varying cotton prices. That so many tenant families moved so often — two years on one plantation was considered average[42] — indicates that few families were able to prosper, and suggests that movement was their form of protest. As far as I can determine, very few debtors were prosecuted. Certainly the landlords could not have put the runaway debtors in jail, for that would have constituted peonage.[43]

By the 1920s, Jim Crow laws prohibiting black people from white public facilities were firmly established down home. That blacks could not eat in the same restaurant rooms, use the same toilets, sit in the same chairs, or drink from the same fountains as white people indicates that the whites thought they were publicly unclean. Privately, of course, blacks were permitted to cook, clean, and watch children in white households. Social distinctions were made in forms of address: black people called whites "mister" or "sir" or "ma'am," but white people called blacks "boy" or "girl," reserving "uncle" or "aunty" for their favorites, regardless of their ages. A taboo, sometimes broken for effect, forbade eating at home with blacks. Whites locked their back doors but left the front open, knowing that blacks dared enter only in the socially acceptable place. Black people shopped in separate stores in the larger towns; in the smaller towns they traded in stores with white clientele, often waiting until the whites were served before they took their turns.

Though most whites just distinguished "good niggers" from "bad niggers" on the criteria of diligence and amiability, the black community made distinctions among themselves on altogether different standards. How responsibly they fulfilled family obligations determined whether they were among the "respectables" or the "no-'counts." Powdermaker distinguished three classes: upper, middle, and lower. Her black informants, most of them women, identified an upper class of landowners, businessmen, teachers, and educational officials. Their family life was stable; they were chaste before and faithful after marriage. Most had at least a high school education. They disapproved of emotional display and were unenthusiastic about church; yet the older people belonged. Going to jail was rare and disgraceful. Values and behavior conformed to white middle-class ideals. Tenant farmers and farm workers made up the middle class; they were joined by townspeople employed as maids, janitors, delivery boys, chauffeurs, "yard" boys, gas station attendants, unskilled plant workers, bootblacks, carpenters, barbers, ministers, and small shopkeepers. Men and women were neither chaste before marriage nor faithful afterward, and many children were born out of wedlock; but the middle class tried to keep their sexual affairs private. Going to jail was undesirable, but sometimes happened and could be condoned. A grade-school education was about as much as a middle-class black could claim. Almost everyone belonged to a church, taking part enthusiastically in the services and other concerns of the congregation. The lower class consisted of drifters, prostitutes, bootleggers, and people who could not support themselves. Having little or no family life, they made no secret of their sexual affairs. Going to jail, while unlucky, was taken for granted. Violent behavior and woman beating were common and expected. Church attendance was sporadic; few went to services regularly, and most waited until the intense atmosphere of the summer revival called them back into the fold. Because their behavior flaunted middle-class values, the bootleggers and the prostitutes, no matter how much money they had, were thought worthless.[44]

How reliable is Powdermaker's analysis? Her general conclusion, that "the most constant class indication among the Negroes has to do with the acceptance of certain modes of behavior formerly restricted to whites,"[45] reflects the liberal, assimilationist thought of her time and is, moreover, exactly what her informants would have wanted a white person of her appearance to believe. A more serious objection to her analysis can be directed at her almost exclusive reliance upon female informants, for she could not possibly have gotten a satisfactory impression of male outlooks except as they were filtered through female perceptions.[46] Her upper class made up only 5 percent of the population, and her lower class comprised only little more than that, leaving a vast and relatively indistinguishable middle class to represent the Indianola blacks.

Whereas Powdermaker gave the impression of a large black middle class attempting to conform to white ideals, Johnson found a large black middle class with ideals of its own. "The essential observation of this study," he wrote, "is that the Negro population of this section of Macon County has its own social heritage which, in relatively complete isolation, has had little chance for modification from without or within."[47] Powdermaker's picture of a middle class trying to keep private its extramarital sexual affairs contrasts sharply with Johnson's portrayal of black family life. Young men and women were not expected to marry early, because their economic contribution to their farm households was too valuable for them to leave. Indeed, if a young woman became pregnant, public opinion did not force the father to marry her to support the child. Instead, the young mother brought her baby into the household, where the maternal grandparents assumed responsibility for support. She did not lose status in the community; neither were her chances for marriage in the future compromised.[48] When a young woman married, her partner usually was a man of middle age who needed a woman to work and care for his children from a previous marriage. A woman in her twenties began a new household with a man she loved by marrying him or entering a common-law living arrangement. Not infrequently he was already the father of one or more of her children. As children were an economic asset, the parents could look forward with confidence toward establishing a farm household. Adoption was common; when families broke up after desertion or migration, the children were distributed among friends and relatives. They all shared in the farm labor; little if any distinction in treatment between natural and adopted children was observed.[49] "There is, in a sense, no such thing as illegitimacy in this community," concluded Johnson.[50]

Separation and desertion were common. Johnson's investigation of the reasons for desertion revealed motives identical to those dwelt on in blues lyrics: mistreatment, which took the form of general dissatisfaction with the relationship, or specific objection to laziness, physical cruelty, adultery, age and color differences,[51] and the tedium of farm life. Yet, since households usually did not break up afterwards, it was "more 'respectable' to separate, and even to experiment further with another mate, than to tolerate [these] conditions with one's legal mate."[52] Because separation was common, there was a ready supply of unattached men and women in the community. Sometimes the successor was chosen before the mate departed. And there was also a supply of "no-'count" philanderers (Powdermaker's "lower class") ready to take advantage of love and money in exchange for the good times they offered.[53]

The divergence between Powdermaker's and Johnson's analyses of Black Belt family social values and behavior is not likely to be explained by differences in geography. Indeed, their descriptions of conditions and behavior in Indianola, Mississippi, and Macon County, Alabama, were similar; the difference lay in people's attitudes towards that behavior. I have already suggested certain difficulties in accepting Powdermaker's view of a vast middle class, one in which tenant farmers were lumped together with barbers and ministers, trying to live by a white middle-class value system. Through Johnson's eyes we view a black middle class made up principally of tenant farmers whose family social values, though in contradiction to white ideals of courtship and marriage, supported well an economic system centered on the maintenance of stable farm households. It matters little that the black sociologist Johnson was ashamed of these social values and behavior, that he laid the blame for them on cultural conditions during slavery and isolation afterwards, and that he looked forward to a time when rural black people would adopt "a different body of sentiments and practices in accord with a more advanced conception of social life and relations."[54]

Powdermaker's analysis supports the conventional view of a Black Belt society divided rather rigidly into a "church culture" and a "blues culture." The all-too-easy conclusion that there were two cultures – one predominantly female and middle class which adhered to white middle-class proprieties, the other predominantly male and lower class which lived to make the most of the moment, valuing whiskey, women, and easy money – supposes that movement from one culture to the other bespeaks a divergence in desires, values, and behavior leading to severe feelings of guilt.[55] Such a portrait may well describe the anxiety of black Americans becoming assimilated into white society, but it does not accord with life down home. If there were "respectables" and "no-'counts," they were forced together by the same outside pressures of white discrimination. People moved often, if not easily, between Saturday night parties and Sunday services; a man or woman who had been mistreated had good reason to meet members of the opposite sex at a Saturday night dance and did not lose status in the community for doing so. Downhome blues lyrics are in absolute accord with the values Johnson reported concerning courtship, marriage, and how people should treat each other when living together. Blues songs and the dances at which they provided entertainment served a positive social function, not a guilt-ridden negative one.[56] Black Belt society was fluid, not rigid; people shared the same experience of "church culture" and "blues culture." Whatever rigidity and guilt was felt by a rising middle class was the province of that small, articulate minority who defined themselves in relation to white standards and perhaps tried to adopt them.[57]

In such a fluid society it is not surprising to find that, as institutions, the church and the blues were structural and functional counterparts.[58] Rod Gruver has written, for example, that blues lyrics express a "secular religion."[59] Charles Keil has noted that the blues lyric and the sermon both show the listener how to confront, analyze, and work through a personal difficulty.[60] The preacher and the blues singer shared similar roles as community spokesmen, telling listeners how to behave. Downhome blues and black oral sermons share structural features: formulaic composition and improvisation; repetition of small textual units in parallel form; ideas that cohere associatively instead of logically or chronologically; and an expressive tone of voice – raspiness – to signify emotion. Many of these common features, including call and response, are so apparent, also, in ordinary black conversation, that oral sermons and blues songs may be considered as increasingly ritualized versions of their source, black speaking.

After the family, the church was the most important black institution down home. Black people controlled their own churches. About 10 percent were members of the Church of God in Christ, part of the Pentecostal movement ("Sanctified" in black parlance, "Holy Rollers" in white), and a higher percentage were Methodists, but the majority belonged to Baptist churches.[61] Approved since early nineteenth-century planters had become convinced that a Christian slave was a more docile slave, black American religion fused African remembrance with evangelical Christian borrowings, creating a vital and unique church. Doctrine, as it appeared in the sermons, was a mixture of works and faith. At the outset of the sermon the preacher read his Bible text and interpreted its teaching, usually by making comparisons between Bible stories and present-day life, with a view toward illustrating proper moral behavior in the face of adversity. The congregation punctuated his pauses with shouts of "That's right" or "Amen" or "Tell 'em 'bout it" and the like. The downhome preachers did not rely upon manuscripts for their sermons; rather, they worked out the basic topic in advance, then relied upon memory and the spirit of the Lord to fill their tongues with speech at the proper moment. Most preachers had a repertoire of subjects and a storehouse of illustrative examples on which they drew freely; in short, they repeated themselves, with variations, over the course of the years. After several minutes of speech cadence, the preacher moved his sermon into a hoarse, tonal chant, the lines of which came out in two- or three-second bursts. If the spoken part had concentrated rationally upon works, now the doctrine shifted to the chanted promise of salvation for those who called upon Jesus. By the end of the chant – which could last for ten or fifteen minutes – preacher and congregation were locked in an emotional, rhythmic communion.[62]

For the young people in the community the church was a prime socializing agent. Not only did they attend Sunday school classes there, but their secular instruction was provided in the same building, with a graveyard waiting outside to urge wandering eyes back into the classroom. More important, when parents told their children the proper way to behave, they relied upon church rhetoric for explanation.

Afraid or convinced he was a sinner, puzzled and anxious over the spirit that filled those who "got religion" at services and revival meetings, the young adolescent moved to the mourners' bench at the front of the church, where preacher and elders prayed close overhead that he might be saved.[63] Not everyone experienced conversion in church. Son House had been to the mourners' bench several times, and he had seen his friends saved; but he doubted the authenticity of their experiences. His own conversion came in an alfalfa field:

When I was a kid, a youngster, a teen – a young teenager and up like that I was more churchified. Then that's mostly all I could see into. 'Cause they'd had us go – we'd had to go to the Sabbath school every Sunday. We didn't miss goin' to no Sabbath school. We'd be into that and then in this church there, some of the ones a little larger than me and like that, and it come time of year for 'em to run revival meetin'. Some pastor come to open up the revival meetin', oh, for a week or more. Well, we'd all be goin' to the thing they call the mourners' bench. Gettin' on your knees, you know, and lettin' the old folks pray for you. Yeah, and in a couple of days or weeks, somebody'd come up, holler out they had something. They had religion. They'd squall 'round, man, go on. So they left me thataway I guess, oh about, near 'bout six or eight months sometime. I didn't fall for it because I – I figured they was puttin' on and I didn't want to be puttin' on. I wanted mine to be real and so I just kept on until finally, the next session, I said, "Is there – this one time I'm just gon' see is – is any, any way to get this thing religion they goin' 'round here, talkin' about, puttin' on, and goin' on." I prayed and prayed, commenced prayin', man, every night, workin' in the field, 'n' plowin' the mule and everything. Work all day hard, 'n' tryin' to pray. And work. So, finally, I kept on like that until they come back home that night, middle of the night after the pastor turned out. So I went on home. And I was livin' down in the lower part the place from where my daddy 'n' them stayed, down to my cousin's. Went down there; I didn't want to be up around the old folks. And, man, I went out back of the house little bit, in this old alfalfa field out there.

I had been scared of snakes, 'cause snakes would be bad in the summertime, you know, crawlin' through them weeds and things. But I wasn't studyin' them snakes then. 'Cause they better get out of the way if they don't want to get their heads mashed off. [Laughs.] I went on. I was there in that alfalfa field and I got down. Pray. Gettin' on my knees in that alfalfa. Dew was fallin'. And, man, I prayed and I prayed and I prayed and – for wait awhile – man, I hollered out. Found out then. I said, "Yes, it is somethin' to be got, too, 'cause I got it now!" Went on back there to that house and told my cousin Robert and all them 'bout that and went – walked about two miles and a little better, and up to another white fellow's house, and woke him up and told him all about it. We was workin' for him, too. But I wouldn't care how tough he was or what. "Now get up out of that bed and listen to what I got to say." [Laughs.] He thought I was crazy! Yeah. Name was – we all called him Mister Keaton, T. F. Keaton. Yeah. I say, "Oh yeah!" Found out better now.[64]

Once in the church, the saved member found, in the words of E. Franklin Frazier, a "refuge from this hostile white world,"[65] temporary release of physical and emotional tension, and the promise of a just reward in heaven. The community was bonded through a shared ceremony: the painful and ecstatic sermon, the joy of the hymns. If the services were the center of the church, the social activities, directed by the ladies' clubs, were nearly as important; picnics and suppers, discussion groups, socials and entertainments, conventions, and relief work gave the women a major role in church activities.[66] The church was a most important agent of social control.

How *effective* an agent it was is open to question. Most children and many adults believed in the rhetoric of the downhome church, which both shaped and reflected the patterns of rural black thought. Nor could they easily deny the power with which the Holy Spirit moved them, when that happened. But several problems undermined the influence of the church. People noticed that the minister sometimes did not practice what he preached. The ministers already were powerful figures in the communities, especially in matters where whites were concerned. Trying to secure and enhance their positions of leadership, they did not always act in the best interest of their congregations.[67] Moreover, in order to retain their membership, the churches had to forgive sexual behavior contrary to Christian doctrine. Frazier relates one method of accommodation in which a minister decided that sexual relations outside marriage were perfectly all right so long as the lovers were Christians.[68] Johnson concluded that the black church in Macon County, Alabama, had to face "a widening gap between doctrine and behavior which leaves the traditional doctrine empty and unconvincing in relation to the normal currents of life."[69] Yet one could leave the church and rejoin it, like the Prodigal Son, the better for having sown wild oats and come to a deeper understanding of the heavenly Father's mercy.[70]

Of course, the church did not provide the sole release from farm routine. Families enjoyed secular picnics and outings, with dancing, flirting, perhaps a baseball game – moot activities at best in the eyes of the church.[71] Men liked to get away by themselves, or with a few friends, and pass the time fishing. Children sang and played games. Few black farm families had radios during their first decade of popularity (the 1920s), but it appears that between 10 and 20 percent had phonographs, and a larger proportion had records.[72] For phonographs were among the most prized pieces of furniture in the tenants' homes. Dickins's 1928 monograph on nutrition in the Yazoo-Mississippi Delta contains a photograph of a farm bedroom with a phonograph pictured on the far right (see fig. 4). Arthur Raper found that 19 percent of the black homes in Macon and Greene counties, Georgia, had phonographs early in the 1930s.[73] The families listened and danced to records made by black blues singers, jazz musicians, preachers, and gospel singers which were aimed directly at the black buying market. Neighbors without phonographs bought records and played them on their friends' machines. Since the record players were actuated by spring motors, the small models could be taken outside to picnics, parties, and other social affairs where music was popular and local singers were unattainable.

Downhome music in the early twentieth century was an integral part of many important sacred or secular activities. In church and at home people sang hymns and religious songs that bore little relation to the Europeanized product of the Fisk University Jubilee Singers.[74] African tradition probably had been responsible for the "hollers" in the fields and the markedly accented worksongs used to propel common tasks on construction gangs.[75] Music provided entertainment, too. Men sang to women while courting; people amused themselves and perhaps a small group of friends by singing on the porch at home. In areas fortunate enough to have them, local musicians provided entertainment at birthday parties, evening suppers, and other festive occasions. Often they simply gathered and went from house to house serenading, perhaps receiving food and drink for their music. Sometimes these serenades resulted in impromptu parties. The musicians enjoyed singing and people enjoyed hearing them. On Saturday afternoons, local musicians sang on the streets of nearby towns. But the most formal musical institution was the Saturday night dance, usually held outdoors in warm weather, or inside a country house or juke joint when it was colder. With a long history of providing entertainment for whites as well as blacks, black musicians drew upon a stock of songs common to both: ballads of heroes and outlaws, fiddle and banjo breakdowns, "Ethiopian airs" from minstrel shows, "coon songs" professionally composed for the parlor, and stage songs, all of which had passed into tradition.[76]

The generation which supplied the entertainment just after the turn of the century played something they called "blues," but the next musical generation belittled their efforts. Son House recalled that his father and uncles "tried" to play blues, but that these songs were not like the songs House learned to call blues at a later date.[77] The Reverend LeDell Johnson remembered that "they had these little old jump-up songs. I don't reckon they was even worth getting a record on if they'd had that up then. . . . The little old blues they had to my idea wasn't worth fifteen cents."[78] The older people preferred traditional music and square dancing at their parties. In Attalla, Alabama, seventy-five-year-old Thomas Hale, Sr., recalled that blues songs were sung in Cherokee County in the first decade of the century, but he added that the country people preferred to square dance to breakdowns, such as "Turkey in the Straw," supplied by fiddler and guitarist, while in town they liked doing "couple dances," such as the waltz and the black bottom, to the music of the latest parlor and stage songs. "We lived in the country, and dancing was the only fun we had," Hale said.[79]

The account of downhome blues development which follows is speculative. Any such account must rely upon the resolution of three issues. The first, of course, is one's idea of the minimum essentials of a downhome blues song. Writers who find the essence of downhome blues in such characteristics as plaintive lyrics and melodies, subjects concerning relations between the sexes, and general melancholy can find reason to believe that a few Afro-American songs of this sort were current not long after the Civil War, though they must admit that the songs were not called blues then. In a curious syllogism, one writer argues that since many twentieth-century blues lyrics describe travel experiences, and since mobility was impossible during slavery, "it seems probable that the blues tradition developed after the Civil War."[80] In fact, blues lyrics express not so much the experience of travel as the desire for it, something significant and symbolic, if not frequent, in slave songs. Finding evidence to support a theory of blues origins is so problematic that one becomes impatient with guesswork and is tempted to agree with Charles Keil that those who seek the origins of blues are sticking their heads in the sand.[81]

A second issue concerns the assumption that musical development is most likely evolutionary, in a direction from simpler forms to more complex ones. It is true that phrases and lines which occurred later in recorded blues were reported before the recognizable three-line, AAB blues stanza was observed. The assumption that the field hollers and worksongs which contained these phrases and lines developed into blues is plausible, but what is plausible is not always true; each might, for example, have drawn independently upon a third source, such as proverbial expression.

A third issue centers on the interpretation of materials collected by folklorists and musicologists before blues appeared on wire or disc, and on the reliability of black singers' and listeners' memories of music from so long ago. When the first ragtime craze swept the country just before the turn of the century,[82] most folklorists and musicologists, thinking it commercialized and "debased" folk music like the minstrel songs of an earlier generation, concentrated their collection and analysis upon black religious music.[83] And since blues songs were being sung from the stage by the time they attracted the collectors' ears, it is understandable why they thought blues unworthy of serious attention. Gertrude "Ma" Rainey, for example, said she began singing blues in her traveling show in 1902.[84] When W. C. Handy published "The Memphis Blues" in 1912 and "St. Louis Blues" in 1914, the music caught the fancy of professional Broadway composers lacking Handy's background; the result was a national enthusiasm for blues as strong as the earlier ragtime craze.[85] But their songs, like Handy's, were vaudeville blues, sophisticated imitations of the folk blues Handy had heard down home.

What did downhome blues sound like? What form did it take? Handy recalled that in 1892 he "heard shabby guitarists picking out a tune called 'East St. Louis.' It had numerous one-line verses and they would sing it all night: 'I walked all the way from old East St. Louis and I didn't have but one po' measly dime.'"[86] This song and others like it were recorded commercially by downhome blues singers in the 1920s. Whereas Handy viewed it as a one-line stanza, most transcribers have heard and rendered it as two lines:

> I walked   all the way   from East St.   Louis town,
> And I   did not have but   one poor lousy dime.

"East St. Louis Blues," "Crow Jane," and several other titles, recorded in the 1920s and still in oral tradition, share the same approximately eight-bar tune and a number of common stanzas. Between 1905 and 1908 Howard Odum collected songs made up of such stanzas.[87] Could this couplet form have expanded into the basic approximately twelve-bar, three-line, AAB form? I don't think so. Repeating the first four bars before rendering the last four would expand the structure to twelve bars and an AAB stanza. But the resulting harmonic support and caesura pattern would be different.

It is possible to argue that the frequent caesuras in "East St. Louis Blues," "How Long – How Long Blues" (see transcr. 14), and other eight-bar songs suggest they were precursors of those twelve-bar stanzas with more than two caesuras per line (see, e.g., transcr. 1, sts. 2 and 3). But very few twelve-bar, AAB stanzas in the common blues stockpile share lines of text with those eight-bar forms. If, for example, "East St. Louis Blues" were a precursor of the AAB form, we should certainly find an AAB stanza with these lines, and the caesura pattern as indicated:

> I walked all the way from   East St. Louis town.
> I walked all the way from   East St. Louis town.
> And I did not have but   one poor lousy dime.

But they are not found in this form.

The three-line, AAB stanza, taking up exactly or approximately twelve bars of $\frac{4}{4}$ meter, was by far the most commonly recorded form of early downhome blues. If it did not develop from a couplet, did it more likely arise from stanzas in which a single line simply was repeated once, twice, or even three times before a one-line refrain? Such stanzas were commonly reported in black spirituals and worksongs during the nineteenth century.[88] Odum collected similar secular songs shortly after the turn of the twentieth century.[89] Handy reported hearing a twice-repeated (i.e., AAA) form as blues from the singing of Phil Jones in Evansville, Indiana, about 1896. Taking this temporarily for a model, he decided it was too monotonous.

> [So I] adopted the style of making a statement, repeating the statement in the second line, and then telling in the third line why the statement was made. Thus I said in *St. Louis Blues:*

> I hate to see de eve'-nin' sun go down
> Hate to see de eve'-nin' sun go down
> 'Cause my baby, he done lef' dis town

> To vary the pattern still further, and to avoid monotony in the music, I used a four line unit in the next part of the lyric.

> St. Louis woman wid her diamon' rings
> Pulls dat man roun' by her apron strings.
> 'Twant for powder an' for store-bought hair
> De man I love would not gone nowhere.[90]

Other vaudeville blues composers used Handy's model, mixing three-line stanzas with other patterns.

But Handy did not invent the three-line, AAB blues stanza form; he reported hearing it while touring with his orchestra in the Mississippi Delta in 1903. Could he have stopped near Drew and listened to Henry Sloan and Charley Patton? In the town of Tutwiler, about fifteen miles north of Drew, Handy saw that "a lean, loose-jointed Negro had commenced plucking a guitar beside me. . . . As he played, he pressed a knife on the strings of the guitar." This singer, who played some of the "weirdest music" Handy had ever heard, sang stanzas in the AAA form.[91] Soon Handy also observed an AAB form:

> In the Delta, however, I suddenly saw the songs with the eye of a budding composer. The songs themselves, I now observed, consisted of simple declarations expressed usually in three lines and set to a kind of earth-born music that was familiar throughout the Southland half a century ago. . . . We heard many song fragments as *Hurry Sundown, Let Tomorrow Come,* or

Boll Weevil, where you been so long?
Boll Weevil, where you been so long?
You stole my cotton, now you want my corn.

[and]

Oh, the Kate's up the river, Stack O' Lee's in the ben'
Oh, the Kate's up the river, Stack O' Lee's in the ben'
And I ain't seen my baby since I can't tell you when.[92]

With an eye as keen for business as for music, Handy also observed, on a trip to Cleveland, Mississippi, just a few miles from Drew, that these songs went over very well with the audience. At an intermission where Handy's band was booked, a "local colored band" (guitar, mandolin, string bass) entertained the audience. "A rain of silver dollars began to fall around the outlandish, stomping feet," wrote Handy. "Then I saw the beauty of primitive music."[93] His comment is self-consciously ironic.

We must conclude from Handy's testimony that in the Delta, downhome blues songs were well known to local entertainers and audiences at least in the Drew-Cleveland area by 1903. This is corroborated by our knowledge of the Sloan-Patton apprenticeship in that region. Odum, collecting songs in Newton County, Georgia, between 1905 and 1908, reported at least one song using a three-line, AAB stanza, titled "Thought I Heard That K.C. Whistle Blow,"[94] and a variant four-line, AAAB stanza.[95] But if the four-line variant is similar to the version recorded in 1929 by the Memphis Jug Band as "K.C. Moan" (Victor v-38558; see transcr. 46), it was an eight-bar form. Regrettably, Odum did not notate the music of the texts he collected, nor did he pay close attention to the number of times a given line was repeated. Primarily interested in words and their meaning, he did not notice the development of blues as a form.

Those are the earliest definitive reports of blues down home. There are reports of blues songs in New Orleans in the 1890s, but most of them are untrustworthy. However, there is good evidence that a woman named Mamie Desdoume (or Desdoumes) was singing a song titled "2:19 Blues" in the standard AAB, approximately twelve-bar format around the turn of the century.[96] The tune of that song is identical to the one used for the widely sung and collected blues ballad "Betty and Dupree" (see transcr. 6 for one version), which suggests that the twelve-bar, AAB format may have been impressed in a few particular songs before it became the mold into which blues improvisations began to pour. Making up lines and stanzas to fit pre-existing tunes was not a new practice; worksongs and fiddle breakdowns, for example, admitted such creativity. (The most fertile improvisers were the fundamentalist preachers, whose oral chant relied partly on stock formulas and partly on spontaneous phrases.)[97]

Big Bill Broonzy believed that blues songs were all derived from "Joe Turner," a song whose first line was repeated twice to make the characteristic AAA stanza:

They tell me   Joe Turner's here and gone
They tell me   Joe Turner's here and gone
They tell me   Joe Turner's here and gone.[98]

Lines which described incidents in Turner's life could be added to form additional stanzas. Another widely reported and collected song in the same AAA form was "Poor Boy Long Ways from Home" (other stanzas were added in random order, most dwelling on the difficulties the "poor boy" faced):

Poor boy   long ways from home
I'm a poor boy   long ways from home
Poor boy   long ways from home.[99]

It is likely that the beginning of the improvised AAB downhome blues song form was marked by the coincidence of these improvised AAA songs with the small number of three-line, twelve-bar, AAB song models whose stanzas were more or less in predetermined order. Singers simply added a rhyming punch line after repeating the first line, and in so doing they formed three-line, AAB songs with improvised, interchangeable stanzas. Sometimes stanzas were "studied" (i.e., made up) by singers in advance, to be fitted in at the proper moment. The new form gave the lyrics the same circular, associative textual coherence the AAA songs had; stanzas could be added, eliminated, or interchanged without ill effect on the sense of the lyrics. At the same time, coherence was achieved at a level more complex than the AAA form. Perhaps associative coherence was more congenial to the worldview of Black Belt culture than was the logical, linear, narrative structure of the ballad.

Where the form appeared first, and when, is open to conjecture; polygenesis is a likely possibility. Wherever it was invented, the tradition developed most fully in east Texas and the Mississippi River Delta region during the first decade of the twentieth century.[100] Its development lagged about a decade in the Southeast, where the influence of Anglo-American traditional music was stronger. Blues was known perhaps as early as 1900 in other sections – New Orleans, for example, and certain midwestern cities – but it did not become the staple of the musical diet that it was down home.[101]

The story of the Johnson brothers and the group of musicians clustered around Charley Patton in the Drew area is instructive. When Tommy Johnson returned to Crystal Springs (near Jackson) in 1917 after two years in the Delta, his repertoire included versions of almost all the blues songs he recorded in 1928 and 1930. His brother LeDell immediately began to "study" these "late blues" which Tommy had learned from Charley

Patton, Willie Brown, and Dick Bankston in the Drew area.[102] If the older generation's blues "wasn't worth fifteen cents," these new ones did amount to something. For now the guitar accompaniments were more complex, relying on single-string work as well as on chording and strumming; and now the looser blues lyric structure encouraged the singer to express himself by making up his own songs. This opportunity for individual creativity cannot be underestimated as a force attracting singers to the blues form.

Most of the downhome blues singers who made commercial recordings in the 1920s had been entertainers at downhome Saturday night parties. They did not sing blues exclusively; their repertoires included the folksongs and popular songs shared by the previous generation. Blind Lemon Jefferson, who became the best-known downhome blues singer before the Depression, was already well known to Texans by 1920 because of his local appearances.[103] Robert Wilkins, born in 1896, grew up in the Hernando, Mississippi, area; he recalled a slightly older generation of guitarists "playing old blues and ragtime . . . and hillbilly stuff."[104] Wilkins began singing regularly in 1913 for white and black audiences alike, using the same basic repertoire for each. He played slow blues songs to accompany a "drag," and medium-tempo music of any sort to accompany a "two-step."[105]

By the time the Eighteenth Amendment became effective in 1920, thirty-three states had already declared themselves dry. Georgia went dry in 1908; Alabama and Mississippi followed in 1909. But since bootlegged whiskey was cheap to make and profitable to sell, bootleggers had been operating long before Prohibition; as Black Belt areas went dry, the bootleggers rejoiced to find themselves with a monopoly. A man could make much money from a small investment by selling the whiskey, which came in gallon or five-gallon jugs and cost twenty-five cents per half-pint.[106] Music and dancing increased its consumption. Sometimes the musicians bootlegged the whiskey themselves.[107] Because the plantation owners condoned (and sometimes underwrote) this practice, there was little trouble from the law. Nevertheless, they had to locate these parties far out in the country, away from potentially complaining whites and, for the sake of form, beyond the view of the sheriff.

During cooler weather, the indoor locations provided separate rooms for eating, gambling, dancing, and making love. Fighting was commonplace. During warmer weather the people went outside these "jukes" to large, cleared fields. Because the locations varied from one dance to the next, it was necessary to use portable instruments. According to Son House, "You couldn't fool with no piano too much, not for country gangs, or gonna have a ball here, yonder, and like that. They couldn't fool with no pianos because they'd be too much to move all the time."[108] No wonder aspiring musicians took up portable instruments. And so the downhome "countrified" sound became associated with the most popular portable instruments, such as the guitar, fiddle, mandolin, and harmonica.

To be sure, other forms of rural entertainment continued: picnics, suppers, serenading, and the like. But the Saturday night whiskey dance became an institution as
important, perhaps, in the social lives of the farmers as the Sunday church service. Not
every locality had nearby musicians skillful enough to entertain at them; but drifting
musicians, like circuit-riding preachers, encouraged these affairs on short notice, while
well-known musicians were brought in from adjacent areas. The Drew group – Patton,
Bankston, Brown, Tommy Johnson – played frequently on Webb Jenning's plantation.[109]
In the 1920s, Roebuck Staples, living on Dockery's plantation, saw Patton playing regularly for local houseparties.[110] Charles S. Johnson described similar parties in Macon
County, Alabama,[111] and Arthur Raper wrote about them in Macon and Greene counties, Georgia.[112] Victoria Spivey recalled seeing Blind Lemon Jefferson providing entertainment for them in the Galveston, Texas, area early in the 1920s.[113] The institution was
widespread down home (and it still exists). Jo Jo Williams remembered seeing House
and Brown, who sang at these dances with Patton in the twenties, providing music for
them in the thirties after Patton had died.[114] House himself, who said, "I could near
about call Charley [Patton] 'papa,'" recalls them fondly today as an old man in his seven-
ties,[115] and so do many musicians of the next generation, like Howlin' Wolf and Muddy
Waters, who grew up during those decades and were indelibly influenced by the blues
played then at the Saturday night dances.

What sort of blues *was* that? Because of the continuous, intense activity, it was
desirable for the music to keep going and going. House said that he and Patton used to
play dance pieces that went on for up to a half-hour without stopping.[116] Breakdowns
and square dances were considered old-fashioned; people wanted to hear the latest music
and do the newest dances. Blues was ideally suited to the purpose. Hence in this atmosphere it flourished. As lyrics could be improvised, and songs could be built of stanzas
whose order need not have been memorized beforehand, singers could string together
whatever stanzas came into their minds, reaching into their stanza storehouses or creating spontaneously. Singers were especially prized if they could keep feeding one stanza
after the next; but when more than one singer was present, they sometimes took turns,
one looking over at the next as a cueing device when he was through with his string.[117]
Another feature of the downhome blues songs made them particularly effective at the
Saturday night dances. Because each stanza expressed a complete thought, a listener
could break off his concentration and pick it up again later in the song without feeling he
had lost the thread. The lyrics most frequently took for their subject relations between
the sexes, with mistreatment and the difficulty of maintaining a stable relationship the
most common themes. Since singers and audience shared the personal experiences and
observations that led to the conventional wisdom of the lyrics, the songs continually
reinforced values and behavior; by expressing how one lover did feel towards the mis-

treating partner, the blues singer showed his audience how they were supposed to feel. Love was not "a trip to the moon on gossamer wings," but "rock me with one steady roll."

Down home is both a place in time and a state of mind. From the Civil War to the Depression most black Americans grew up in it. Holding it together was the plantation system based in a tenant-farming cotton economy. Tenants usually could not make enough money from their share of the crop to buy satisfactory food, clothing, or shelter. Very often the landlords cheated them, it would appear; but the one-crop economy was uncertain anyway. Tenant behavior was in part a response to oppressive white society, which controlled the law and had the sole power to enforce it. The black tenant family, close and strong, centered upon the farm household; if values and behavior did not conform to white middle-class standards, they were well suited to the economic system and to the culture it carried. People moved frequently, if not easily, from Saturday night dances to Sunday services; structural and functional similarities made the transition more comfortable. As the preacher voiced the ethic of the church community, the blues singer expressed the aspirations of the blues culture. The ethic, if not the worldview, they reinforced were identical. Interpreted as secular ceremony, the Saturday night dancing acted out the sexual embrace, while communal eating and drinking symbolized the bonding of the group. Fighting and gambling tested one's luck, measured how one stood at the moment with Fate. Though the worldviews of blues song and sermon differed, they preached the same advice: treat people right. Blues song lyrics teased the boundary between religion and magic, where supplication turned to demand, as the mistreated lover, after reciting his bill of indictment, decided whether to beg, bully, or leave – with an ironic parting shot. The large number of singers and listeners who have testified to feeling better after blues performances indicates that the ceremonies were effective, that people were renewed.

2 THE SINGERS' PERSPECTIVE

Where do blues songs come from? Most singers take credit for making up songs, but many feel that the songs ultimately derive from outside sources. Indeed, singers in tribal societies generally distinguish between personal songs and those which come from the natural or supernatural world (e.g., from birds, animals, gods, or spirits), usually attaching more importance to the latter. W. C. Handy wrote in his autobiography:

> As a child I had not heard the pipes of Pan, but pastoral melody was nevertheless a very real thing to me. Whenever I heard the song of a bird and the answering call of its mate, I could visualize the notes in the scale. . . . Although, as I fancied, they belonged to a great outdoor choir.

There was a French horn concealed in the breast of the blue jay. The tappings of the woodpecker were to me the reverberations of a snare drum. . . . In the raucous call of the distant crow I would hear the jazz motif. . . . All built up within my consciousness a natural symphony. This was the primitive prelude to the mature melodies now recognized as the blues. Nature was my kindergarten.[1]

But this is the only report of its kind that has come to my attention. To the reader versed in pre-Romantic English thought, it will sound familiar. That Handy must have been acquainted with some version of its ideas is clear from his response to a criticism of his manuscript: "I disagree with you in the matter of deleting the reference to birds and animals in the second chapter. By all means keep that in, it establishes a very important fact. The genius doesn't find his music in books and notes but in nature. He hears the music of the stream, the brook, the ocean, and makes notes out of them. I would not consent to take this out."[2]

Handy's schoolteacher disapproved of the young boy's ambition, saying that "musicians were idlers, dissipated characters, whisky drinkers and rounders. They were social pariahs. Southern white gentlemen . . . looked upon music as a parlor accomplishment, not as a means of questionable support. Such men should be examples." Handy's father, a minister, claimed, "Becoming a musician would be like selling my soul to the devil."[3]

Black Belt churchgoers commonly believed that blues was a sinful music and that to sing it one must be in league with the devil. The Reverend Robert Wilkins, at one time a blues singer, explained: "Now, the difference between blues and spiritual songs . . . you can only sing the one and not the other. . . . See, the body is the temple of the spirit of God, and it ain't but one spirit can dwell in that body at a time. That's the good spirit or the evil spirit. . . . Blues are songs of the evil spirit."[4] Tommy Johnson's bargain with the devil for the blues singer's ability to make up songs and play them expressed a widely held belief about their origin:

Now if Tom was living, he'd tell you. He said the reason he knowed so much, said he sold hisself to the devil. I asked him how. He said, 'If you want to learn how to play anything you want to play and learn how to make songs yourself, you take your guitar and you go to where a road crosses that way, where a crossroad is. Get there, be sure to get there just a little 'fore twelve o'clock that night so you'll know you'll be there. You have your guitar and be playing a piece sitting there by yourself. . . . A big black man will walk up there and take your guitar, and he'll tune it. And then he'll play a piece and hand it back to you. That's the way I learned how to play anything I want.[5]

Johnson learned to play spirituals that way, casting doubt on their holy origin. And blues songs bore evil fruit. Charles Love, a ragtime and jazz musician born in 1885, expressed these views: "You see blues is the evil of music, evil spirited music. Why I say that is because whenever the blues is played there's a fight right after. You know the blues apt to get them all bewildered some kind of way, makes 'em wild, they want to fight."[6] Whether blues and alcohol were the cause, reports indicate plenty of violence at the Saturday night juke parties.

Like the church spirituals, blues had power over its listeners. George "Mojo" Buford thought the power was in the words: "Both [blues and spirituals] make you cry. Quick, too."[7] Their similarities even led a few singers to suggest that blues songs grew out of the church. An anonymous singer interviewed by William Ferris in the Delta said:

> Now if blueses had originated in the church, which it might have, as far as I know . . . you take the . . . basic beat behind your blues records you will also find behind a lot of spiritual tunes. The people git happy in church just like they'll git happy at a dance. It's the same thing. They can't dance, but they pat their feet and clap their hands and enjoy it. It's not that much difference between the types of music. It's just where you are and who you're playing for, your audience.[8]

Baby Doo Caston made a persuasive case for the source of blues in the tone and cadence of the preacher's voice: "The blues mostly derive out of the Baptist churches. Because a preacher, if he's preaching gospel, he doesn't have to be making no particular sound as long as he was preaching from the Bible, right? But in those days a preacher could do that until he'd get warmed up and get a certain sound going; I mean, they wouldn't consider him a good preacher." Here Caston broke into an imitation of a chanting preacher delivering his lines in short bursts, then continued: "And people got to feeling these things. Unless this preacher had a certain sound in his church they didn't consider him as a good preacher. But he had to have a certain tone quality in order for the people to consider him a good preacher." The power in the preacher's voice made the congregation "start whooping, hollering, screaming, and fainting; they'd have to pass them out the windows! And they was serious." Afterwards the relieved congregation broke into song. The next morning, Caston said, people exclaimed – just as others spoke about a dance party the morning after – "Oh! Did they have a good service last night!"[9]

Tempting as the analogy between service and dance party might have been, churchgoers rejected it. Wilkins theorized: "In blues it's what you call a felt-inward feeling – of your own self. It's not a spiritual feeling that you have. . . . It's something that happened to you and cause you to become sorry. . . . Then you would compose the song to that feeling that you have. And then you would sing it and after you begin to sing it, then you become accustomed to it through psychology that 'most anybody could have that same feeling as you did. It's universal, but it don't bring joy in the spirit." To bring true joy in the spirit, Wilkins thought, one must sing God's praises: "Singing blues helps to relieve your natural soul – from your natural soul – but not from a spiritual soul. The only thing you can get relief from in the spiritual soul is by praising God. . . . It don't say nothing in the Bible about playing any blues. All it says is 'Praise the lord with string instruments' in the *Psalms*. . . . It says praise the Lord with them, not the devil."[10]

Wilkins's distinction could not relieve the blues singer worried about the state of his soul. To find another answer, he pondered the source of his power. Wilkins himself believed that "it was impossible . . . to play like I did unless it was a gift from my birth."[11] Sam Chatmon thought inheritance accounted for his ability: "We started out from our parents – it's just a gift we had in the family. Our father and mother could both play."[12] Jo Jo Williams agreed: "A lot of my foreparents was musicians, as far as I can understand, so for that particular reason I guess it's just something that fell on me."[13] It was a short step from something that just "fell" unasked on someone to the belief that blues-singing ability was God given. Babe Stovall said, "God gave me a talent. Everybody has a talent. Smoking and drinking are habits. God gives talents. These others are from the devil."[14] Yet other singers felt it sufficient merely to keep the Sabbath holy. Blind Lemon Jefferson refused to sing blues on Sunday.[15] Skip James sang at Saturday night parties and went "up the road" to preach the next day.[16] Many blues singers became preachers later in life, acting out the parable of the Prodigal Son.

Whether blues singers inherited their gift or received it from a supernatural source, they took pride in their ability to create songs. In fact, audience demands for continuous dance music encouraged singers to make up lyrics. By adding on traditional blues stanzas, they could extend a piece as long as their memories might serve. Sometimes, instead of combining and recombining traditional lyrics, they invented lines and stanzas on the spot; but this sort of spontaneous improvisation was rare. When the audience expected shorter songs, or if the singer's memory was unequal to the task of creating longer ones,[17] they usually responded with stanzas built upon the same theme.

Even so, the storehouse habit was so thoroughly ingrained that singers rarely sang a song the same way twice. Most often the song was built on a foundation stanza, usually the first one, which established the song's title and announced a basic situation. A good example is "Pony Blues" (transcr. 1):

> Hitch up my pony   saddl' up my   black mare
> Hitch up my pony   saddl' up my black mare
> I'm gon' find a rider ooh   baby in the   world somewhere

Charley Patton probably sang this stanza first each time he performed "Pony Blues." Eventually, the song "Pony Blues" became associated with Patton, and whoever else sang it had to include that initial, identifying stanza. But after the first stanza established the song, the singer was free to mix in other stanzas, some associated with the "pony" theme or the basic situation, some not. Together with the foundation stanza, a small group of two or perhaps as many as five stanzas were linked in the singer's mind; the combination formed the supporting structure on which additional, unlinked stanzas could extend the song for as long as the dancers could stay on their feet or until the singer(s) ran out of lyrics. The interchangeability of the stanzas gave the long blues song a different shape each time Patton, or anyone else, sang it; the habit of interchange made it likely that even a short blues song would exhibit alternate lyrics and a differing stanzaic order each time it was sung.

Lester Melrose, a semi-independent recording director and "A & R" (artist and repertoire) man who was responsible for most of the blues recording done by Columbia and RCA Victor from 1934 to 1951, recalled that this composing technique caused consternation in the recording studios: "Some of the artists who could not read or write made it very difficult to record them. Every time they would record a number they could never repeat the same verses. The result would be to record the number about four times and select the one with the best verses. . . . They would sing two or three different verses for each song."[18]

When multiple "takes" of the same title have been preserved, we can compare lyrics and observe something of the process of blues composition. In April, 1927, probably on the same day, Blind Lemon Jefferson recorded two takes of "Match Box Blues"; a month earlier he had recorded the same title for a different company. Here is the earlier version:

FIGURE 5. "Match Box Blues" (OKeh 8455, March 14, 1927)

1. I'm goin' to the river goin' walk down by the sea
   I'm goin' to the river   walk down by the sea
   I've got those tadpoles and minnows eyein' over me

2. Standin' here wonderin' will a matchbox hold my clothes
   I was settin' here wonderin' will a matchbox hold my clothes
   I ain't got so many matches but I got so far to go

3. Lord mama   who may your manager be
   Hey hey mama   who may your manager be
   Reason I ask so many questions can't you make 'rangements for me

4. I got a girl cross town she crochet all the time
   I got a girl cross town crochet all the time
   Baby if you don't quit crochetin' you're gon' lose your mind

5. I wouldn't mind marryin'   but I can't stand settlin' down
   I don't mind marryin'   but lord settlin' down
   I'm gon' act like a preacher so I can ride from town to town

6. I'm leavin' town   cryin' won't make me stay
   I'm leavin' town eeee cryin' won't make me stay
   Baby the more you cry   the further you drive me away

Below are the two takes which Jefferson recorded a month later (figs. 6 and 7).[19] Stanzas 2, 3, and 4 in figure 5 recur here in slightly modified form and in a different order.

FIGURE 6. "Match Box Blues" (Paramount master number 4424-2, April, 1927)

1. I'm settin' here wonderin' will a matchbox hold my clothes
   I'm settin' here wonderin' will a matchbox hold my clothes
   I ain't got so many matches but I got so far to go

2. Girl cross town gonna be my teddy bear
   Girl cross town gonna be my teddy bear
   Put a chain on me and I'll follow you everywhere

3. And a peg leg woman man she can't hardly get her dough
   I say a peg leg woman just can't hardly get her dough
   I left one in Lakeport last night I been – and I'm servin' jelly roll

4. I don't see why   these women treats me so mean
   I don't see why these   gals treat me so mean
   Sometime I think I'm some man that the women ain't never seen

5. Well I got up this morning with my sure enough on my mind
   Got up this morning   same thing on my mind
   The woman I love   she keep a good man worried all the time

6. Now tell me mama   who may your manager be
   Now tell me   who may your manager be
   Reason I ask so many questions can't you make 'rangements for me

FIGURE 7. "Match Box Blues" (Paramount master number 4446-4, April, 1927)

1. I'm settin' here wonderin' will a matchbox hold my clothes
   I'm settin' here wonderin' will a matchbox hold my clothes
   I ain't got so many matches but I got so far to go

2. I said fair brown   who may your manager be
   Oh mama who may your manager be
   Reason I ask so many questions can't you make 'rangements for me

3. I got a girl cross town she crochet all the time
   I got a girl cross town crochets all the time
   Mama if you don't quit crochetin' you're gon' lose your mind

4. I can't count the time   I've stole away and cried
   Can't count the times I've stole away and cried
   Sugar the blues ain't on me but things ain't goin' on right

5. If you want your lover   you'd better pin her to your side
   I said if you want your baby   pin her to your side
   If she flag my train papa Lemon's gon' let her ride

6. I ain't seen my good gal   in three long weeks today
   Ain't seen my good gal in three long weeks today
   Sugar it's been so long seem like my heart gon' break

7. Now excuse me mama   from knockin' on your door
   Well excuse me mama from   knockin' on your door
   My mind gon' change   I'll never knock here no more

In all three versions the "matchbox" stanza establishes the title and introduces an underlying theme. The singer possesses so few clothes that he asks whether a suitcase the size of a matchbox might not hold them; then he announces that he has a long journey ahead. Loneliness and poverty are underlying ideas which find specific expression in this stanza. Two additional stanzas recur in the three versions to form the supporting structure on which the other stanzas are built: the stanza in which the singer speaks of his girl across town, and the stanza in which he addresses a woman and asks who her manager (pimp) is. The rest of the stanzas are all, in one way or another, about woman trouble; there are, apparently, several women, and it is not always clear which one is being addressed at a given moment. Nor is it clear that the stanzas have any chronological progression. The order of the stanzas could be – and has been – changed with no apparent ill effect.

Yet we should not be hasty in ascribing textual incoherence to the songs. It is reasonable to suppose that there is some reason why the singer follows one stanza with another; it would be unusual if it were a wholly random process. Associative coherence suggests itself as one alternative: something in one stanza signals the singer; the signal reminds him of something else; that something else finds expression in the following stanza. Since this coherence differs from the logical and temporal kind which a Westerner expects from a tale, anecdote, or narrative song, we might suppose that it is not random, but unconscious.

We do not know precisely why Jefferson moves from one particular stanza to the next in any version of "Match Box Blues." In some cases we remain baffled; in others we may guess. A rare temporal connection probably exists between stanzas 6 and 7 in figure 7: the singer, who has not seen his lover for three weeks, knocks on her door. The ensuing dialogue is confusing in the context of the absence. We may try to make sense of it by filling in the lacuna, but that is unnecessarily speculative; all that is needed is temporal coherence. In fact, supplying logical coherence is a dangerous undertaking when it is the singer's, not the analyst's, mental processes that are at issue.

One kind of associative composition may be responsible for the progression from stanzas 1 to 3 in figure 6. Thought of travel in stanza 1 signals the "across town" lines of stanza 2. The girl of stanza 2 is likened to a teddy bear. If I understand correctly, it is she who speaks in the third line of that stanza, asking for a chain and promising to follow the singer. That language, with its overtones of sadomasochism and the suggestion of a pimp-prostitute relationship, may trigger stanza 3, where the singer takes on the role of pimp and introduces a peg-legged woman whose handicap jeopardizes her profession. It is characteristic of this kind of associative composition that one stanza signals the stanza directly following.

For another kind of associative composition, we may return to the notion of an underlying idea, or theme, such as loneliness, the desire for travel, the desire for sex, and so forth. A single theme or group of related ideas may find specific expression in a successive series of stanzas. The desire for sex may be the associative link among, and the idea which generates, stanzas 2 through 6 in figure 6. The singer's assumed role of pimp may have been the underlying idea giving rise not only to stanzas 2 and 3, as noted, but also to stanza 6. Indeed, if we compare the three versions, we find that these are the three stanzas common to all, although the idea of pimping is not apparent behind the "crocheting" stanza (fig. 5, st. 4; fig. 7, st. 3).

These hypotheses of associative composition have something in common with the Parry-Lord theory of composition by oral formula and by theme, and with Noam Chomsky's theories of transformational-generative grammar; I take up these similarities in chapter 5.

Associations based on other factors are likely – rhyme, for example. The pressure of finding a third line that rhymes with the first two constrains the singer, while it also directs him. The same assonant rhyme (*time/mind*) is used in stanzas 4 and 5 of figure 5, but the stanzas are quite different. Moreover, the movement from one stanza to the next may have a subtle phonetic pressure; it is unusual, for example, to find two successive stanzas that use the same rhyme.

Some of Jefferson's stanzas in the three versions of "Match Box Blues" reappeared in identical or slightly altered form in his other recordings. He included the "teddy bear" stanza to establish the title of a song he recorded two months later, "Teddy Bear Blues" (Paramount 12487); but here the roles are reversed:

> I said fair brown let me be your teddy bear
> Oooh   can I be your teddy bear
> Tie a string on my neck and I'll follow you everywhere[20]

Jefferson employed the "crocheting" stanza in "Easy Rider Blues," recorded immediately before the second version of "Match Box Blues" (fig. 7) and released as the other side of the disc. In a similar fashion, but one which I will not discuss here, Jefferson's guitar accompaniment consisted of several interchangeable sequences which he varied from one song to the next.

In the preceding analysis of the way stanzas are fitted together in the composition of downhome blues songs, I have been aware that coherence is something we are likely to find if we are looking for it. But the alternative assumption – incoherence – proceeds equally to a foreordained conclusion. It is a fact that the stanzas follow one upon the other; associative coherence suggests one way in which they do so.

Blind Lemon Jefferson's method of fitting together stanzas to build blues songs at the moment of performance was typical of most early downhome blues singers and a good many later ones. Recordings, however, slowly exerted an opposing influence. Blues singers who were drawn to recordings, who listened to them, studied them, and imitated them, usually tried to achieve logical, temporal, and thematic coherence among the six or seven stanzas that made up their own separate compositions. Often those who could do so wrote out the lyrics beforehand, composing them over a period of time and practicing them in advance to make certain they fit the $3\frac{1}{2}$-minutes-per-side time limit. Different takes of Robert Johnson's blues songs, recorded one just after another, reveal only slight changes in the texts. Moreover, once a singer had made a record, the audience expected to hear it again in a live performance.[21] But traditional methods of blues composition were encouraged by the continuing institution of the Saturday night juke dance party. The older singers were fixed in their habits; like Charley Patton or Tommy Johnson, they probably viewed recording as incidental to their main activity. Even many of the younger singers, like Son House, who admired recordings and tried to keep lyrics to a single theme, simply failed to do so. The power and exhilaration provided by the traditional methods of improvisation and the opportunity to continue them at the dance parties prevented these singers from attaining their ideal. Lyrics were invented and shared; they passed into tradition, where they appeared and reappeared in the recorded and unrecorded repertoire that makes up the corpus of the blues.

Although most singers relied heavily on traditional lyrics, they prized (and sometimes overestimated) their ability to make up their own. Those who made records convinced the company talent scouts that the songs were indeed original. If the songs were not wholly theirs, they usually did include a few original stanzas. It is virtually impossible to pinpoint the first occurrence of a particular phrase, line, or stanza; locating its first recorded appearance does not guarantee that the singer on that record originated it. A singer could declare a song his own by reworking traditional material that he mistakenly thought was original, by alternating it with stanzas he knew he had borrowed from other singers, and, of course, by making up new lyrics. Skip James reported, "I composed my own music and songs, wordings, I have rhymed up my own words and the biggest amount of playing and music and version is from self experience."[22] Many times the singer relied on his own experiences to find subjects and feelings to put into his lyrics: "Maybe it wasn't exactly then but I had the experience of things. You find that it's easier to tell the truth about your life so you sing about it."[23]

But blues songs do not always represent the direct experiences or emotions of the singer. The Reverend Rubin Lacy, a former blues artist, explained: "Sometimes I'd propose [lyrics] as [if] it happened to me in order to hit somebody else, 'cause everything that happened to one person has at some time or other happened to another one. If not, it will."[24] Lacy said his composition "Mississippi Jailhouse Groan" did not derive from a long stretch *he* spent in prison. "St. Louis Jimmy" Oden remembered how his famous song "Goin' Down Slow" was inspired by the experience of a friend: "Of course all blues singers make up their own blues. . . . And my blues came mostly from women . . . 'Goin' Down Slow' started from a girl in St. Louis – it wasn't me – I've never been *sick* a day in my life, but I seen her in the condition she was in – pregnant, trying to lose a kid, see. And she looked like she was goin' down slow. And I made that remark to my sister and it came in my mind and I started to writin' it. . . . I looked at other people's troubles and I writes from that, and I writes from my own troubles."[25] Victoria Spivey recalled how her mother became worried when she heard her daughter's hit record "T.B. Blues": "I'll never know what made me make that record. Cause when my mother heard it . . . she . . . ask if I was sick, if I had the T.B. . . . But at that time I had been lookin' at people who had the T.B. in part of the country . . . so I figured it was a nice thing to write about."[26] The Reverend Robert Wilkins, recalling his days as a blues singer, "asserted that one need not personally undergo the experiences related in a blues song; the singer often can take as his song material occurrences that have befallen others."[27]

I have belabored the point that blues singers do not always sing about experiences they themselves have undergone, because the assumption that blues lyrics are factually autobiographical remains common in blues scholarship.[28] Yet, like autobiographies, blues lyrics contain an "I" who is a character, an actor, a persona created by the singer.[29]

Not only have some writers assumed that blues songs must reflect the singers' direct experiences; they have also asserted, as they have been told by several musicians, that one should "have" the blues in order to sing blues well. This self-fulfilling prophecy accounts for lackadaisical-sounding performances and establishes a ludicrous listener's aesthetic principled on the amount of observable agony in the singer's cry. It is not true that downhome blues singers who provided regular entertainment felt the blues every time they sang such songs. How could they? Rubin Lacy expressed a reasonable judgment:

> I've sung [blues] on many a day and never thought I had 'em. What did I want to have the blues for, when I had everything I wanted, all the liquor, all the money I needed, and more gals than I needed? . . . I was playing because everybody loved to hear me play 'em and I loved to play 'em . . . I was having fun. Sometimes I'd be kind of bothered and worried as any other man would be. I wasn't lively all the time. . . . But as a whole I had more blues since I been preaching than I ever had when I was playing the blues.[30]

Singers sometimes feel melancholy when they sing blues, and sometimes the singing helps them feel better. Singers sometimes make up blues songs about personal experiences, happy ones and sad ones, and sometimes they think back to those experiences when singing about them, feeling the associated emotions. That much should be clear to anyone who gives the matter a little thought. But reconstruction of a singer's life or personality solely from his songs seems to me ill advised.

Downhome blues singers learned by imitating others, usually local musicians. Because instruments were personal possessions, the novice tried to buy or trade for his own, or convinced his family to do it. If he could not get a "legitimate" instrument, he rigged up a substitute. Although more cigar-box guitars were recalled than played, the one-string "diddly-bow," derived from an African musical bow, was abundant.[31] It consisted of a piece of broom wire strung up on a wall, kept a few inches off the wall by bottles or cans or pieces of wood at each end. The wire was plucked; its pitch could be varied by sliding a smooth object, like a bottle, up and down its length. (Here, rather than in Hawaii, is the logical source of Afro-American slide guitar playing.)

Once the learner had an instrument, he approached the skilled musician for help. The expert, like the devil which Tommy Johnson saw at the crossroads, showed him how to tune it and how to accompany songs. Usually there was no singing instruction. Though some musical vocabulary was exchanged, the terminology consisted of nomenclature incorporating half-correct borrowings from Western musical vocabulary, inventions, and, possibly, African-derived terms. Of the Delta terminology used by Skip James and Son House, Al Wilson wrote:

> Unlike most bluesmen, Son calls each of the standard tuning keys by their right names, save for C, which he calls F. (Booker White calls E G, G cross-G, and A A♭ or D♭; Robert Pete Williams, Rubin Lacy and Skip James all refer to E as C natural.) However, in other matters Son approaches the delta blues norm. For instance "minor" means any note or chord on or above the fifth fret, and "major" any note or chord below it. . . . In addition, Son uses a rather vague system of string classification, using soprano, alto, tenor, and bass. Skip is more definite; from the sixth string to the first they are 6) bass or subtone, 5) baritone, 4) alto, 3 + 2) tenors, 1) soprano. Skip also refers often to triplets, 16th, 32nd, and 64th notes, tonics, subdominants, and $\frac{2}{4}$ and $\frac{4}{4}$ time, all incorrectly. It turns out he bought an "Exegesis of Musical Knowledge" from H. C. Speir in 1931 and skimmed it.[32]

There was no written system of musical notation; the learner simply watched and imitated the expert's movements as best he could. Since repetition of the accompaniment unit, the stanza, could serve throughout a given song, the learner needed to master only a few of these before he was able to give rudimentary performances to support his lyric invention. The novice often sat at the master musician's feet during a Saturday night dance. If he was bold enough, he picked up the master's guitar or used his own during an intermission to test the crowd's reaction. Son House recalls that Robert Johnson drove away the audience the first time he played at an intermission between sets by House and Willie Brown.[33]

It took up to a year of steady practice before a novice could consider himself an adequate guitarist; it took longer for him to build up a large stock of blues stanzas, although he could perform one or two songs in a matter of days or a few weeks after he began. Records made either by novices or by studio-shy professionals enable us better to observe the retrieval of stanzas from the singer's mental stockpile, because in such instances the procedure does not work very well. Memphis Minnie's first recording of "Bumble Bee" (see transcr. 16) is a useful illustration; she repeats lines and stanzas, hesitating occasionally, having difficulty finding formulas that rhyme. Some singers never got over these problems, even after they had been singing for quite some time (see transcrs. 12 and 13 for Tommy Johnson's blunders). The more skillful a singer, the better he was at manipulating traditional formulas to his own ends.

The guitar was the chief accompanying instrument in early downhome blues recordings. The guitar was more popular down home than the piano because it was portable and less expensive. Easier to play than the fiddle, and easier to sing along with than the fiddle or banjo, it offered a fuller sound besides. Guitars were relatively new, having become widely available at the very end of the nineteenth century;[34] their rise in popularity coincided with the growth of downhome blues. Even if downhome blues singers did not favor guitar accompaniments, however, an overwhelming number of early recordings featured them simply because the companies sought to duplicate the commercial success of singer-guitarist Blind Lemon Jefferson.

Pocket knives, bottlenecks, and other smooth devices were slid on top of the strings of the guitar, as on the diddly-bow, to produce whining sounds. A musician could thus obtain degrees of pitch between the common Western semitone divisions of the finger-board. (Sliding fingers achieved similar effects on the fiddle and fretless banjo.) Musicians were able to raise or lower pitch microtonally by pushing the string to the side and stretching or releasing it. The guitar could thereby produce the same dips, glides, and shadings as the voice. Because the guitarist could supply a rhythmic pulse at the same time he could produce melodies or riffs, the guitar provided a satisfyingly complex accompaniment.

For downhome blues the guitar was sometimes tuned outside the standard concert guitar tuning (E-A-D-G-B-E). The so-called Spanish tuning (D-G-D-G-B-D), in which the open strings were tuned to a G-major triad (or, a whole tone higher, to an A-major triad), was the most widespread nonstandard tuning, used from Texas (Ramblin' Thomas) to Atlanta (Blind Willie McTell, Barbecue Bob). It was similar to a standard banjo G tuning and may have gotten its name from a piece often called "Spanish Fandango" which employed it.[35] Another important tuning was the "cross-natural" or "Vastopol" tuning to a D-major triad (D-A-D-F♯-A-D) or an E-major triad. It probably was derived from "The Siege of Sebastopol," a song popular in the 1880s.[36] Both of these open tunings facilitated playing with a slide device, because major triads could be sounded by laying it straight across the strings. Another advantage of open tunings was that the guitarist, pitching his song in the key of the chord to which the strings were tuned, could easily pick out melodies or riffs using his fingers or a slide device on the treble strings while he kept a rhythmic pulse on the unfretted bass strings. This arrangement encouraged accompaniments which differed from the already standardized "three-change" harmony based on tonic, subdominant, and dominant-seventh chords. The guitarist, by holding a drone bass on the keynote, created a much more ambiguous overall harmonic structure by merely suggesting the changes in the treble. Sometimes guitarists attained this same harmonic ambiguity by playing in the key of E in standard tuning and using the lowest-pitched bass string (E) to suggest the tonic, and the next-lowest bass string (A) to suggest the subdominant. Because it was unnecessary to fret the bass strings, the fingers of the left hand were free, as they were in open tunings, to play complex figures all over the fingerboard on the treble strings.

Recent downhome blues scholarship has established geographical "guitar style areas." Except for a few Atlanta guitarists, East Coast accompanists favored complex "ragtime" accompaniments, usually played in standard tuning, without harmonic ambiguity, in the keys of C or G. Complex and versatile, this style could be used to advantage for blues, ballads, ragtime, and poplar songs. The outstanding East Coast guitarist of the 1920s was Blind Blake. At the other pole is the "Delta blues" style, played either in open tunings (usually Spanish), or in standard tuning in the keys of E or A. I find these accompaniments deceptively simple. Harmonically ambiguous and polyrhythmic, they are among the most interesting Afro-American musical achievements. But stylistic distinctions do not always correspond to geographical ones; hence, their superimposition must be taken only as a rough and general guide.[37]

Not all musicians were eager to teach others how to play, especially when they thought songs "belonged" to them. Nonetheless, reticence seems the exception rather than the rule; in a Black Belt community there was a good deal of musical borrowing, much of it probably unconscious. Fred McDowell said, "I never could hardly learn no music by nobody trying to show me. Like, what I hear you play tonight, well, next week sometime it would come back to me – what you was playing. I'd get the sound of it in my head. Then I'd do it my way, from what I remembered."[38] McDowell's initial instruction came by demonstration. He learned from his uncle, and from two local guitarists: Raymond Payne, who never recorded commercially because he was afraid other singers might "steal" his songs, and Vandy McKenna. After McDowell or any other downhome musician learned a rudimentary style, his future learning became more selective.

Once blues records became available in the 1920s, guitarists familiar with the idiom could learn from them. Although exceptional accompaniments were admired, and imitated, if possible, it was easier just to learn the words and the tune while working out a suitable accompaniment in one's habitual style. Some of the downhome recording artists – not just vaudeville singers – toured on a small scale, and musicians who could see what they were doing might learn from them. Blind Lemon Jefferson, for example, spent a week with Rubin Lacy in Itta Bena, Mississippi; they could hardly have helped exchanging songs and guitar techniques.[39]

Without question, downhome blues singers of the 1920s were influenced by vaudeville blues singers. The antics that went with the music and the general "show" atmosphere carried over into the Saturday night dance parties and country suppers. (Of course, they may also have begun there.) When I asked Son House if he thought he learned anything from Ma Rainey and Bessie Smith's music, he replied, "Well, yeah, some things. No music, but their singing. Old Bessie Smith used to be our favorite. . . . [She] had the best voice – and words."[40] Even so, the downhome blues singers did not develop the studied control that Bessie Smith had.[41]

A surprising number of blues singers shared with vaudeville musicians similar ideals of music and musicianship, even though their practice was further from those ideals. These singers valued the ability to read and thus perform any kind of music. Blues was all right in its place, but grand opera was the highest vocal art. The aesthetic criteria can be detected behind the Perfect Voice Institute advertisement which appeared among the blues record ads on the entertainment page of the November 5, 1927, *Chicago Defender* (fig. 8). The black "artistic metropolis" was responsible for continuing the "legitimate" ideal.[42] Dave Peyton, who took over in 1925 as the *Defender's* major entertainment columnist after Tony Langston, steadily told his readers that musical achievement came from formal education, apprenticeship, and experience in the "classics."[43] Perry Bradford, the promoter responsible for the initial appearance of vaudeville blues on commercial recordings, articulated this attitude in his autobiography: "[The young jazz musician] should study how to play and develop the sound of his instrument to blend with the legitimate musician and make some of the billion of dollars that is rolling right under his nose by the 'square' musicians."[44] If Bradford's motive was to gain a fair share of the money, others believed that vaudeville singers and musicians should serve as models because they were better artists. That assumption underlies Edith Johnson's recollection of Ethel Waters:

> Years ago at that time blues singers on the stage were real new around here and each week at the Booker Washington they would feature some blues singer like Ida Cox or Clara Smith or Bessie Smith, Ma Rainey, Blind Lemon and . . . oh my, Ethel Waters . . . I always thought she was one of the better singers that we had. . . . If you don't have no personality with your singing, your singing is enjoyed but you are soon forgotten.[45]

A close look at evaluative remarks by many downhome blues singers reveals their similar aspirations. Son House was impressed with his partner Willie Brown's ability to "second" another guitarist and play in any key all over the fingerboard. Brown's ability with the flat pick also impressed him.[46] Sam Chatmon's "main criticism of Charley Patton and the older generation was that they only knew how to play in the key of E and in 'Spanish.'" Chatmon thought that "the [Mississippi] Sheiks and Charley McCoy were much more proficient, versatile, and talented. The Chatmon brothers' recordings are characterized by group sessions, complex chords, more use of the major IV and major V chords in the same song – in general, a more sophisticated sound than that of Patton and his musical generation."[47] The Chatmon groups were closer than Patton to Anglo-American string-band style and the East Coast style just described. Although downhome musicians shared a desire to "improve" their country style, they often were unable to do so. If they were older, they were settled in their musical habits. If they were young, they had to travel to the cities to get instruction – and many did just that. Curiously, then, although downhome blues does not sound genteel, many singers believed

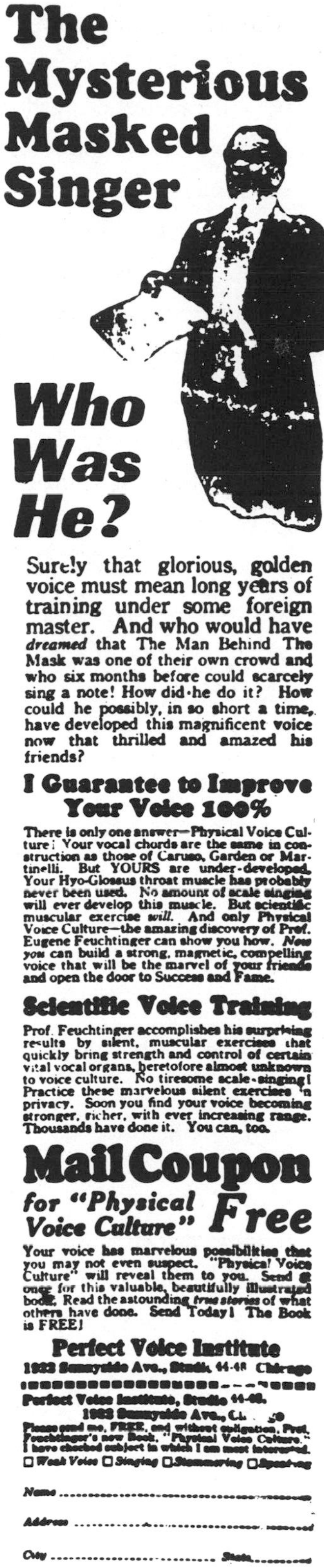

FIGURE 8. *From the* Chicago Defender, *November 5, 1927*

in a matrix of standards set by vaudeville taste ultimately traceable to genteel white aesthetic criteria.

Even though the singers knew they were far from their ideal, they maintained it. A good singer must know many different songs, said Son House.[48] Rubin Lacy asserted that "the blues is not sung for the tune. It's sung for the words, mostly."[49] House was critical of songs which did not stick to a single subject; Charley Patton's main trouble, he said, was that he felt free to put almost any stanza into a song. House offered this brief for textual coherence: "The main thing – what you start on in a song anyhow what it's about, what it means, the more words you could get on that same song with a different verse about the same thing, oh man, that went, they liked that."[50] Furry Lewis believed that some musicians were poor singers; they made mistakes and got the order of the stanzas and the words themselves mixed up. Each stanza must rhyme and make its point, Lewis said. "It's like when you cook; you have to put in all the ingredients and have to put 'em in the right order or it won't come out right." He told me he disagreed with House's contention that each stanza should be about the same subject, but in another interview he expressed the opposite opinion.[51] Though House admitted that not everyone could hold songs to a single theme, he maintained that ideal. And though he believed he succeeded in doing it in his records, for which he studied the stanzas in advance, it is clear that he failed to achieve the kind of coherence – mainly temporal and logical – which the vaudeville blues writers provided for their singers. Probably House was most sensitive to this criterion because he himself had such difficulty meeting it. He criticized Tommy Johnson's records:

> [He] would go over and over a song, you know, the same verse he'd say just a little while ago and then directly he'd go back over the same one way back on the end. I never did believe in that; I didn't figure the [record] buyer could get no sense out of that. I figured the buyer, he wants, since you're singing about such and such a thing, this rooster or this puppy, that it consist of him. Don't start about the puppy and then go on later up on about the hen.[52]

By his own standards, Lewis would have criticized Johnson's repetitions, too. Lewis declared that a singer should memorize his words before the recording session; studying a song, he said, was as hard as working on a job.[53]

It was important not to alter a song's steady pulse. When I asked Lewis whether, if he had to make a mistake, he would prefer it to be in the beat or the words, he replied that he would rather err in the words.[54] Robert Pete Williams asserted that it was very important not to "break time," and the Reverend Robert Wilkins was quick to agree.[55] Son House criticized Blind Lemon Jefferson for being a "time-breaker"; people who danced to his records had trouble getting back in step. "It was a bother, it absolutely was," House complained.[56] Yet a skilled musician such as Jefferson could pause or "stop-time" and come back as if the beat had not disappeared.

Most downhome blues singers believed lines should rhyme their last syllables. House pointed out that rhyme added impact to meaning: "I had sense enough to try to make 'em rhyme 'em so they'd have *hits* to 'em with a meaning, some sense to 'em, you know."[57] Furry Lewis said, "If it ain't rhymed up, it don't sound good to me or nobody else."[58] On another occasion he observed, "If you don't rhyme it up, you don't understand nothing and you ain't getting nowhere."[59] Robert Pete Williams said lines need not rhyme (and his do not); but Wilkins, who overheard my question, and believes that Williams is "countrified," disagreed.[60]

Musical taste sometimes reflected practical matters. It was important to have a voice which could be heard above the volume of the instruments. If a man could not sing loud, "they wouldn't want to be bothered with you."[61] According to Baby Doo Caston, a vibrato was particularly good because it made one's voice carry.[62] Both Caston and House emphasized that a wide vocal range was an asset. Many listeners have commented on the hoarse or raspy quality in the voices of some blues singers. Some downhome singers did strive for a low, raspy voice, while others preferred a high, thin one. Most vaudeville blues singers had high, clear voices and precise diction; most downhome blues singers valued clear enunciation but were not trained to produce it. When I asked Son House to listen to a particular line from a song by Charley Patton that I could not make out, House laughed. He said, "You could sit at Charley's feet and not understand a word he sang."[63]

Skeptics may suggest that divergence between downhome blues theory and practice is more apparent than real, emphasized for the sake of interviewers who might be expected to hold genteel views themselves. But that skepticism has to face continued pronouncements from a variety of musicians, a well-known vaudeville aesthetic, and the fact that many downhome blues singers traveled to the cities to undertake formal musical training.

Besides learning down home from local or traveling musicians, the blues singer could spend time in a large town or city with a constant musical turnover. If he went to a very large city, especially one in the North, he might learn a new style of accompaniment and increase his musical knowledge. During the 1920s and 1930s several "guitar methods" – instruction books, some still in print – promised the faithful student mastery of the most modern instrumental styles. Typical instruction began with the proper letter names of the individual notes as the guitarist played them on the strings with his flat pick – finger-picked accompaniments were said to be old-fashioned – but soon progressed to the melody-chord style of accompaniment, in which he played the melody on the treble strings when it was moving quickly, and played chord inversions emphasiz-

ing the melody note at the highest-pitched string when it was moving slowly enough. For orchestral or "combo" work, the style recommended was a four-to-the-bar chopping right hand, sounding "power chords" formed by the left, to supply a solid pulse for the band. Particularly exciting were the different chord substitutions available. The mark of the good guitarist was his ability with various altered chords: ninths, elevenths, diminished chords, augmented chords, chords with flatted fifths, and so on, instead of "straight" triads or dominant-seventh chords. In a four-to-the-bar accompaniment the guitarist usually switched chords every second beat. These guitar methods always told the student that the "old-fashioned" ways of playing guitar – and, by implication, downhome music – were "corny." What they did not tell the student was that the new style would quickly prove corny itself. How perplexed the instructors would have been trying to explain what was dull about the guitar style of a Blind Blake or a Charley Patton, had they even been aware of them.

The principal "modern" blues guitarist of the 1920s was Lonnie Johnson. His records inspired young guitarists who wanted to learn something different from the downhome styles. Scrapper Blackwell, Leroy Carr's guitarist, was another. The story of Carl Martin (fig. 9) and Ted Bogan (fig. 10), musicians who grew up just outside Knoxville, Tennessee, learning the old-fashioned, East Coast, string-band style, and then decided to improve, is typical of many downhome musicians who migrated to the cities. Wanting a full-time career in music, they rightly observed that the more versatile they became, the more work they could get. At first they traveled throughout their region, even venturing into Ohio and Michigan, playing for picnics, dances, Rotary Club suppers, and the like, for white as well as black audiences. After they learned to read music and acquired "fake books," which contained lyrics, melodies, and guitar chords to current popular songs, they could play practically any request. Martin proudly explained, "If you asked me a request today and I didn't know it, I'd go get the sheet music tomorrow and learn it so I wouldn't be caught the next time."[64] After 1933 they made their home in Chicago and learned songs of various ethnic groups – Polish, Italian, German – so they could play at their weddings and parties. They once played for Ralph Capone, Al Capone's brother.[65] Charley McCoy, a guitarist from Jackson, Mississippi, who accompanied Tommy Johnson and made several downhome blues records by himself, moved to Chicago and found work with the Harlem Hamfats, a hokum-jazz group of the 1930s whose music was well ahead of its time. Several downhome musicians, inspired by guitarists in touring jazz bands, went to northern cities to learn how to play in that style. Floyd Smith, one of the earliest guitarists to use electric amplification, was featured in the 1930s with Andy Kirk's Twelve Clouds of Joy; Baby Doo Caston's move to Chicago was decided when he saw Smith in person.[66] Much of the information about downhome

FIGURE 9. *Carl Martin, Lexington, Massachusetts, June 16, 1973.*
Photograph by the author.

FIGURE 10. *Ted Bogan, Lexington, Massachusetts, June 16, 1973.*
Photograph by the author.

blues musicians who left the country and the blues to become jazz musicians or cocktail pianists has not come to blues researchers because they generally have not sought it.

Though many downhome musicians who came to the city did not take up formal musical training, they usually acquired other styles unconsciously and produced a hybrid. By the late 1920s a definite "city" influence could be heard on records, if by that one understands a number of tendencies: small instrumental groups, instead of soloists accompanying themselves; songs which reflected urban concerns (house-rent, policy) and omitted rural references (mules, chopping cotton, floods) in their lyrics; a higher proportion of stanzas concerned with humor and sex; accompaniment techniques employing numerous chord changes and substitutions in a still-recognizable blues form; precise diction; vocal styles which were less raspy and hurried, more relaxed and "laid back" than their downhome counterparts, and in which the words were delayed for dramatic effect (surely Bessie Smith's singing was a major influence here). This kind of blues might be called "urbane blues" because of a self-conscious polish and elegance coupled with a tongue-in-cheek bawdiness.

The old-fashioned, countrified musician became an object of ridicule. Even now, for one black musician to call another countrified is not only to insult his ability, but also to belittle his intelligence and worldly wisdom. The Reverend Gary Davis, a guitarist who played in a complex East Coast ragtime style, scornfully labeled rediscovered Mississippi John Hurt's songs countrified and not worth trifling with.[67] Lazy Bill Lucas regularly called blues piano styles of the 1920s and 1930s countrified and old-fashioned even though he could not execute them. But Lucas's own technique appears countrified to more versatile and modern pianists like Baby Doo Caston, who mixes blues songs, boogie-woogie, light classical pieces, and country-western songs in his cocktail bar performances. Because Caston has been working steadily and successfully in piano bars for many years, whereas Lucas just recently began to get work – unsteady, at that – in the blues revival aimed at young white audiences, Lucas admires Caston's abilities and would imitate him if he could. Yet some folklorists and blues scholars will call Lucas an honest artist and Caston a slick entertainer. This paradoxical situation – that researchers sometimes hold values exactly opposite from the "commercial" aesthetic of many blues singers – is, I think, basically responsible for many of the misperceptions and misrepresentations which occur when blues singers are presented to a white audience.

But downhome musicians, even in the days before commercial recordings, were playing whatever their audiences wanted to hear. Most of the singers who recorded downhome blues in the 1920s, who were certainly countrified by the standards of vaudeville singers, included blues songs in their wide repertoires, but did not specialize in them. They did not record their whole repertoires, as a rule, because company officials did not want them to. As late as the early 1940s, when Brownie McGhee asked to record some hillbilly songs he regularly performed, he was told that it was not "[his] kind of music."[68] In the 1920s black musicians rarely were recorded playing the hillbilly music they provided for white dances.[69] Record companies wanted blues, for blues sold. If they needed hillbilly music, they might as well turn to hillbillies. Most older black musicians were nonetheless proud of their ability to entertain whites and stressed that their repertoires were complete enough to do so. Many had toured with small medicine or minstrel shows, where they picked up humorous songs they were able to use later. Furry Lewis still sings them at blues festivals.[70] Mack McCormick believes that Mance Lipscomb, born just before the turn of the century, was the typical downhome songster of his generation. His repertoire included ragtime pieces like "Alabama Jubilee" and popular songs like "Shine On, Harvest Moon," besides blues, ballads, and spirituals.[71] A few singers, such as Charley Patton, managed to record a wide repertoire; many others gave some recorded indication of their ability as songsters. Most blues recording artists born before 1900, in fact, seem to have been songsters.[72]

Ishmon Bracey, Son House, Sam Chatmon, Fred McDowell, and Howlin' Wolf all commented on Charley Patton's habit of clowning with the guitar: playing it behind his head, twirling it, rapping it, dancing around it, often interrupting the continuity of the accompaniment, but not the performance, to do so.[73] Tommy Johnson played the guitar "behind his head, between his legs, or on the floor."[74] Babe Stovall and Furry Lewis still do tricks with the guitar.[75] Howlin' Wolf, who learned from Patton, carried on that tradition in his live performances; he crawled and lurched around the stage, using the microphone's visual similarity to the penis in his act. Such antics illustrate that these musicians, at least, thought their prime task was entertainment. How widespread clowning was in the Southeast awaits further research. Not all performers in the Memphis area and the Delta were given to it, and some there (Son House, for example) disapproved of it.

Depending on personal preference and the kind of entertainment involved, the downhome musician performed sitting or standing in front of a crowd. Assuming that performance postures in the past were the same as today, the musician's feet and legs were relaxed, often moving in rhythm to the pulse of his music; his chest was somewhat rigid, probably to control his breath; often, but not always, he shook his head. At times he looked out at the audience and sang to one person or to a small group.[76] If he was standing and clowning around, his movements were sudden and rapid, his pose comical and exaggerated. He sang with an open throat, letting his tongue stay well back and low in his mouth.

Alan Lomax, the first ethnomusicologist to pursue in a systematic manner relations between performance practice and social institutions, has compared body posture and facial expression between "American white folk" and "American negro folk" singers. The white person's body "is held tensely, the singer sits or stands stiffly erect. The head is often thrown far back." The black singer's body "moves sinuously or in relaxed easy response to the beat. He dances his song." The white's "singing expression is mask-like and withdrawn, normally, and agonized on high notes." The black's "expression changes with the mood of the song, line by line; there is a great deal of smiling and even laughing in many performances."[77] Lomax ties these distinctions to sexual behavior, suggesting that they are culturally (not racially) determined.[78] This divergence of behavior may account for cultural misperception.

Posture and instrument choice influenced the degree of interaction the downhome singer was able to achieve with his audience. The piano, for example, hides the musician unless he turns and looks over his shoulder. Seated, a musician is less mobile and must depend on facial expressions and head gestures to make audience contact. The performer who must look at his instrument has very little visual interaction with his audience; some instruments demand more attention than others. But the downhome musician, by habit or design, used his body to communicate with his audience as well as to produce sounds. The same observation can be made for other black "performers" – preachers, for instance. Body movement appears to be particularly expressive in black social interactions. Whether it is more significant among Afro-Americans than among Anglo-Americans awaits study.

Musicians play roles and enjoy a particular status in any society; in turn, the society expects certain kinds of behavior from them because they are musicians. The American jazz-musician stereotype – lazy, addicted to alcohol and other drugs, constantly in debt, irresponsible, sexually amoral – resembles stereotypes held by many societies toward their musicians. Even though these performers are held in low regard, however, they are considered important by the community; their talent and function take precedence over their personal idiosyncracies.[79]

Many downhome musicians were given special treatment, by both whites and blacks, for their musical abilities. Alan Weathersby and Baby Doo Caston, for instance, found an extremely appreciative audience for their serenading in the 1920s near Natchez, Mississippi:

> We used to go to different people's houses, you know. In those days I mean they could hear music and – if somebody could play an instrument, man, they would get up at night, from one o'clock; and they'd fix food and they'd have drinks and they'd stay up till five, six o'clock in the morning and give you money. It wasn't a dance but a serenade; we'd go from house to house. In those days there wasn't too much things like juke boxes, high fidelity sound, wasn't nothing like that then; and whenever somebody could play and could play well, he was considered as *somebody;* he could go anywhere and he had it made, you know?

So I used to follow [Weathersby] around, and everybody'd know him, and everybody was crazy about him; but he was the type of guy that wouldn't work for nobody. He didn't have much money because there wasn't no money to be made then; but he'd never have to worry about food or nothing because everybody liked him, White and Colored; he was the type of musician whom everybody heard and respected him for what he was doing.[80]

Caston compared the life of a farmer with the life of a musician and chose the latter. Although not so well treated as Weathersby in their pastoral idyll, he does not regret his decision. He did not become rich or famous, but he was able to make a comfortable living and raise two families. Down home, Charley Patton "spent most of his adult years as a semi-professional, paid (or kept) entertainer. There was room in this economy for a few full-time professional entertainers, and although the entertainer did not earn a sumptuous living, he made a decent one relative to the standards of the time and place. If he was supported by numerous roadhouses and corn liquor salesmen, these roadhouses and bootleggers in turn were dependent upon the (sometimes) wealthy plantation owners."[81]

Other musicians down home drifted from one place to the next, occasionally taking on part-time work in town or on a farm, but usually supporting themselves through music. Even churchgoing families provided a blind child with a guitar or piano if they could afford it, so that he might be able to make his way in the world. Not all downhome musicians avoided farming; Son House, for example, was a well-respected tractor driver, and it was this skill which kept him out of serious trouble with the law.[82] The farmer-musicians were paid for making music, even if the pay was only a few dollars and some food and whiskey. Because downhome musicians were remunerated and given special treatment, one must conclude that they were considered specialists and at least semi-professionals by the communities which valued their services.

The social function of the downhome musician was, outwardly, to provide entertainment. People in the blues culture received emotional relief from the drudgery of plantation routine by moving to the music and enjoying the lyrics. While during certain musical occasions – serenading, for example – the audience paid especially close attention to the words, many musicians insist that they always listened seriously to the words. Yet a number of blues scholars recently have stressed the "pure" entertainment quality in the downhome blues, denying claims that the music expressed deep sadness and that performances were social rituals purging sadness from singer and audience alike. Nick Perls, founder of Yazoo Records' blues reissue series, asserted, "Country blues lyrics are meant to be coy – make people laugh with it or at it. The whole sadness thing about country blues is white publicity bullshit."[83] Of Charley Patton, John Fahey wrote:

Patton was an entertainer, not a social prophet in any sense. He had no profound message and was probably not very observant of the troubles of his own people. He was not a "noble savage." Least of all did he try to express the "aspirations of a folk." His lyrics are totally devoid of any protesting sentiments attacking the social or racial *status quo*. In fact, according to Son House, Patton had very good relations with White people many of whom helped to support him in return for his services. They liked not only his folksongs but also his blues. Both Patton and House were frequently received into White homes, slept in them, and ate in them.[84]

Black Belt musicians were, in other words, a coddled crew, valuable members of their society. Their behavior was supported by white landowners, who probably felt that their tenants needed some safety valve for their energy. As long as that energy was channeled in a safe direction inside the black community, the landowners had less to worry about. A parallel case can be made for the support given by white landowners to black churches. Actually, it does not matter whether the safety-valve theory is accurate; as long as the landowners acted as if it were, musicians received special treatment.

To be sure, the musicians acted to preserve the status quo. Yet it is also true they ultimately encouraged solidarity within the culture and kept the community together, helping to provide a supportive alternative to white middle-class beliefs. Without the blues, the black experience down home would have been significantly closer to white middle-class behavior, making it infinitely more difficult for black people today to find a separate identity in an Afro-American culture distinct from Anglo-American culture. If downhome blues singers conceived of their function as entertainment, it does not necessarily follow that they failed to express significant ideas and emotions, standards and behavior directives, which the community felt very deeply. If they did not think of the Saturday night juke parties as ritual, it does not mean that the parties did not serve that purpose.

PART III THE SONGS

3 EARLY DOWNHOME BLUES ON RECORD: A REPRESENTATIVE SAMPLE

Approximately two thousand downhome blues titles were issued on record between 1926 and 1930, their period of peak sales; they were promoted in the black press and sold throughout the United States. Early in the Depression, however, the record companies sharply reduced the number of titles produced for the race market. The first downhome blues singer to enjoy commercial success, Blind Lemon Jefferson, became the model followed by the record companies when they sent portable field equipment to southern cities or invited downhome singers north to their home studios. The model Jefferson provided was quite a contrast to the vaudeville sophistication of the blues-singing queens. Contemporaries noted the difference; Fred McDowell, for example, recalled that Bessie Smith "sang a different kind of blues, a piano blues. I never heard of her being backed by a guitar itself."[1] Unlike Smith and the other vaudeville singers, who relied on professional songwriters and a stride piano or jazz-band accompaniment, Jefferson sang from memory and accompanied himself on the guitar. He never adopted the vaudeville framework device of the sung, explanatory introduction to let the listener know why he was blue (though he did offer spoken introductions on one or two occasions); ordinarily he began his singing in the three-line, AAB stanza form, and adhered to it throughout. He included Texas placenames in his lyrics; he did not enunciate clearly; he varied the length of his lines and the timing of his music. Presented to the listening audience as an old-fashioned singer, he did seem artless and plain.

Because the record companies generally were successful in their attempts to find and record singers who, like Jefferson, provided downhome entertainment, it is not difficult to choose a representative sample of early recorded downhome blues. Of course, the records do not provide a representative survey of black American folk music, for the companies specifically sought blues songs; nor do they offer a reliable guide to performance context, for they were limited in length and, since they were made in studios, they do not indicate audience reaction. It might also be charged that the records were censored, either by the companies or the singers themselves; thus they may not have preserved obscene lyrics or protest themes. I consider the matter of censorship at some length in chapter 5 and conclude that the charge cannot be substantiated. What the recordings finally do provide is a useful inventory of the texts and tunes of early downhome blues songs, together with an indication of performance styles.

I transcribed forty-four representative early downhome blues texts and tunes for the sample in this book. In addition, I transcribed three vaudeville blues songs: "Me and My Gin" and "Poor Man's Blues" by Bessie Smith, and "Lost Wandering Blues" by Ma Rainey. "Original Blues," by Bayless Rose, brings the count to forty-eight; though Rose appeared in the Gennett race series, the evidence indicates that he was white. These four additional texts and tunes are included to provide comparative information.

I sought geographical representation in the sample roughly in proportion to the amount of early downhome blues recorded in a given region; as a result, more singers from Mississippi and Tennessee are represented than from, say, the Carolinas or Georgia. Some important singers who turned their contemporaries into followers have been allowed more than one song: Blind Lemon Jefferson, Charley Patton, Blind Willie McTell, Son House, Blind Blake, and Tommy Johnson. For the most part I chose songs which were recorded at the singers' first recording sessions, on the assumption that these had already been their most popular down home. I took a few songs into the sample which did not fit the three-line blues-stanza pattern: "K.C. Moan," "Bootlegging Blues," "That Will Be Alright," "How Long – How Long Blues," and "Cottonfield Blues," part 2. A few borderline songs extended the first line of the stanza directly into the second: "My Black Mama," part 1, and "Maggie Campbell Blues," for example. While these few songs are also representative, they stand as exceptions to the formal blues-stanza model proposed in chapter 4.

The majority of early recorded downhome blues songs did fit that model. Moreover, most blues songs, whether downhome or vaudeville, had the word *blues* at the close of their titles. "Ragtime" songs,[2] popular songs and show tunes, spirituals, and Anglo-American folksongs recorded by black people rarely included *blues* in their titles. Evidently people thought the category "blues" made sense then; we may hope it makes sense now. Exactly what sense it makes can either be uttered whole – that is, by performing – or found by analysis, broken into signs which provide a description of the musical style called blues. The analysis is proved correct if those signs can be brought together in a model which accounts for blues songs already in existence and which shows how to produce new and acceptable blues songs. I attempt a limited version of such a model in the following chapter.

General Notes on the Transcriptions

The primitive recording equipment used in the 1920s squeezed the sound into a narrow frequency range. Since many of the master recordings were lost when record companies changed hands or went bankrupt, collectors' copies often are the best obtainable, and in some cases these are well worn and scratched after years of use and storage. A majority of the early downhome blues records have been reissued on long-playing albums, though the sound quality is rough in many places. Happily, the transcriber gets used to the hiss and scratch and, yearning for even more, turns up the treble control and alters the equalization to get a sharper, more intelligible sound.[3]

I listened to each song several times, then selected a typical stanza for transcription. Generally, if the singer altered the melody radically, as in "Pony Blues" (transcr. 1), I transcribed more than one stanza. Next I determined the tonal center of the song, not a difficult task, since most lines gravitated toward it and ended on it.[4] I transposed each melody so that its final tone fell on C or C'. (Notes on the staff are named as in figure 11; it will be helpful to return to this nomenclature during the analysis sections in chapter 4.) To check the melodies, I used a guitar put into concert pitch with a tuning fork. The major advantage of the guitar over the piano is that by sliding a knife or bottleneck

FIGURE 11.

lightly over the strings, one can produce intervals smaller than the Western twelve-tone octave divisions.

In working out the stanza's metrical scheme, I marked the accents in a rhythmic outline above the text as I transcribed it. I found rhythm more difficult to transcribe than pitch. Downhome blues singers frequently attack their tones between pulse beats. The accompaniment usually supplies the pulse beat, however, often dividing it in twos or threes, which makes marking the vocal rhythm easier. To check the rhythm of difficult passages, I slowed down the tape recorder, using a variable speed control. I marked the tempo for the first and final stanzas with a stopwatch, then checked these figures with a metronome.

Supplementary musical notation symbols are shown in figure 12.

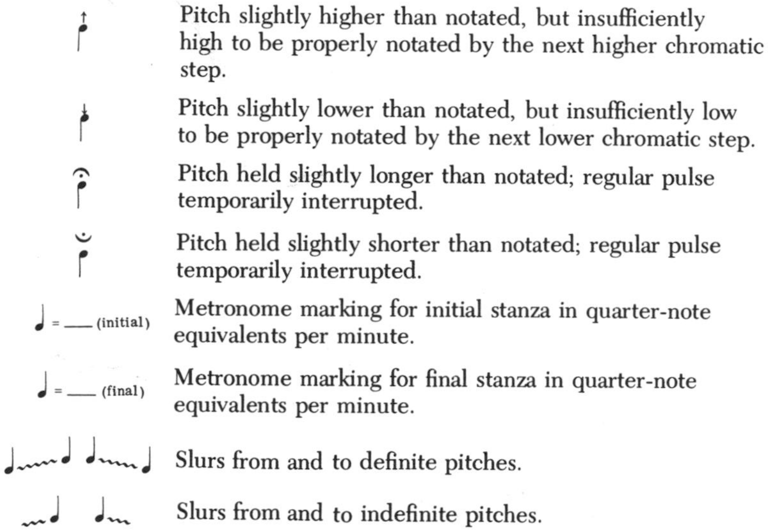

♪	Pitch slightly higher than notated, but insufficiently high to be properly notated by the next higher chromatic step.
♪	Pitch slightly lower than notated, but insufficiently low to be properly notated by the next lower chromatic step.
♪	Pitch held slightly longer than notated; regular pulse temporarily interrupted.
♪	Pitch held slightly shorter than notated; regular pulse temporarily interrupted.
♩ = ___ (initial)	Metronome marking for initial stanza in quarter-note equivalents per minute.
♩ = ___ (final)	Metronome marking for final stanza in quarter-note equivalents per minute.
♩⌣♩ ♩⌣♩	Slurs from and to definite pitches.
⌣♩ ♩⌣	Slurs from and to indefinite pitches.

FIGURE 12.

David Evans provided invaluable assistance with the texts, suggesting alternate readings of certain difficult passages. Many of the tune transcriptions were checked, and in a few cases corrected, by Alan Kagan and Johannes Riedel. Transcription is not, however, an exact science; it is expected that two ethnomusicologists will transcribe the same piece somewhat differently. Ultimately, any transcription is valuable to the extent that it identifies performance elements useful in analysis; transcription and analysis provide material for musical description, comparison, and the construction of song-producing models. Of course, motional and rhythmic elements, the ones best indicated by Western staff-scale notation, are not the only ones which may be identified; one can mark such items as tone of voice, posture, and interaction between singer and audience, though many of these are best checked at a live performance.

The forty-eight musical and textual transcriptions follow. At the head of each I have identified the singers and accompanying instruments, indicated as closely as possible the date of the recording, and named the record company and release number of the original issue.[5] I have also indicated the LP reissue from which I made the transcription.[6] Textual transcription follows each headnote. Vocal lines are broken to indicate something of the singer's timing; thus each stanza attains a spatial form on the page reflecting the temporal utterance.[7] But it is still a convention tied to the printed page; a roll of paper extending sideways would be more useful. Words of which I am uncertain are italicized. I will be grateful to have any mistakes or alternate readings called to my attention. Following the textual transcription of the selected stanza appears its musical transcription. In three instances I transcribed entire songs: "Lonesome Blues," take 1 (transcr. 12), "Lonesome Blues," take 2 (transcr. 13), and "Got the Blues, Can't Be Satisfied" (transcr. 10).

1. "Pony Blues"

Charley Patton (vocal and guitar), "Pony Blues," Paramount 12792.
Richmond, Indiana, June 14, 1929. Yazoo L-1020.

Hitch up my pony   saddl' up my   black mare
Hitch up my pony   saddl' up my black mare
I'm gon' find a rider ooh   baby in the   world somewhere

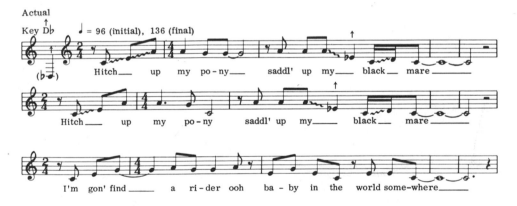

Hello central   'sa matter with your line
Hel- lo central   matter now   with your line
Come a storm last night   tore the   wires down

Hel - lo cen-tral   mat-ter now_____ with your line_____

Come a storm___ last _ night ____ tore_____ the wir - es down_____

Bought a brand new shetland   man already trained
Brand new shetland   baby al- ready trained
If you get in the saddle   tighten up   on your rein

And a brownskin woman like   somethin' fit to eat
Brownskin woman like   somethin' fit to eat
But a jet black woman   don't put your hand on me

Took my baby   to meet the mornin' train
Took my baby   meet that mornin' train
And the blues come down   baby like   showers of rain

I got something to tell you   when I gets a chance
Somethin' to tell you   when I get a   chance
I don't want to marry   just want to   be your man

I got some - thing to tell you_ when I_____ gets a___chance.____

Somethin' to tell you____ when I get a_____ chance.____

I_____don't want to mar-ry_____ just want to be your man.____

The three musical stanzas transcribed here have distinctly different tonal sequences. This kind of variance was more common in vaudeville blues than in down-home blues.

The best single source of information on Patton's life and music is John Fahey, *Charley Patton,* where another transcription of "Pony Blues" may be found (pp. 74–75). See also David Evans, "Blues on Dockery's Plantation, 1895 to 1967," and "Charley Patton's Life and Music." Most of Patton's recorded output, together with textual transcriptions, is available on Yazoo L-1020, *Charley Patton: Founder of the Delta Blues.* Practically everyone I have spoken with who recalls Patton associates "Pony Blues" with him. According to Fahey, it was his best-selling record as well as his most frequently requested song in live performances. Patton's idiosyncratic "gallop" rhythms are apparent in the accompaniment:

Recorded songs derived from Patton's "Pony Blues" are Big Joe Williams, "My Grey Pony" (Bluebird B5948); Johnny Temple, "My Pony" (Decca 7817); Son House, "Pony Blues" (Herwin 92401); and Howlin' Wolf, "Saddle My Pony" (Chess 1515).

2. "Banty Rooster Blues"

Charley Patton (vocal and guitar), "Banty Rooster Blues," Paramount 12792.
Richmond, Indiana, June 14, 1929. Yazoo L-1020.

I'm gonna buy me a banty   put him in my back door
I'm gonna buy me a banty   put him in my back door
'Cause he see a stranger comin'   he'll flop his wings and crow

What you want with a rooster   he won't crow 'fore day
What you want with a rooster   he won't crow 'fore day
What you want with a man   when he won't do nothin' he say

What you want with a hen won't   cackle when she lay
What you want with a hen won't   cackle when she lay
What you want with a woman   when she won't do nothin' I say

I take my picture   hang it up in Jackson's wall
I take my picture   hang it up in Jackson's wall
If anybody ask you what about it   tell 'em that's all that's all

My hook in the water   and my cork's on top
My hook in the water   and my cork's on top
How can I lose   lord with the help I got

I know my dog any-   where I hear him bark
I know my dog any-   where I hear him bark
I can tell my rider   if I feel her in the dark

Because the text of Patton's song is almost identical with Walter Rhodes's 1927 record "The Crowing Rooster" (Columbia 14289-D), it has been suggested that Patton learned his song from Rhodes's recording. (One implication is that seemingly unrelated stanzas – here, the fourth, fifth, and sixth – become definitive when committed to the phonograph record.) However, Bengt Olsson (*Memphis Blues and Jug Bands*, p. 72) reports that Rhodes lived in Cleveland, Mississippi, the vicinity where Patton resided for more than a quarter-century. It is possible, therefore, that Patton learned the song from Rhodes in person, or that Rhodes learned it from Patton.

3. "Dead Drunk Blues"

Lillian Miller (vocal), Papa Charlie Hill (guitar), and George W. Thomas (speech), "Dead Drunk Blues," Gennett 6518. Richmond, Indiana, ca. May 3, 1928. Origin Jazz Library OJL-6.

[spoken by Miller:] I'm dead drunk this morning daddy be yourself
You knowed I was drunk when I laid down across your bed
You knew I was drunk when I laid down across your bed
All the whiskey I drank it's   gone right to my head

Oh give me Houston that's the place I crave
Oh give me Houston   that's the place I crave
   [spoken by Thomas:] Oh play it Papa Charlie Hill
So when I'm dry I can   get whiskey that's just made

Whiskey whiskey   it's some folks' downfall
   [spoken by Thomas:] It's not my downfall don't put that washin' out
Oh whiskey whiskey   it's some folks' downfall
But if I don't get whiskey I ain't no good at all
   [spoken by Thomas:] You ain't by yourself neither

When I was in Houston drunk most ev'ry day
When I was in Houston   drunk most ev'ry day
I drank so much whiskey I thought I'd pass away

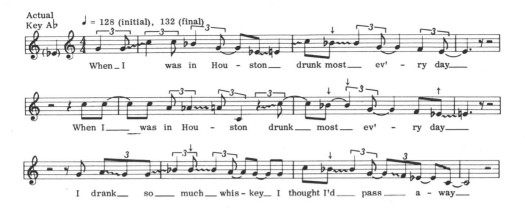

Actual
Key Ab   ♩ = 128 (initial), 132 (final)

When I was in Hou - ston drunk most ev' - ry day

When I was in Hou - ston drunk most ev' - ry day

I drank so much whis - key I thought I'd pass a - way

Have you ever been drunk and slept in all your clothes

    [spoken by Thomas:] No sir I ain't never did that no sir

Have you ever been drunk and   slept in all your clothes

When you wake up feel like you out of doors

I'm gonna get drunk   daddy just one more time

    [spoken by Thomas:] Go ahead and get drunk and stay drunk

I'm gonna get drunk   daddy just one more time

    [spoken by Thomas:] Just stay drunk I don't care

'Cause when I'm drunk   nothin' don't worry my mind

Almost nothing is known about Lillian Miller. Her ragged vocal suggests a down-home background, though most of her slender recording output employed vaudeville-styled accompaniments. Two vaudeville singers released versions of "Dead Drunk Blues" in 1927: Margaret Johnson (Victor 20982) and Sippie Wallace (OKeh 8499). The texts are similar in all three versions, and the logical inference is that Miller's derives from one of the other two.

4. "Stranger Blues"

Rosie Mae Moore (vocal) and Charlie McCoy (guitar), "Stranger Blues," Victor 21408. Memphis, Tennessee, February 3, 1928. Origin Jazz Library ojl-6.[8]

[spoken:] Oh play it mister Charlie a long time and a heap of it

If I feel tomorrow   like I feel today

If I feel tomorrow   like I feel today

Before I stand to be mistreated girls I'll   take morphine and die

Actual
Key Bb   ♩ = 94 (initial), 104 (final)

If I feel ___ to-mor-row ___ like I ___ feel ___ to-day

If I feel ___ to-mor-row ___ like I ___ feel ___ to-day

Be-fore I stand ___ to be mis - treat-ed girls ___ I'll take mor-phine and die ___

Now my daddy's got something it's a   brand new thing to me
Now my daddy's got something girls it's a   brand new thing to me
I just want to tell you it   sure stings good to me

I'm a poor old stranger girls and I   just rolled in your town
I'm a poor old stranger girls I   just rolled in your town
Lord I just come here to   ease my troublin' mind

Lord I'm so heartbroken girls I   cannot cry at all
Lord I'm so heartbroken girls I   cannot cry at all
But if I find my man girls I'm gon'   nail him to the wall

Say I'm poor old stranger and I   just rolled in your town
Lord I'm poor old stranger girls and I   just rolled in your town
Lord I   find my man I'm gonna   nail him to the wall

Ishmon Bracey recalled that Rosie Mae Moore lived in Hazlehurst, Mississippi, and that she toured with traveling shows (David Evans, liner notes to Origin Jazz Library OJL-17, *The Mississippi Blues, No. 3*). For more information on Moore, see Bob Groom, "The Georgia Blues, Part 7."

5. "Jacksonville Blues"

Nellie Florence (vocal) and Charley Lincoln (guitar), "Jacksonville Blues," Columbia 14342-D. Atlanta, Georgia, April 21, 1928. Origin Jazz Library OJL-6.[9]

Let me be your wiggler   until your wobbler come
Let me be your wiggler   until your wobbler come
If she beats me wigglin'   she got to wobble some

Women cryin' danger   but I ain't raisin' my hand
Women cryin' danger   but I ain't raisin' my hand
I got a way of lovin they   just can't understand

Men they call me oven they says that I'm red hot
Men they call me oven   they say that I'm red hot
They say I've got somethin' the other gals ain't got
     [Lincoln laughs]

I can strut my pudding   spread my grease with ease
I can strut my pudding   spread my grease with ease
Cause I know my onions that's why I always please

Wild about coffee but I'm crazy 'bout   China tea
Wild about my coffee but I'm crazy 'bout my   China tea
But this sugar daddy is   sweet enough for me
     [spoken:] And I got ————

Men they call me oven   they says I am red hot
Men they call me oven   they say that I'm red hot
They say I've got somethin'   the other gals ain't got
     [Lincoln laughs; Florence laughs]

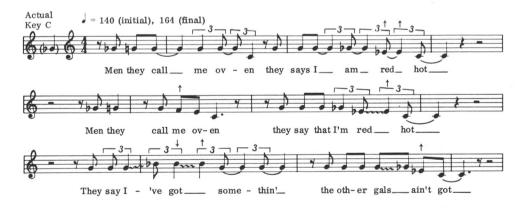

Actual Key C
♩ = 140 (initial), 164 (final)

Men they call__ me ov-en they says I__ am__ red__ hot__

Men they   call me ov-en   they say that I'm red__ hot__

They say I-'ve got__ some-thin'__ the oth-er gals__ain't got__

One John in the city one lives up on a hill
Oh John's in the city one lives up on the hill
But the man I'm lovin' lives down in Jacksonville

Reports indicate that Jacksonville, Florida, was Nellie Florence's home, but it is likely that she spent considerable time in Atlanta (where this recording was made). The same tune was employed by Atlanta-based Barbecue Bob (Robert Hicks), "Laughing

Charley" Lincoln's brother, in several songs (for example, "Blind Pig Blues" [Columbia 14372-D]). Other textual transcriptions may be found in Eric Sackheim and Jonathan Shahn, *The Blues Line,* p. 40, and Paul Oliver, *The Meaning of the Blues,* p. 216.

6. "Dupree Blues"

Willie Walker and Sam Brooks (vocals and guitars), "Dupree Blues," Columbia 14578-D. Atlanta, Georgia, December 6, 1930. Yazoo L-1013.

Betty told Dupree	I wants me a diamond ring	oh baby
Betty told Dupree	I wants me a diamond ring	oh sugar

Now listen   mama   your daddy bring you mostly any thing

He had to kill a policeman   and he wound a detective too   oh sugar
Killed a detective   wounded a policeman too   oh babe
See here mama   what you caused me to do

Hired him a taxi   said can't you drive me back to Main   say taxi
Then he hired him a taxi   said carry me back to Main   oh baby
I've done a hangin' crime   yet I don't never feel ashamed

Standin' there wond'rin'   will a matchbox hold my clothes   oh baby
Standin' there wond'rin'   matchbox hold my clothes
Said a trunk was too big   to be bothered on the road

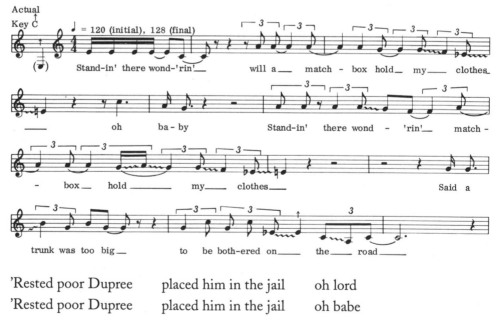

'Rested poor Dupree   placed him in the jail   oh lord
'Rested poor Dupree   placed him in the jail   oh babe
He had the mean old judge   went and refuse to 'sign him any bail

Wrote a letter to Betty   and this is the way the letter read   oh baby
He wrote a letter to Betty   and this is the way the letter read   oh lord
Come home to daddy   I'm almost dead

Betty went to the jailer   cryin' mister jailer please   oh baby
Betty went to the jailer   cryin' jailer please   oh lord
Please mister jailer   let me see my used to be

This is the well-known blues ballad "Betty and Dupree," collected in AAB stanza form, AB form, and AABB form. See Howard Odum and Guy B. Johnson, *Negro Workaday Songs,* pp. 56–59; and G. Malcolm Laws, Jr., *Native American Balladry,* pp. 251–52, where it is listed as Laws I 11. It has the same tune as "2:19 Blues," for which Mamie Desdoume was famous in New Orleans, and with which, in a version reported by Odum and Johnson, it shares a similar line: "Michigan water tastes like sherry wine." Leroy Carr's "Midnight Hour Blues" (Vocalion 1703) used the same melody; similar melodies may be heard in Charley Patton's "Tom Rushen Blues" (Paramount 12877) and "High Sheriff Blues" (Vocalion 02680).

Walker was born in 1896; he was the most highly regarded singer in the Greenville, South Carolina, region until his death in 1933. For more information on Walker and Brooks, see Bruce Bastin, *Crying for the Carolines,* pp. 71–72.

7. "Original Blues"

Bayless Rose (vocal and guitar), "Original Blues," Gennett 7250.
Richmond, Indiana, June 7, 1930. Yazoo L-1013.

Said I didn't come here baby to take nobody's brown
Said I didn't come here honey take nobody's brown
I'm just a poor man babe I just walked in your town

From ashes from ashes mama from dust to dust
From ashes from ashes woman from dust to dust
Just show me a woman that any poor man can trust

Says I laid and talked with my brown all night long
Says I laid and talked to my woman all night long
Tried to teach that woman teach her right from wrong

Says I laid ____ and ____ talked ____ to my wom-an ____ all night ____ long ____

Tried to ____ teach that ____ wom-an ____ teach her ____ right ____ from wrong ____

Mississippi River woman is deep and wide
Mississippi River   deep and wide
Couldn't see my brownie from this other side

Said lord woman look what you've done done
Said run here woman look what you've done done
Said run here woman look what you've done done
You made me love you now your man done come

She's your 'n' she's mine she's someone else's too
She's your 'n' she's mine she's someone else's too
She's your 'n' she's mine she's someone else's too
Just any woman good lord she will do

It is likely that Bayless Rose was white, though there is little in the musical transcription to indicate that. Instead, one must turn to aspects of performance which are not transcribed in standard notation, such as pronunciation and accent. Rose tended to keep his tongue towards the front and roof of his mouth when he pronounced vowels, and he has a nasal quality to his voice which most black downhome blues singers lacked.

8. "Early Morning Blues"

Blind Blake (vocal and guitar), "Early Morning Blues," Paramount 12387.
Chicago, Illinois, ca. September, 1926. (Dutch) Riverside RM 8804.[10]

Early this mornin'   my baby made me sore
Early this mornin'   my baby made me sore
I'm goin' away to leave you   ain't comin' back no more

Tell me pretty mama   where did you stay at last night
    [spoken:] Tell me where did you stay last night
Tell me pretty mama   where did you stay at last night
It ain't none of your business   daddy since I treat you right

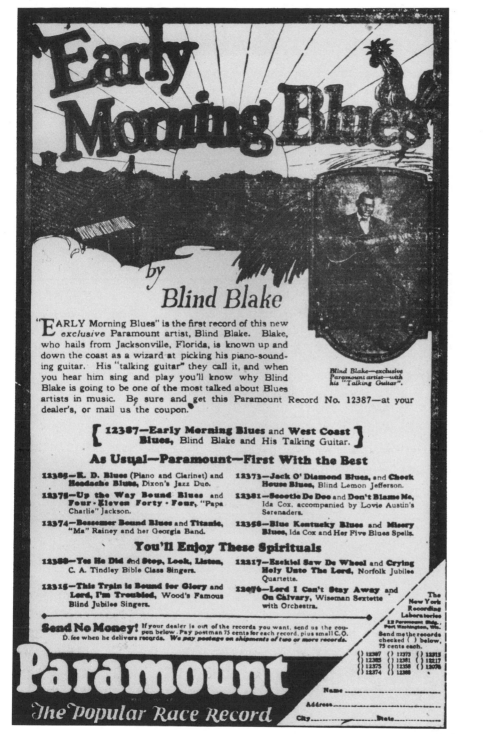

FIGURE 13. *Paramount's advertisement for Blind Blake's first record. From the* Chicago Defender, *October 2, 1926.*

When you see me sleepin'   baby don't you think I'm drunk

    [spoken:] No I'm not drunk not a bit of it

When you see me sleepin'   baby don't you think I'm drunk

I got one eye on my pistol   and the other on your trunk

    [spoken:] Play that thing low and lonesome boy

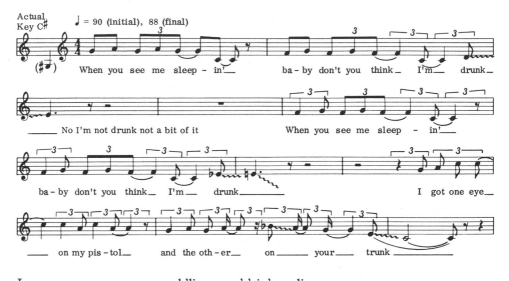

Love you pretty mama   b'lieve me 't'ain't no lie

    [spoken:] I mean it 't'ain't no lie

I love you pretty mama   b'lieve me 't'ain't no lie

The day you try to quit me   baby that's the day you die

Blind Blake's first record – a best seller – introduced him to the national audience for race records. Based in Jacksonville, Florida, Blake sang and played along the East Coast. He moved to Chicago in 1926 and became a Paramount studio musician. From 1926 to 1932 he recorded more than eighty separate titles under his own name, and he accompanied other singers or jazz bands on several more. His "ragtime" style of guitar playing inspired many young musicians. Biograph records has reissued most of his recordings on LP.

Stanzas similar to those in "Early Morning Blues" appear in Rosie Mae Moore's 1928 recording "Staggering Blues" (Victor 21280). George Williams used the same tune in his 1924 recording of "Chain Gang Blues" (Columbia 14049-D).

9. "One Time Blues"

Blind Blake (vocal and guitar), "One Time Blues," Paramount 12479.
Chicago, Illinois, ca. April, 1927. (Dutch) Riverside RM 8804.

Blind Blake

E have all heard expressions of people "singing in the rain" or "laughing in the face of adversity," but we never saw such a good example of it, until we came upon the history of Blind Blake. Born in Jacksonville, in sunny Florida, he seems to have absorbed some of the sunny atmosphere — disregarding the fact that nature had cruelly denied him a vision of outer things. He could not see the things that others saw—but he had a better gift. A gift of an inner vision, that allowed him to see things more beautiful. The pictures that he alone could see made him long to express them in some way — so he turned to music. He studied long and earnestly — listening to talented pianists and guitar players, and began to gradually draw out harmonious tunes to fit every mood. Now that he is recording exclusively for Paramount, the public has the benefit of his talent, and agrees, as one body, that he has an unexplainable gift of making one laugh or cry as he feels, and sweet chords and tones that come from his talking guitar express a feeling of his mood.

FIGURE 14. *From* The Paramount Book of Blues, *p. 15*

Ah   the rising sun goin' down
Ah   the rising sun goin' down
I ain't   got nobody   since my baby blowed this town

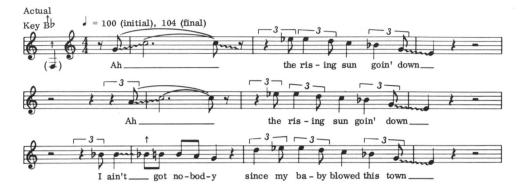

Ah   mama love me one more time
Ah   mama love me one more time
You gimme little chance   maybe you will change your mind

I done called you   but I've almost lost my mind
I done called you   mama   but I almost lost my mind
I ain't gon' call no more   good man is hard to find

Ah   mama who can your reg'lar be
Ah   who can your reg'lar be
When you got no reg'lar   baby please take me

Take me   mama I'll tell you what I'll do
Take me   mama I'll tell you what I'll do
I'll get up every mornin'   work hard all day for you

"One Time Blues" and "Early Morning Blues" show Blind Blake to be a skillful lyricist. In these instances the singer discovers his woman's adultery, but he loves her so much anyway that he can only make empty threats or debase himself.

10. "Got the Blues, Can't Be Satisfied"

"Mississippi" John Hurt (vocal and guitar), "Got the Blues, Can't Be Satisfied," OKeh 8724. New York City, December 28, 1928. Origin Jazz Library OJL-5.

Got the blues   can't be satisfied
Got the blues   can't be satisfied
Keep the blues   I'll catch that train and ride

Whiskey straight will drive the blues away
Whiskey straight will drive these blues away
That be the case I wants a quart today

Bought my gal a great big diamond ring
Bought my gal   great big diamond ring
Come right back home and caught her shakin' that thing

I said babe what makes you act this a way
I said baby why did you act this a way
Says I won't miss a thing she gives away

Took my gun   and I broke the bar'l down
Took my gun   broke the barrel down
Put my baby   six feet under the ground

I cut that joker   so long deep and wide
Cut that joker   so long deep and wide
Yes got the blues and I still ain't satisfied

3. Bought my gal a great big dia-mond ring___ Bought

___ my___ gal___ great___ big di - a-mond ring___

Come___ right___ back___ home___ and___ caught her shak-in' that thing___

♩ = 184

4. I___ said babe what makes you act this a way___

I___ said ba-by why___ did___ you act this a___ way___

Says I won't___ miss a___ thing she gives___ a-way___

5. Took my gun and I___ broke___ the bar'l down

Took my___ gun___ broke the bar - rel___ down___

Put my ba-by___ six feet un - der the ground___

♩ = 192

6. I cut that jo-ker so long deep and wide___

Cut that jo-ker so___ long deep___ and wide___

Yes got the blues_ and I still ain't sat - is - fied

John Hurt's 1964 "rediscovery" in Avalon, Mississippi – "Avalon's my home town, always on my mind," he had sung in his 1928 "Avalon Blues" (OKeh 8759) – was one of the high points of the recent blues revival. His gentle, melodic fingerpicking guitar style was exceptional among Mississippi blues singers. The songs he recorded for Piedmont, Gryphon, and Vanguard after his rediscovery are virtually identical with those he recorded almost forty years earlier. I have transcribed his "Got the Blues, Can't Be Satisfied" in its entirety to reveal the subtle tune variations which Hurt utilizes in each stanza. For another textual transcription, see Sackheim and Shahn, *The Blues Line,* p. 230.

11. "Number Three Blues"

Walter "Buddy Boy" Hawkins (vocal and guitar), "Number Three Blues," Paramount 12475. Chicago, Illinois, ca. April, 1927. Yazoo L-1010.

I done lost all my money   I got nowhere to go
I said I lost all my money   ain't got me nowhere to go
I believe to my soul   I'm about to lose my brown

All these women gets mad   'cause I want *what what what what*
All you women gets mad   'cause I want *want want want want*
All you women gets mad at Buddy Boy 'cause   I want me *da da da*

I say I flagged number four mama   she kept on wheelin' by
I flagged number four   she kept on wheelin' by
I couldn't do anything partner but   fold my little arms and cry

Here come number three   with her headlight turned down
I say here come number three   with her headlight turned down
I believe to my soul   she's Alabama bound

FIGURE 15. *Buddy Boy Hawkins. From the* Chicago Defender, *May 14, 1927.*

Apples on my table   peaches on my shelf
Apples on my table   peaches on my shelf
I got to stay there   couldn't eat 'em all by myself

Buddy Boy Hawkins is one of the more puzzling figures in the history of down-home blues. What is known about him is summarized by Jerome Epstein in the liner notes to the Yazoo records reissue *Buddy Boy Hawkins and His Buddies* (L-1010). Hawkins favored Spanish tuning, but came up with more complex accompaniments in it than his peers used, developing three-voice counterpoint. He recorded ragtime and hokum pieces as well as blues.

12. "Lonesome Blues," take 1

Tommy Johnson (vocal and guitar), "Lonesome Blues," take 1, unissued Victor master number 45463-1. Memphis, Tennessee, August 31, 1928. Historical HLP-31.

Won't you iron my jumper   starch my overalls
I'm gon' find my woman said she's   in this world somewhere

Well it's good to you mama   sure lord killin' me
Well it's good to you mama   sure lord killin' poor me
Well it's good to you mama says it's   sure lord killin' me

I wonder do my   rider think of me
I wonder do my   rider think of poor me
Cryin' if she did she would   sure lord feel my care

I woke this mornin'   said my mornin' prayer
I woke up this mornin' I   said my mornin' prayer
I woke this mornin' babe I   said my mornin' prayer

I ain't got no woman   *speak in my behalf*
I ain't got no woman now   *speak in my behalf*
I ain't got no woman to   *speak in my behalf*

Won't you iron my jumper   starch my overalls
Won't you iron my jumper   starch my overalls
I'm gon' find my woman said she's   in this world somewhere

She don't like me to holler   tried to murmur low

Actual
Key A ♩ = 112

1. Won't you iron my____ jum - per starch my____ o - ver-alls____

I'm gon'____ find my wom-an said she's____ in this world____ some-where____

2. Well it's_____ good to you ma - ma sure____ lord kill-in' me_____

Well it's_____ good to you ma - ma____ sure lord kill - in' poor me____

Well it's_____good to you____ma-ma says it's____ sure lord____ kill-in'____ me____

3. I _____won-der do my_____ rid - er think of me_____

I_____ won - der do____ my____ (uh) rid - er think____ of poor me____

Cry - in'____ if she did____ she would sure lord_____ feel my____ care____

4. I_____woke this morn-in'____ said____ my morn-in' prayer____

I_____woke up this morn - in'____ I said my_____morn - in' prayer

I_____woke this morn-in' babe I____ said my_____morn-in'____ prayer____

5. I ain't ____ got no wom-an____ *speak* ____ in my be - half____

I ____ ain't____ got no wom-an now____ *speak in _____ my_____ be - half* ____

13. "Lonesome Blues," take 2

Tommy Johnson (vocal and guitar), "Lonesome Blues," take 2, unissued Victor
master number 45463-2. Memphis, Tennessee, August 31, 1928. Historical
HLP-31.

Won't you iron my jumper   starch my overalls
I'm gon' find my woman said she's   in this world somewhere

I wonder do my   good gal think of me
I wonder do my   good gal think of poor me
Cryin' if she did she would   sure lord feel my care

Honey good to you mama   sure lord killin' me
Honey good to you mama   sure lord killin' poor me
Say good to you mama   but it's sure lord killin' me

I woke up this mornin'   said my mornin' prayer
I woke up this mornin' I   said my mornin' prayer
I ain't got no woman to   *speak in my behalf*

Cryin' good to you   sure lord killin' me
Well it's good to you mama   sure lord killin' poor me
Hey good to you mama says it   sure lord killin' me

Iron my jumper   starch my overalls

Won't you iron my jumper   starch my overalls

Gon' find my woman said she   in the world somewhere

Won't you iron my jumper   starch my overalls

Both takes of Tommy Johnson's "Lonesome Blues," made one right after the other, have been transcribed in their entirety so that the reader may observe the course of its complex melody from one stanza to the next, and compare analogous stanzas in the different takes. David Evans, *Tommy Johnson*, pp. 58–60, includes textual transcriptions.

14. "How Long – How Long Blues"

Leroy Carr (vocal and piano) and Francis "Scrapper" Blackwell (guitar), "How Long – How Long Blues," Vocalion 1191. Indianapolis, Indiana, ca. June, 1928. No reissue.

How long   babe how long
Has that evenin'   train been gone
How long   how how long   baby how long

FIGURE 16. *From the* Chicago Defender, *September 1, 1928*

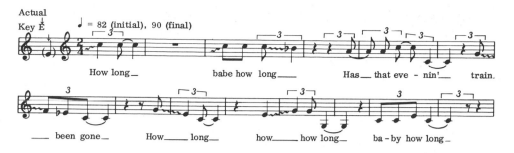

Here and I stood at the station   watched my baby leavin' town
Blue and disgusted   nowhere could peace be found
For how long   how how long   baby how long

Now I can hear the whistle blowin'   but I cannot see no train
And it's deep down in my heart baby   there lies an achin' pain
For how long   how how long   baby how long

Sometimes I feel so disgusted   and I feel so blue
That I hardly know what in this world   baby just to do
For how long   how how long   baby how long

And if I could holler   like I was a mountain jack
I'd go up on the mountain   I'd call my baby back
For how long   how long   baby how long

I know someday you're gonna be sorry   that you done me wrong
Well it be too late baby   I will be gone
For so long   so long   baby so long

My mind get to ramblin'   I feel so bad
Thinkin' about the bad luck   that I have had
'Cause how long   how how long   baby how long

Leroy Carr is generally credited (or blamed) for introducing the relaxed blues vocal style which became dominant in the 1930s. Born in Tennessee, he grew up in Indianapolis. His repertoire included pop songs and novelty items as well as blues, and his approach was considerably more sophisticated than that of the normal downhome blues singer or barrelhouse pianist. Many of his best performances have been reissued on Columbia C 30946, *Blues before Sunrise.* In the words of Mike Stewart and Stephen Calt, "He was a shade slicker than most country bluesmen but far raunchier than the average vaudeville blues singer" (liner notes to Yazoo L-1036, *Leroy Carr and Scrapper Blackwell*).

"How Long – How Long Blues" surely was one of the best-selling blues records of any period. Carr and Blackwell had to be recalled to the studio on three occasions to record a new master because the old one had worn out from so many pressings. While the song may derive from Ida Cox's 1925 recording "How Long Daddy, How Long" (Paramount 12325), my guess is that it was already thoroughly traditional.

15. "Prison Bound Blues"

Leroy Carr (vocal and piano) and Francis "Scrapper" Blackwell (guitar), "Prison Bound Blues," Vocalion 1241. Chicago, Illinois, December 20, 1928. No reissue.

Early one morning   the blues came falling down
Early one morning   the blues came falling down
All locked up in jail   and prison bound

All last night I   sat in my cell alone
All last night oooo –   I sat in my cell alone
Thinkin' of my baby   and my happy home

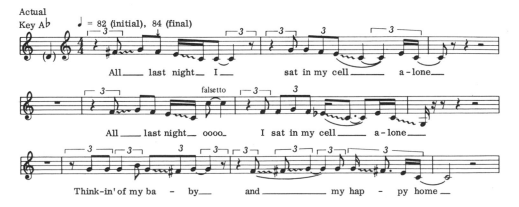

When I had my trial baby   you could not be found
When I had my trial baby oooo –   you could not be found
So it's too late now mistreating mama   I'm prison bound

Baby you will never   see my smiling face again
Baby you will never   see my smiling face again
But always remember   your daddy has been your friend

Sometimes I wonder   why don't you write to me
Sometimes I wonder   why don't you write to me
If I been a bad fellow   I did not intend to be

Duncan Schiedt reports that Carr spent time in an Indianapolis jail for bootlegging whiskey (liner notes to Columbia CL 1799, *Blues before Sunrise*). "Prison Bound Blues" was another enormously popular and influential song which found its way into the repertoires of many blues singers in the 1930s. Carr used a similar tune in his 1934 recording of "Southbound Blues" (Vocalion 03107).

16. "Bumble Bee"

Memphis Minnie (vocal and guitar) and Kansas Joe McCoy (guitar), "Bumble Bee," Columbia 14542-D. New York City, June 18, 1929. No reissue.

Bumble bee bumble bee   please come back to me
Bumble bee bumble bee   please come back to me
He got the best old stinger any bumble bee that I ever seen

He stung me this mornin' I been lookin' for him all day long
Stung me this mornin'   been lookin' for him all day long
Lord it got me to the place hate to see my bumble bee leave home

Bumble bee bumble bee   don't be gone so long
Bumble bee bumble bee   don't be gone so long
You's my bumble bee   and you're needed here at home

I can't stand to hear him   buzz buzz buzz
Commence bumble bee I want you to stop your fuss
You's my bumble bee   and you know your stuff
Oh sting me bumble bee until I get enough

Bumble bee bumble bee   don't be gone so long
Bumble bee bumble bee   don't be gone so long
You's my bumble bee and you're needed here at home

I don't mind your goin'   ain't *gon' stay so long*

Don't mind your goin'   don't be goin' so long

You's my bumble bee and you needed here at home

I can't stand to hear him   buzz buzz buzz

Commence bumble bee I want you to stop your fuss

You's my bumble bee   and you know your stuff

Oh sting me bumble bee until I get enough

    Minnie Douglas was born on June 3, 1896. "In 1929," wrote Mike Leadbitter in "My Girlish Days," "a talent scout spotted [Joe McCoy and Kid Douglas] playing for dimes on Beale [Street, in Memphis] and took them to New York to record for Columbia. A man with the company dubbed them Kansas Joe and Memphis Minnie, and it was the instant success of 'Bumble Bee' that really started their professional careers" (p. 8).

    The transcription, from Memphis Minnie's first recording of "Bumble Bee," shows her sounding hurried; she forgets lyrics and has to repeat. But evidently the sexual metaphor made the song a great success, for she recorded several new versions: Vocalion 1476 (1930); Vocalion 1556 (1930), as "Bumble Bee No. 2"; Vocalion 1618 (1930), as "New Bumble Bee." She was able to sustain a highly successful recording and performing career throughout the 1930s and 1940s. Her earlier recordings may be sampled on Blues Classics BC-13, *Memphis Minnie, Vol. 2;* her later ones, on Blues Classics BC-1, *Memphis Minnie, Vol. 1.* She had few equals on guitar, and once bested Big Bill Broonzy in a blues guitar-playing contest. Broonzy fixes the date of the contest at 1933 (Yannick Bruynoghe, *Big Bill Blues,* pp. 138–40); however, I assign it a date in the early 1940s, when both Broonzy and Memphis Minnie were the most popular blues singers in Chicago, because she won with two songs she first recorded in 1941. She died in Memphis on August 6, 1973.

17. "M. and O. Blues"

Willie Brown (vocal and guitar), "M. and O. Blues," Paramount 13090.
Grafton, Wisconsin, May 28, 1930. Origin Jazz Library OJL-5.

I leave here I'm gonna   catch that M. and O.
Now when   I leave here I'm gonna   catch that M. and O.
I'm goin'   way down south where I ain't   never been before

'Cause   I had a notion   lord and I b'lieve I will
'Cause   I had a notion   lord and I b'lieve I will
I'm gonna   build me a mansion   out on Decatur hill

Now it's   all of you mens   ought to be 'shamed of yourselves
She says   all of you mens   ought to be 'shamed of yourselves
Goin' round here swearin' 'fore God you got a   poor woman by yourself

I start' to   kill my woman till she   lay down 'cross the bed
I start' to kill my woman till she   lay down 'cross the bed
And she looked so ambitious till I   took back ev'rything I said

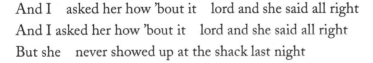

And I   asked her how 'bout it   lord and she said all right
And I asked her how 'bout it   lord and she said all right
But she   never showed up at the shack last night

And –

Willie Brown was born about 1895. A pupil of Charley Patton, he sang with his
teacher and the Drew group of musicians. He supplied entertainment for dances in the
Delta from about 1910 through the 1940s (Patton died in 1934). Unfortunately, only one
of the two records Brown made has been found. See Al Wilson, *Son House,* and Evans,

"Blues on Dockery's Plantation," for further information on Brown. Another transcription of the text appears in Sackheim and Shahn, *The Blues Line,* p. 202. For my transcription of Brown's guitar accompaniment, see pp. 148–49.

18. "Lonesome Home Blues"

Tommy Johnson (vocal and guitar), "Lonesome Home Blues," Paramount 13000. Grafton, Wisconsin, ca. January, 1930. Yazoo L-1007.

Lonesome place don't seem like home to me
Now it's a lonesome place don't mama seem like home to me

I woke up this mornin' blues all round my bed
Mm woke up this mornin' blues all round my bed
Had the blues so bad mama till I couldn't raise up my head

If you want to live easy pack your clothes with mine
Mm want to live easy pack your clothes with mine
S'if you want to live easy just pack your clothes with mine

Mm mm soon one mornin' blues come fallin' down
Mm mm soon one mornin' blues come fallin' down
Said they fell so heavy till it caused my heart to moan

Well I'm goin' back home gon' fall down on my knees
Mm mm goin' back home gonna fall down on my knees
Says I'll 'knowledge now *pretty* baby that I treat you mean

The theme of leaving is prominent here and in several other blues records Johnson made. Although this tune is related to Johnson's "Lonesome Blues," his guitar accompaniment is quite different. For another transcription of the text, see Evans, *Tommy Johnson,* pp. 64–65.

19. "The Jail House Blues"

Sam Collins (vocal and guitar), "The Jail House Blues," Gennett 6167.
Richmond, Indiana, April, 1927. Origin Jazz Library OJL-2.

When I was layin' in jail with my   back turned to the wall
When I was layin' in jail with my   back turned to the wall
I could lay down and dream I could   hear my good gal squall

Lord she brought me coffee   and she brought me tea
Lord she brought me coffee   and she brought me tea
Fell dead at the door   with the jailhouse key

I'm going down to the courthouse   see the judge and the chief police
Goin' down to the courthouse   see the judge and the chief police
My good gal fell dead and I   sure can't see no peace

I tell you what I'll do an' I   sure God I won't tell no lie
Tell you what I'll do an' I   sure God ain't gon' lie
I b'lieve I'll lay down   take morphine and die

What little is known of Sam Collins can be found in Pete Whelan's brochure notes
to Origin Jazz Library OJL-10, *Crying Sam Collins and His Git-Fiddle,* and in Samuel
Charters, *The Bluesmen,* pp. 122–23. Reports indicate that Collins was born in McComb,
Mississippi. For another transcription of the text, see Sackheim and Shahn, *The Blues
Line,* p. 145.

20. "Cottonfield Blues," part 2

Garfield Akers (vocal and guitar) and Joe Calicott (guitar), "Cottonfield Blues,"
part 2, Vocalion 1442. Memphis, Tennessee, September 23, 1929. Origin Jazz
Library OJL-2.

I got something to tell you – oo   mama keep it all to yourself

Don't you tell your mama – ah   don't you tell nobody else

I'm gon' write me a letter oo – oo –   I'm gon' mail it in the air

I'm gon' write me a letter – oo –   I'm gon' mail't in the air

Actual Key D

♩ = 134 (initial), 136 (final)

I'm gon' write me a let-ter oo oo I'm gon'

mail it in the air I'm gon' write me a let-ter

Transcribed by Alan Kagan and Jeff Titon

oo I'm gon' mail't in the air

Said I know you will catch it   babe in this world somewhere

Said I know you'll catch it   mama in the world somewhere

And I'm gon' write me a letter – oo –   I'm gon' mail it in the sky

Mam' I know you'll catch it   when the wind go rollin' by

Oo – oo – oo   mama I don't know what to do

I said oh baby – ee   gal I don't know what to do – oo – oo

I know sugar *it be on account of you now*

Oo – oo – oo   that's the last word she said

And I just couldn't remember – oh   babe it's the last old word you said

Whenever a song was too long for the $3\frac{1}{2}$-minute limit of one side of a 78 rpm record, it was recorded in two parts, to fill both sides.

Garfield Akers lived in Hernando, Mississippi. In its rhythmic insistence, his "Cottonfield Blues" is intense even by Delta standards. The freely embellished melody, the drawn-out phrases, and the two-line stanza structure are characteristic of field hollers; thus the title may be generic. One imagines that Akers, in the studio, was asked the name of the song he had just sung: "Oh, that's just an old cottonfield blues." See Charters, *The Bluesmen*, pp. 118–19.

21. "Maggie Campbell Blues"

Tommy Johnson (vocal and guitar) and Charlie McCoy (guitar), "Maggie Campbell Blues," Victor 21409. Memphis, Tennessee, February 4, 1928. Origin Jazz Library OJL-2.

Cryin' who's that yonder   comin' down the road   comin'   down the road
Mm who's that yonder   comin' down the road
Well it look like Maggie baby   but she walk too slow

Now sun gon' shine   my back door someday   my back   door someday
     mm mm
Sun gon' shine in   my back door some   day
And the   wind gon' change gon'   blow my blues away

Now see see rider   see what you done done   see what   you done done   mm
See see rider   see what you done done
You done   made me love you now you're   tryin' to put me down

Well I'm goin' away lord   won't be back till fall   won't be   back till fall
Well I'm goin' away lord   won't be back till fall
If I   meet my good gal mama   won't be back at all

Now who's that yonder   comin' down the road   comin'   down the road   mm
Who's that yonder   comin' down the road
Well it look like Maggie baby   but she walk too slow

Mm – goin' away   won't be back till fall   won't be   back till fall
Well I'm goin' away lord   won't be back till fall
Said if I   meet my good gal mama   won't be back at all

Tommy Johnson married Maggie Bidwell (or Bedwell) from Crystal Springs, Mississippi, in 1914 or 1915; they separated between 1917 and 1919. The Victor recording director probably thought Johnson gave the title of this blues as "Maggie Campbell" rather than "Maggie Bidwell." Other transcriptions of the text may be found in Sackheim and Shahn, *The Blues Line*, p. 154, and, with discussion of the lyrics, in Evans, *Tommy Johnson*, pp. 52–54. Charters has transcribed the melody of stanza 2 in *The Bluesmen*, p. 134. "Look Who's Coming Down the Road" (Champion 50041) by the Georgia Pine Boy (Kansas Joe McCoy) is derived from "Maggie Campbell Blues." For the tradition Johnson probably started, see David Evans's liner notes to Yazoo L-1007, *Jackson Blues, 1928–1938*, and his *Tommy Johnson*.

22. "Whiskey Moan Blues"

Clifford Gibson (vocal and guitar), "Whiskey Moan Blues," QRS R7087.
Long Island City, New York, June, 1929. Yazoo L-1006.

I been drinkin' and gamblin'   bar'lhousin' all my days
Mm drinkin' and gamblin'   bar'lhousin' all my days
But I have found someone to love me   I'm goin' to change my ways

I've always heard it   but now I know it's true
I've always heard it   but now I know it's true
If you mistrust a good woman   she'll turn her back on you

If your woman loves you   she'll stand by you to the end
Mm if your woman loves you   she'll stand by you to the end
Nobody can steal your place   you can leave her with a bunch of men

If you got a jealous hearted woman   be careful what you do
If you got a jealous hearted woman   be careful what you do
'Cause there's always somebody   tell her lies on you

Whiskey has been my pleasure   good time places I've always found
Whiskey has been my pleasure   good time places I've always found
But it seems so different now   since I have settled down

Just where Clifford Gibson came from remains uncertain. Henry Townsend and Big Joe Williams reported that he was from Mississippi (Pete Welding, "Henry Townsend," p. 11), although Richard Noblett heard Williams say that Gibson was from Arkansas ("American Folk Blues Festival 1968," p. 10). Humphrey Higgins's liner notes to Yazoo L-1006, *The Blues of Alabama,* indicate that Gibson was an Alabamian (Higgins is a pseudonym, possibly for Steve Calt or Nick Perls). But Godrich and Dixon, in *Blues and Gospel Records,* place Gibson from Louisville, Kentucky. It is nonetheless clear that Gibson lived for a long time in St. Louis. His tunes show the influence of Leroy Carr and Scrapper Blackwell. Gibson used the "Whiskey Moan Blues" tune on other records, such as "Jive Me Blues" (Victor v-38572).

23. "Mean Conductor Blues"

Ed Bell (vocal and guitar), "Mean Conductor Blues," Paramount 12546.
Chicago, Illinois, September, 1927. Yazoo L-1006.

The same train same engineer
The same train same engineer
Took my woman 'way lord left me standin' here

My *stroller* caught a passenger I caught the mamlish blinds
My *stroller* caught a passenger I caught the mamlish blinds
Hey you can't quit me ain't no need of tryin'

Hey mister conductor let a broke man ride your blinds
Hey mister conductor let a broke man ride your blinds
You better buy your ticket know this train ain't mine

FIGURE 17. *Ed Bell. From the* Chicago Defender, *October 8, 1927.*

Hey——mis-ter con-duc-tor—— let a—— broke— man ride— your—— (blinds)

You bet-ter buy your—— tick - et—— know this train ain't— mine——

I just want the blinds as far as Hagerstown
Say I just want the blinds as far as Hagerstown
When she blow for the crossing I'm gon' ease it down

I pray to lord that Southern train would wreck
I pray to lord that Southern train would wreck
'Cause it kill that fireman break that engineer's neck

I'm standing here looking up at the risin' sun
I'm standing here looking up at the risin' sun
The train don't run why there'll be some walkin' done

Ed Bell was born about 1905 and raised in rural Lyons County, Alabama, reports Bengt Olsson ("Ed Bell," p. 31). Moving to Greenville, Alabama, when he became "old enough to make his own decisions," he was the most popular singer there until he became a preacher, a profession he practiced from 1930 until his death in 1960. Charters has transcribed part of the text of "Mean Conductor Blues" in *The Bluesmen,* p. 154. *Mamlish,* wrote David Evans, is probably an intensifier like *doggone* (letter to me). See also the brochure notes by Stephen Calt to Origin Jazz Library OJL-14, *Alabama Country.*

24. "Lost Wandering Blues"

Gertrude "Ma" Rainey (vocal), Miles Pruitt (banjo), and Milas Pruitt (guitar), "Lost Wandering Blues," Paramount 12098. Chicago, Illinois, ca. March, 1924. (Dutch) Riverside RM-8807.

I'm leavin' this mornin'   with my clothes in my hand
Lord I'm leavin' this mornin'   with my clothes in my hand
I won't stop goin'   till I find my man

I'm standin' here wond'rin will a   matchbox hold my clothes
Lord I'm stand'n' here wond'rin   will a matchbox hold my clothes
I've got a trunk too big to be bothered with on the road

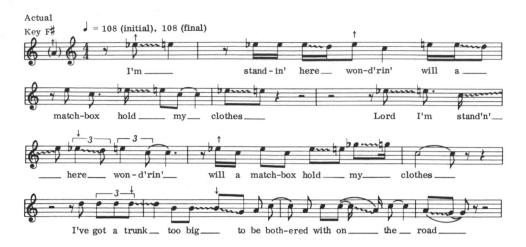

Actual
Key F#   ♩ = 108 (initial), 108 (final)

I'm _____ stand-in' here_ won-d'rin' will a _____
match-box hold _____ my_ clothes _____ Lord I'm stand'n'
_____ here_ won-d'rin'_ will a match-box hold_ my_____ clothes _____
I've got a trunk_ too big_ to be both-ered with on _____ the_ road_

I went up on the mountain   turned my face to the sky
Lord I went up on the mountain   turned my face to the sky
I heard a whisper it said   mama please don't die

I turned around   to give him my right hand
Lord I turned around   to give him my right hand
When I looked in his face I was   talking to my man

Lord look a yonder people my love has been refused
    [spoken:] Lord
I said look a yonder people   my love has been refused
That's the reason why mama's   got the lost her man blues

Gertrude Rainey, the "Mother of the Blues," was one of the first singers to feature blues songs in her stage act. When she and her husband, William "Pa" Rainey, were with the Tolliver Circus and Musical Extravaganza between 1914 and 1916, they were billed as "Rainey and Rainey, Assassinators of the Blues" – that is, "killers" or "knockouts," superior performers. The banjo and guitar accompaniment by the Pruitt Twins gives "Lost Wandering Blues" a downhome flavor.

For a good general introduction to the vaudeville blues singers, see Derrick Stewart-Baxter, *Ma Rainey and the Classic Blues Singers*. See also Paul Oliver, *Bessie Smith*, and Chris Albertson, *Bessie*. LeRoi Jones, in *Blues People*, develops the thesis, advanced first by Samuel Charters in *The Country Blues*, that vaudeville blues singers were slick professionals far removed from the folk roots of downhome blues. The matter needs reexamination.

25. "Mama 'T'ain't Long fo' Day"

Blind Willie McTell (vocal and guitar), "Mama 'T'ain't Long fo' Day,"
Victor 21474. Atlanta, Georgia, October 18, 1927. Yazoo L-1005.[11]

Wake up mama   don't you sleep so hard
Wake up mama   don't you sleep so hard
For it's these old blues   walkin' all on your yard

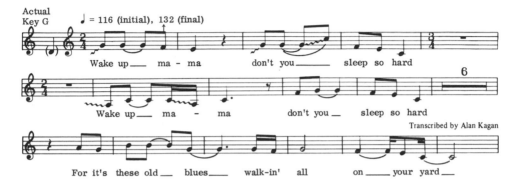

Transcribed by Alan Kagan

I've got these blues   reason I'm not satisfied
I've got these blues   I'm not satisfied
That's the reason why I   stole away and cried

Blues grabbed me at midnight and didn't turn me loose till day
Blues grabbed me at midnight   didn't turn me loose till day
I didn't have no mama to drive these blues away

The big star falling   mama it ain't long 'fore day
The big star falling mama 't'ain't long 'fore day
Need a little sunshine to drive these blues away

[spoken:] Oh come here quick   come on mama you know I got you

Mm mm mm   mm mm mm mm mm
Mm mm mm   mm mm mm mm mm
Mm mm   mm mm mm mm mm

Blind Willie McTell was born on May 5, 1901, probably in Statesboro, Georgia. His career as a street singer in Atlanta spanned five decades; he managed to make records during most of that period, whether for commercial companies or for folklorists and blues collectors. Albums which represent his early music are available on Roots and Yazoo; later efforts are on Biograph, Prestige, and Atlantic. His 1940 Library of Congress recordings are on Melodeon. McTell is presumed to have died about 1960, but there is no official record of his death.

For other textual transcriptions of "Mama 'T'ain't Long fo' Day," see Samuel Charters, *The Poetry of the Blues,* p. 51, and Tony Travers, "Lyric Transcript No. 17." The tune was widespread, usually known as "Poor Boy"; hear Sam Butler, "Poor Boy Blues" (Vocalion 1057), and Gus Cannon, "Poor Boy Long Ways from Home" (Paramount 12571), for early recordings of the melody. Thunder Smith's 1947 recording "Big Stars Are Falling" (Gold Star 615) contains similar lyrics.

26. "Barbecue Blues"

Barbecue Bob (vocal and guitar), "Barbecue Blues," Columbia 14205-D. Atlanta, Georgia, March 25, 1927. Piedmont PLP-13159.

Woke up this morning gal   'twixt midnight and day
I woke up this morning   'twixt midnight and day
With my head around my pillow where my brownie used to lay

I know I ain't good looking   teeth don't shine like pearls
I ain't good looking   teeth don't shine like pearls
So glad good looks don't take you through this world

Go starch my jumper mama   iron my overalls
Go starch my jumper   iron my overalls
My brown done quit me God knows she had it all

FIGURE 18. *From the* Chicago Defender, *May 21, 1927*

I'm gon' tell you now gal   like *gypsies* told the Jews
Gon' tell you now gal   like *gypsies* told the Jews
If you don't want me it's a cinch I don't want you

Did you ever dream lucky   wake up cold in hand
Did you ever dream lucky   wake up cold in hand
That's a mighty true sign your brown's got some other man

My mama told me   papa told me too
My mama told me   papa told me too
Some brownskin woman   gon' be the death of you

Barbecue Bob (Robert Hicks) was born in 1902 and raised on a farm in Walton County, Georgia, twenty-five miles east of Atlanta. In 1920 he settled in that city and found work as a car-hop in a restaurant which featured barbecued beef. Pneumonia resulting from influenza was the cause of his death on October 21, 1931. For biographical information, see Pete Lowry, "Some Cold Rainy Day," p. 15, and Samuel Charters's brochure notes to RBF 15, *The Atlanta Blues*. Other textual transcriptions may be found in the brochure notes to Piedmont PLP-13159, *Kings of the Twelve-String*, and in Sackheim and Shahn, *The Blues Line*, p. 318.

27. "Poor Man's Blues"

Bessie Smith (vocal), Porter Grainger (piano), Ernest Elliott and Bob Fuller (saxophones), and Joe Williams (trombone), "Poor Man's Blues," Columbia 14399-D. New York City, August 24, 1928. Columbia G 30450.[12]

Mister rich man rich man   open up your heart and mind
Mister rich man rich man open up your heart and mind
Give a poor man a chance help stop these hard hard times

While you're livin' in your mansion   you don't know what hard time mean
While you're livin' in your mansion   you don't know what hard time mean
Old workin' man's wife is starvin'   your wife is livin' like a queen

Please listen to my pleading   'cause I can't stand these hard times long
Oh listen to my pleading   can't stand these hard times long
They'll make an honest man   do things that   you know is wrong

Please lis-ten to my plead-ing— 'cause I can't stand these hard— times—
long Oh——— lis-ten to my plead-ing can't—
——————— stand these hard— times long— They'll make
an hon - est— man — do things that you know is wrong———

Old man fought all the battles   old man would fight again today
Old man fought all the battles   old man would fight again today
He would do anything you ask him in the name of the U.S.A.

Now the war is over   old man must live the same as you
Now the war is over   old man must live the same as you
If it wasn't for the poor man   mister rich man what would you do

Chris Albertson credits Smith with these protest lyrics, but it is not clear that she
was the author. He writes: "Bessie Smith's recorded repertoire radiated black pride. As
English blues scholar Paul Oliver has pointed out, one might easily substitute the term
'white' for 'rich' in her *Poor Man's Blues,* but racial references are strangely absent from
her recordings, although it is said that she frequently alluded to the subject on stage.
This was not due to any restrictions put on her by Columbia, for the subject crops up
on many recordings by other artists of that time, especially male Country blues singers"
(liner notes to Columbia G30450, *Empty Bed Blues*). But Albertson is wrong; one simply
cannot support a case that a significant amount of social or racial protest lyrics appeared
in early recorded downhome blues.

As for Smith's authorship of this social protest song, the *Catalog of Copyright
Entries* indicates that the original copyright listed credit for composition of words and
melody to Frankie Marvin (E U.S. unpub. 621; Oct. 26, 1928), and that, two years later,
Bessie Smith copyrighted the song in her name, receiving credit for composition of "song
and melody," a highly unusual assignation. There are three possibilities: that Frankie
Marvin wrote the words; or that Bessie Smith wrote the words, and the assignation
"song" so indicates; or that Bessie Smith wrote the words, but Frankie Marvin received
credit for them in the original copyright entry. Since she was in fact acknowledged in

copyright notices as the author of other songs she sang, one cannot assume that composer credit was routinely stolen from her. Thus the issue of authorship remains in doubt.

28. "Me and My Gin"

Bessie Smith (vocal), Porter Grainger (piano), and Joe Williams (trombone), "Me and My Gin," Columbia 14384-D. New York City, August 25, 1928. Columbia G 30450.[13]

Stay 'way from me   'cause I'm in my sin
Stay 'way from me   'cause   I'm in my sin
If this place gets raided   it's me and my gin

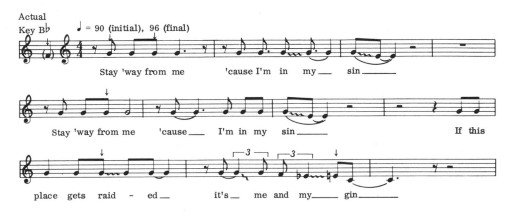

Don't try me nobody   'cause you will never win
Don't try me nobody   'cause you will never win
I'll fight the army and navy   just me and my gin

Any bootlegger   sho' is a pal of mine
Any bootlegger   sho' is a pal of mine
'Cause a good old bottle o' gin   will get it all the time

When I'm   feelin' high   't'ain't nothin' I won't do
When I'm feelin' high   't'ain't nothin' I won't do
Keep me full of liquor   and I'll sure be nice to you

I don't want no *cloak*   and I don't need no bed
I don't want no *cloak*   and I don't need no bed
I don't want no porkchop   just give me gin instead

"Me and My Gin" and "Poor Man's Blues" reveal some of the stylistic differences between Bessie Smith and the downhome blues singers. Smith employed a narrow melodic range, usually of a fifth, though in some stanzas she expanded it and introduced melodic variations. She toyed with the fifth and flatted it microtonally; because her melodies were streamlined and simplified, such subtle effects as microtonal variation appeared more emphatic. Downhome blues singers were impressed with Smith's delivery (and her lyrics); some tried to imitate her, but few were successful. Today's listeners who prefer downhome blues find Smith's singing predictably dull. But that very predictability testifies to her tremendous influence upon popular singing style in the years following her revolutionary innovations.

For biographical information, see Albertson, *Bessie*.

29. "That Will Be Alright"

Kansas Joe McCoy (vocal and guitar) and Memphis Minnie (guitar), "That Will Be Alright," Columbia 14439-D. New York City, June 18, 1928. Origin Jazz Library OJL-21.

Well look here mama see what you've done done
Took all my money put me on a bum
But that'll be all right
Oh no but that'll be all right
Oh no don't you hear me talkin' to you   mama that'll be all right

Now you wore your dresses up above your knees
Serve some jelly to whom you please
But that'll be all right
Oh no but that'll be all right
Oh no don't you hear me talkin' to you   mama that'll be all right

Gon' buy me a dog   *wire the nose*
Keep these men from m' jelly roll

And that'll be all right

Oh no but that'll be all right

Oh no don't you hear me talkin' to you   mama that'll be all right

[spoken:] All right now

I knew we was gon' play it again

Now my baby said she loved me don't see why she can

Caught her on the corner with another man

But that'll be all right

Oh no but that'll be all right

Oh no don't you hear me talkin' to you   mama that'll be all right

Now you're talkin' 'bout jelly you ought to see mine

Spreadin' her jelly all over town

But that'll be all right

Oh no but that'll be all right

Oh no don't you hear me talkin' to you   mama that'll be all right

I had a good *chance* not sleeping by myself

Now she gone got somebody else

But that'll be all right

Oh no but that'll be all right

Oh no don't you hear me talkin' to you   mama that'll be all right

Gon' build me a house out on the sea

So these women come see poor me

And that'll be all right
Oh no but that'll be all right
Oh no don't you hear me talkin' to you   mama that'll be all right

Me and my brother went round the bend
Held my gal and couldn't drive her in
But that'll be all right
Oh no but that'll be all right
Oh no don't you hear me talkin' to you   mama that'll be all right

Downhome singers knew other songs besides blues and sometimes got the opportunity to record them. An example is this folksong by Memphis Minnie's partner, Kansas Joe McCoy. For information on McCoy, see Bruynoghe, *Big Bill Blues,* pp. 119–20. Songs similar in tune and text are Clifford Gibson, "She Rolls It Slow" (Victor 23290), and John Lee "Sonny Boy" Williamson, "G.M. and O. Blues" (Victor 20-2369).

30. "Sunshine Special"

Blind Lemon Jefferson (vocal and guitar), "Sunshine Special," Paramount 12593. Chicago, Illinois, ca. October, 1927. Roots RL-312.

Burn the railroad down   so that Sunshine Specials can run
Burn the railroad down   so that Sunshine Specials can run
I got a gang of womens man they ride from sun to sun

Same old fireman   we'll keep the same old engineer
Got the same old fireman   same old engineer
So that Sunshine Special's girls run me all the way from here

Blind Lemon Jefferson

AN anyone imagine a fate more horrible than to find that one is blind? To realize that the beautiful things one hears about — one will never see? Such was the heart-rending fate of Lemon Jefferson, who was born blind and realized, as a small child, that life had withheld one glorious joy from him — sight. Then — environment began to play its important part in his destiny. He could hear—and he heard the sad hearted, weary people of his homeland, Dallas — singing weird, sad melodies at their work and play, and unconsciously he began to imitate them — lamenting his fate in song. He learned to play a guitar, and for years he entertained his friends freely — moaning his weird songs as a means of forgetting his affliction. Some friends who saw great possibilities in him, suggested that he commercialize his talent — and as a result of following their advice — he is now heard exclusively on Paramount.

FIGURE 19. *From* The Paramount Book of Blues, *p. 3*

Gonna leave on the Sunshine Special   gon' leave on the Santa Fe
Leave on the Sunshine Special   goin' in on the Santa Fe
Don't say nothin' about that Katy because it's taken my brown from me

Arrives at ——— Texas   set on to San Anton'
Arrives at ——— Texas   right on to San Anton'
Somebody's been satisfyin' your engine man ever since you been gone

Cotton Belt is a slow train   also that *I. and G.N.*
I said Cotton Belt is a slow train   also that *I. and G.N.*
If I leave Texas anymore I'm gonna leave on that L. and N.

Charters discusses Jefferson's vocal style in *The Bluesmen,* pp. 177–86, and includes a scalar analysis. Another transcription of this text appears in Bob Groom, *Blind Lemon Jefferson,* p. 10. Jefferson employed the same tune and accompaniment in "Lock Step Blues" (Paramount 12679), recorded in 1928, and in several other titles. This common practice suggests that singers thought of new songs as new texts which could be fitted to old tunes and accompaniments.

A monograph on Jefferson's life and music is badly needed. He was born in the mid-1890s in the Texas farm country about seventy-five miles south of Dallas. As a young man he played and sang on the streets of Wortham. Before the start of World War I, he and Huddie Ledbetter traveled and sang together in the Dallas area, playing for suppers, dances, and country balls, as well as entertaining in juke joints and on the streets. After Leadbelly was sent to prison in 1917, Jefferson continued singing in Texas, where he gained local renown. Although Leadbelly sang blues, he did not favor it; nor did his guitar style display the virtuosity of the performing bluesman. It is logical to infer that Jefferson did not specialize in blues, either. But by the time he was asked to come to Chicago and make records for Paramount, he had developed a fluent and apparently idiosyncratic blues guitar style. His lyrics were among the most inventive in the blues genre. Between 1926 and 1930, when he reportedly froze to death one night on a Chicago street, he recorded ninety-seven titles. Most of these were issued, and because of their wide distribution, he became the best-known downhome blues singer of his time.

31. "Got the Blues"

Blind Lemon Jefferson (vocal and guitar), "Got the Blues," Paramount 12354. Chicago, Illinois, ca. March, 1926. Biograph BLP-12000, mistakenly identified as "Long Lonesome Blues."

Well the blues come to Texas   lopin' like a mule
Well the blues come to Texas   lopin' like a mule
You take a high brown woman man she's hard to fool

You can't ever tell what a woman's got on her mind
Man you can't tell what a woman's got on her mind
You might think she's crazy 'bout you she's leavin' you all the time

She ain't so good looking   and her teeth don't shine like pearls
She ain't so good looking and her teeth don't shine like pearls
But that nice disposition carries a woman all through the world

I'm goin' to the river   gonna carry my rocker chair
Well I'm goin' to the river   carry my rocker chair
——————————————— have the worried blues right here

I think I heard my   good gal   callin' my name
Hey hey   good gal called my name
She couldn't call so loud but she called so nice and plain

I was raised in Texas   schooled in Tennessee
I was raised in Texas   schooled in Tennessee
Now sugar you can't make no fatmouth out of me

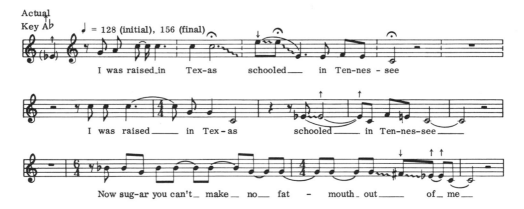

Said a woman act funny   quit you for another man
Yeah a woman act funny   quit you for another man
She ain't gon' look at you straight but she's always raisin' sand

A "fatmouth" is a fool. "Raising sand" is an idiom like "stirring up trouble"; it means arguing and fighting. There is no evidence that Jefferson was "schooled" in Tennessee; the line is traditional and is found in many blues stanzas.

32. "Long Lonesome Blues"

Blind Lemon Jefferson (vocal and guitar), "Long Lonesome Blues," Paramount 12354. Chicago, Illinois, ca. March, 1926. Biograph BLP-12000, mistakenly as "Got the Blues."

I walked from Dallas   I walked from Wichita Falls
I said I walked from Dallas I walked from Wichita Falls
After I lost my sugar that was no walk at all

Woman see you comin' man   go get the rocker chair
Woman see you comin'   go get the rocker chair
I want to fool this man and make out he's welcome here

So cold in China the birds can't hardly sing
So cold in China   birds can't hardly sing
You didn't make me mad till you broke my diamond ring

Hey   papa mama papa papa do double do love you
Doggone my side papa do your mama papa do double do love you
What you cryin' 'bout sugar papa don't care what you do

I know my baby   she gon' jump and shout
I said I know my baby   she gon' jump and shout
When she gets that letter Lemon have wrote a few days out

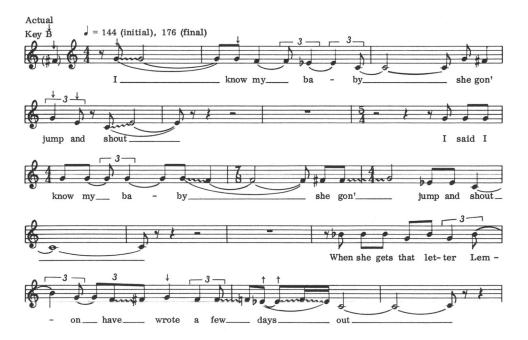

Tell me what's the matter that I can't get no mail

Won't you tell me what's the matter papa Lemon can't get no mail

I was said last night 'cause a black cat crossed your trail

I got up this mornin'   these blues all 'round my bed

I got up this morning   these blues all 'round my bed

Couldn't eat my breakfast and there's blues all in my bread

Music and lyrics for "Long Lonesome Blues" appear in *The Paramount Book of Blues*, p. 5. For an imitation, hear "It's Cold in China Blues" (Vocalion 03166) by the Mississippi Moaner (Isaiah Nettles).

33. "44 Blues"

Roosevelt Sykes (vocal and piano), "44 Blues," OKeh 8702. New York City, June 14, 1929. Historical Vol. 5.

Lord I walked all night long   with my forty-four in my hand

Lord I walked all night long   my forty-four in my hand

I was lookin' for my woman   found her with another man

Lord I wore my forty-four so long   lord it made my shoulder sore

Lord I wore my forty-four so long   lord it made my shoulder sore

After I do what I wants to   ain't gon' wear my forty-four no more

I heard my baby say   she heard that forty-four whistle blow

Lord and my baby say   she heard that forty-four whistle blow

Lord it sounds just like   't'ain't gon' blow this whistle no more

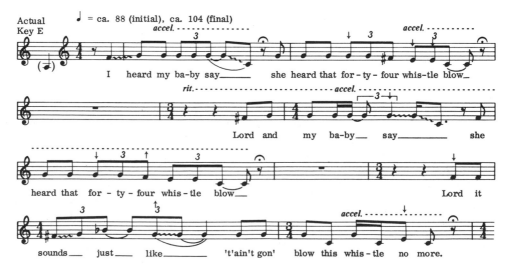

FIGURE 20. *Roosevelt Sykes at the 1970 Ann Arbor Blues Festival.*
Photograph by the author.

Now I got a little cabin   lord it's number forty-four
Now I got a little cabin   lord it's number forty-four
Lord I wake up every morning   the wolf is scratching on my door

Paul Oliver has a thorough discussion of the "Forty-four Blues" song family in
Screening the Blues. His definition of song family is much broader than my definition of
blues family (see pp. 141, 163–64). Sykes is still active, making records and appearing
at festivals, clubs, and colleges. He was born in West Helena, Arkansas, on January 31,

1906. As a young boy he listened to traveling pianists in the town juke joints. At fifteen he ran away from his grandfather's farm and traveled with pianist Lee Green in a juke-joint circuit along the Mississippi River from New Orleans to St. Louis. After a few years he settled in St. Louis, where he subsequently met Jesse Johnson, who arranged his recording dates (see chap. 6). "Forty-four Blues" is a very popular blues song even today; Howlin' Wolf recorded a hit version of it in 1954 (Chess 1584). The difficult left-hand piano part makes it a benchmark among blues pianists.

34. "My Black Mama," part 1

Eddie "Son" House (vocal and guitar), "My Black Mama," part 1, Paramount 13042. Grafton, Wisconsin, May 28, 1930. Origin Jazz Library OJL-2.

Well black mama what's the　matter with you said that it
Ain't satisfactory don't care　what I do hey mama
What's the matter with you
Said it ain't satisfactory baby I don't care　what I do

You take a brownskin woman would make a rabbit　move to town said well a
Jet black woman would make a mule kick his　stable down a brownskin woman
Would make a　rabbit　move to town
Oh but a *real* black woman'll make a mule kick his stable down

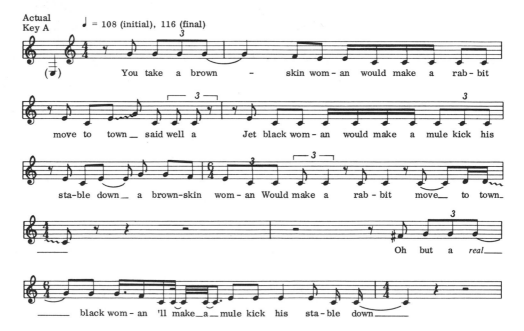

FIGURE 21. *Son House, Minneapolis, Minnesota, May 8, 1971. Photograph by the author.*

Hey there   ain't no heaven there ain't no   burnin' hell said a
Where I'm goin' when I die can't no-   body tell oh it ain't no heaven now
Ain't no burnin' hell
Oh where I'm goin' when I die can't nobody tell

Well my black mama's face shines   like the sun
Oh lipstick and powder sure won't   help her none my black mama's face
Shines like the sun
Oh lipstick and powder well it sure won't help her none

Well you see my milkcow tell her t'   hurry home
I ain't had no milk since that   cow been gone if you see my milkcow
Tell her to hurry home
Yeah I ain't had no milk since that cow been gone

Well I'm   goin' to the race track to see my   pony run
He's the best in the world but he's a runnin' son-of-a-gun I'm goin' to the
    race track
To see my   pony run
He's the best in the world but he's a runnin' son-of-a-gun

Oh lord have mercy on my   wicked soul
Wouldn't mistreat you baby for my   weight in gold oh lord have mercy
On my   wicked soul
Mm mm mm mm mm mm mm mm mm

Son House was "rediscovered" in 1964. From then until a few years ago, he performed at colleges and festivals; presently he resides in Rochester, New York. He was

born in 1902, but he did not learn to sing and play blues until 1927 because he was "churchified" (his expression). "Just puttin' your hands on an old guitar, looked to me like that was a sin," he told me. Once he began, he progressed quickly, and in 1930 he joined the Charley Patton–Willie Brown group, keeping the tradition of Mississippi Delta, Saturday night, bootleg-whiskey blues parties going strong throughout the Depression. For further information, see Wilson, *Son House*. Other transcriptions of the text of "My Black Mama" can be found in *Blues World*, no. 14, pp. 19–20, and in Charters, *The Poetry of the Blues*, pp. 25–26. The strength of House's fully resonant voice was unequaled among downhome blues singers recorded in the early period.

35. "Dry Spell Blues," part 1

Eddie "Son" House (vocal and guitar), "Dry Spell Blues," part 1, Paramount 12990. Grafton, Wisconsin, May 28, 1930. Origin Jazz Library OJL-11.

The dry spell blues are falling   *drove* me from door to door
Dry spell blues are falling   *drove* me from door to door
The dry spell blues have put everybody   on the killing floor

Now the people down South   soon won't have no home
Lord it's people down South   soon won't have no home
'Cause this dry spell has   parched all their cotton and corn

Hard luck's on ev'rybody   ain't missing but a few
Hard luck's on ev'rybody   ain't missing but a few
Now been tryin' to shower   *and kind of heavy too*

Lord I fold my arms   and I walked away
Oh I fold my arms   lord 'n' I walked away
Just like I tell you   somebody's got to pray

Pork chops forty-five cents a pound   cotton is only ten
Pork chops forty-five cents a pound   cotton is only ten
I can't keep no women   no no not one of them

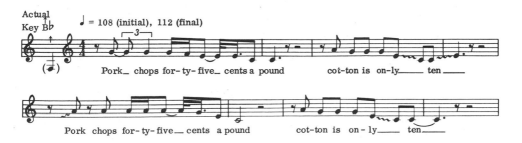

I can't keep no___wom-en_____   no___ no_ not one___ of them_

So dry old boll weevil   turn up his toes and die
So dry old boll weevil   turn up his toes and die
Now ain't nothin' to do   bootleg moonshine and rye

Another transcription of the text of "Dry Spell Blues," part 1, may be found in *Blues World*, no. 8, pp. 22–23; see also Charters, *The Bluesmen*, p. 62. When I played House's old recording of the song for him and asked him to tell me the words to the third stanza, he could no longer make them out.

36. "Minglewood Blues"

Cannon's Jug Stompers (Ashley Thompson, vocal and guitar; Gus Cannon, banjo and jug; Noah Lewis, harmonica), "Minglewood Blues," Victor 21267. Memphis, Tennessee, January 30, 1928. Folkways FA 2953.[14]

Don't you never   let one   woman rule your mind
Don't you never   let one   woman rule your mind
Said she keep you worried   troubled all the time

Don't you think your fairer was   li'l and cute like mine
Don't you wish your fairer was   li'l and cute like mine
She's a mar-   she's a married wom'n but she's come to see me all the time

Actual
Key A♭   ♩ = 100 (initial), 136 (final)

Don't you think   your fair - er was____ li'l and cute____ like___ mine_

Don't you wish   your fair - er was____ li'l and cute ___ like_____ mine____

She's a mar- she's a mar-ried wom'n_ but she's come to see ___ me_____ all the time

Don't you never   let no   woman rule your mind
Don't you never   let no   woman rule your mind
She keep you troubled   worried all the time

Well I got a   letter mama and you   ought to heard it read
Well I got a   letter lord and you   ought to heard it read
If you comin' back   baby   now be on your way

Many of the members of the Memphis jug bands had backgrounds in minstrel and medicine shows. Cannon's Jug Stompers began as a group in 1916, with the same personnel who appear on "Minglewood Blues." For further biographical information, see Olsson, *Memphis Blues,* pp. 52–62. Mengelwood is a small suburban district outside Memphis.

37. "Roll and Tumble Blues"

"Hambone" Willie Newbern (vocal and guitar), "Roll and Tumble Blues," OKeh 8679. Atlanta, Georgia, March 14, 1929. Roots RL-307.

And I   rolled and I tumbled and I   cried the whole night long
And I rolled and I tumbled and I   cried the whole night long
And I rose this mornin' mama and I   didn't know   right from   wrong

Did you ever wake up and find your dough roller gone
Did you ever wake up and find your dough roller gone
And you wring your hands and you   cry the   whole day   long

And I told my woman lord   'fore I left the town
And I told my woman just be-   fore I left the town
Don't she let nobody   tear her   barrelhouse   down

And I fold my arms lord and I walked away
And I   fold my arms and I   slowly walked away
Said that's all right sweet mama your   trouble gon'   come some   day

This is the first recording of one of the more durable blues songs. For other versions and variants, hear Robert Johnson, "If I Had Possession over Judgment Day" (recorded in 1936, but first issued thirty years later, on Columbia LP 1654); Sleepy John Estes, "Brownsville Blues" (Decca 7473, 1938); John Lee "Sonny Boy" Williamson, "Lord Oh Lord Blues" (Bluebird B7847, 1938); Baby Face Leroy, "Rollin' and Tumblin'" (Parkway 501, 1950); Sunnyland Slim, "Going Back to Memphis" (Blue Lake 105, 1954).

Estes thought Newbern was born near Ripley or Brownsville, Tennessee, in 1899. He died about 1947 in the Marked Tree, Arkansas, state prison farm.

38. "Fo' Day Blues"

Peg Leg Howell (vocal and guitar), "Fo' Day Blues," Columbia 14177-D. Atlanta, Georgia, November 8, 1929. Roots RL-309.

I woke up this mornin'   'tween midnight and day
I woke up this mornin'   'tween midnight and day
I woke up this mornin'   'tween midnight and day
I felt for my rider   she done eased away

Sweet mama sweet mama   your papa double do love you
Sweet mama sweet mama papa double do love you
Just crazy about the way sweet mama do

My rider got something   I really don't know what it is
My rider got something   I really don't know what it is
She's wake up in the morning   can't keep my body still

"PEG LEG" HOWELL

WHEN "Peg Leg" Howell lost his leg, the world gained a great singer of blues. The loss of a leg never bothered "Peg Leg" as far as chasing around after blues is concerned. He sure catches them and then stomps all over them.

Nobody ever knows just what will happen next when "Peg Leg" Howell is let loose with a guitar, but it always is sure to be good.

"Peg Leg" Howell is an Exclusive Columbia Artist

NEW JELLY ROLL BLUES—*Accompanied by His Gang* . . . . BEAVER SLIDE RAG—*Accompanied by His Gang*	14210-D	75c
TISHAMINGO BLUES . . . . COAL MAN BLUES	14194-D	75c
NEW PRISON BLUES . . . . FO' DAY BLUES	14177-D	75c

HOWELL, HORSLEY AND BRADFORD

HARRY WILLS, the Champion . . . . WASN'T IT NICE—Vocals	14168-D	75c

FIGURE 22. *From* The Latest Blues by Columbia Race Stars, *p. 13*

wake up in the morn-ing___ can't keep my___ bod - y___ still

My rider got something they call it the stingaree
My rider got something   they calls it the stingaree
I wake up ev'ry morning it worryin' worryin' poor me

I'm goin' I'm goin' mama ain't comin' here no more
I'm goin' away mama ain't   comin' here no more
I'm goin' away mama ain't   comin' here no more
When you see me leavin' pin crepe on your door

Say the Mississippi River mam' it's long and deep and wide
The Mississippi River   long and deep and wide
Mississippi River   long and deep and wide
I got a lovin' fairer she's on the other side

I'm goin' up the country mama   honey an' I would carry you
I'm goin' up the country   mama I would carry you
Ain't nothin' up the country sweet mama you can do

I'd rather drink muddy water   sleep in a hollow log
Rather drink muddy water   sleep in a hollow log
Than to be in Atlanta treated like a dog

Peg Leg Howell was born in 1888 on a Georgia farm. He learned to play guitar in 1909 and by 1924 had settled in Atlanta. Most of what is known about his life appears in George Mitchell's liner notes to Testament T-2204, an album Howell recorded shortly before his death.

Paul Oliver observed that Howell's blues "are of special interest because they clearly represent the transition from old songs, work songs and ballads, to blues" (*The Story of the Blues*, p. 43). Certainly, Howell used widely collected traditional texts and tunes, borrowing from Anglo-American tradition as well as from Afro-American. But whether that proves that he represents a transition from worksongs and ballads to blues – if there was such a transition – is arguable.

39. "It Won't Be Long"

Charley Patton (vocal and guitar), "It Won't Be Long," Paramount 12854. Richmond, Indiana, June 14, 1929. Yazoo L-1020.

I b'lieve sweet mama   *gon'* do you like she says baby

I b'lieve sweet mama   *gon'* do you like she says baby

Gonna cook my supper   lord   put me in   her bed

If you ever go down Memphis   stop by Mengelwood baby

If you ever go down Memphis   stop by Mengelwood baby

You Memphis women don't mean   no man   no good

She's got a man on *a man*   *got a kid on her kid* baby

She's got a man on *a man*   *got a kid on her kid* baby

Done got so bold   lord she won't keep   it hid

Ah rider   ain't gon' be here long baby

All right all right   ain't gon' be here long baby

Cryin' ah rider   daddy'll   be here   long

I believe sweet mama   sure was kind   to me baby

I believe sweet mama   sure was kind   to me baby

She's up at night like a po-   lice on   his beat

I'll tell you something   keep it to   yourself   baby

I'm gon' tell you something   keep it to   yourself   baby

Don't you tell your husband lord   and no   one else

It's a long tall woman   tall like a cher-   ry tree   baby

Got a long tall woman   tall like a cher-   ry tree   baby

She gets up 'fore day and she puts   that thing   on me

For a recent version of "It Won't Be Long," hear Clarence Edwards, "Cooling Board" (Excello LP 8021). "Mengelwood" (st. 2) is the "Minglewood" in "Minglewood Blues" (transcr. 36). Another transcription of the text and tune may be found in Fahey, *Charley Patton*, p. 76.

40. "Writin' Paper Blues"

Blind Willie McTell (vocal and guitar), "Writin' Paper Blues," Victor 21474.
Atlanta, Georgia, October 18, 1927. Yazoo L-1005.[15]

I wrote you a letter mama   put it in your front yard
I wrote you a letter   put it in your front yard
How I'd love to come to see you but your   good man's got me barred

Ah you wrote me a letter   to come back to Newport News
You wrote me a letter mama   come back to Newport News
To leave the town   and don't spread the news

I wrote you a letter mama   sent you a telegram
I wrote you a letter mama and   sent you a telegram
Not to meet me in Memphis but   meet me in Birmingham

Mm   hear my weep and moan
Mm mm   hear my weep and moan
Won' you hear me pleading   hear my grieve and groan

Now if I could get me   one more drink of booze
If I could get me   one more drink of booze
I guess it would ease   these old writin' paper blues

I caught a freight train special mama   mama caught a passenger behind
I caught a freight train special ma-   mama caught a passenger behind
'Cause you can't quit me papa   there's no need in tryin'

Another transcription of this text can be found in *Blues World,* no. 38, p. 22.

41. "I'm So Glad I'm Twenty-one Years Old Today"

Joe Dean (vocal and piano), "I'm So Glad I'm Twenty-one Years Old Today,"
Vocalion 1544. Chicago, Illinois, August 7, 1930. Yazoo L-1028.

Well I'm so glad I'm twenty-one years old today
Lord I'm so glad I'm twenty-one years old today
Lord I'm so glad my baby can't treat me thataway

Ah babe   what you want poor me to do
Ah babe   what you want poor me to do
Drive a coal wagon babe give all of my money to you

That's why I'm so glad I'm twenty-one years old today
That's why I'm so glad I'm twenty-one years old today
Lord I'm so glad my baby can't treat me thataway

Ah babe   don't play me for no fool
Ah babe   don't play me for no fool
Lord I ain't no plumber 'n' I ain't nobody's tool

That's why I'm so glad I'm twenty-one years old today
That's why I'm so glad I'm twenty-one years old today
Lord I'm so glad my baby can't treat me thataway

From St. Louis to the river river to the deep blue sea
From St. Louis to the river river to the deep blue sea
Glad your monkey ways babe don't take no 'fect on me

That's why I'm so glad I'm twenty-one years old today
That's why I'm so glad I'm twenty-one years old today
Lord I'm so glad my baby can't treat me thataway

Ah babe   don't make no fool of me
Ah babe   don't make no fool of me
Lord I'm three times seven babe why can't you see

That's why I'm so glad I'm twenty-one years old today
That's why I'm so glad I'm twenty-one years old today
Lord I'm three times seven and I'm going to have my way

Joe Dean made one record for Vocalion, in August, 1930. No more is known of him than that he was called "Joe Dean (from Bowling Green)" on the record label.

42. "Biddle Street Blues"

Henry Spaulding (vocal and guitar), "Biddle Street Blues," Brunswick 7085. Chicago, Illinois, May 6, 1929. Roots RL-310.

Hey Biddle Street blues babe   is easing down on me
Hey Biddle Street blues babe   is easing down on me
'Cause my best baby have quit me   and no one to care for me

Now well it's please be kind babe   let me speak just one more time
Will you please be kind babe   let me speak just one more time
'Cause I have something to tell you baby   will ease your troublin' mind

[spoken:] Ah babe   ah baby

Now I'm goin' back to Biddle Street   to wear you off my mind
Now I'm goin' back to Biddle Street   to wear you off my mind
'Cause I have another woman on Biddle Street   will treat me nice and kind

Biddle Street Biddle Street now   is only twenty-six blocks long
Biddle Street Biddle Street now   is only twenty-six blocks long
And the women on Biddle Street   just won't leave me alone

That's why I'm goin' back to Biddle Street   I swear 'n' it won't be long
That's why I'm goin' back to Biddle Street   I swear 'n' it won't be long
'Cause I know my baby's there   she will take my lovin' on

long · · · · That's_ why I'm goin' back to Biddle Street

I_____ swear_____ 'n'it won't be long · · · · 'Cause I know

my ba-by's there_ · · · she will take_ my lov-in' on

Henry Spaulding was born in Mississippi and settled in St. Louis.

43. "Mistreatin' Mamma"

Walter "Furry" Lewis (vocal and guitar), "Mistreatin' Mamma," Victor v-38519. Memphis, Tennessee, August 28, 1928. Roots RL-323.[16]

Babe if your heart ain't iron   it must be marble stone
If your heart ain't iron   it must be marble stone
For you're a mistreatin' mama baby sure as you born

I can tell from a little   just what a whole lot means
I can tell from a little   just what a whole lot means
You treat me just like somebody you ain't never seen

I got a woman in Cuby I   got a woman in Spain
Woman in Cuby   got a woman in Spain
I got a woman in Chicago and I'm scared to call her name

I got nineteen women   all I want's one more
I got nineteen women   all I want's one more
Just one more sweet mama and I'll let the nineteen go

I could had religion   lord this very day
I could had religion   lord this very day
But the womens and whiskeys lord won't let me pray

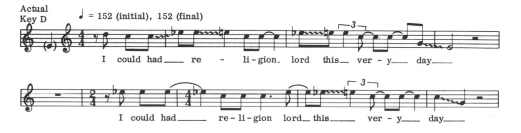

Actual Key D   ♩ = 152 (initial), 152 (final)

I could had_____ re - li-gion. lord this_ ver-y_ day_____

I could had_____ re-li-gion lord_ this_____ ver-y_ day_____

FIGURE 23. *Furry Lewis in an unorthodox left-hand "over the top" position at the 1970 Wisconsin Delta Blues Festival. He is using a piece of tubing on the little finger of his left hand as a slide. Photograph by the author.*

But the wom - ens and —— whis-keys —— lord won't —— let me —— pray ——

I can set right here look on   Jackson Avenue
I can set right here look on   Jackson Avenue
I can see everything that my good woman do

Sometime I b'lieve I will sometime I believe I won't
Sometime I b'lieve I will sometime I believe I won't
Sometime I b'lieve I do sometime I believe I don't

Furry Lewis, a veteran of medicine shows, lives in Memphis, where he has been an entertainer for many years. In the 1960s he rerecorded many of his old songs on LP for Folkways and Prestige. He performs in many different styles with a large and varied repertoire.

44. "Dying Pickpocket Blues"

Nolan "Barrel House Welch" Welsh (vocal and piano), "Dying Pickpocket Blues,"
Paramount 12759. Chicago, Illinois, January, 1929. (Dutch) Riverside RM 8809.

It was in New York City workhouse on a cold December day
'Twas in New York City workhouse on a cold December day
'Twas in a dirty cell   where a dying pickpocket lay

And his buddy stood besides him with his long dark drooping hands
And his buddy stood besides him with his long dark drooping hands
Listened to the last words that the dying pickpocket sang

He said tell my babe back in Cinci' although I know she will feel blue
Yes tell my baby back in Cinci'   although I know she will feel blue
That I got this *dose* on a hundred and I cannot pull it through

I'm long gone partner   going to a better land
Oooh   partner I'm goin' to a better land
I ain't gonna pick no more pockets   I'm gon' be a reg'lar man

Although she have been a real pal and she answered to all my calls
Although she have been a real pal and she answered to all my calls
Yeah I've ruined her health   tryin' to spring me from this fall

Nothing is known of Nolan "Barrelhouse" Welsh. The text is a variant of "The
Dying Hobo," indexed as H 3 in Laws, *Native American Balladry*.

45. "Bootlegging Blues"

Jim Jackson (vocal and guitar), "Bootlegging Blues," Victor 21268.
Memphis, Tennessee, February 14, 1928. Roots RL-323.

Since   corn liquor came in style   there's plenty   money to be made
Just get a job at   one of these stills and you'll surely   will be paid

I tell you it's a mighty   risk to run   and a mighty   chance to take
To spend your money for the corn that the   boot- leggers make

The bootleggin' man's   got his bottle in his hand
And all he needs   a little more speed
So he can outrun the revenue man

When the bootlegger goes   to his still   gets ready   to make his stuff
He's got his concentrated lye   cocaine   and his snuff

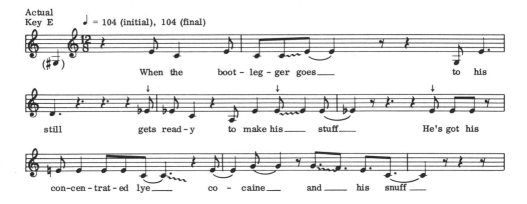

He'll fix you a drink that just won't quit
It'll make you fight a *circle saw*
Make you slap the lady down
And make you pick a fight with your pa

The bootleggin' man's   got his bottle in his hand
And all he needs   is a little more speed
So he can outrun the revenue man

I went home   the other night   I'd swore I wouldn't drink no more
Until s'loons come back with   with bottled-in-bond   and the days of long ago

But I see   that will never be   so I   just got   drunk again
I have nothing as long as corn liquor   last 'cause I got no money to spend

The bootleggin' man   got his bottle in his hand
Now all he needs   is a little more speed
So he can outrun the revenue man

The bootleggin' man   got his bottle in his hand
And all he needs   is a little more speed
So he can outrun the revenue man

Jim Jackson was born in the 1880s in Hernando, Mississippi. His recorded repertoire included many traditional minstrel songs, but his "Jim Jackson's Kansas City Blues" (Vocalion 1144) was one of the best-selling race records of the decade. "Bootlegging Blues" bears some similarity to the tune used for the "Crow Jane" family (see p. 166).

The melody for stanzas 3, 6, 9, and 10 is different from that for stanza 4; the melody for stanza 5 is related to this "chorus."

46. "K. C. Moan"

Memphis Jug Band, "K. C. Moan," Victor v-38558. Memphis, Tennessee, October 4, 1929. Folkways FA 2953.[17]

I thought I heard that K.C. when she blowed
Oh I thought I heard that K.C. when she blowed
Oh I thought I heard that K.C. when she blowed
Yes she blowed like my woman's on board

When I get back on that K.C. road
Oh when I get back on that K.C. road
Oh when I get back on that K.C. road
Gonna love my baby like I never loved before

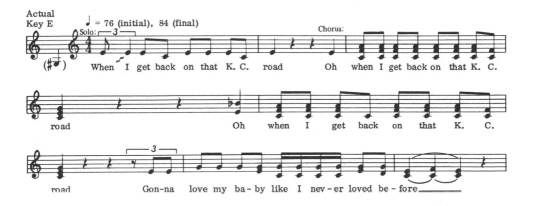

Mm mm mm mm mm mm mm mm mm
Mm   mm mm mm mm mm mm mm mm mm
Mm   mm mm mm mm mm mm mm mm mm
Mm mm mm mm mm mm mm mm mm

"K.C. Moan" is another song whose form bears a superficial similarity to the approximately twelve-bar, AAB blues stanza, but which cannot be proven to have undergone a metamorphosis into it. An empirical approach identifies elements – typical phrases and lines used in blues songs – in the earlier forms, and asserts merely that they were congenial to the blues form. Howard Odum collected a very similar song between 1905 and 1908; see p. 23.

47. "James Alley Blues"

Richard "Rabbit" Brown (vocal and guitar), "James Alley Blues," Victor 20578. New Orleans, Louisiana, March 11, 1927. Folkways FA 2953.[18]

Oh times ain't now nothing like they used to be
No times ain't now nothing like they used to be
And I'm telling you all the truth   oh take it for me

I done seen better days but I'm puttin' up with these
I done seen better days   but I'm puttin' up with these
I would have a much better time but these girls now are so hard to please

'Cause I was born in the country   she thinks I'm easy to rule
'Cause I was born in the country she thinks I'm easy to rule
She try to hitch me to her wagon she want to   drive me like a mule

You know I bought the groc'ries   and I paid the rent
Yeah I buys the groc'ries   and I pays the rent
She tried to make me wash her clothes but I got good common sense

I said if you don't want me   why don't you tell me so
You knowed if you don't want me   why don't you tell me so
Because it ain't like a man that ain't got nowhere go

I been giving you sugar for sugar   let you get salt for salt
I'll give you sugar for sugar   let you get salt for salt
And if you can't get along with me   well it's your own fault

How d'you want me to love you and you treat me mean
How do you want me to love you   you keep a treat' me mean
You my daily thought   and my nightly dream

Sometime I think that you too sweet to die
Sometime I think that you too sweet to die
And another time I think   you ought to be buried alive

Richard Brown was one of the few downhome blues singers to record in New Orleans. His guitar style and vocal delivery suggest that he spent some time entertaining in minstrel and medicine shows.

48. "Yellow Girl Blues"

Alger "Texas" Alexander (vocal) and Lonnie Johnson (guitar), "Yellow Girl Blues," OKeh 8801. San Antonio, Texas, March 9, 1928. Historical HLP-31.

Some of these womens   I just can't understand
Lord some of these womens   I just can't understand
They run around here   with one another's man

Oh black woman evil   brownskin's evil too
A black woman's evil   brownskin's evil too
Gonna get me a yellow woman   see what she will do

Mm mm mm mm   mm mm mm
Mm mm mm mm   mm mm mm
Gonna get me (a) yellow woman   see what she will do

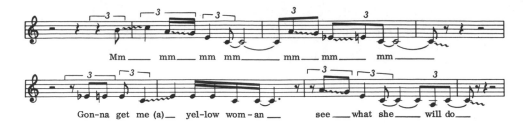

Mm___ mm___ mm mm___ mm___ mm___ mm___

Gon-na get me (a)___ yel-low wom-an ___ see ___ what she ___ will do ___

Gonna get me a heaven   have a kingdom of my own
Gonna get me a heaven   have a kingdom of my own
So these brownskin women   can cluster 'round my throne

Mm mm mm mm   mm mm mm
Mm mm mm mm   mm mm mm
So these brownskin women   can cluster 'round my throne

[spoken:] Let me down easy

Texas Alexander's vocal style is loose even for someone who does not accompany himself. It is a field-holler style, freely decorative. He recorded forty-two titles, all of which were issued, before 1930; most were blues songs.

MUSICAL ANALYSIS: TOWARD A SONG-PRODUCING SYSTEM

Theoretical Assumptions

The listener who advocates pure and simple enjoyment of music without the encumbrance of analysis probably does not realize that he analyzes music each time he listens to it, for otherwise he could not distinguish one kind of music from another. In this chapter I am primarily concerned with a kind of musical analysis that leads to a performance model, a set of instructions for producing early downhome blues songs. From the transcriptions of the previous chapter I derive a grammar of downhome blues melody and demonstrate a song-making model which, given words, will produce an acceptable blues melody and set those words to it.

What is the meaning of meaning in music? Besides personal implications for singer and audience, musical performances enjoy functional and structural social consequences. Worksongs, for example, channel energy into common tasks; music as a form of ritual imitation of life anticipates, directs, and reinforces the symbolic social order. The structure of musical performance reflects the social pattern of human interaction. Complex societies, for example, exhibit a constellation of precise, individualized features in their performance styles: a tendency toward solo performance, combined with considerably more verbal information per unit line of text than is found in simple societies. Mbuti Pygmy musical performance, on the other hand, reflects the cohesion and integration of their small-band egalitarian society. Such structural generalizations, however, operate upon a gross cultural level; meaning is forced upon correlations between music and culture, which become interculturally significant. Intraculturally, if the music has an intelligible text, the words carry direct symbolic meaning, since they stand for objects, ideas, and feelings. But the music itself – a mere succession of musical tones – has an additional musical meaning, and it is this which must be apprehended if one is to work within the musical system as a viable composer.

Laying aside the perennially attractive idea that the mathematical relations between musical tones reveal structural design in the universe, or, by Levi-Straussian extension, in the human mind, the most common view is that music is a kind of nonverbal symbolism: music is said to express emotion or represent events. Of course, the emotion wells up in the listener while the events take place, aided by program notes or by convention, in his mind's eye. Imagine, for example, a motion picture showing a young woman going up the stairs to her bedroom. The sound track can arouse the viewer's expectations only in a general sense. Dissonant sounds with sharp dynamic variations imply impending difficulty, but the tones themselves cannot specify it – a sudden fall? a burglar in the bedroom? fire on the landing? – unless a recurrent sound sequence in the film prefigures a recurring event. The language of music is symbolic, but in a less meaningful sense than the language of words, for it can offer a fixed referent only when it employs a recognized convention, such as the tolling of the death bell or the sounding of taps on a bugle.

Yet there exists a more specific kind of musical significance than the symbolic, though it is not translatable into words. Consider a sequence of sounds in a purely musical context. Here the significance of a musical sound is that it points to other musical sounds. A linguistic analogy may make musical signification clearer. Consider the incomplete sentence "The cat is on the ———." The five initial words imply a sixth word or word cluster in the sequence; *mat* or *grass* or *table* or *rocking chair* would complete the sentence. But not any kind of word will serve. Some words, in this situation, would be ungrammatical; one could not say "The cat is on the lightly." The word which completes the sentence must be a noun or noun phrase. But not all nouns are logical in the context; one could not say "The cat is on the ceiling" and expect to make sense.

As a series of words implies consequential words, so a series of musical tones implies consequential tones; given a context, or sense-making language, only certain consequent tones will make musical sense. What determines that language? Convention of customary use makes consequent tones probable, just as it makes consequent words probable. When a listener becomes aware that certain musical tones imply other tones, he operates on a musical probability associated with a particular musical style. Tones, therefore, do not merely imply tones which are consequent in temporal sequence. They also point to a set of related tones, whose organization as a whole accounts for the musical style; and that musical style exists as an abstraction – a model – apart from any single piece of music in that style. Just as anthropologists say that individuals in a society carry a personal culture, while the society carries a whole culture, so we can say that individual pieces of music in a related group carry an individual style, while the group of related pieces carries a whole style.

A singer fluent in downhome blues style knows how to give performances of downhome blues songs which make musical sense to him and to his audience. He is not born with this knowledge, though he may have been blessed with the capacity to acquire it. He learns by listening to a number of downhome blues performances, from which he derives the materials to fashion his songs. How can he make up songs no one has ever sung before? We must suppose he has fashioned inside himself some sort of creative apparatus. It should be clear that the principles of its operation are predominantly unconscious, for the singer cannot explain precisely how it works, even though he can make up songs with it.

Downhome blues singers patch and fit their words and music at the moment they sing them. Sometimes, of course, they memorize stanzas; but only rarely can they sing a song exactly the same way twice. Nor, in many cases, do they intend to. The first stanza ordinarily establishes the title of the song and introduces a tune, but succeeding stanzas do not use precisely the same tune. The number of syllables varies in each textual line; accent shifts; sometimes the melody changes drastically when the singer wants to employ a "different" tune (e.g., sts. 1 and 2 in "Pony Blues" [transcr. 1]). But the singer is unaware of minor variations; he operates unconsciously.

To test the unconsciousness hypothesis, I convinced Lazy Bill Lucas to sing a blues song for me over and over, so that I might transcribe it for copyright purposes. He observed that I could have had him sing it once into a tape recorder, but I told him that I did not have access to any machines that afternoon and it was imperative that the song be transcribed and sent in as soon as possible.

As Lucas repeated the stanzas for me to write down, he realized he sometimes sang them to slightly different tunes. He noticed that he could end his lines either on the keynote or on the major third above it; this unnerved him a little. When I asked him what might account for the variation, he said, "It doesn't really matter which way you put it down because the tune is basically the same."

"But why does it come out different?" I asked.

"I'm not thinking about it when I do it, it just comes natural."

"How come you can sing different words to the same tune, so that sometimes you'll sing two notes where you only sang one before with a different word?"

"Well, yeah, I do that," he said. "I remember the tune from the first verse. It just comes natural. I must have it somewhere at the back of my mind. Not from the notes, you see, I don't do it like that."[1]

Musical analysis is incomplete unless it shows how the parts broken down by the analytical procedure may be put into various combinations to form acceptable musical wholes. As the biologist, for example, is not content merely with morphology, so the musicologist cannot rest satisfied with description and comparison. As the biochemist proposes theories of cell metabolism to account for the life of the organism, so the musicologist must pursue music as process, and propose theories of origin and growth. And as the scientist attempts – however crudely – to verify his theories by synthesizing life in the laboratory, so the musicologist moves toward certainty as his theories are able to synthesize acceptable music.

Musical analysis requires, therefore, not only identification of musical elements (a style lexicon), but also a set of instructions for creating complete performances from them. The song-producing system should be based on models which are fleshed into performances by the application of the proper principles to the musical elements.[2] Furthermore, elements, models, and principles must be derived from a finite group of performances which one judges intuitively to share a common musical style. Without the song-producing system, description of the style remains partial, though in fairness it must be said that identification of elements and musical characteristics of various styles has had some comparative usefulness.

A very large number of observations conceivably could be made about early downhome blues style. It is useful to distinguish between stylistic components which belong to the performance situation and those which pertain to the music sound. The analyst seeking to describe early downhome blues style using commercial recordings from the 1920s soon realizes that these documents do not preserve live performances. Of course, those components can be recaptured to some extent by questioning singers and listeners who recall them, and by observing contemporary performances. For example, in live performances of early downhome blues at the Saturday night parties, the audience was noisy. Some people clustered around the singer, shouting encouragement; some danced; some paid little attention to the music while they drank, conversed, or gambled nearby. Considered as an event, the live performance has, obviously, social interactions which are important parts of the musical situation, yet are divorced from the music sound. But a blues song does not cease to be a blues song when it is put on record. To be sure, the performance and listening situations are altered (see chap. 6 for a discussion of recording studio conditions, and Appendix A for a discussion of audience reaction to records); but the musical system remains constant.

Form

By observing features shared by a finite but representative group of early downhome blues songs, one can ultimately infer models, which I shall call *blues families*. These blues families must, by definition, be capable of producing, according to a derivable set of instructions, a large number of blues songs. Some of those features and instructions are fairly obvious. For example, a downhome blues song (S) consists of several stanzas $(z_1, z_2, z_3$, etc.). This may be expressed according to the following notation, in which the symbol → means "can be written as":

$$S \rightarrow z_1 + z_2 + z_3 \text{ etc.}$$

Taking the three-line, approximately twelve-bar, AAB stanza for the development of the model,[3] we can say that a stanza consists of three lines (1, 2, 3). This may be expressed thus:

$$z \rightarrow 1 + 2 + 3$$

These generalizations occur on the level of musical form; form is a representation of the overall structure of a piece of music. Structure is posited from divisions within the piece, that is, units marked off by repetition, by rests, and by textual groups. A strophe is a repeated musical section; recorded downhome blues songs share, with most forms of Western folk and popular music, strophic form. But the three-line, AAB stanza belongs, as far as I know, solely to blues. In the text transcriptions presented in chapter 3, I divided the songs into stanzas, and divided most stanzas into three lines, each beginning at the left-hand margin. Here each stanza is a strophe, ordinarily containing different words each time the music is repeated. The strophic form is carried to the line level as well; the stanzaic AAB form, with the rhymed ends of A and B, is marked by repetition and balance, but not by symmetry.

In virtually every downhome blues song I transcribed, the first (and second) lines of the stanzas fall into two distinct parts. This division is accomplished melodically in one of three ways: by a rest (* in fig. 24); by an end pitch held longer than a quarter-

FIGURE 24. *"Pony Blues" (transcr. 1), st. 1, l. 1*

FIGURE 25. *"Got the Blues" (transcr. 31), st. 6, l. 1*

FIGURE 26. *"Dead Drunk Blues" (transcr. 3), st. 4, l. 1*

note (* in fig. 25); or by an intervallic skip, usually upward, of at least a minor third (* in fig. 26). Sometimes singers use two division signals at once. If the line is divided by a rest, the singer usually takes a breath there. The third line of each stanza is similarly divided into two parts in most, but not all, cases.[4]

The units resulting from these line divisions can be regarded as musical phrases. Line 1 is divided into phrases a and b:

$$1 \rightarrow a + b$$

Line 2 is divided into phrases c and d:

$$2 \rightarrow c + d$$

Line 3 is (usually) divided into phrases e and f:

$$3 \rightarrow e + f$$

The formal divisions indicated here stress certain positions in the melody and certain words in the text: those tones and syllables which end phrases and lines, and those which begin them. Of course, various additional musical and textual factors besides formal division combine to emphasize or deemphasize these positions.

Basic harmonic support in recorded downhome blues was the (by 1926) standardized "three-change" harmony employing the I, IV, and V chords. Since many of the songs are heterometric (that is, with a change of meter during the stanza), it is better to think of the stanza as three lines of variable measure, instead of three lines of four measures each (the standard twelve bars). The basic harmonic support for the three lines is indicated in figure 27; each beat is represented by a slash (/). Line 1 begins on the I triad (C in the key of C, to which the transcriptions were transposed), either in the pickup measure or at the start of the first full measure, and continues on that triad through the rest which precedes

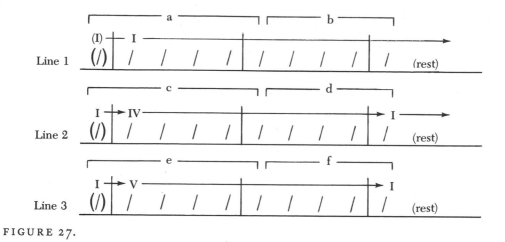

FIGURE 27.

line 2. Line 2 begins on the I triad in the pickup measure and moves to the IV chord (F in the key of C), remaining there until phrase d crosses the bar line, moving then to a I triad (a IV-I cadence). The I chord continues through the pickup measure of line 3. It moves to the V chord (G, or often G⁷, in the key of C), which is sustained until phrase f crosses the bar line. Then the V chord moves to a I triad (a V-I cadence), which remains until the next stanza, unless the musicians play a stanza instrumentally. These instrumental breaks are infrequent in early recorded downhome blues songs; when they occur (in "That Will Be Alright" [transcr. 29], for example) they usually take the form of a stanza (without words) with normal harmonic support and additional complexity in the accompaniment.

Thus far the song-producing system lacks the lexical elements. Elements of tone have three fundamental attributes: pitch, duration, and quality. Quality will be treated only briefly here, as it is an attribute difficult to transcribe. Duration will be treated under the general heading of rhythmic organization; pitch will be considered under the general heading of motional organization.

Tone Quality

The tone quality of early downhome blues singing largely resulted from the way the singer enunciated his words. Singing with an open throat, he relaxed his lips and mouth and kept his tongue loose, low, and toward the back of his mouth. This position favored certain kinds of vowels and consonants and made it somewhat difficult to produce others. Thus the singers favored the low, back vowels [o], [a], and especially [ɔ], and tended to change other vowel sounds into these, while [o] and [a], in turn, gravitated toward [ɔ].[5] For example, *home* became not [hom] but [hɔm]. With the lips relaxed and the tongue low and back, certain consonants were difficult to produce: the bilabial stops [p] and [b], the bilabial nasal [m], the dental fricatives [θ] and [δ],[6] the alveolar stops [t] and [d]. Unable to accent the melody with forceful consonants, downhome blues singers gave certain tones strength by singing them very loudly. An expert like Charley Patton, whose singing is virtually unintelligible to some people, was able to give a sequence of dynamic accents to a vowel sound held through successive pitches, lending a percussive rhythmic effect which could – and did – contrast with the rhythm of his guitar accompaniment. Some singers, particularly those close to the Mississippi Delta, used a good deal of vibrato and raspiness in their singing voices which was not present in their speech – at least, not in their spoken asides on records. They sang nasally, but not so much as the hillbilly singers or popular crooners of the 1920s. These techniques, all told, raised problems for recording engineers, who had to be very careful about microphone placement and volume level in the studio. Indeed, in some instances the engineer turned the volume control up and down during the performance, compressing the dynamic range that could be recorded without distortion. (The same compression was used for recordings of opera singers.)

Rhythmic Organization

Rhythm is generally regarded as time-measured movement. In music, the notion of rhythm indicates a succession of sounds and silences whose time-lengths form a duration pattern. If meter is defined as the measurement of the number of pulse beats between more or less regularly recurring accents, the typical meter in downhome blues songs is marked by the accompaniment, which supplies the pulse beats with the right-hand thumb playing the bass string(s) of the guitar. Often these beats are reinforced by simultaneous foot-stomps.[7]

Downhome blues accompaniment meter is $\frac{4}{4}$; that is, the beats are grouped in fours. The first pulse beat is heavily stressed; the third beat also is stressed, but not so heavily; the second and fourth beats, while clearly marked, are unstressed. Of the forty-four downhome blues songs in the sample, fourteen are heterometric. Metrical changes ordinarily occur at phrase beginnings; typically, the singer rests two extra beats before initiating a phrase (fig. 28) or comes in two beats early (fig. 29). In the latter instance, the

FIGURE 28. *"Mean Conductor Blues" (transcr. 23), st. 3, ll. 1–2*

FIGURE 29. *"Minglewood Blues" (transcr. 36), st. 2, l. 3*

two-beat anticipation can cause confusion between the singer and the accompanying group. Stanza 2 in "Sunshine Special" (transcr. 30) is in no discernible meter during lines 1 and 2; but this stanza is metrically atypical in the song. Twenty-nine downhome blues songs in the sample are isometric; that is, the meter remains constant during the stanza.

Although instrumental accompaniments provide a four-beat measure in $\frac{4}{4}$, the melodies sometimes suggest a four-beat measure in $\frac{12}{8}$, that is, four groups of triplets, each beat being divided into three equal parts. (For a transcription in $\frac{12}{8}$, see "Bootlegging Blues" [transcr. 45].) I regularly transcribed the melodies in $\frac{4}{4}$, however, to illustrate the polyrhythmic passages. A full discussion of downhome blues polyrhythm (cross- or contrasting rhythms within the same meter) must consider not only melody, but also the relation of melody to accompaniment. I will treat these points shortly in my discussion of "M. and O. Blues."

The most common rhythmic unit in downhome blues melodies is the eighth-note. The quarter-note is next. Triplet rhythms are common; the patterns most often encountered, in decreasing order of frequency, are shown in figure 30.

FIGURE 30.

Dotted quarter-notes or their equivalents are reasonably common, while half-notes and sixteenth-notes occur less frequently. More rarely encountered still are dotted eighth-notes, dotted half-notes, whole notes, dotted sixteenth-notes, and thirty-second notes. Enumeration of these rhythmic units helps build the blues lexicon, but how they are *used* is the main concern of a song-producing system. Tones of longer than quarter-note duration come regularly at the ends of phrases b, d, and f. Sometimes triplet rhythms occur in sequence, and once a singer gets into them, he may move into $\frac{12}{8}$ meter. But just as often the singer moves back out of the triplet rhythm after a few beats, into duple rhythm once more.

Most downhome blues melodic phrases begin directly between two pulse beats (or on the third unit of a triplet). Often phrases b, d, and f are begun just after the bar line, as illustrated in figure 31. Phrases a, c, and e often begin on unstressed positions in

FIGURE 31. *"Dry Spell Blues" (transcr. 35), st. 1, l. 1*

the third or, less frequently, the fourth beat of the measure (fig. 32). Beginning a phrase thus off the beat lends emphasis to the following beat, in these cases either the normally weak fourth or the normally stressed first.

FIGURE 32. *"Whiskey Moan Blues" (transcr. 22), st. 1, l. 2, phrase c*

Singers frequently anticipate the beat elsewhere in the phrase also. They start singing a syllable on the last, unstressed eighth-note of the previous pulse and hold it over
to its normal stress position, that is, into the beat. Such anticipation occurs regularly
across bar lines and at the close of phrases b, d, and f, as illustrated in figure 33 (marked

FIGURE 33. *"Minglewood Blues" (transcr. 36), st. 1, l. 1*

by *). This type of syncopation is also characteristic of "ragtime" songs and the treble
part of finger-picked styles of guitar accompaniment which follow the melody, such as
that used by Mississippi John Hurt in "Got the Blues, Can't Be Satisfied." While his
thumb supplies a steady 1-2-3-4 series of beats, his fingers play the treble strings, following the melodic syncopation at the close of phrases b, d, and f (see transcr. 10).

When the syncopation is continuous, the natural result is a conflict of pulse patterns (polymeter) between the vocal and the accompaniment (fig. 34). But polymeter

FIGURE 34. *"Got the Blues" (transcr. 31), st. 6, l. 3*

usually does not last longer than two and a half beats (or two beats plus one-third of a
triplet).

The contrast between duple and triple patterns is another principle of rhythmic
organization. Sometimes a melody alternates duple and triple rhythms (fig. 35). More

FIGURE 35. *"Long Lonesome Blues" (transcr. 32), st. 5, l. 1*

often, as I indicated earlier, when a downhome blues singer moves into a triple rhythm
he stays there a while, suggesting a $\frac{12}{8}$ metrical signature (figs. 36 and 37). Once singing in triplets, he tends to switch his bass accompaniment from the duple ♩ ♩ to the
triple ♩³♪ ♩³♪. The slower the tempo, the greater the tendency to divide the beat in
thirds; in tempos below ♩ = 84, this is hard to avoid.

FIGURE 36. *"Bumble Bee" (transcr. 16), st. 5, l. 1, phrase a, written in $\frac{4}{4}$ meter*

FIGURE 37. *"Bumble Bee" (transcr. 16), st. 5, l. 1, phrase a, written in $\frac{12}{8}$ meter*

Vocal and accompaniment sometimes cross differing rhythms, usually duple versus triple. Of course, cross-rhythm arises when even a single triplet occurs in the melody against a duple accompaniment – and this occurs frequently – but it seems better to reserve the designation polyrhythm for that situation in which the crossing is sustained for at least a beat.

David Evans first noted that alternation between duple and triple rhythms typified the blues songs of singers living in Jackson, Mississippi, in the 1920s.[8] In the sample presently under consideration, this principle is most apparent in Jackson singer Tommy Johnson's "Maggie Campbell Blues" (transcr. 21). The accompaniment starts in a smooth duple rhythm, then changes to a triple rhythm in the first stanza when Johnson begins humming (fig. 38). Johnson's vocal occasionally works a triple rhythm against a duple in his guitar accompaniment (fig. 39).

FIGURE 38.

FIGURE 39.

Although both duple and triple rhythms may appear in the same downhome blues song, one rhythm predominates. Consider Blind Blake's "Early Morning Blues" (transcr. 8). Blake carries over an unmatched steadiness of accompaniment pulse and inventive, off-beat treble combinations from his ragtime playing to his blues. His blues accompaniment is often grounded in a stated or implied triplet bass figure played either by the right-hand thumb alone or by first finger and thumb (fig. 40). In "Early Morning Blues" Blake begins singing in a duple rhythm against the triplet bass, but by phrase b the vocal is in triplets, and it continues thus throughout the stanza.[9]

FIGURE 40.

An examination of the vocal and the accompaniment in a stanza of Willie Brown's "M. and O. Blues" (transcr. 17) will cast further light on rhythmic organization. Some comments on the harmonic support are also in order. In figure 41, the vocal melody is written stem up, at the top of the system. The guitar accompaniment is written in two parts: a bass part, played by the right-hand thumb, and a treble part, played with the

FIGURE 41. *"M. and O. Blues"* (transcr. 17), st. 4

fingers of the right hand; these are written stem down to distinguish them from the vocal. Lines and measures are numbered; phrases are lettered.

Brown's guitar accompaniment throughout the stanza is in duple rhythm. He begins singing in duple in the pickup measure. In measure 1 he sings a brief triplet, but in measure 2 he crosses the rhythm dramatically, holding the triple rhythm in the vocal against the duple accompaniment. Combined with the direction of the melody, the contrast produces a tumbling sequence of sounds.

Harmonically, the accompaniment is simple. Brown holds a low C pedal point in the bass, while he plays the treble in counterpoint to the vocal. (This low C is actually F, the key in which Brown sings "M. and O. Blues" and plays it on the guitar; the instrument is tuned so that he can use the open sixth string, nominally E, to produce the low C. He "chokes" (stretches) a string to slur upward from E♭′ to E′ (which I call the E′ complex), contrasting it with G′ or C′; played against G′, this creates a dissonance of a second with the A′ in the vocal. Although the support is on the I chord throughout the line, the passing F in the last beat of measure 2 hints at the IV chord. Just before line 2, Brown moves to the I⁷ chord, as expected (see fig. 27).

A subtly different and unexpected line 2 follows. The melodic triplet rhythm occurs but once in each measure – sufficient, nonetheless, to lend cross-rhythmic contrast. Starting on the I⁷ chord, Brown moves expectedly to the IV chord at the beginning of measure 5, holding the F in the bass. Halfway through measure 5 he surprises the listener by returning to the low C and the I chord, using the same bass slide previously employed in the pickup measure. At the close of line 2 he provides another hint of the IV chord with the F passing tone, while moving to the usual I chord at the beginning of measure 7 and to the I⁷ chord on the pickup in line 3.

Line 3 is also harmonically ambiguous, here between the I and the V chords. In phrase e, one expects a V or a V⁷ chord; Brown's bass-note G at the beginning of measure 9 supplies its root, but he plays the typical I-chord, E′-complex, treble accompaniment used in phrases a, b, and d. The melody dips to G′ on the second beat, suggesting the V-chord harmony. Of course, G is the fifth of the tonic chord as well. However, the treble accompaniment part does not move upward to the melodic G′, and the melody returns to the dissonant A′ heard so often before. Suddenly an unprecedented bass-note A appears, as the triplet melody in G′ finally confirms the V chord in the vocal line. While the counterpoint continues, Brown crosses triple vocal rhythm against duple accompaniment rhythm once more, beginning on the word *ambitious* (a good term to describe Brown's art as well as the woman's appearance).

He ends the stanza by contrasting complex triplets-within-triplets against the duple accompaniment. The added D′ in the cadence suggests the V⁷ chord or possibly the IV⁶ chord; it reminds the listener that he may have been listening to V⁷-I cadences all the time. The simplification and ambiguities are deliberate and controlled, not accidental and unsuccessful attempts to achieve the standard progression.

This detailed analysis of "M. and O. Blues" has revealed a significant amount of vocal/accompaniment polyrhythm. Within the vocal itself, Brown uses syncopative devices: he begins phrases on unstressed notes, anticipating the beat both in duple and triple rhythms across bar lines and within measures. Polyrhythm is found most frequently in recorded early downhome blues from the Mississippi Delta area and the Memphis area. But it is not infrequent elsewhere. In the main, duple and triple rhythms are crossed only temporarily; while the effect is not one of continuous polyrhythm, its occurrence as part of the variation encouraged by instructions in the song-producing model is significant. *Metrical* conflict between vocal and accompaniment (polymeter) is rare in downhome blues, however.

To my knowledge, no systematic analysis of rhythm in early downhome blues songs has been published. Excellent rhythmic analysis of a closely related music, however, appears in Winthrop Sargeant's *Jazz*. Sargeant locates what he terms polyrhythm in a three-over-four superimposition (fig. 42). The descending three-note melodic com-

FIGURE 42. *"I Can't Give You Anything but Love, Baby"*

binations cross against implicit combinations of four notes (in the $\frac{4}{4}$ meter). Most often he finds three-over-four superimposition in smaller units (fig. 43). (I have re-notated

FIGURE 43. *"Bugle Call Rag"*

his example to conform to the downhome blues transcriptions in this book.) This sort of rhythm – a tendency to anticipate a forthcoming beat – I have termed merely syncopative, reserving the label polyrhythm for cross-rhythms which last for longer periods. Cross-rhythms which last so long that the listener perceives not merely conflicting rhythm, but also conflicting pulse patterns, I refer to as polymeter. Sargeant, admitting that it "is, perhaps, merely a matter of definition," asserts that "the principle of polyrhythm would seem, none the less, to be a syncopative principle." Taking note of Aaron Copland's definition of polyrhythm as "a play of two independent rhythms," he argues that "syncopation in any extended form also constitutes a play of two independent rhythms"; hence, three-over-four syncopation is polyrhythm, because "the accents of the superimposed rhythm are spaced differently from those of the basic rhythm."[10]

Downhome blues tempo usually accelerates as a song continues. The accelerations may come gradually, or they may occur abruptly at stanza beginnings. Most often, the accompanying instruments are responsible for the quickening pace; infrequently, the voice rushes the tempo. The average initial-stanza tempo in the early recorded downhome blues sample under consideration is 119 quarter-note equivalents per minute; the average tempo of the final stanza is 136.5. The slowest tempo is 68 for the initial stanza and 76 for the final (both in "Lonesome Home Blues" [transcr. 18]), whereas the highest initial-stanza tempo is 184 ("Barbecue Blues" [transcr. 26] and "I'm So Glad I'm Twenty-one Years Old Today" [transcr. 41]) and 194 for the final ("Barbecue Blues" [transcr. 26]). The greatest acceleration takes place in "Writin' Paper Blues" (transcr. 40), from 112 to 168. Two songs, "Early Morning Blues" (transcr. 8) and "Mean Conductor Blues" (transcr. 23), decelerate slightly. Tempo in vaudeville blues songs is considerably slower than in downhome blues, and it tends to hold constant.

Before I take up the organization of melodic motion, a summary of the rhythmic analysis is in order. The basic rhythmic principles and elements which have so far been identified are outlined in figure 44. I do not mean by these conventions to exclude songs from the category of downhome blues which do not fit them. At the same time it is doubtful that a downhome blues song can violate more than one or two of them.

FIGURE 44.

   I. The meter is $\frac{4}{4}$.

      A. A song is normally isometric.

      B. A song may be heterometric, with a $\frac{2}{4}$ measure at the beginning of a phrase.

  II. Phrases normally begin on an unstressed note.

      A. Phrases b, d, and f begin after an initial eighth-note rest (or quarter-note rest in a triplet) in the first beat after the bar line.

      B. Phrases a, c, and e begin after an initial eighth-note rest (or quarter-note rest in a triplet)

         1. on the third or, less frequently, the fourth beat of the measure;

         2. on the first beat of a heterometric $\frac{2}{4}$ insert.

 III. Syncopation may occur on any beat.

      A. Beats are frequently anticipated across bar lines at the close of phrases b, d, and f.

      B. Continuous syncopation, which yields polymeter between vocal and accompaniment, is infrequent.

 IV. Duple and triple rhythmic contrast may exist

      A. between successive parts of the vocal;

      B. between the vocal and the accompaniment (polyrhythm).

  V. The tempo normally accelerates.

      A. Initial stanzas range from ♩ = 68 to 184 (average ♩ = 119);

      B. Final stanzas range from ♩ = 76 to 194 (average ♩ = 136.5).

A final point about downhome blues rhythmic organization is worth emphasizing: while the accompaniment marks the pulse beats, the vocal gives the impression of floating above them. Freed from strict square time, the singer moves through time near the rhythm of speech, apparently hurrying his phrases. This contrasts with the delay and hold-over characteristic of vaudeville blues singing.

Motional Organization

A scale is simply the listing of pitches used in a piece (or pieces) of music without any indication of how they are used. A blues scale, like scales for other types of music, constitutes a pitch lexicon. In theory, any pitch within vocal range may be sung; in practice, singers are limited by the proprieties of their musical tradition, usually codified by the tuning systems and the pitches available on instruments. Downhome blues accompanying instruments were set to the fixed Western division of the octave into twelve chromatic tones, but this did not prevent musicians from obtaining other tones. Pianists, for example, by "crushing" notes (playing adjacent keys), made particular pitches ambiguous; guitarists slid a bottleneck on top of the strings to obtain infinite gradations of pitch; fiddlers had no frets to worry about; wind musicians "bent" notes in the Western twelve-tone scale by changing the force of their breath or manipulating the shape of the tongue, lips, and mouth.

To obtain a scale for each downhome blues song, I counted the number of stems for each pitch, including the tones altered by marks such as ↑ or ↓. One theory of counting simply tallies each pitch in order to find out which are more important. A better theory maintains that since pitches of longer duration are more important, the counting should be weighted by duration to obtain, say, quarter-note equivalents. I do believe that longer tones are more important than shorter ones in downhome blues songs, but I do not believe that a quarter-note is precisely twice as important as an eighth-note. Counting the stems provides a compensating intermediate theory. In the transcriptions, in order to reveal the pulse clearly, I made it a point to tie eighth-notes from one beat to the next, rather than combine, say, two eighth-notes into a quarter-note, or an eighth and a quarter into a dotted quarter. Thus quarter-notes (including in that category quarter-note equivalents) are given more emphasis than eighth-notes, but less than twice the emphasis. Because quarter-notes and eighth-notes predominate, I feel safe in this procedure.

All stem-counts in the downhome blues sample are summed up in figure 45. This

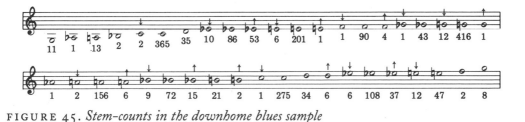

FIGURE 45. *Stem-counts in the downhome blues sample*

scale includes important pitches, unimportant pitches, and mistakenly sung pitches. From the frequency with which they occur, I determined which pitches are important for establishing a downhome blues scale. In an earlier report of these findings,[11] I confined the scale to one octave, considering E and E′, for example, to be the same pitch. But I think now that that was unwise. Twenty-one of the forty-four downhome blues songs have a range of a tenth or more, and twelve of those include the range from C to E′, thus allowing the opportunity – exercised in about a half-dozen cases – of using the pitches from C to E and from C′ to E′ for different melodic purposes. It is also clear that C and C′, occurring together in twenty-seven of the forty-four songs, are used differently. Because pitches an octave apart are used differently, the scale must be greater in range than an octave. The downhome blues scale – the pitch lexicon – is illustrated in figure 46. Numbers below each pitch tally the stem-counts. I call the series of pitches between E♭ and E the E complex; the series between G♭ and G, the G complex; the

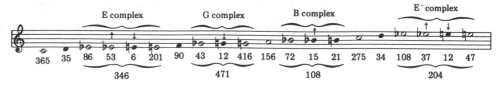

FIGURE 46. *Downhome blues scale*

series between B♭ and B, the B♭ complex; and the series between E♭′ and E′, the E′ complex. Other analysts often have termed the complexes "blue notes."[12]

The downhome blues scale has a range of a tenth. This is the most common vocal range in the sample, usually from C to E′. Seventeen songs have the range of a tenth; twelve have the range of an octave, usually from C to C′; six have the range of a fifth, usually from C to G; four have the range of a sixth, usually between C and A; four have a range greater than a tenth, usually between G and C′; and one has the range of a minor seventh, from C to B♭.

Identifying the pitches used in downhome blues songs merely establishes the elements of the pitch lexicon. The scale (fig. 46) may be compared with scales used in other musics of the world. For example, the classical Hindustani (north Indian) scale consists of twenty-two pitches to each octave, but no melody uses them all. All the pitches in the Western twelve-tone scale may be used in a melody; in fact, Schoenberg's twelve-tone system was based on the principle that no pitch could be repeated until the other eleven had appeared. While a *scale* simply identifies the pitches in a group of songs, a *mode* indicates their potential uses. To construct a downhome blues mode, I listened carefully and continuously to the sample, regarded the transcriptions, and referred to the scale I had extracted. (Recall here and in the following discussion that I transposed each transcription so that it ended on C or C′.) The most important pitches in the mode are the keynote C and its octave C′, the group of pitches in the E complex, the group of pitches in the E′ complex, and G. Slightly less important are A, F, the G complex, and the B♭ complex. Least important, but significant nonetheless, are D and its octave D′. I determined this hierarchical arrangement from the pitches' weighted frequency of appearance, their typical positions in melodic phrases, and their typical uses. For example, although A has a higher stem-count than B♭, the latter has a typically stronger phrase position, often as the highest pitch in phrase e.

The following discussion of melodic motion takes up this basic question: which tone follows any given tone? The answer depends, of course, on the position in the melodic phrase which the given tone occupies. But because certain tones characteristically do follow other tones, I can specify melodic motion with reasonable accuracy.

Melodic motion is more frequent and more gradual in the downward direction than in the upward. The melody is likely to leap upward and descend stepwise, pausing at the complexes on the way. Here are the ways in which the important pitches are used.

The keynote C and its octave C′ are most frequently tonal rest points at the close of phrases b, d, and f. C is used with the E complex above, and it is usually approached from that complex (see fig. 47; Δ indicates a complex without specifying parts). C′ is also

FIGURE 47. *"Dying Pickpocket Blues" (transcr. 44), st. 2, l. 1, phrase b*

used in connection with the E′ complex above, in a like manner, but it differs from its lower octave in that it functions with the G, A, and B♭ below it. Motion upward from G to C′ (sometimes through A) is common, especially at the beginnings of phrases a and c (fig. 48).

FIGURE 48. *"Maggie Campbell Blues" (transcr. 21), st. 2, l. 1, phrase a, showing common motion with C′*

The E and E′ complexes are most often alternated with the keynotes C and C′. However, there are significant differences in the complexes. When the E′ complex is reached from C′ below, the E′ itself is rarely reached first, that honor usually going instead to E♭′ or Ê♭′ (fig. 49). But when the E complex is reached from C below, the E is

FIGURE 49. *"Mistreatin' Mamma" (transcr. 43), st. 5, l. 1*

often reached directly, and the typical movement is an upward arpeggio to G or pendular motion back to the keynote (fig. 50). When it is E♭ which is reached from C, there

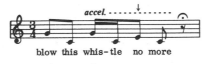

FIGURE 50. *"44 Blues" (transcr. 33), st. 3, l. 3*

rarely is movement within the complex, and the melody typically moves back to C, E♭ operating again as a pendulum point. And although the E′ complex is almost never reached from above, the E complex is reached thus very often, usually from G (sometimes through G♭ and/or F) (fig. 51). In such cases there is at least the occasion for

FIGURE 51. *"My Black Mama" (transcr. 34), st. 5, l. 3*

motion within the G complex. Common uses of the E complex and the E′ complex are summarized in figure 52. I will have more to say about motion within complexes shortly.

FIGURE 52. *Common uses of the E complex and the E′ complex*

G may be reached in a variety of ways: for example, from C′ above, often through the B♭ complex or A (fig. 53), or directly from the B♭ complex or A (fig. 54). Or it may be reached from below, from F (sometimes through F♯) or E (fig. 55), or, less fre-

FIGURE 53. *"Stranger Blues" (transcr. 4), st. 1, l. 1, phrase a*

FIGURE 54. *"Fo' Day Blues" (transcr. 38), st. 3, l. 3*

FIGURE 55. *"It Won't Be Long" (transcr. 39), st. 2, l. 3*

quently, from C, but almost never from E♭. G is a versatile pitch of great importance, acting as a temporary resting place in some phrases, especially when several syllables must be sung in a short time, and figuring as the highest, most emphatic pitch in others (fig. 56). As the root of the dominant chord, which often supplies the harmonic support

FIGURE 56. *"Biddle Street Blues" (transcr. 42), st. 5, l. 2, phrase c*

for phrase e, it is regularly contrasted with B or B♭ (sometimes through A) in pendu-lar motion (fig. 57). G also designates an important group of pitches in close proximity

FIGURE 57. *"Writin' Paper Blues" (transcr. 40), st. 1, l. 3, phrase e*

which function together; in this case the G complex pitches are G, Ǧ, and G♭. The singer in a sequence of G pitches "leans" on some of them, lowering them for empha-sis and contrasting them against the G. This "leaning" was a vaudeville blues technique which rubbed off on the downhome singers, though it is not found in great abundance in their songs. Bessie Smith was particularly proficient at leaning on the fifth (her prac-tice [see transcrs. 27 and 28] was not counted in the downhome blues scale, of course). Leaning on the fifth was more commonly employed by singer-pianists than by singer-guitarists, more by women than by men. But Roosevelt Sykes illustrates it well (see fig. 58). The common uses of G are summarized in figure 59.

FIGURE 58. *"44 Blues" (transcr. 33), st. 3, l. 2*

FIGURE 59. *Common uses of G*

The keynote, major third (E), and fifth (G) degrees of the scale are easily sung, for they make up the tonic triad which closes out each line and weights the song heavily. Since F (the fourth) can be sung easily near the start of phrase c – it is the root of the subdominant triad, which is the typical harmonic foundation for this phrase – one would expect F to be common there. But it is not, for singers prefer to repeat the phrase-a melody against the odd subdominant support. F is most often a passing tone between the E complex and G, but F' is almost never used with the E' complex. Common uses of F are indicated in figure 60.

FIGURE 60. *Common uses of F*

The sixth, A, functions principally as a passing tone between the G and the B♭ complex, or between G and C′ (fig. 61). Whereas D is rarely used, and then only as a

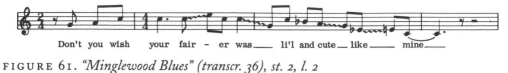

Don't you wish   your fair - er was___ li'l and cute__ like_____ mine___

FIGURE 61. *"Minglewood Blues" (transcr. 36), st. 2, l. 2*

pendulum point with C, D′ occurs both as a pendulum point with the E′ complex and as a passing tone from the E′ complex to C′ (fig. 62).

Tell you what___ I'll _____ do__ an' I_____

FIGURE 62. *"The Jail House Blues" (transcr. 19), st. 4, l. 2, phrase c*

The B♭ complex functions like a combination of the G and the E complexes. It may be approached from C′ above, usually in phrases a and c, less often in b and d (fig. 53). In phrase e, as noted (fig. 57), it plays a role as the highest and as a frequently employed pitch, usually approached from G or A below. The singer, leaning on the B, sometimes produces $\hat{B}♭$ or B♭. Singers sometimes even lean on C′ and produce $\check{C}′$ for contrast.

Stepwise motion in a single direction is more characteristic of downhome blues melody than pendular motion is. Equally common, however, is repetition of the previous pitch, especially, as noted, on the fifth degree of the scale. Skips upward are larger than those in the downward direction; descent takes place by smaller intervals, rarely by more than thirds (except in slurs to the keynote C).

In the forty-four downhome blues songs transcribed, twenty-two contain E (or E′) complexes consisting of the E♭, $\hat{E}♭$, and E (or their octaves) – that is, all three pitches – while thirty-one contain these complexes with at least E♭ and E (or their octaves). Motion within the E and E′ complexes is not perfectly consistent; singers vary it to some extent to suit themselves, but certain tendencies are clear. Movement within the E complex is taken more slowly, and most often in an upward direction. If E is reached, that is a signal for exit downward, usually directly to C; but the singer does not need to reach E before moving out. When the E complex is reached from G above, a typical movement is G to E♭, up through E and down to C (fig. 61). In general, there is not so much movement within the E complex as within the E′ complex, because E is a much more important pitch than E′; the downhome blues scale (fig. 46) shows E′ only 47 times, while E figures 201 times. Stated differently, while E is sung more often than E♭ and $\hat{E}♭$, E♭′ is sung much more often than E′. In short, E is the basic pitch in the E complex, but E♭′ is the basic pitch in the E′ complex. Indeed, E′, unlike E, is not a signal for direct exit downward (to C′); the melody may progress downward within the complex, and the release may be from any of the pitches within it. Motion within the E and E′ complexes is summarized in figure 63.

FIGURE 63. *Motion within the E complex and the E′ complex*

John Fahey has suggested that in Charley Patton's repertoire Ê♭ and Ê♭′ are mistakenly sung pitches.[13] Perhaps the Ê♭′ is a mistake, since Patton and other singers are straining at the top of their register, but I do not believe so. Most often I have heard Ê♭ (and Ê♭′) a quarter-tone between E♭ and E (or between E♭′ and E′), and I have checked the location carefully with a slide device. In fact, in some instances I have heard Ě′ (microtonally between Ê♭′ and E′ here, though in some notations Ě′ might be the same as Ê♭′) when the singer was leaning slightly on E′. To argue that these are mistakenly sung pitches does not take into account the singers' habits of leaning on B and G. Besides, the singers approach Ê♭ and Ê♭′ directly from intervals as much as a third away without "correcting" the pitch upward or downward. But the most important argument that these quarter-tones form distinct pitches in a downhome blues mode is that singers enter and move within the complexes in a manner reasonably consistent from phrase to phrase, line to line, and stanza to stanza throughout a given song.

The downhome blues mode, with the most important pitch movements indicated by arrows, appears in figure 64. But no downhome blues song in the sample takes advan-

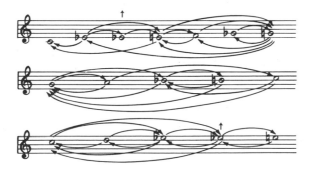

FIGURE 64. *Early downhome blues mode*

tage of all the possibilities. Knowing that one pitch may move to certain other pitches is helpful, but not sufficient for a song-producing model; one wants to know under which circumstances a given tone is likely to move to a *particular* tone. To determine these circumstances, we can investigate the shape of the melody in the phrase, line, and stanza units. It turns out that downhome blues melodies do have characteristic shapes in these units; hence, we can predict melodic motion.

The general shape of a sequence of pitches – rising, falling, terraced, undulating, level, and so on – is called melodic contour. Alan Kagan has suggested to me the following scheme to describe contour. If we consider a sequence of pitches, the ones which define its shape are the starting, highest, lowest, and final pitches. Let us take as melodic contour I a generally falling contour (fig. 65); that is, the starting pitch in the

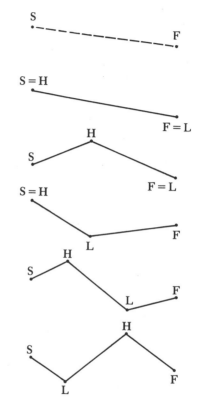

General case I: Starting pitch S is higher than final pitch F: S > F

Specific cases:

IA: Starting pitch S = highest pitch H; final pitch F = lowest pitch L

IB: Final pitch F = lowest pitch L; highest pitch H > starting pitch S

IC: Starting pitch S = highest pitch H; final pitch F > lowest pitch L

ID_a: Highest pitch H > starting pitch S; final pitch F > lowest pitch L; H is achieved before L

ID_b: Highest pitch H > starting pitch S; final pitch F > lowest pitch L; L is achieved before H

FIGURE 65. *Melodic contour I*

sequence is higher than the final. Let us take as melodic contour II a generally rising contour (fig. 66); that is, the starting pitch in the sequence is lower than the final. In the only other possible case, melodic contour III, the starting pitch is identical to the final (fig. 67). These contours are considered "general cases"; the "specific cases" depend upon the location of the highest and lowest pitches. Consider, for example, "Number Three Blues" (fig. 68). The first phrase begins on G and ends on E′, with an indefinite downward slur. The starting pitch, G, is the lowest in the phrase, while the final E′ (slurs after finals are not counted) is the highest. This rising contour fits specific case IIA. In the second phrase, the starting pitch, C′, is the highest and the final C is the lowest; its contour fits specific case IA. Now consider the sequence of pitches in the line as a

General case II: Starting pitch S is lower than final pitch F: S < F

Specific cases:

IIA: Starting pitch S = lowest pitch L; final pitch F = highest pitch H

IIB: Starting pitch S = lowest pitch L; highest pitch H > final pitch F

IIC: Starting pitch S > lowest pitch L; final pitch F = highest pitch H

IID$_a$:   Starting pitch S < highest pitch H; final pitch F > lowest pitch L; H > F; H is achieved before L

IID$_b$:   Starting pitch S < highest pitch H; final pitch F > lowest pitch L; H > F; L is achieved before H

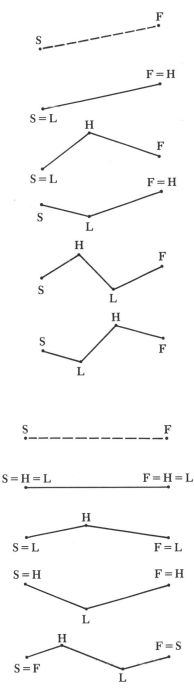

FIGURE 66. *Melodic contour II*

General case III: Starting pitch S is the same as final pitch F: S = F

Specific cases:

IIIA: Starting pitch S = highest pitch H = lowest pitch L

IIIB: Starting pitch S < highest pitch H; starting pitch S = lowest pitch L

IIIC: Starting pitch S = highest pitch H; starting pitch S > lowest pitch L

IIID$_a$:   Starting pitch S < highest pitch H; starting pitch S > lowest pitch L; H is achieved before L

IIID$_b$:   Starting pitch S < highest pitch H; starting pitch S > lowest pitch L; L is achieved before H

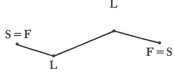

FIGURE 67. *Melodic contour III*

FIGURE 68. *"Number Three Blues" (transcr. 11), st. 4, l. 1*

whole. The starting pitch is G and the final is C. The lowest pitch is identical to the final, but the highest pitch, E', comes at the close of the first phrase. The contour of the entire line fits specific case IB. The entire stanza has a contour which fits specific case IB. This is, in fact, the most common stanzaic contour in downhome blues.

To determine characteristic contours of the phrase, line, and stanza units, I counted, in each transcribed stanza, the number of occurrences of each specific contour case. Certain exceptional phrases I did not count.[14] The characteristic contours are shown in figure 69. I did not determine a separate contour in phrases e and f, because

Specific Contour Case	Number of Occurrences							
	Phrase a	Phrase b	Line 1	Phrase c	Phrase d	Line 2	Line 3	Whole stanza
IA	10	18	8	12	20	7	6	3
IB	9	9	17	9	13	23	19	17
IC	2	4	3	0	2	3	2	3
ID_a	1	2	3	0	3	2	3	4
ID_b	1	0	0	0	0	1	0	2
IIA	9	1	0	8	0	0	0	0
IIB	3	0	3	2	1	2	0	2
IIC	0	0	0	2	0	0	0	0
IID_a	1	1	0	0	0	0	2	3
IID_b	0	0	0	0	0	0	0	0
IIIA	1	0	0	1	0	0	0	0
IIIB	2	3	3	5	0	2	7	2
IIIC	1	0	0	1	0	0	0	0
$IIID_a$	0	0	0	0	0	0	0	1
$IIID_b$	0	0	1	0	0	0	0	0

FIGURE 69. *Melodic contour of phrases, lines, stanzas*

this kind of phrase division in line 3 is not always accomplished (see p. 142); but I did ascertain the contour of line 3 as a whole. Figure 69 shows that the shape of all three structural units in downhome blues melody is well defined.

In the stanza unit, the predominant contour is general case I, a falling contour. By far the most common stanzaic contour is IB, a generally falling contour which rises from the starting pitch to the highest and falls eventually to the lowest, final pitch (fig. 70). Melodic contour of the line unit is similar to stanzaic contour; that is, it is described by general case I and specific case IB. In the phrase unit, melodic contour shifts depending on the phrase. In phrase a, the first part of line 1, a rising contour is almost as frequent as a falling one. In phrase c, the first part of line 2, the same rising contour is significant.

FIGURE 70. *Downhome blues melodic contour: stanza*

In phrases b and d, the second parts of lines 1 and 2 respectively, a falling – often directly falling – contour predominates. It becomes clear from figure 71 that the predominant

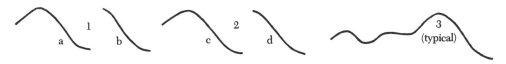

FIGURE 71. *Downhome blues melodic contour: phrase sequence*

stanzaic contour (fig. 70) is not able to do justice to the balanced, yet nonsymmetrical, tension which the succession of phrase contours yields.

Blues Families

Several of the forty-four downhome blues songs in the sample share similar melodies.[15] From these melodies, blues families may be derived as follows. The transcriptions and contour diagrams show that in a given stanza in a particular song, phrases b, d, and f are usually identical, or nearly so; and that phrases a and c are very close. This enables further simplification of stanza models. From the stanza model suggested earlier (summarized in fig. 72), we can combine lines 1 and 2 (ignoring, since we are considering melo-

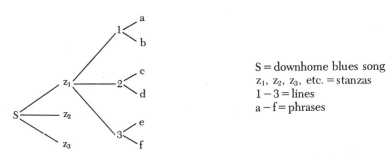

S = downhome blues song
z_1, z_2, z_3, etc. = stanzas
1 – 3 = lines
a – f = phrases

FIGURE 72.

dies only, their different harmonic support) and indicate that the second half of line 3 is derived from the same part of the skeleton as the second half of lines 1 and 2 (fig. 73).

Then we can concentrate on the skeletal structures and generative principles of phrases a, b, and e. These structures should be able to account for the minor differences observed between phrases b, d, and f, and those between a and c. When phrase f does differ from phrases b and d significantly, it is usually in a line 3 with no break into e/f

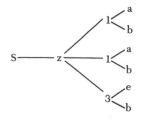

FIGURE 73.

phrases; even so, the latter part is at least similar to phrases b and d (sometimes transposed a third lower, for example) and resolves to the tonic as do b and d. Phrase e, on the other hand, varies seemingly independently of the other phrases. There is even an interesting relation between the halves of lines 1 and 2: many times when the contour of phrase a taken from the first full measure is a falling one, the phrase b following is virtually identical (except that whereas phrase b falls to the keynote, phrase a does not regularly do so) (fig. 74). Another example is shown in figure 75, in which the pickup measure leads into the directly falling melody in which phrase b imitates phrase a.

FIGURE 74. *"Pony Blues" (transcr. 1), st. 2, l. 1*

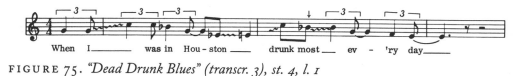

FIGURE 75. *"Dead Drunk Blues" (transcr. 3), st. 4, l. 1*

In the forty-four-song downhome blues sample, I was able to discern four blues stanza families. Songs in the sample outside these families doubtless fall into other families that would have become obvious in a larger sample. Each family can be defined by a model. Blues family I includes "The Jail House Blues" (transcr. 19), "Whiskey Moan Blues" (transcr. 22), "Bumble Bee" (transcr. 16), "Barbecue Blues" (transcr. 26), and "Mistreatin' Mamma" (transcr. 43). Related to this family is the two-line "Cottonfield Blues," part 2 (transcr. 20). Ma Rainey's vaudeville "Lost Wandering Blues" (transcr. 24) is also in this family. These tunes characteristically begin phrases a and c in the E' complex, moving around within it for two or more beats, and end the phrases on C'. Phrases b and d are similar to a and c, involving the E' complex, but often come to rest on C. Phrase e is variable, and phrase f often follows the pattern of phrase d. The model for this and succeeding blues families is illustrated in figure 76.

Closely related to blues family I is blues family II, which includes "Minglewood Blues" (transcr. 36), "Number Three Blues" (transcr. 11), "It Won't Be Long" (transcr. 39),

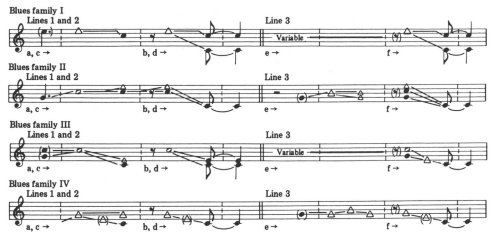

FIGURE 76. *Early downhome blues families as models*

"One Time Blues" (transcr. 9), "Banty Rooster Blues" (transcr. 2), "Got the Blues" (transcr. 31), and "Roll and Tumble Blues" (transcr. 37). Whereas in blues family I the first heavily accented pitch is in the E' complex, in blues family II it is C', and it is approached by an anacrusis beginning in the previous measure on G. What follows takes place within a few variations. The stressed C' may rise to the E' complex, or it may stay the highest pitch in line 1. If it rises to the E' complex, it usually does so at the end of phrase a or the very beginning of phrase b; then phrase b descends to C. If it does not rise to the E' complex, it continues as the most important pitch in line 1, descending to C in phrase b. Phrases c and d are similar to a and b, respectively. Interestingly, phrase e takes on a characteristic form in this family, with the B♭ complex the stressed upper bound, sometimes alternating with G. "I'm So Glad I'm Twenty-one Years Old Today" (transcr. 41) would be in this tune family had its phrase e not included the precipitous drop of a sixth (often referred to as the "Leroy Carr special" because of his frequent use of it). Phrase f in blues family II usually follows phrase d.

Blues family III includes "Pony Blues," stanza 2 (transcr. 1), "Writin' Paper Blues" (transcr. 40), "Dead Drunk Blues" (transcr. 3), "James Alley Blues" (transcr. 47), and "Stranger Blues" (transcr. 4). "Mean Conductor Blues" (transcr. 23) and "Yellow Girl Blues" (transcr. 48) are related to it. These tunes share with blues family II a C' as the first stressed pitch; unlike blues family II, phrases a and c descend, to close at E or C. The first stressed C' is sometimes, but not always, preceded by an anacrusis. Phrases b and d generally follow a and c, but without the anacrusis (fig. 75). Phrase e is variable. Phrase f descends variably to the keynote, C, from C', A, G, or in pendular motion with the E complex.

Blues family IV includes "Jacksonville Blues" (transcr. 5), "Prison Bound Blues" (transcr. 15), and "44 Blues" (transcr. 33). "Biddle Street Blues" (transcr. 42) and Bessie

Smith's two vaudeville blues songs (transcrs. 27 and 28) are related to it, differing in an uncharacteristic phrase e. The first heavily stressed pitch in this family is a G, often preceded by a brief rise. This is the family which includes the characteristic leaning on G. Phrase a may stay on G or close with a descent to C, while phrase b begins with a G and descends to G. Phrases c and d are similar to a and b, respectively. Phrase e of blues family IV is similar to phrase e of blues family II; but whereas in II the B♭ complex is stressed, the G is more important in IV. Phrase f always starts on G and descends to the keynote, C.

I mentioned earlier that the remaining, unaffiliated songs in the downhome blues sample will probably fall into other blues families when a larger number of songs is considered. For example, "M. and O. Blues" (transcr. 17) and "Pony Blues," stanza 1 (transcr. 1), share virtually identical tunes. As for blues families based on forms other than the three-line, AAB stanza, the matter should be simpler. Anyone wishing, for example, to start an investigation of two-line, approximately eight-bar blues families might begin with the "Crow Jane" family, represented in the sample by stanzas 1, 2, 4, 7, and 8 of "Bootlegging Blues" (transcr. 45). Some of the songs he will find in the "Crow Jane" family include "Gang of Brown Skin Women" (Gennett 6122), "Brown Skin Girls" (ARC 6-11-66), "Coffee Pot Blues" (Paramount 12264), "Frank Stokes' Dream" (Victor 23411), "Dry Land Blues" (Victor 23345), "Married Woman Blues" (ARC 7-08-57), "Somebody's Been Talkin'" (Vocalion 05527), "Mill Man Blues" (Columbia 14381-D), various versions of "Slidin' Delta" (e.g., Mississippi John Hurt's on Piedmont LP 13161), the various versions of "Key to the Highway" (e.g., Jazz Gillum's on Bluebird B8529). And there are many, many more. The relation between the "Crow Jane" family and the "How Long – How Long Blues" family would be interesting to pursue, for while the tunes are very close melodically and rhythmically, they call for considerably different harmonic support. They are also related to songs known variously in white tradition as "In the Pines" and "The Longest Train I Ever Saw." But it is remarkable that out of a sample of forty-four downhome blues songs, twenty fall distinctly into four blues families.

Text and Tune

It is simple enough to extract blues families and to suggest basic principles of melodic organization which operate retrodictively. But a retrodictive model is not a song-producing system. It may be explanatory, but it is not predictive. One wants a model that produces *new* blues melodies.

Blues singers fit different stanzas of text to "the same tune" throughout a blues song. Of course, they do not use the exact same tune; they modify it according to the words they sing and, possibly, purely by improvisatory play. Since lines and stanzas of blues text "float" from one tune to the next as they move from song to song, the same blues lyrics must be fitted to several different tunes. In the adjustment of text and tune one finds the song-producing system in action.

The blues singer employs the following general principles to adjust text and tune: for a given song, he holds a skeletal tune in his mind; he tries to manipulate the skeletal tune, fleshing it into the actual tune for each line and stanza, so as to give pitch, rhythmic, and dynamic emphasis to those syllables which receive textual stress. But on occasion he is constrained to emphasize weak syllables of text in order to maintain the integrity of the skeletal tune.

The skeletal tune may provisionally be defined as the melody which a stanza would take were it not for the demands of stress. For the analyst, it most likely will remain a construct, for it is doubtful that a skeletal tune is ever sung. In principle, however, the skeleton is derivable from the stanzas in a song which are, in fact, sung. Whereas it is tempting to regard a stanza which is hummed as a skeletal tune, there is no reason why this must be so; for metrical imperatives, habits of accompaniment technique, and the play of improvisation lend stress and may produce a hummed tune as fully fleshed as one which is sung. The transcriptions do reveal three hummed stanzas: stanza 5 of "Mama 'T'Ain't Long fo' Day" (transcr. 25), stanza 3 of "K.C. Moan" (transcr. 46), and the first two lines of stanzas 3 and 5 of "Yellow Girl Blues" (transcr. 48). Yet when I compared these hummed lines with their sung counterparts, it was clear that they could not be considered the skeletal tunes which had generated those counterparts.

A blues family, in outline form, is capable of generating several related skeletal tunes for the various songs that fall into the family. It is, therefore, useful to consider a blues family a skeletal structure at a level of abstraction once removed; and it is true that blues families can generate tunes without the intermediate skeletal tune. But the intermediate seems both reasonable, for it indicates what is in the back of the singer's mind, and useful, for it resembles "the tune" of a given song more closely than the blues family does and thus, because of its greater detail, is a more dependable generator of acceptable variations.

Stress is regularly achieved in blues tunes in the following ways. Rhythmic emphasis is applied by placing a syllable on a tone of long duration, often incorporating syncopation. Blues singers infrequently attack stressed syllables on metrically strong beats (in the common $\frac{4}{4}$ blues meter, the first and third beats are metrically strong). Instead, they habitually place stressed syllables on offbeats or weak beats and tie them over to strong beats. Pitch emphasis is applied by placing a syllable on the highest pitch in a given sequence. Additionally, a sudden drop will provide pitch prominence and thereby lend emphasis. Syllables placed on the initial or final tone of an E or E' complex also receive considerable pitch emphasis. A particular tone receives dynamic emphasis if it is sung more loudly than the tone which precedes it. Voicing a syllable after a rest gives it dynamic emphasis. A skeletal tune will, therefore, already have built into it certain emphasis points; the singer's skill enables him to place textually stressed syllables at these points and to create other emphases where appropriate. The singer will modify the skeletal tune in order to fit the proper number of syllables and accommodate a stress pattern which varies from stanza to stanza. (But sometimes he cannot alter it sufficiently, either because he lacks the skill or because his alteration would change the tune significantly.)

A given line of text may, of course, be understood to contain several equally sensible stress patterns. But when the line is uttered it has only one pattern. Consider line 1 from stanza 2 of "Banty Rooster Blues" (transcr. 2) (the sign ′ over a syllable indicates that it receives stress):

What you wánt with a róoster   he won't crów 'fore dáy
Whát yóu want with a róoster   hé wón't crów 'fore dáy
Whát you wánt with a róoster   hé won't crów 'fóre dáy

These are all sensible stress patterns. But here is how Charley Patton sings it:

Whát you want with á róoster   hé won't crów 'fore dáy

Why does Patton stress *a?* It is unlikely that he wants to distinguish one rooster from several roosters. Instead, it is likely that a constraint of the basic tune accounts for this accent. But this is the only position in the stanza where Patton is forced into emphasizing a textually weak syllable.[16] Its consistent appearance in the stanza further suggests its melodic importance:

Whát you want with á róoster   hé won't crów 'fore dáy
Whát you want with á róoster   hé won't crów 'fore dáy
Whát you want with á mán   when he wón't do nóthin' he sáy

Now consider (figs. 77–82) the transcriptions of several line 1's from the two takes of "Lonesome Blues" (transcr. 12 and 13). Here are six different texts fitted to "the same tune." Clearly, the fit is near perfect in the phrase b's. But the texts for the several phrase a's vary in the number of syllables they contain and in their stress patterns. The phrases contain five, six, or seven syllables. If for the moment one considers the first example (fig. 77) to display the skeletal tune of the pickup measure, then it appears that extra syllables are fitted into this measure by two methods: doubling the number of tones and halving their value (figs. 79 and 81), or placing the syllable on a significant melismatic tone (figs. 78 and 82). My guess is that one method takes precedence over the other depending on the sound of the syllable which precedes the "extra" one. If it is a sound of relatively long speed duration (these usually contain a long vowel, a nasal, or a sibilant),

FIGURE 77. *"Lonesome Blues" (transcr. 12), st. 3, l. 1*

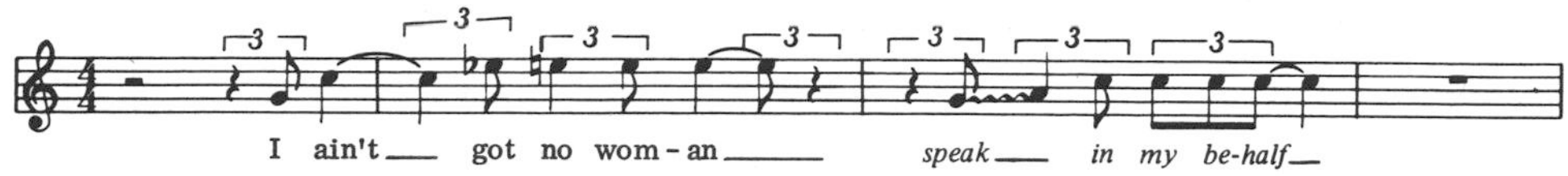

FIGURE 78. *"Lonesome Blues" (transcr. 12), st. 5, l. 1*

FIGURE 79. *"Lonesome Blues" (transcr. 12), st. 2, l. 1*

FIGURE 80. *"Lonesome Blues" (transcr. 13), st. 2, l. 1*

FIGURE 81. *"Lonesome Blues" (transcr. 13), st. 3, l. 1*

FIGURE 82. *"Lonesome Blues" (transcr. 13), st. 5, l. 1*

then its time value must not be lessened to such an extent that it becomes unintelligible; conversely, if it is a sound of relatively short duration, it may be lessened. Since shortening *I* (fig. 78) or *cry-* (fig. 82) further would render them unintelligible, the extra syllable is inserted on the following beat. On the other hand, since shortening *well* (fig. 79) or *hon-* (fig. 81) would not prevent their being understood, it is preferable to double the number of tones and halve their value, thus preserving the melodically significant melisma from G through A to C and emphasizing the glide by introducing no new syllables.

If the extra syllables were placed according to their speech stress instead, a different pattern would ensue; one could hardly rest content emphasizing *-in'* (fig. 82) or *-ey* (fig. 81). But as they are sung in these examples, they are most assuredly given durational and syncopative emphasis. Clearly, the tune, having been established, does not permit sufficient alteration here. But consider the second example (fig. 78): here *ain't* receives the emphasis which speech stress suggests it should have. Evidently it is more important to give emphasis to speech-stressed syllables than to remove it from weak ones. (Cf. Charley Patton's "What you want with á rooster.")

Similar principles account for the structures taken by the phrase a's after the pickup measure. Doubling the number of tones and halving their value places *good to* (figs. 79, 81, and 82) in the duration occupied by *won-* (fig. 77) or *got* (fig. 78). After the first beat of this measure, three syllables must be accommodated in all the phrases save that in figure 82. In the latter example, the text is shortened and the tone carrying *you* is lengthened to fill out the tune. (Such treatment is expected because "Cryin' good to you" is a truncation of the seven-syllable "Honey good to you mama" [fig. 81]. The alternative, placing "Cryin' good to you" on the five-syllable "I wonder do my" [fig. 77], is less likely.) The three syllables after the first beat (figs. 77–81) are accommodated by virtually the same rhythmic pattern, one which lends particular emphasis to the third syllable by its length and initial placement on a strong beat. *Wom-* (fig. 78) and *ma-* (figs. 79 and 81) do not receive the emphasis one could expect from their speech stress, but since the syllables which precede them (*no* and *you*) could just as well receive speech stress, no violence is done to the textual stress pattern.[17]

I have remarked that any skeletal tune will have built into it certain points of emphasis; because these skeletal tunes must conform to a family pattern, many of these points are fixed. In blues family I, lines 1 and 2, great pitch and dynamic emphasis is given to the syllable which begins each phrase, while durational emphasis is given to the syllable which ends phrases b and f. In blues family I, line 3, great pitch and dynamic emphasis is given to the syllable which begins phrase f, while the syllable which ends the stanza receives durational emphasis. Similar examination reveals that in every blues family the syllable which ends phrases b, d, and f receives durational emphasis; that in every blues family the syllable which begins phrases b, d, and f receives pitch and dynamic emphasis; that in families II and III the syllable which initiates the pickup measure receives dynamic emphasis; that in families I and IV the initial syllable in phrases a, b, c, d, and f receives pitch and dynamic emphasis.

At last the model is sufficiently detailed to generate tunes and set texts. From a given blues family a skeletal tune may be produced; with text and tune in mind and a set of directions for fitting one to the other, the song-producing system may now be demonstrated.

Let the given blues family be the one which I have called II; let it produce a skeletal tune for phrase a (fig. 83) similar to that which was just illustrated by the phrase a's in "Lonesome Blues" (figs. 77–82). To make matters more complex (and to reveal the melodic operation of the generative model), let the skeletal tune for phrase b be no more detailed than the family model (fig. 84).

FIGURE 83. *Production of phrase a of a skeletal tune from blues family II*

FIGURE 84. *Production of phrase b of a skeletal tune from blues family II*

To find a text, I have just pulled down a book from the shelf and opened to a random page; the first sentence which catches my eye is this: "Esperanza swings her great arm in a contemptuous arc."[18] Let this unlikely sentence be set to the skeletal tune. A sensible phrase division, with stress marked wherever it could sensibly fall, is as follows:

Ésperánza swíngs hér gréat árm   ín a contémptuous árc

The four points of emphasis which blues family II necessarily provides are (1) on *Es-;* (2) wherever in phrase a the E′ complex is entered; (3) on *in;* (4) on *arc*. As the singer fits text to tune, he supplies additional emphasis, trying to make the emphasis coincide with a sensible, meaningful pattern of speech stress. Consider the text for phrase a: it contains eight syllables; but blues singers usually would shorten *Esperanza* to *Esp'ranza,* which reduces the text to a more manageable seven syllables. Of those seven, six conceivably could receive stress, but not simultaneously; American metrical speech rarely contains more than two stressed syllables in succession. Let emphasis be placed upon *Es-, swings, great,* and *arm.* Were emphasis placed additionally on *-p'ran-,* something like the setting in figure 85 would be the best obtainable. To be sure, *swings* receives

Es-p'ran - za swings her great arm ___

FIGURE 85.

pitch emphasis as the entry into the E′ complex, *great* receives rhythmic emphasis by its placement on a strong (third) beat, and *arm* receives durational, syncopative, and pitch emphasis. But *swings* is the syllable which receives the most textual stress; it is a one-syllable word whose sibilance and nasality give it great duration. As it is set in figure 85, it receives insufficient duration and emphasis. But if *-p'ran-* were not emphasized (and there is no semantic reason for stressing it), *swings* could be set as in figure 86 and receive not only pitch but also syncopative and durational emphasis.[19]

The tune in figure 86 moves to E♭′ at the same relative point that the "Lonesome Blues" tunes (figs. 77–82) do;[20] but the tune in figure 85 does not, thus seeming to violate

Es-p'ran -za _____ swings ___ her great arm ___

FIGURE 86.

the integrity of the skeletal structure. Phrase a of the "Esperanza" tune was generated from the family outline and examination of the "Lonesome Blues" tunes; movement within the E′ complex was obtained from the appropriate section of the model (fig. 63) and could have been far more complicated than it was written in figure 86. That movement is not identical with the E′-complex movement in the "Lonesome Blues" tunes; but it could be made identical easily enough, were it true that the skeletal tune for phrase a of "Lonesome Blues" contained specific directions for movement within the E′ complex. The matter is in doubt because, while the movement in the several phrase a's of "Lonesome Blues" is consistent over the first two beats of the measure in which the E′ complex appears, it is inconsistent over the last two beats (see n. 17).

Now consider the text for phrase b. Blues singers usually would shorten *contemptuous* to *contempt'ous* and reduce the line to six syllables. Let emphasis be place on *-temp-*; the blues family structure has already seen to it that *in* and *arc* will also receive stress.

For a tune outline, the blues family provides a descent from the E′ complex or from C′ to C; let the descent begin from C′. In order that the syllable *-temp-* receive sufficient emphasis, let it not be buried tonally in the descent to C; therefore, fix its pitch at C′. So fixed, it suggests that those tones in phrase b which precede it should also be placed on C′ (fig. 87). The simple rhythmic setting indicated in figure 87 has the virtue

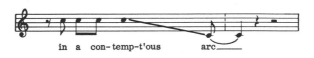

in a con-temp-t'ous   arc___

FIGURE 87.

of emphasizing *-temp-* even more by placing it on a strong (third) beat. The melody must descend an octave from *-temp-* to *arc;* where are the likely stopping places? The diagram indicating the most common motion with C′ (fig. 48) shows a descent to G and to the B♭ complex. For an octave descent over such a short time period, an initial descent to G is more sensible, for two reasons: there is no temptation to pause at the B♭ complex; and the larger skip makes the subsequent drops less precipitous, hence more easily intoned. The diagram for motion with G (fig. 59) suggests a descent to E. The E-complex diagram (fig. 63) confirms E as a good choice (E♭ would have had a tendency to move upward to E before exiting the complex, and there is insufficient time for that here) and clinches the final descent to C. The two tones to be used in the descent (G and E) require melismata, because the number of syllables left is insufficient to carry them one per syllable. Figures 88 and 89 show two alternate descents. The first (fig. 88) achieves satisfactory emphasis on *-temp-* by placing it on a metrically strong

in a con- temp-t'ous arc_____

FIGURE 88.

beat and excellent emphasis on *arc* in a typical melismatic finish. The second descent (fig. 89) achieves satisfactory emphasis on *arc* and arguably better emphasis on *-temp-*.

in a con-temp - t'ous arc_____

FIGURE 89.

If the skeletal tune demanded emphasis on the third beat of the measure, either of these two patterns would be satisfactory. However, one condition for setting this particular text was that the skeletal tune for phrase b should be no more detailed than the family structure; and since the family structure demands no emphasis on the third beat, that constraint may be abandoned. A setting which gives excellent emphasis to both *-temp-* and *arc* may be obtained by singing *-temp-* on the unaccented second half of the second beat and tying it through the third beat, thus achieving durational and syncopative emphasis. The emphasis on *arc* shown in figure 88 may be retained, but a slight adjustment is necessary at the beginning of the measure to squeeze in the extra syllable (fig. 90).

in a con-temp - t'ous arc_____

FIGURE 90.

Relying on the transcriptions in the previous chapter, I have derived a melodic grammar of early downhome blues: a tonal lexicon and a set of instructions for using it to produce acceptable blues melodies. The instructions are suggestive, not exhaustive; they are trial-and-error principles, not rules; and, limited as they are to melodic material, they do not pretend to be a complete performance model. But, given words, the song-making model I have just demonstrated will produce a melody and set those words to it (fig. 91), just as a downhome blues singer, having found words, may be expected to

Es-p'ran-za____ swings_ her great arm____ in a con-temp-t'ous arc____

FIGURE 91.

find an appropriate melody, or set the words to a tune he is already using. In the following chapter I consider those words, taking up the subjects of blues texts and the ways they might enter the singer's mind.

5 FORMULAIC STRUCTURE AND MEANING IN EARLY DOWNHOME BLUES LYRICS

Downhome blues phrase units ordinarily last two to three seconds each. Unlike Tibetan Buddhist chanters, downhome blues singers do not continue a phrase until they run out of breath; nor do they take in air each time they pause. Rather, their relatively short bursts of text suggest that they compose (or at least recall) the song in the midst of performance and put it together piece by piece. The time they take between phrases enables them to think about what is coming next. *How* do they think about it?

Anyone who listens to downhome blues lyrics for a while notices the repetition of certain phrases, such as "have you ever been mistreated" or "I'm goin' away, babe." He also notices variant expressions of them, such as "I been mistreated," "my gal mistreats me," "she's a mistreatin' mama," and so on. Since each of these phrase examples is regularly repeated by downhome blues singers, each is a formula. The classic definition of a song formula is Milman Parry's: "a group of words which is regularly employed under the same metrical conditions to express a given essential idea."[1] Related formulas may be based on some single underlying idea which takes variant expressions. In his discussion of formula, Parry's colleague Albert Lord emphasizes the creative aspect of formula making. Formulas are not invariant, memorized clichés, but new words in established patterns:

> Were he merely to learn the phrases and lines from his predecessors, acquiring thus a stock of them, which he would then shuffle about and mechanically put together in juxtaposition as inviolable, fixed units, he would, I am convinced, never become a singer. He must make his feeling for the patterning of lines, which he has absorbed earlier, specific with actual phrases and lines, and by the necessity of performance learn to adjust what he hears and what he wants to say to these patterns.[2]

So, too, the blues singer adjusts his formulas depending on context. Those contexts involve the subject of the stanza, its syntax, the audience, the occasion, and so on.

Lord views the patterns as "substitution systems." Once the novice singer "has the basic pattern [of the formula] firmly in his grasp, he needs only to substitute another word for the key one."[3] Blues singers do not use formulas so strictly. The Serbo-Croatian epic singers upon whom Lord based his model had to fit their utterances into a fixed ten-syllable line, with a caesura after the fourth. It is no wonder that they employed simple substitutions. But blues singers are not bound by such syllabic constraints. It is true that they operate under given metrical conditions, if by that one understands musical meter. But they are free to use a greater or lesser number of syllables in each line, depending upon the rhythmic combinations they choose. Instead of a mere substitution system, a blues singer possesses a generating system, something that can produce, from a single idea, a variety of formulaic and nonformulaic word groups which carry a variety of rhythmic combinations that may be accommodated to a given tune.[4] This text-generating system is intimately related to the tune-producing system, as I have shown in the previous chapter: the melody is adjusted insofar as possible to the natural spoken rhythm of the text, while particular text formulas may be chosen because they are easily accommodated, more so than other formulas, to the rhythm of the melody. Let us now look at some of the formulas generated in the representative sample of downhome blues songs transcribed in chapter 3.

Here are two examples of formula lines which appear to be based on simple substitutions: "my woman" for "a rider," "this world" for "the world," and "ooh baby in" for "said she's" (although the phrasing is different):

I'm gon' find a rider ooh   baby in the   world somewhere[5]

I'm gon' find my woman said she's   in this world somewhere[6]

But phrases like "ooh baby" and "said she's" are filler formulas, interchangeable in a great many phrases; they fulfill the skeletal tune model's demands. Of course, the variants are meaningful; "a rider" (a sexual partner) is more specific than "my woman," even though possession is confirmed only in the latter. To account for the different words, one must move beyond viewing them simply as formulaic substitutions. If they are achieved semantically at the level of an underlying idea capable of generating surface variants, then the different formulas are phenomena of a surface structure, dependent upon the demands of the melody, perhaps suited to the decorative mood of the singer. Thus a kind of meaning – say, "I want to and shall find a woman who will be a good sexual partner" – is brought into the singer's mind, although he does not think it in words. The thought, however inchoate, is transformed into whatever formula is appropriate in the song and its context, and that is the formula which is sung.

Next, some formulas which resemble those just cited, but which are not the same:

I've got these blues   reason I'm not satisfied
I've got these blues   I'm not satisfied[7]

Got the blues   can't be satisfied
Got the blues   can't be satisfied[8]

"I'm gon' find a rider" is different in its surface structure from "got the blues," but it shares the same pattern: "I" (either uttered or understood) + verb phrase. This is apparently the simplest pattern in which to fit formulas. "Reason" in "I've got these blues reason I'm not satisfied" is a most interesting utterance of the relation between the two phrases that make up the line; it is an example of something from the generating idea itself, brought to the surface.

Let us now examine a series of formulaic lines about waking up in the morning and finding the blues turned into particles in the surrounding atmosphere:

Early one morning   the blues came falling down[9]

Mm mm   soon one mornin'   blues come fallin' down[10]

And the blues came down   baby like   showers of rain[11]

Note how the simile in the third line – "like showers of rain" – explains the meaning of blues "coming down" in the first two lines. This is further evidence of an underlying thought (in this case that blues are things which can fall on someone like raindrops) generating related formulas. In another set of lines, the thought of waking up in the morning is followed by the notion of blues occupying space around the bed:

> I woke up this mornin'   blues all 'round my bed
> Mm woke up this mornin'   blues all 'round my bed [12]

> I got up this mornin'   these blues all 'round my bed
> I got up this morning   these blues all 'round my bed
> *Couldn't* eat my breakfast and there's blues all in my bread [13]

A kind of personification of the blues unites and relates all these phrases. The blues, almost like a cloud of germs, hovers around and enters familiar objects, threatening the singer. Morning is an appropriate time for this new vision. Here are some more waking-up formulas from the sample:

> Woke up this morning gal   'twixt midnight and day
> I woke up this morning   'twixt midnight and day [14]

> I woke up this mornin'   'tween midnight and day [15]

> Wake up mama   don't you sleep so hard [16]

> Early this mornin'   my baby made me sore [17]

> I woke up this mornin'   said my morning prayer
> I woke up this mornin' I   said my morning prayer
> I woke up this mornin' babe I   said my mornin' prayer [18]

Such formulas as "I woke up this morning," "got up this morning," "soon one morning," and "early this morning" certainly are related. The deep structure for this series of formulas has been examined by Michael Taft in what is, as far as I know, the only application of transformational-generative grammar to blues lyrics.[19] I believe that a modified generative approach to blues lyric formulas should reveal something about how the texts are created. Groups of formulas should fall into blues lyric families in a manner analogous to the way sequences of musical tones fell into blues tune families (as shown in the previous chapter). As generative models, the lyric families should be able to produce innovative utterances as well as clichés. Yet there is no need to abandon the Lord-Parry concept of formula because it does not quite fit conditions for which it was not designed.

Related formulas do not always carry the same tune, nor are they found only in songs of the same tune family; they are adaptable. The appearance of related formulas in different songs may result from selective learning; Atlanta singers Barbecue Bob and Peg Leg Howell, in the lines just discussed, sang "'twixt midnight and day" and "'tween midnight and day." Other formulas set to different tunes were traditional and widespread. Barbecue Bob sang:

> Go starch my jumper mama   iron my overalls[20]

whereas Tommy Johnson, characteristically jumbling his lyrics, sang

> Won't you iron my jumper   starch my overalls[21]

Similar lyrics appear in "common stock" songs with different tunes shared by blacks and whites at the turn of the century. Many other formulas are evident just from the sample in chapter 3; if the totality of downhome blues lyrics were considered, a high percentage of phrases in the sample would turn out to be formulaic.

What are the themes of early downhome blues songs? What are the songs about? Conventional wisdom has it that they are laments which call attention to social injustice, racial discrimination, and the trials and tribulations of being black in America. In the standard work on black folk music in this country, Harold Courlander states that "the blues have provided a convenient outlet for protest against racial injustice."[22] Recorded early downhome blues songs do not support this assertion with overt protest. Son House explained their subject matter: "You know sometime – I don't know who it was that started this thing, this blues business. You know it ain't but one way you – the blues exists, and that comes between male and female bein' in love. Uh-huh. And when one has been deceived by the other. And then he gets the blues, that is, if they love each other. Yeah. Then they get the blues."[23] Early downhome blues songs as a genre were overtly concerned with love between men and women, while social and racial protest found other outlets, whether in tales, sayings, and conversation, or in direct action.

In the downhome blues sample in chapter 3, several recurring ideas and attitudes are voiced by the singers. The basic unit of complete thought is the stanza, wherein situations are described, feelings expressed, threats made, resolutions stated, and so on. The linkage of stanzas into songs, however coherent, adds complexity to the relations among the thoughts. I shall take up the most important attitudes now, roughly in decreasing order of frequency.[24]

Perhaps the most frequently expressed stanzaic idea is the difficulty of keeping a lover:

> I'm gonna buy me a banty   put him in my back door
> I'm gonna buy me a banty   put him in my back door
> 'Cause he see a stranger comin'   he'll flop his wings and crow[25]

This stranger is the proverbial "back door man" who sneaks in to seduce one's lover. One must always be on guard. Bribing her with presents makes no difference:

Bought my gal a great big diamond ring
Bought my gal   great big diamond ring
Come right back home and caught her shakin' that thing[26]

If one has no money, it is even more difficult:

I done lost all my money   I got nowhere to go
I said I lost all my money   ain't got me nowhere to go
I believe to my soul   I'm about to lose my brown[27]

Almost equally common are stanzas expressing regret over the loss of a lover. Leroy Carr sang:

How long   babe how long
Has that evenin'   train been gone
How long   how how long   baby how long

Here and I stod at the station   watched my baby leavin' town
Blue and disgusted   nowhere could peace be found
For how long   how how long   baby how long[28]

(Trains appear frequently in early downhome blues songs. They are neither iron monsters chewing up pastoral landscapes nor heralds of advancing industrialization; the trains simply separate ex-lovers and enable drifters to move on.) In "Bumble Bee," Memphis Minnie compares a departed lover to a bumble bee with a superior "stinger" (penis) and pleads for his return:

Bumble bee bumble bee   please come back to me
Bumble bee bumble bee   please come back to me
He's got the best old stinger any bumble bee that I ever seen[29]

Barbecue Bob sang of a man who wakes up in the early hours reminded of his lost brown-skinned woman:

Woke up this morning gal   'twixt midnight and day
I woke up this morning   'twixt midnight and day
With my head around my pillow where my brownie used to lay[30]

Another commonly expressed attitude is the desire to enjoy a free and happy union, without mistreatment. The "mistreatin' mama" of Furry Lewis's song is scolded:

Babe if your heart ain't iron   it must be marble stone
If your heart ain't iron   it must be marble stone
For you're a mistreatin' mama baby sure as you born[31]

In "Pony Blues," Charley Patton asks for an untrammeled relationship:

> I got something to tell you   when I gets a chance
> Somethin' to tell you   when I get a   chance
> I don't want to marry   just want to   be your man[32]

"Fo' Day Blues" incorporates a folk saying used to protest, among other things, racial injustice:

> I'd rather drink muddy water   sleep in a hollow log
> Rather drink muddy water   sleep in a hollow log
> Than to be in Atlanta treated like a dog[33]

Closely related is the celebration of a happy alliance. In the role of back door man, Blind Willie McTell sang:

> The big star falling   mama it ain't long 'fore day
> The big star falling mama 't'ain't long 'fore day
> Need a little sunshine to drive these blues away
>   [spoken:] Oh come here quick   come on mama you know I got you[34]

Charley Patton rejoiced in a sexually enthusiastic mate:

> It's a long tall woman   tall like a cher- ry tree baby
> Got a long tall woman   tall like a cher- ry tree baby
> She gets up 'fore day and she puts   that thing   on me[35]

Next in frequency of expression, and closely related to the specific desire for a free and happy relationship, is the general desire for a good lover. This stanza from Tommy Johnson's "Lonesome Blues" is typical:

> Won't you iron my jumper   starch my overalls
> Won't you iron my jumper   starch my overalls
> I'm gon' find my woman said she's   in this world somewhere[36]

The expression is particularly strong because the lines do not rhyme.

Threats of reprisal for mistreatment are more common than acts. Blind Blake sang of a light sleeper:

> When you see me sleepin'   baby don't you think I'm drunk
>   [spoken:] No I'm not drunk not a bit of it
> When you see me sleepin'   baby don't you think I'm drunk
> I got one eye on my pistol   and the other on your trunk

Love you pretty mama   b'lieve me 't'ain't no lie
   [spoken:] I mean it 't'ain't no lie
I love you pretty mama   b'lieve me 't'ain't no lie
The day you try to quit me   baby that's the day you die[37]

Richard "Rabbit" Brown envisioned a grisly death for a lover:

Sometime I think that you too sweet to die
Sometime I think that you too sweet to die
But another time I think   you ought to be buried alive[38]

"44 Blues" is also concerned with revenge:

Lord I walked all night long   with my forty-four in my hand
Lord I walked all night long   my forty-four in my hand
I was lookin' for my woman   found her with another man[39]

The threat is carried out in "Got the Blues, Can't Be Satisfied":

Took my gun   and I broke the bar'l down
Took my gun   broke the barrel down
Put my baby   six feet under the ground[40]

A general complaint that the singer feels blue or "has" the blues, as one has a disease, is reasonably common. As I pointed out in the discussion of formulas earlier in this chapter, blues can fall like raindrops, hover like germs in a room, enter food, and infect the eater. But this metaphorical complaint is more significant as a generative idea than as an actual expression; having the blues serves as a foundation on which the narrator lays his specific difficulties with his lover. Though some blues songs express satisfaction and others are resolved happily, most concentrate upon trouble. To feel blue is not merely to feel sad; it is to feel a complex of emotions, as the narrator begs, brags, threatens, cries for help, stoically accepts his situation, or exits with an ironic parting shot.

In *Urban Blues,* Charles Keil has found that lyrics boasting of sexual prowess were less common in the urban blues of the 1960s than in the city blues of the 1940s and 1950s. Instead, Keil continues, contemporary blues singers analyze problems and close with a call to the lover for help so they can work toward a common solution. This shift to problem solving is a sign of growing solidarity in the black community.[41] In early recorded downhome blues, boasting and cries for help were about equally common, but the cries lacked the sophistication of Keil's rational, problem-solving model. (That sophistication may reflect the ability of the professional composers who supply lyrics for contemporary urban blues singers.) Nellie Florence sang:

Men they call me "oven" they says that I'm red hot
Men they call me "oven"   they say that I'm red hot
They say I've got somethin' the other gals ain't got

I can strut my pudding   spread my grease with ease
I can strut my pudding   spread my grease with ease
'Cause I know my onions that's why I always please [42]

Henry Spaulding boasted:

Biddle Street Biddle Street now   is only twenty-six blocks long
Biddle Street Biddle Street now   is only twenty-six blocks long
And the women on Biddle Street   just won't leave me alone [43]

The call for help is sounded no less often. Leroy Carr asked for letters to a prisoner:

Sometimes I wonder   why don't you write to me
Sometimes I wonder   why you don't write to me
If I been a bad fellow   I did not intend to be [44]

In "One Time Blues," Blind Blake sang:

Ah –   mama love me one more time
Ah –   mama love me one more time
You gimme little chance   maybe you will change your mind [45]

Later in the song the singer declares that he will be around when the woman's regular man has departed; he asks to be taken in at that time, putting himself in a helplessly debased position (the boaster would try to convince the woman that he was a better lover). Of course, whenever a singer expresses regret over the loss of a good woman or desire for one, he is asking, however indirectly, for help. But it is not the kind of "help us" that Keil sees in contemporary black music; the cry for help in early downhome blues is "help *me*."

Whiskey is an important motif in the sample, though different attitudes are expressed about its worth. In a stanza from the common stock, Furry Lewis sings of the power of whiskey (and women) to draw one from a religious life:

I could had religion   lord this very day
I could had religion   lord this very day
But the womens and whiskeys lord won't let me pray [46]

In "Whiskey Moan Blues" the singer resolves to refrain from alcohol once he has settled down with his good woman:

I been drinkin' and gamblin'   bar'lhousin' all my days
Mm drinkin' and gamblin'   bar'lhousin' all my days
But I have found someone to love me   I'm goin' to change my ways[47]

While some singers expressed pleasure over whiskey's effects, Lillian Miller sang of a woman who regrets the loss of her senses when drunk:

You knowed I was drunk when I laid down across your bed
You knew I was drunk when I laid down across your bed
All the whiskey I drank it's   gone right to my head

When I was in Houston drunk most ev'ry day
When I was in Houston   drunk most ev'ry day
I drank so much whiskey I thought I'd pass away[48]

She admits that she isn't much good without it, either:

Whiskey whiskey   it's some folks' downfall
Oh, whiskey whiskey   it's some folks' downfall
But if I don't get whiskey I ain't no good at all[49]

Whiskey can get rid of the blues:

Whiskey straight will drive the blues away
Whiskey straight will drive these blues away
That be the case I wants a quart today[50]

Now if I could get me   one more drink of booze
If I could get me   one more drink of booze
I guess it would ease   these old writin' paper blues[51]

Whiskey is dangerous to the bootlegger as well as to the drinker:

When the bootlegger goes   to his still   gets ready   to make his stuff
He's got his concentrated lye   cocaine   and his snuff

He'll fix you a drink that just won't quit
It'll make you fight a *circle saw*
Make you slap the lady down
And make you pick a fight with your pa

The bootleggin' man's   got his bottle in his hand
And all he needs   is a little more speed
So he can outrun the revenue man[52]

Nevertheless, it remains attractive:

> I went home   the other night   I'd swore I wouldn't drink no more
> Until s'loons come back with   with bottled-in-bond   and the days of long ago
>
> But I see   that will never be   so I   just got   drunk again
> I have nothing as long as corn liquor   last 'cause I got no money to spend[53]

But the narrators the blues singers create do not seem to me as pathological as those of modern country singers, whose mixture of religion, alcoholism, and divorce bespeaks an extraordinary cultural breakdown.

Finally, one often encounters a general desire to leave and find better times (as against a desire to leave with a specific purpose, such as to find a lover). Willie Brown sang:

> I leave here I'm gonna   catch that M. and O.
> Now when   I leave here I'm gonna   catch that M. and O.
> I'm goin'   way down south where I ain't   never been before[54]

Peg Leg Howell sang of a man who directed his woman to put crepe on her door – to signify a death – when he left her:

> I'm goin' I'm goin' mama ain't comin' here no more
> I'm goin' away mama ain't   comin' here no more
> I'm goin' away mama ain't   comin' here no more
> When you see me leavin'   pin crepe on your door[55]

(To ask a woman to mourn for her departed lover, who may be on the next plantation, is defiant indeed.) If there were "good times here," they were "better down the road":

> If you   want to live easy   pack your clothes with mine
> Mm   want to live easy   pack your clothes with mine
> Said if you   want to live easy just   pack your clothes with mine[56]

Roger Abrahams distinguishes two black masculine approaches to urban life: that of the gorilla, who directly overpowers obstacles, and that of the cat, who gains his ends by deception and indirection. Both "agree . . . that women exist to be exploited. But not only do men commonly have this attitude – they also expect it from the women in return. Indeed, the women expect it of themselves it would appear."[57] Does the predominantly male outlook of early downhome blues lyrics express this fatalistic sexism? "Early Morning Blues" (transcr. 8) begins as the singer wakes up to find his "baby" coming home after spending the night elsewhere; he threatens to leave her. But in the next stanza he softens and asks her where she was, hoping she has an excuse. She will have none of his whining, for she tells him that where she went is "none of your business daddy since I treat you right." The singer continues with a threat in the last two stanzas: he loves his "mama," but he will kill her if she tries to leave. What could be more sexist? But the woman exploits the singer, not the other way around. If he *were* going to shoot her, he might have done so when she told him that her affairs were none of his business. No, this is an empty threat; the singer loves her too much to kill her. The case, then, is not so simple. The selfish brag turns out to be a bluff; and a complaint, in a pattern noted by Keil, is simply covered up with bravado.[58] This is not to say that the singer may not be exploiting the woman; we get only his side of the story. Nor is it to say that blues lyrics do not portray an exploitative culture, or that the cat and the gorilla do not exist as characters in blues songs (the gorilla is usually a cat bluffing in disguise).

The blues singer's cry to his woman – "treat me right" – seems less omnivorously self-centered than the cry of white American popular music, "Give me love." S. I. Hayakawa advanced the thesis that "the words of true jazz songs, especially the Negro blues, tend to be unsentimental and realistic in their statements about life. . . . The words of popular songs, on the other hand, largely (but not altogether) the product of white song-writers . . . tend towards wishful thinking, dreamy and ineffectual nostalgia, unrealistic fantasy, self-pity, and sentimental cliches masquerading as emotion."[59] Hayakawa's observations about white popular songs, at least those from about 1850 to 1950, seem correct. His further observation that, as socializing agents, these songs badly prepared young people for the realities of adult love, is certainly true. But are downhome blues songs realistic? Hayakawa's choice of recent songs to support his thesis is fortunate, for there is a large body of songs, particularly among the later city blues, to bear him out. But the lyrics of early downhome blues songs – at least in my sample – exhibit wishful thinking and unrealistic fantasy. Hayakawa asserts that fantasy may lead to the "IFD disease" – idealization giving way to frustration and then demoralization.[60] Certainly, responding to despair with false bravado is not a realistic solution. Since blues lyrics *start* from trouble, they sometimes display a reverse of the IFD disease: demoralization leading to frustration, leading to idealization, as the singer thinks of finding a good woman or leaving the plantation, or boasts of his prowess. Yet it need not lead to that, for if Keil is correct about contemporary blues lyrics, then the songs become, to use Kenneth Burke's phrase, viable equipment for living.[61]

Fantasy in blues lyrics may be linked to racial protest. Listeners have been perplexed because they cannot find much overt racial or social protest in blues lyrics. A number of explanations are possible. It has been argued that blues singers were not angry, since they were well treated, entertaining whites as well as blacks. But the assumption that the singers did not feel white hostility and the constraints of the plantation system, or that they were not aware of the anger of their fellows, goes against so much else in oral black culture that it is most unlikely. Rather, this is the wishful thinking of those who would turn downhome life into plantation pastoral.

If the blues singer did feel anger, why did he not express this overtly in his lyrics? I suggested earlier that as long as there were other outlets for protest, the relatively newer blues songs may simply not have been thought of as a proper protest vehicle. Because blues, at an early stage in its development, was made available by vaudeville singers and then through W. C. Handy's popular songs, their themes as well as their forms were fixed in the minds of others who took blues up. Singers learned that the proper subject of a blues song was the pain and joy of love, not racial protest. One possible explanation for the paucity of protest themes in *recorded* blues is that since the singer, whose name was on the record, could be traced, caught, and punished, he would have exercised self-censorship. While this is a reasonable argument, singers probably did not censor their lyrics in the recording studio. For one thing, the formulaic process of blues composition makes it difficult to ascribe to the singer the ability to censor lyrics at will. Undoubtedly, some protest phrases would have crept in despite the singers' best efforts. Furthermore, where we know that lyrics were substituted, anti-black phrases were, as Tony Russell has pointed out, "usually directed against sections of the black public."[62] Here, for instance, is a common-stock American folksong couplet at least as old as its appearance in the 1867 collection *Slave Songs of the United States:*

> Some folks say a Nigger won't steal
> I caught one in my cornfield.[63]

In his 1931 recording of "Preachers Blues" (Vocalion 1643), Kansas Joe McCoy used the line

> Some folks say a preacher won't steal

which fits the folk stereotype (one that crosses racial boundaries) of the preacher. This does not rule out the possibility that the line was on occasion sung

> Some folks say Mister Charlie won't steal

in live performance to black audiences, confirming their suspicion that the white boss was not to be trusted.

In a recent essay, William Ferris, Jr., attempts to show that blues singers' repertoires for black audiences contain obscene lyrics and racial protest not sung in front of white audiences.[64] But his case is clouded by the history of black singers like Leadbelly and Big Bill Broonzy, who composed blues songs on protest subjects after they were discovered by white folklorists and promoted for northern, white audiences sympathetic to the Civil Rights movement and other liberal causes. Even so, their repertoires did not contain very much overt protest. And who can imagine that Leadbelly did not have some help composing "Bourgeois Blues"?[65] That is not to deny that he was angry about housing discrimination in Washington, D.C., but it is to suggest that his expressing that anger in a blues song may have issued from his desire to please his new audience.

If blues lyrics contain little overt protest, could they contain coded messages, covert protest? If so, the messages are so well hidden that one doubts the code's existence. Blues songs carry sexual messages, often obscene by contemporary standards, in a series' of quite obvious and frequently hilarious metaphors for the sex act (e.g., Memphis Minnie's "Sting me bumble bee until I get enough" [transcr. 16]). But part of a code's effectiveness in songs, or in any form of entertainment designed to please a large audience, depends upon most of the audience deciphering it. Besides occasional reference to "Mr. Charlie," I can find little evidence of a protest code in the vast majority of blues lyrics.

Covert protest need not be presented in code; its expression may be unconscious. It might be argued, for example, that the songs offer an unwitting allegory in which deception in love signifies treachery in race relations. Perhaps the boasts and bluffs of the singer are sublimations of racial hostility. Richard Wright observed that "a submerged theme of guilt, psychological in nature, seems to run through [blues songs]. Could this guilt have stemmed from the burden of renounced rebellious impulses?"[66] Paul Oliver goes a step further, claiming that in the blues of lost love the "singer has found, consciously or subconsciously, a vehicle for protest. . . . Neither the blues singer or his listener is likely to be aware of the function of the songs as a sublimation of frustrated desires. . . . But . . . they sublimate hostility and canalize aggressive instincts against a mythical common enemy, the 'cheater.'"[67]

This is an appealing theory. The mistreating lover is transformed into the mistreating white plantation owner, the sheriff, and other authority figures, while the drama of the song revolves around the victim's response to mistreatment. Experiments have shown that people who are nonaggressive tend to exhibit more aggression in Thematic Apperception Tests than do people who are aggressive.[68] But plantation-system blacks had outlets among themselves for aggression even if they had to show deference among whites. There is hostility expressed between lovers in blues songs; but it may simply be a reflection, not a sublimation, since, after all, lovers did mistreat one another, argue, and fight. Nor is aggression a dominant theme in early downhome blues lyrics. (It becomes much more important in blues songs of the Depression and the post-World War II era.) Finally, it is one thing to say that aggression is a sublimation of racial hostility, and quite another to speculate that it must therefore be an expression of racial *protest*.

Viewed as a sublimator of racial hostility, the blues singer performs a negative role in the black community, feeding fantasies and diverting energy into forms (including art) which allow racial injustice to continue. The character Clay in LeRoi Jones's play *Dutchman* observes, for example, that if Charlie Parker had not blown his violence into his horn, he would have murdered whites on the street. But viewed as an artist, the blues singer plays a positive role. He offers his listeners an imitation of life, an imitation so real that the traditional wisdom of blues lyrics becomes proverbial expression and offers explanations as well as directives. Linear, temporal logic is replaced by an endless circular structure, the parts of which may be interchanged to provide different perspectives each time they are sung, each time they are lived. James Baldwin's account of the novelist as artist serves also to indicate the positive function of the blues singer (or the preacher, for that matter) in the black community:

> You [the artist] are compelled . . . into dealing with whatever it is that hurts you. . . . You must find some way of using this to connect you with everyone else alive. . . . You must understand that your pain is trivial except insofar as you can use it to connect with other people's pain; and insofar as you can do that with your pain, you can be released from it. And then hopefully it works the other way around, too; insofar as I can tell you what it is like to suffer, perhaps I can help you to suffer less.[69]

Art gives us order. But it also gives us disorder – a great deal more than life does, for we put life's perceptions into preconceived constructions of reality. The disorder of painful experience, the gap between what we hope for and what happens, can be prolonged and experienced at will only through art. The more we experience it – connect our pain with other people's pain – the more we can adjust and adapt, learn and grow.

PART III THE RESPONSE

6 RECORDING THE BLUES

Little genuine black music appeared on phonograph records before 1920. Minstrel skits, "coon" songs, and "Ethiopian airs" were listed in the catalogs, but as often as not they were performed by white singers and comedians. Making fun of the "child-like" black, these discs reinforced the stereotype at the same time they continued it.

Record advertisements from those days transported the reader to the worlds the music conjured up. Opera stars' faces looked out forbiddingly (fig. 92) to assure the high standards of the product. Surely one's social standing could be secured upon purchase of the proper records (fig. 93). Though opera was given the most honored position, a wide variety of other material was recorded. It was possible to hear the most recent songs

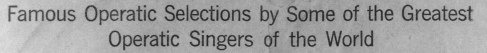

FIGURE 92.

and imitate the dancing of Vernon and Irene Castle in one's own home, or march to the music of John Philip Sousa's band.

Sousa himself opposed phonograph records. Writing in *Appleton's Magazine* on the "menace of mechanical music," he warned:

> I could not imagine that a performance by [a record] would ever inspire embryotic [*sic*] Mendelssohns, Beethovens, Mozarts, and Wagners to the acquirement of technical skill, or to the grasp of human possibilities in the art. . . . Under such conditions the tide of amateurism cannot but recede, until there will be left only the mechanical device and the professional executant. Singing will no longer be a fine

FIGURE 93.

accomplishment! vocal exercises will be out of vogue! Then what of the national throat? Will it not weaken? What of the national chest? Will it not shrink?[1]

Had Sousa peered into the future, he would have seen the national throat imitating recorded bird calls, while the national chest was expanding to the rhythms of recorded exercises.[2] Sousa's anti-mechanical attitude was shared by most folklorists, who deplored the new medium and predicted the imminent death of folk music[3] – though they were not averse to using the equipment to make field recordings of the music before it expired, in order to preserve it for analysis. Instruction and amusement were the major purposes of records in the early period.

When commercial recording began in 1890, the equipment was sensitive only to the middle frequencies of the audio spectrum. Records had to be made one at a time, and the cost of the listening equipment was beyond most people's reach.[4] Realizing that few families could afford the phonograph's $190 price, the industry contemplated uses for it outside the home. Tycoons, it was hoped, might record their correspondence, thus disguising their presumed illiteracy. Retail stores put phonographs where customers, by pressing a button to turn them on, could hear snatches of music or humor interspersed with advertisements for goods in the store.[5] McLuhan to the contrary, then, the record medium did not begin as a copy of another medium – live entertainment – though that was included soon enough.

As the price of phonographs gradually dropped to twenty-five dollars by the end of the decade, more and more families bought them. The 1891 Columbia catalog was ten pages long and included a "Negro novelty" section. By mid-decade, spoken records had become popular; humorous skits, monologues, dramatic readings, and ethnic humor were the staples. Current hit songs as well as old American favorites were on wax. In addition, the industry aimed records at the various immigrant groups, in their native languages. Len Spencer sang "darky" ditties, and George W. Johnson, a black man, became famous for his record "The Whistling Coon."[6] To the record industry, blacks were just another ethnic group, albeit an especially humorous one. As far as I can determine, though, whites, rather than blacks, bought those records.

At first, the poor frequency response of their equipment kept the industry away from opera, but improvements in the recording process in the first few years of the new century led to the release of several arias (fig. 94). Although sales were disappointing, the companies, proud of their new product, wanted to expand. To increase sales they offered a greater number and variety of records, put their phonographs in decorative cabinets, and stepped up their advertising.[7]

By 1912, Victor's advertising budget was more than $1.5 million annually. The era of mass newspaper and magazine circulation was now two decades old; practically every issue contained an advertisement for a phonograph with an announcement of the latest opera records and the Victor dog listening to "his master's voice."[8] Catalogs and supplements illustrated these serious recordings with sketches of opera and concert stage scenes. A national ballroom dance craze was most responsible for the sharp rise in record sales between 1913 and 1915 (fig. 95).[9] The industry kept growing: in 1914, 18 phonograph manufacturers sold half a million phonographs, and in 1919, 200 manufacturers sold two million phonographs.[10]

The black middle and upper classes living in northern cities wanted black music on record, but blues was not what they had in mind. The *Chicago Defender*, largest and most

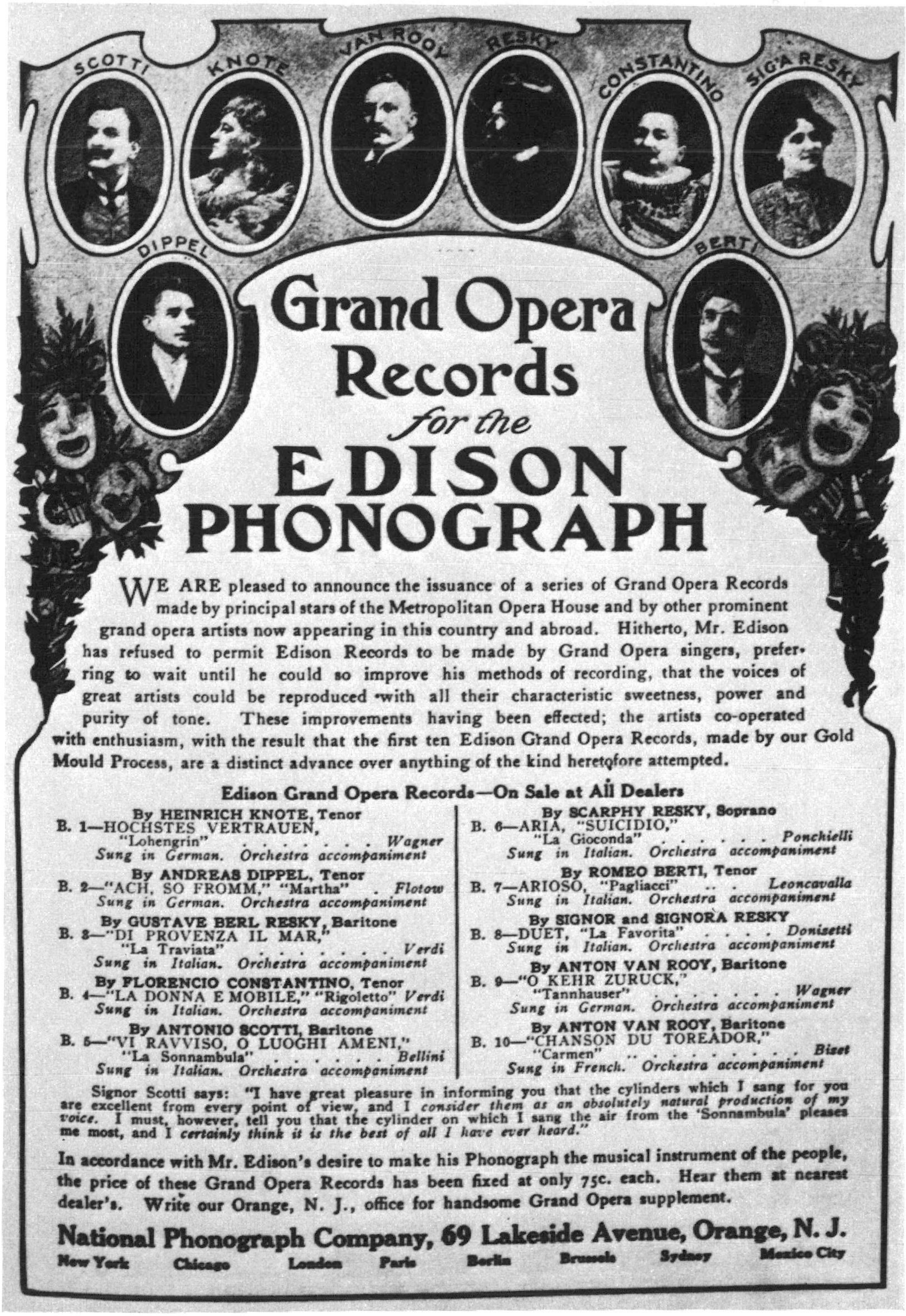

FIGURE 94. *A 1906 Edison opera record advertisement*

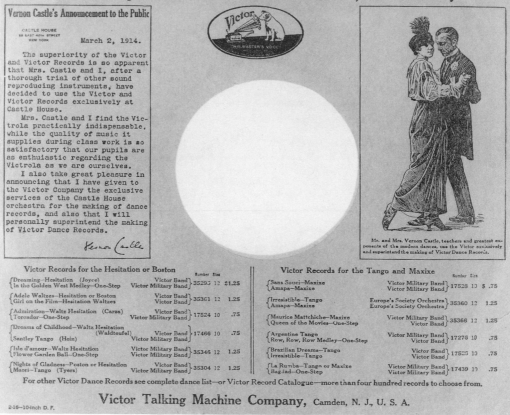

FIGURE 95. *The "2-16" at the lower left probably indicates the date this sleeve was released – February, 1916.*

influential of the black newspapers, campaigned in 1916 and the following year for the inclusion of black concert artists in the recording industry's prestigious opera series. (In 1920, Roland Hayes and Anita Patti Brown did record for Columbia – but they had to put up the money.)[11] The *Defender* proudly followed the career of black society orchestra leader James Reese Europe, whose recordings, skill with the latest dance rhythms, and successful European tour had alerted a number of whites to black talent in a field previously thought too sophisticated for their undisciplined nature.[12]

As more and more black people came to the urban ghettos – major migrations took place during World War I – it became clear that the move was not going to quicken black integration into white American society. Two kinds of separatism emerged. The black establishment view was that the ghettos must become self-sufficient economic and political units.[13] Counter to this idea of a black metropolis (which embraced the economic assumptions of an outdated small-business capitalism) ran a more militant separatism. Blacks must rebel psychologically, take pride in their differences from whites, and, by refusing to imitate white middle-class standards, break the white value systems. This mass movement, centered on Marcus Garvey, foundered when he was imprisoned for mail fraud in 1925 and deported in 1927, after his sentence was commuted.[14] The movement represented then, as it did in the late 1960s, a direct assault on the white culture.

On the whole, the black press approved of this "ignominious climax to Garvey's meteoric career," for its lot was already cast with the black metropolis.[15] The idea of a black "artistic metropolis" was a natural outgrowth. Yet, just as economic and political success in the black metropolis was defined in traditional American terms, so black artists and critics measured artistic success by genteel white standards. W. C. Handy, for example, believed he had refined black folk music by "polishing" and publishing compositions based on the blues songs he had heard as a boy.[16] Entertainment columnists, such as the *Chicago Defender*'s Tony Langston, urged black vaudeville and variety show performers to discard "crude" routines and develop skill and subtlety in their presentations. Orchestras were cautioned not to play too loudly or too quickly.[17] The same attitude was responsible, if not for the music, at least for the artist identification – "Mamie Smith, contralto" – on the label of the first blues record.

Perry Bradford must be given credit for the recording breakthrough. "I had traveled all over the country singing and playing the blues," wrote Bradford in his autobiography. "I tramped the pavements of Broadway with the belief that the country was waiting for the sound of the voice of a Negro singing the blues with a Negro jazz combination playing. . . . For our folks had a story to tell and it could only be told in vocal – not instrumental – recordings."[18] There is some evidence that other promoters, scouts, and record dealers had the same idea; but they were unsuccessful.[19] In February, 1920, Bradford persuaded Fred Hager, recording director for General Phonograph Corporation's OKeh label, that blues records would be profitable. The recording companies had been reluctant to issue this type of material. Some feared a white boycott, while others wondered if blacks had enough money to buy phonographs and records. But Mamie Smith was brought in to sing – backed by a white studio orchestra – "That Thing Called Love" and "You Can't Keep a Good Man Down." Released in August and publicized in the black communities, the record (OKeh 4113) sold well enough for Hager to invite Smith back into the studio. This time Bradford supplied a black jazz band to accompany her: cornet, trombone, clarinet, violin, and piano. Though Bradford wrote that the band used "hum and head arrangements"[20] (that is, they played by ear), they did rehearse for two days beforehand outside the studio.[21]

The result, "Crazy Blues" and "It's Right Here for You" (OKeh 4169), was the first commercial blues record. There was such a demand for it that record dealers who did not hold an OKeh franchise sold it under the counter to their black customers.[22] OKeh had opened a promising market, and other companies were quick to imitate a successful formula. In 1921, Arto, Emerson, Pathe, Perfect, Black Swan, and Columbia issued blues records featuring black women vocalists accompanied by black jazz groups or pianists. By 1923, Paramount, Victor, Ajax, and Vocalion had joined the bandwagon.

The introduction and quick acceptance of a new medium, radio, which gave listeners fidelity superior to that of acoustic records and which provided constantly changing live programming, was responsible for the sudden decline in record sales at the beginning of the 1920s. In 1919, Columbia's net income before taxes was $7 million; in 1921 it lost $4.3 million, and its stock dropped from 65 to $1\frac{5}{8}$.[23] In 1923 it filed for bankruptcy and went into receivership, while continuing to produce records. Victor, the largest company, watched sales decline from $51 million in 1921 to $25 million in 1925.[24] Pecuniary motives, rather than altruism or product approval, were responsible for the enthusiasm with which the companies embraced black music.

There was practically no blues radio programming in the 1920s to compete with record sales.[25] The number of blues and gospel titles released each year grew from about 50 in 1921 to 250 in 1925 and 500 in 1927.[26] Sales were phenomenal. Howard Odum and Guy B. Johnson, writing in 1925, estimated that blacks were buying five or six million records each year – and their figures must have been low.[27] Adjusted to reflect the increase in titles by 1927 and to include the companies Odum and Johnson omitted, the estimate comes to ten million records, a number approximately equal to the black American population counted by the census takers. Sheer quantity made the records significant; and because the other mass media – radio, motion pictures, newspapers – neglected black American culture, the impact of the discs was strengthened ever further. We are not, in short, dealing with a small, isolated phenomenon. It is no wonder that the names Bessie Smith, Blind Lemon Jefferson, and the Reverend J. M. Gates are well known to black people old enough to have heard their records when they first appeared.

In 1923, OKeh opened up a parallel market for what came to be known as hillbilly (later, country) records. From *The Victor Master Book, Vol. 2: 1925–1935,* which lists all Victor recordings except opera sets, the importance of the different kinds of records in that period may be calculated from the number of issues. In 1928, for instance, 22.9 percent of the records listed were hillbilly; 21.7 percent were black.[28] Without knowing how many opera sets were produced, it is difficult to put these figures in perspective, though they may be contrasted with the 36.4 percent figure for popular, show, novelty, and (white) jazz records. Even if the industry did not hold black music in high esteem, it could not deny that it made up a significant proportion of the records sold and thus deserved careful production, advertising, and marketing.

When the companies saw that there would be a continuing market, they set aside special numerical series for black records. A generic name was needed to identify the already segregated offerings. Ralph Peer, head of OKeh's 8000 series, claimed to have coined the name which stuck: "race records." "We had records by all foreign groups: German records, Swedish records, Polish records, but we were afraid to advertise Negro records, so I listed them as 'Race' records and they are still known as that."[29] Peer probably was afraid to advertise "Negro" records because that term was not then in favor with the black leadership; several writers in the *Defender* had expressed the opinion that the word *Negro* was meaningless and, worse, could easily be changed into the pejorative *nigger*. Whether or not Peer invented the term "race records," the phrase "the race" was widely used by black people to identify themselves long before it was used to identify records. It was not a derogatory term; instead, it signified group solidarity.[30] Though the record companies classified Afro-Americans with immigrant groups for whom special series would be provided, they took pains, in the early marketing period, not to insult consumers with an offensive generic name for the records. By 1923 "race records" was the established identification in advertisements, although Columbia did not use it very often.[31] (The tag "hillbilly music," thought to be a pejorative, was never established through advertisements, but it was common in trade talk.)[32]

Distribution and advertising methods were simple and direct. Most records were distributed nationally through regional jobbers, and from there to local dealers, who sold them to customers. Some record companies enjoyed an additional mail-order business from blanks at the bottom of their newspaper advertisements. By 1923 race records were available in most American cities.[33] As the decade went on, dealerships were set up in smaller towns to take advantage of the local appeal of downhome blues records. In early advertisements Paramount asked customers to become sales agents. Records were sold in drugstores, furniture stores, bookstores, department stores, music stores, and theaters. They were also sold by peddlers and hawked from traveling shows. Although most race records were distributed nationally, many downhome blues records were marketed primarily in those localities where the singers were already well known.[34]

Advertising was directed by a company "publicity man," or it was farmed out to an agency. As far as I can determine, the illustrators who sketched the singers and drew cartoons, and the photographers who took the singers' pictures, were either free-lancers hired by the record company or artists working for the advertising agency. Black consultants whose opinions were considered in the selection of recording artists were also asked to help find appropriate language for the advertising copy. The advertisements reveal white uncertainties about the increasing visibility of black people in the urban North, and by extension in the life of the nation. Chapter 7 assesses this cultural impact.

When a customer walked into a record store, he saw banners, streamers, posters, photographs, catalogs, supplements, handbills, and, of course, records. If he could not read, his eye was caught by the illustrations. The dealer was happy to play the latest releases on his store machine; that way he might even sell a phonograph. Outside the store, the buyer was attracted by large displays hung in the windows. Lantern slides projected in theaters announced the latest discs; record sleeves presented miniature catalogs and sometimes provided order blanks. Few store displays have been preserved, but because their illustrations usually were taken from newspaper campaigns, we can easily imagine what they looked like. Since the *Chicago Defender* was read widely in the South as well as in the North (even though some southerners tried to suppress its distribution because of its unsettling opinions), the newspaper ads reached black people down home.

When in 1921 it became clear that Mamie Smith's recording of "Crazy Blues" was a hit, she went on tour with her Jazz Hounds, the orchestra Bradford had provided, to capitalize on her success and promote the record. In every city she was entertained by the cream of black society. For her stage performances she was elaborately gowned; mellow lighting and tasteful scenery surrounded her. The *Defender*'s Tony Langston praised her refined style. She did not shout, she did not dance, she did not even snap her fingers.[35]

Vaudeville blues songs formed the largest class of race records issued, but there were other offerings: spirituals, sermons, jazz, skits, show songs, and even a few operatic arias. Black Swan records, then the only black-owned and -operated company, proclaimed that it would emphasize blues but release "many numbers of a higher standard."[36] The company announced the "First Grand Opera Record Ever Made By A Colored Singer" in the April 15, 1922, *Defender*. But it misjudged the market, and in 1924, in financial trouble, it was absorbed by Paramount.

Unquestionably, Ma Rainey and Bessie Smith, the two best-remembered vaudeville blues singers, sounded more down home and sang more blues than their competitors, though they all possessed similar backgrounds; it was their vocal style – a certain tone of voice, a way with pronunciation, a kind of delivery – which set them apart. Both Smith and Rainey were recorded for the first time in 1923. Smith had been refused recording contracts with OKeh and Black Swan earlier because her singing was thought insufficiently refined.[37] If Smith's style was crude, Rainey's was even more so. Her background with virtually every kind of touring show had left its mark on her appearance but had given her a kind of majesty. Photographs of her from the period (e.g., fig. 96) show a middle-aged, short, stocky woman with a round face, clear complexion, and beautifully expressive eyes and mouth. In these photographs she usually is dressed in a sequined gown, jeweled with a necklace (sometimes of twenty-dollar gold pieces),

FIGURE 96. *Ma Rainey*

tasseled earrings, and a wide headband. Evidently, the "Mother of the Blues" could be forgiven her old-fashioned vulgarity. Al Wynn remembered how she made her stage appearance: "I was asked to join the Rainey organization just after she was forming a new group in '23 or '24. . . . Her entrance was – she would come out of a large victrola – it was made just like a old-style phonograph and she would walk out of that singing 'Moonshine Blues' which was her big hit at the time."[38] Rainey's entrance – a strong contrast with Mamie Smith's tasteful stage act – befit someone who was called "Madame 'Ma' Rainey" on the label of her early records. Like Bessie Smith, Rainey had a raspier voice than the other vaudeville singers, and she sang more blues songs. Her singing was generally free from melodic embellishment, and she also placed her vocal attack more solidly on the beat than Smith or the downhome singers did. Smith, whose record sales made her the most popular race artist of the decade – even white southerners bought her records[39] – wore simple dresses and little or no jewelry during her performances.[40] Her relaxed, loose delivery, coupled with a rasp she could turn off and on for emphasis, her play with embellishment, especially around the third and fifth of the blues mode, and her dramatic sense of timing and dynamics gave her a marvelous and distinctive style. But there is little evidence that the other vaudeville singers, except perhaps Ida Cox, imitated either Rainey, whom they must have thought old-fashioned, or Smith, whom they probably thought insufficiently refined. Bessie Smith's impact on downhome blues singers was substantial, I am convinced.

As the decade reached its midpoint, the jazz groups whose main interest was instrumental music began to receive more promotion in the newspaper advertisements. The ads show a modest boom in recorded jazz from mid-1925 to mid-1926, though the records were identified as "instrumental blues" to take advantage of the much larger blues market. Suddenly, beginning in 1926, both recorded sermons with singing and downhome blues records were promoted with overwhelming frequency in the newspapers, an advertising concentration which continued until the end of the decade. Jazz and vaudeville blues records continued to sell at least as well as downhome blues records,[41] although in the late 1920s race record sales generally declined. The industry could have continued its insistent jazz and vaudeville blues record advertising in the black press. While it is reasonable to suggest that the companies did not do so because they felt no need – after all, the records were selling as it was – their pattern had *always* been to advertise race records heavily to keep the flow of new releases moving into their customers' hands. More probably, advertisement concentration on downhome blues and religious records toward the end of the decade has a psychological explanation: the record companies felt more comfortable with illustrations of black people down home.[42]

Recordings of spiritual-singing quartets had been available before the 1920s, and they were continued on a small scale in the early race series. The phenomenal sales success of the Birmingham Jubilee Singers led the industry to release more than seventy recordings of this type during 1927 alone. Husband-and-wife teams and solo evangelist singers also were popular. But the most important religious records were the sermons with singing. From September, 1926, to June, 1927, "sixty records of sermons were put out by the various companies, and no less than forty of them were by Rev. J. M. Gates."[43] Gates was not the only successful preacher; sermons by the Reverend J. C. Burnett on Meritt and Columbia sold well, while the two-part "Black Diamond Express to Hell" (Vocalion 1098) by the Reverend A. W. Nix was the most popular sermon record of the decade (fig. 97). Later Gates recorded a series of "secular" sermons – humorous moral lessons without singing, in which the preacher poked fun at the escapades of members of his "congregation," who often embarrassed him in return by accusing him of similar practices. Although the demand for recorded sermons with singing lessened toward the end of the decade, the religious records had a large impact.

As early as 1923, Black Swan and OKeh thought there might be a market for blues less sophisticated than the vaudeville variety. A Black Swan advertisement for Josie Miles's "Love Me in Your Old Time Way" read: "Have you ever heard the snatches of songs sung by Negro section hands on Southern railroads? Do you recall how their plaintive melodies struck a responsive chord in you? Generally termed blues, yet how strongly contrasted are these songs springing from the depths of the laborer's soul to the commonplace dance tunes that we are accustomed to call BLUES. LOVE ME IN YOUR OLD TIME WAY is in the vein of the laborer's songs."[44] Miles was a vaudeville singer, and her song was merely "in the vein of" the "songs springing from the depths of the laborer's soul." Black Swan did not use the urban jive talk employed by OKeh and Paramount; its approach was consistently refined, its impulse characteristically genteel. The record, released on the Black Swan label in 1923, a year after it was made, and re-issued on Paramount in 1924, when the latter company absorbed the former, evidently was successful, but it did not lead to imitations. In 1923, OKeh A & R director Ralph Peer took portable equipment to Atlanta, ostensibly to record hillbilly musician Fiddlin' John Carson. Atlanta's OKeh jobber, Polk Brockman, thought Carson's records would be successful locally. They were. But neither Peer nor Brockman predicted what happened next: Carson's record opened a hillbilly market as lucrative as the race market.[45] And though Peer had recorded Birmingham blues singer Louise Bogan on the Atlanta trip,[46] the idea of making field trips to record blues singers in southern cities was forgotten in the rush to capitalize on the new hillbilly market.

The downhome impulse was undoubtedly responsible for Paramount's promotion of Ma Rainey as a southern-styled singer. It was also responsible for the publicity surrounding that company's "discovery" of Papa Charlie Jackson – "the only man living who sings, self-accompanied, for Blues records" – who was introduced in a *Defender* ad-

FIGURE 97. *From the* Chicago Defender, *October 1, 1927*

vertisement as if he were a relic of a bygone era (fig. 98). Since his records sold well, he is a likely candidate to honor as the first downhome blues singer, but others have classified him as a vaudeville singer because he accompanied his songster's repertoire (which did include some blues) on a six-string banjo-guitar, which gave it an unmistakable minstrel-show sound.[47] Although he was a minstrel-show veteran, his downhome blues credentials are at least as good as those of some, such as Jim Jackson, who had the good fortune to record after Blind Lemon Jefferson.

What was different about Jefferson? Local record dealers in the South had been suggesting downhome singers for some time before Sam Price sent a letter to Paramount recommending Jefferson, who was already well known throughout Texas. A. C. Laibley, Paramount recording director, claimed that he found Jefferson on the streets of Dallas and late in 1925 invited him to Chicago.[48] The music of the vaudeville blues singers was close enough to Tin Pan Alley for the record companies to feel familiar with it; and the music of singers like Papa Charlie Jackson and Daddy Stovepipe was close enough to the common stock of folk and minstrel song shared, at the turn of the century, by Anglo- and Afro-Americans for the record companies to recognize *that*. The inescapable conclusion is that Jefferson's music confused them. Unsure at first what to do with the blind singer, Paramount had him record a spiritual under the pseudonym "Deacon L. J. Bates," but its release was delayed.[49] In March, 1926, he recorded four blues songs. For the first release, "Booster Blues" and "Dry Southern Blues" (Paramount 12347), Paramount introduced him in an April 8, 1926, *Defender* advertisement as "a real, old-fashioned Blues singer" singing "a real, old-fashioned Blues" (fig. 99). The point was emphasized in succeeding sentences, which called his songs "old-time tunes" and his guitar playing "in real Southern style." It is difficult to imagine a better word to describe Paramount's judgment of Jefferson's songs than the one they used continually in their publicity about him: *weird* (e.g., fig. 19). They could not understand his words; they had never heard anyone play the guitar as he did. Even his appearance must have been startling – a blind, black street-singer of enormous girth with tiny, steel-rimmed glasses perched on his nose. So striking was his appearance that the advertising illustrators forgot their rule of avoiding cartoon caricatures of the singer's likeness when it came to his advertisements (see figs. 123 and 124).

Yet Jefferson's downhome style was familiar to almost anyone from the Black Belt. His first record sold moderately well, but his second, "Got the Blues" and "Long Lonesome Blues" (Paramount 12354), became the best seller (transcrs. 31 and 32). Paramount's success with Jefferson led the other record companies to work the same vein, and they quickly sent scouts south looking for downhome blues talent. The naïveté of the companies' scouting behavior indicates unfamiliarity with the music; they sent their representative directly to Dallas, Jefferson's home city. Dallas pianist Alex Moore described

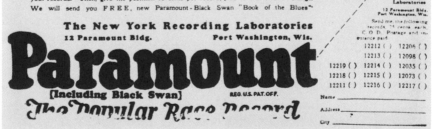

FIGURE 98. *This first advertisement for records by Papa Charlie Jackson appeared in the August 23, 1924,* Chicago Defender.

"Booster Blues"
by
Blind Lemon Jefferson

HERE'S a real, old-fashioned Blues by a real, old-fashioned Blues singer — Blind Lemon Jefferson from Dallas. This "Booster Blues", and "Dry Southern Blues" on the reverse side are two of Blind Lemon's old-time tunes. With his singing, he strums his guitar in real southern style — makes it talk, in fact. Be sure to get this Paramount Record No. 12347—at your dealer's, or send us coupon.

12347—Booster Blues and **Dry Southern Blues,** Blind Lemon Jefferson and His Guitar.

12338—Chain Gang Blues and **Wringing and Twisting Blues,** "Ma" Rainey with Her Georgia Jazz Band.

12335—I'm Going Where The Chilly Winds Don't Blow and **Texas Blues,** "Papa" Charlie Jackson.

12336—He Likes It Slow and **Black Bottom Hop,** Trixie Smith, accompanied by Fletcher Henderson's Orchestra.

〔12344—I'm Leaving Here Blues and **Trouble, Trouble〕
Blues,** Ida Cox, accompanied by Lovie Austin's Serenaders.

12337—When Your Man Is Going To Put You Down, "Coot" Grant, with Cornet and Piano Accompaniment and **Find Me At The Greasy Spoon,** "Coot" Grant and "Kid" Wesley Wilson with Fletcher Henderson's Orchestra.

12305—Mama, Don't You Think I Know and **Hot Papa Blues,** "Papa" Charlie Jackson.

12345—Shake That Thing and **Quit Knocking On My Door,** Viola Bartlette with piano accompaniment.

"I couldn't buy no ticket,
    I walked to the door;
My baby's left town,
    She ain't coming here no more."

Instrumentals

12340—Shake That Thing, Jimmie O'Bryant's Famous Original Washboard Band and **Pump Tillie,** Blythe's Sinful Five.

12330—My Man Rocks Me (for dancing) and **Chicago Skiffle,** Jimmie O'Bryant's Famous Original Washboard Band.

Spirituals

12342—Pharaoh's Army Got Drowned and **Great Jehovah,** Norfolk Jubilee Quartette.

12331—Tell Me, Where Are You Building and **When the Gates Swing Wide,** The C. A. Tindley Bible Class Gospel Singers.

12221—Jerusalem Morn and **Do You Call That Religion,** Sunset Four.

Send No Money!

If your dealer is out of the records you want, send us the coupon below. Pay postman 75¢ for each record plus sma'l C. O. D. fee when he delivers records. *We pay postage on shipments of two or more records.*

The New York
Recording Laboratories
  12 Paramount Bldg.
  Port Washington, Wis.

Send me the records checked
(✓) below, 75 cents.

12347 ( )	12344 ( )	12342 ( )
12338 ( )	12337 ( )	12331 ( )
12335 ( )	12305 ( )	12221 ( )
12336 ( )	12345 ( )	12346 ( )
	12339 ( )	

Name..............................

Address...........................

City...................State...........

Paramount
The Popular Race Record

FIGURE 99. *From the* Chicago Defender, *April 3, 1926*

this activity: "Specialty Records, OKeh, Vocalion, Decca Records, Columbia Records, all had talent scouts in Dallas . . . [they] were in and out of Dallas every 15 to 30 days. You can't imagine how they were, savaging [sic] up songs for recordings. Dallas was a noted town for piano players and guitarists, blues and boogiewise, good ones like Blind Lemon Jefferson, Lonnie Johnson."[50]

To take advantage of downhome talent, the larger record companies sent portable recording equipment to southern cities, while the smaller ones paid singers' traveling expenses to have them record in their northern studios.[51] Late in 1927 another downhome blues record paid off well when Jim Jackson, accompanying himself on guitar, sang "Jim Jackson's Kansas City Blues" (Vocalion 1144). By the end of the decade a few hundred downhome singers had made blues records. Those whose records fell flat were not invited back into the studios; those whose records sold well, or even moderately well, and who gave evidence of a large repertoire, were recalled for additional recording sessions. The new downhome blues releases were advertised heavily in the black press; although vaudeville singers and jazz ensembles continued to make successful recordings, most of the promotion went to downhome blues singers, preachers, and singing evangelists. In 1928, Leroy Carr and Scrapper Blackwell's "How Long – How Long Blues" (transcr. 14), a well-known song given Carr's easygoing vocal and piano treatment and backed by Blackwell's sophisticated single-string guitar work, inaugurated a successful piano-guitar accompaniment formula for blues records and launched the duo on a profitable recording career. In the same year, guitarist Tampa Red (Hudson Whittaker) and pianist "Georgia Tom" Dorsey recorded "It's Tight like That" (Vocalion 1228), a bawdy ragtime song. "It's Tight like That" and subsequent recordings by Tampa Red's Hokum Jug Band, had a house-rent party flavor with a decidedly downhome string-band instrumentation. Although some blues historians see degeneration caused by commercialism in the large number of bawdy records that followed, obscene and double-entendre lyrics had for many years been common in the country juke joints.

The first major period of downhome blues recording extended from 1926 until 1930. (The second occurred from 1947 until 1955.) Talent scouts secured primarily local and regional southern blues singers who had been entertaining in juke joints, in barrelhouses, and at suppers, picnics, and country dance parties. Most of these entertainers were songsters whose repertoires included many kinds of songs besides blues, but the scouts were looking for original blues songs. Many of the singers had just one recording session, in a makeshift studio in a southern city. Others, like Blind Blake, were so successful that they were invited to make records on a regular basis.

Race record sales fell as the decade drew to a close. Although about five hundred blues and gospel titles were released each year from 1927 until 1930, the number of copies of each record pressed declined sharply toward the end of that period.[52] The sales decline has been attributed to black poverty in the Depression,[53] but this explanation is insufficient, for the Depression came to the Black Belt farm country at least six years before the stock market crash of 1929.[54] Rather, as the industry retrenched it adopted several economy measures that worked against securing a continuing supply of down-home blues singers – measures that initiated a self-fulfilling prophecy. The expensive field trips were cut back severely. Professional singers with wide repertoires and practiced efficiency promised to be the most productive, as studios came to operate on assembly-line techniques, processing songs very quickly. Under these circumstances, for example, one take instead of two became normal procedure. As long as their records sold reasonably well – Carr and Blackwell, Tampa Red and Georgia Tom, Memphis Minnie and Kansas Joe were selling consistently in the early 1930s – it was foolish to take chances on unknown singers or to keep issuing records of established performers, like Blind Blake, whose sales figures suddenly dropped. Although the industry continued to issue down-home blues records, and although new singers like Big Bill Broonzy, Bumble Bee Slim (Amos Easton), and John Lee "Sonny Boy" Williamson established their reputations in the 1930s, the intense activity was over.

There was a redefinition of the downhome style, as the younger singers felt the influence of recordings and as jukeboxes began to displace live entertainment in the juke joints. Solo singers accompanying themselves on guitar seemed archaic, though some (like Blind Willie McTell) would continue to record, and others (like Robert Johnson, Tommy McClennan, and Robert Petway) would break into the race market. If the guitar had been the major downhome blues instrument in the recordings of the 1920s, the piano replaced it in the following decade. As Bessie Smith's generation of vaudeville blues singers aged, the featured spot they had held was taken over by the jazz band itself, and singers became attached to bands, instead of the reverse. There was a sharp decline in race titles issued, both in overall quantity and as a percentage of all records issued. But in the Black Belt, juke parties continued, and downhome musicians with portable instruments were still in demand to provide entertainment at them. When, after World War II, small record companies sprang up, breaking the major companies' virtual monopoly, they found plenty of black singers accompanying themselves with guitars. And some of the more successful ones, like Lightnin' Hopkins and John Lee Hooker, sounded very much like their counterparts twenty years earlier – after their electric guitars were unplugged by folk music enthusiasts.

The recording directors who authorized the late-1920s field trips which resulted in such an extraordinary collection of Afro- and Anglo-American music probably did not intend the preservation of a musical heritage. Yet it is unfair to imagine them as greedy exploiters, certain to cheat the artists and taint the music. Often their commercial considerations served the combined interests of obtaining quality performances, satisfying the artists, and pleasing the purchasing public. A closer look at the way they treated downhome blues singers will reveal their operating procedure and something of their values. There is no reason to believe they were anything but typical representatives of the predominantly white, middle-class, urbanizing, business-oriented America of their time.

Frank Walker, Columbia's recording director, recalled that his company's field trips were announced in advance by local newspapers and by Columbia record dealers.[55] Other companies followed the same practice. They believed, correctly, that good singers would be attracted by money and the prestige of making records.[56] Carl Martin affirmed that he learned of a Brunswick field trip to his hometown (Knoxville) in 1930 through "letters"[57] – by which he probably meant newspaper advertisements or handbills. Often local record dealers auditioned to attract, screen, and select singers in advance. Peg Leg Howell said, "The man from Columbia records found me there in Atlanta. A Mr. Brown – he worked for Columbia – he asked me to make a record for them. I was out serenading, playing on Decatur Street and he heard me playing and taken me up to his office and I played up there."[58] Other dealers arranged for skilled singers to travel to the home-city studios. Roosevelt Sykes recalled that "Jesse Johnson in St. Louis in 1929 . . . had a record shop there and he was looking for different artists and to take 'em to different places to record. So . . . I done a few tunes over for him so he seemed to like this tune – the '44 Blues.' . . . So he decided that [all my] numbers were all right and that they would go. So he asked me would I go over to New York with him. . . . So we goes to . . . the OKeh record company."[59]

Henry C. Speir owned a music store in Jackson, Mississippi, but traveled all over the South to find downhome blues talent. He arranged sessions for several record companies, including Columbia, OKeh, and Paramount. "With blues singers," wrote Gayle Dean Wardlow,

> he usually used an approach similar to the following: "I hear you're a good singer, how about singing some of your songs for me?" After the singer finished, he would tell him "You sound pretty good. You know, I make records; if you will keep practising and get your songs together real good and come to Jackson in a couple of days, I see that you get on records." If the singer balked at Speir's legality as a record scout, he would then tell the singer a long line of musicians he was responsible for recording. . . . When the singer showed up in Jackson he reimbursed him for his travel expenses and gave him a couple of extra dollars for spending money while going to a session.[60]

Of all the downhome blues singers Speir "discovered," in his estimation Patton ranked highest.[61]

Speir, and other major talent scouts and recording directors, must have used certain criteria to determine a singer's suitability. Though their standards are difficult to reconstruct, it appears that they wanted singers with a substantial repertoire of original material and a distinctive performance manner. Though these criteria seem obvious, they were sufficient to eliminate many local entertainers from consideration. Speir once met Ralph Peer at an audition for Victor and was struck by his inscrutability during the trials; Peer showed no emotion either during the performance or afterward, when he accepted or rejected the songs. Speir had no formal musical training; he simply relied on his musical taste. Unlike other scouts, he placed no weight on the prospective singer's popularity in his community. He observed that singers who were effective in person could lose their effectiveness on record. Perhaps he was thinking of Patton, whose clowning and antics could not be transferred to disc, although enough people were satisfied with the music to make his records sell moderately well. Speir admitted, however, that it was impossible to predict which singers would succeed.[62]

As the decade wore on, most industry scouts, who stood to profit from their charges' record sales, grew used to downhome blues and more confident that they could pick out the best singers. Still, they and the recording directors employed well-known recording artists as subsidiary talent scouts. Roosevelt Sykes said, "[The company director] wrote me a letter of introduction to different places that I would go out to in the countries. I had to have the letter because in certain places we'd go fellas be workin' in — you go in and ask them for an audition and the boss would think you come to steal the guy away. . . . [Sometimes I couldn't get a singer I wanted to come with me] but still I found some good talent."[63] Patton brought Willie Brown and Son House to Speir's attention, and Speir soon arranged a recording session for them.

The talent scout had to show the potentially successful blues singer some respect. Often he had to convince a reluctant plantation landlord to allow the singer to travel hundreds of miles to make a record, with no other guarantee than his word that he would return. W. R. Calaway of the American Record Corporation had to bail Charley Patton out of jail for his 1934 session.[64] Some scouts, like Speir, were genuinely fond of downhome blues. But the majority of industry figures thought the rubes laughable and their music decidedly inferior to vaudeville blues. They treated the singers like children, taking the care that adults take to keep children protected and ignorant. Polk Brockman, Atlanta's OKeh jobber and a general talent scout, believed that the field trips were successful enterprises because singers flocked like sheep to the makeshift studios for the chance to make a record.[65] Brockman probably had in mind black singers as well as hillbilly singers. Frank Walker expressed the following opinion of guitar-evangelist Washington Phillips's "dulceola," surely one of the most ethereal instruments to be heard on race records: "He had no name for it; it was something he had made himself. Nobody on earth could use it except him. Nobody would want to, I don't think."[66] Written in a Gennett ledger beside an unissued hillbilly title were words to this effect: "too good for this kind of music."[67] Downhome blues fared little better in their estimation.

But if the record companies did not think highly of downhome blues, they had to take it seriously, because it accounted for a significant portion of record sales and profit. Sale of more than 5,000 copies of a record made money for the company, and selling the masters to dime-store labels (just as publishing houses today sell paperback rights) for a flat fee increased their profit.[68] In addition, a royalty of two cents per record sold went to the copyright holder.[69] Peg Leg Howell said he received $50 for his first record ($25 per side) and an additional royalty check twice a year.[70] But few downhome blues singers were given copyrights to their material, although they were given authorship credit on the record label. They were paid traveling expenses and a lump sum for each song accepted by the company, in exchange for which they signed over the copyright to the company's music-publishing agent. Certainly, the musicians did not grow rich from such arrangements. Booker White, whose memories are often exaggerated, reported being paid $240 for eight sides he made for Victor in 1930; in fact, he recorded fourteen sides, four of which were accepted and issued.[71] Son House told John Fahey that A. C. Laibley promised him $15 per side; he told Al Wilson that he got $40 for the nine sides Paramount accepted in 1930.[72] Mississippi John Hurt was assured in a letter from OKeh recording director T. G. Rockwell that he would be paid traveling expenses and $20 per accepted side; six weeks later he recorded twelve sides in New York, ten of which were issued.[73] Jaybird Coleman claimed he was not paid for a 1926 Gennett session in Birmingham. Actually, he had four sessions there for Gennett, but in 1927. Nothing was accepted from Coleman's first session; since he would not have been paid for it, this is probably the one he had in mind (whether he was paid for the other three, I do not know).[74] Apparently, the fees paid to hillbilly singers were higher. Blind Alfred Reed, for instance, said the standard was $50 per selection plus traveling and hotel expenses.[75] The contrast with vaudeville blues was even more striking. Bessie Smith received $125 per song at first; in 1924, when her records were selling very well, she was getting $200 per song.[76]

It would be easy to conclude that the record industry exploited downhome blues singers by denying them artist royalties, stealing composer copyrights, and paying them a pittance for their talent. Against this, it should be pointed out that sales income from most downhome blues records was insufficient to meet the expense of their recording, manufacture, and distribution. The company was not required to pay the artists any flat fee for their services. By trading a lump sum for copyrights and artist royalties, the singers were assured of immediate cash, no matter how badly their records performed on the market. Considering the difficulties of a royalty arrangement for downhome singers

– bookkeeping, informing the record company of new addresses, the possibility of being cheated when the royalty checks were cashed – it is no wonder that singers as well as company men preferred the lump-sum cash arrangement.[77] The industry hoped that income from best-selling records would cover losses on poor sellers, finance the search for new talent, and pay its own salaries. The result was that singers who turned out a string of hit songs (like Blind Lemon Jefferson and Blind Blake) were denied a large share of the profits.

Once the singers were in the recording studio, it was to everyone's advantage that they perform at their best. Son House said that he and other musicians he knew were "high as a Georgia pine" when making records, and that they received a drink after each take. A session lasted from about 9:30 in the morning until one o'clock in the afternoon. Two microphones – one for the voice and one for the instrument – were used to record the singer.[78] Skip James confirmed the two-microphone arrangement, saying that when he played piano, the engineer placed a third microphone near his feet.[79] In "Hot Dogs" (Paramount 12493), Blind Lemon Jefferson's feet were not only given a microphone but also credited on the record label: "Blind Lemon Jefferson and His Feet" (or "Foot," on some labels!).[80] James also recalled being well "lickered up" for his sessions.[81] Invariably, the recording engineer signaled the singer with a blinking red light that the end of his allotted three minutes was drawing near. After his performance, the singer settled back with his drink and listened to the playback while the recording engineer asked his opinion of it.[82] Ordinarily, no more than two takes of any one song were recorded at a single session. If the song held promise but the takes were unsatisfactory, the artist was asked to practice and to return the following day to try again.

In their efforts to obtain the best possible performances, it is clear that the companies tried to recreate, in the studio, something of a live-performance atmosphere to help the singers overcome their nervousness. A few downhome blues records have encouraging chatter from background "commentors" brought along as accompanists to fill the role of a responsive audience. But sometimes the artists resisted what they perceived as paternalism from company men who knew little about the music. Bo Carter recalled: "Tell ya, we was the Mississippi Sheiks and when we went to make records in Jackson, Mississippi, the feller wanted to show us how to stop and start the records. Try to tell us when we got to begin and how we got to end. And you know . . . I started *not* to make 'em 'cause he wasn't no musicianer, so how could he tell *me* how to stop and start the song? We was the Sheiks, Mississippi Sheiks and you know we was famous."[83] Big Bill Broonzy's recollections of his 1927 and 1928 sessions for Paramount more typically describe an ordinary studio session, except that he read lyrics: "They had my head in a horn of some kind and I had to pull my head out of the horn to read the words and back in it to sing. And they had [John] Thomas put on a pillar about two feet high and they kept on telling us to play like we would if we was at home or at a party, and they kept on telling us to relax and giving us moonshine whiskey to drink – and I got drunk."[84]

It is hard to estimate the extent to which the companies succeeded in creating a true performance atmosphere, and harder still to determine the degree of freedom the singers felt – or were allowed – to sing the songs they regularly performed live to a black audience. Art Satherley, an English immigrant who supervised many vaudeville and downhome blues recordings for Paramount, recalled his approach to the musicians in the studio:

> I didn't just say, "Sing this and go out and have a drink somewhere." I spent my time in that studio getting them ready for the people of the world. . . . When I spoke to those Negroes, I would talk to them, I would tell them something about my background as an immigrant. I would tell them what we had to expect. Then when I found that I had these Negroes in a feeling, I would ask, "Before we sing this spiritual . . . which one of you have lost a loved one in the last year or so?" And one would step forward. Then I would say to the fellow that had some preaching experience, "Just say a little short prayer before we start preaching." This was not an act on my part. It was the simplicity of a simplicity to be an honest man, to give them what they wanted back. And the only way to get it back was to get what they felt in their souls. How many recording men know that? . . . It's all a study. You just don't go in like animals and talk to people, whether they're white, black, pink, or any color. You just have to know their life a little bit, and they have to know that you're not going to hurt them, too.[85]

I do not know what Satherley said to downhome blues singers; perhaps he asked them to think of someone they loved who had left them.

It is difficult to know how free from constraints the singers felt. I asked Son House, "Did you feel that there were certain things that you *couldn't* sing about that you might sing back home because, well, they just shouldn't be put on record?" He answered, "Well, we got to the place once, there, we kind of, some of us, we was thinkin' like you was thinkin' just then, but a little later on, after then, then these [company men] tell us, say, oh, then, that don't make no, go on, say it, do what, say what you want, and then they told us we didn't [have to worry]."[86] Since we had just been talking about blues singers recording lyrics which contained humorous sexual metaphors, House probably had these in mind. Whether or not his sense of propriety was the reason, House's lyrics have generally been free from sexual metaphors.[87] It is difficult to believe that the record companies were unaware of the sexual metaphors since their advertising shows they knew what the lyrics meant (see chap. 7). In "My Black Mama," part 1 (transcr. 34), House sang, "Well you see my milkcow tell her t' hurry home / I ain't had no milk since that cow been gone." H. C. Speir denied knowing about a "nature code" which translated this line to mean that the narrator had not had intercourse since his lover had left.[88] But I believe Speir was the exception, not the rule.

I have already discussed the possibility of racial protest codes in which the "mistreater" stood for the white man. Lacking sufficient evidence, it is difficult to affirm that the codes existed. I wanted to ask House whether he had ever censored racial protest lyrics in the recording studio, but I thought I had not developed sufficient rapport for such a sensitive question. His hesitancy in answering the general probe suggested that he was already cautious. However, I may have mistaken fatigue for caution, and I regret not questioning him further, for he had already discussed quite openly the irregular procedures by which he and his friends were thrown into and released from jail and made to owe the landlord an imaginary fine. I did ask Lazy Bill Lucas, the blues singer to whom this book is dedicated, if he knew of racial protest in blues lyrics, direct or in code. I had known Bill for four years, playing in his band for two of them, when I brought up the subject. He said he had never known of a racial protest code in blues songs, for blues was about the troubles men and women have getting along. But he affirmed overt and encoded protest in conversation, stories, sayings, and folksongs other than blues.

It is difficult to escape the conclusion that recording downhome blues was a little bizarre. The industry was forced to adopt an operating procedure inconsistent with its values. The music was unfamiliar, seemed archaic, probably was worthless; yet it sold millions of records. Singers were carefully scouted and scrupulously auditioned; but it was impossible to predict those who would be successful. The musicians were black, inscrutable, presumably inferior; yet their performances had to be coaxed in the recording studios, for company profits ultimately depended on them. Given these ponderables, the industry dealt with the singers as carefully as it knew how – as the guardian of a trust might treat an underage ward, or as a scientist might examine moon rocks brought back from a mechanical space probe.

7 THE CULTURAL SIGNIFICANCE OF RACE RECORD ADVERTISEMENTS

Of the several problems the recording industry faced with race records, perhaps the most difficult was how to advertise them in the black press. Because new records were released every week, sales had always depended heavily on advertising. The continuously changing product was not a great burden to the companies' advertising departments (or the agencies to which they sometimes farmed work out), as long as they used prepared mats into which the week's new releases and a few from the backlist could

Versions of this chapter were read at a colloquium in American Studies at Hobart and William Smith Colleges in March, 1972, before the Folklore and Mythology Group at Harvard University on November 14, 1973, and before the Colloquium in the History of American Civilization at Brandeis University on October 10, 1974. I am grateful for comments and suggestions from those audiences.

be placed. But here were a music and a consumer the industry did not wholly understand. Though company executives were delighted with the prospect of an eager community of black consumers, the enthusiastic response had come as a surprise; a poorly designed advertising campaign now would fail to sustain and develop the market. Should they advertise the singers or emphasize the songs? Perhaps they should merely illustrate the phonographs and relegate information about new releases to a listing of titles. The American entertainment industry, in which the record companies played a large part, had done as much as any institution – if not more – to keep the plantation stereotype before the general public. Anyone who bothered to read what the black leaders said knew that they resented it. But popular novelty music had almost always received humorous illustration. As far as the record companies could observe, rank-and-file black people laughed at the minstrel shows and plantation stereotypes as heartily as anyone else. After all, didn't blacks don blackface and play their minstrel shows to black audiences as well as white?

The record companies were among the first white American institutions to try to sell black Americans a product they could refuse to buy. Their advertising, while not surprisingly incorporating deep-seated racism, also revealed careful attempts to understand black people and their music. It exhibited the ambivalent feelings, ambiguous symbols, and contradictory activities which white Americans continue until this day. Because advertising is (and was recognized then to be) an attempt to create and sustain a community of consumers based upon an image of who they are and who they should like to become,[1] advertisements are a particularly rich source of information about how people are perceived and the directions in which they are pushed. A simple example will illustrate. In the black press during the 1920s, only the cosmetic advertisements were produced on as large a scale as those for race records. They promised either a lighter complexion or straighter hair. Sometimes the illustrations were crude but unintentionally revealing. The skin lightener Bleach-O, for example, pictured a smudged "before" face and a blank "after" face. It is not surprising that the woman in the Nadinola Bleaching Cream advertisement (fig. 100) has a light complexion, presumably the result of applying the ointment; her straight hair, thin lips, and Roman nose suggest the metamorphosis from black to white that the advertisers wanted the consumer to perceive. In the cosmetic ads the advertisers did not, of course, have to create a need; the circumstances of American life had seen to that. But race records were something new, and no specific black need for them was apparent.

Illustrating race record advertisements with cartoons – what the industry settled on – developed a set of variations on the black stereotype which never, even in the cover illustrations for minstrel sheet music, had been so elaborately drawn. It seemed that a cartoon was available to fit any situation a record's title suggested. The singers themselves ordinarily escaped caricature; instead, they were praised, and usually paid the

Bleach
Your Skin This Quick, Sure Way

NOW science has found an amazing new way to whiten your skin more quickly, safely, surely! In Nadinola are secretly combined the fastest, most powerful skin-whitening ingredients known. It never fails. The minute you apply this marvelous super-bleach, it begins to lighten your skin—give you new beauty.

You will be amazed how fast Nadinola works. Almost overnight you will note the change. Instant improvement, then day by day fresh beauty, new loveliness, until in a very short time you have the light fair skin everybody admires.

And Nadinola does more —it banishes pimples, closes enlarged pores, clears up eruptions, refines the texture, removes oiliness —without fail or your money back. Remember, Nadinola *always* gets results. Positive, written, money-back guarantee (together with simple directions) in every package.

Begin this very night—learn the real power of beauty—the power to attract and hold men who admire a fair light skin. At all drug stores and toilet counters, 50c. Extra large, save-money size, $1. If you cannot buy it where you live, send us 50c or $1 and we will promptly send it, postpaid, together with dainty gift sample box of Nadine Face Powder and free beauty booklet. Address Dept. D, National Toilet Company, Paris, Tenn., U. S. A.

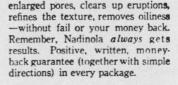

Use these Nadine Beauty Aids, too:
Nadine Face Powder, 50c; Rouge, 25c and 50c;
Vanishing Cream, 50c; Soap, 25c.

Nadinola Bleaching Cream

FIGURE 100. *From the* Chicago Defender, *April 30, 1927*

compliment of a photographic insert. Moreover, black consultants (such as Paramount's race series recording director, Mayo Williams) helped the advertising copywriters describe the singer and his song in a fitting vernacular: urban jive talk.

Ronald C. Foreman, Jr., claims that the overwhelming number and variety of race record ads in the black press indicate accommodation of the buyers.[2] Correct as far as it goes, Foreman's thesis does not touch on the industry's increasing anxiety toward the stylish city black man, or the strategy it used to befriend him and, at the same time, to avoid facing his real image. Considering him a member of a folk society, the industry concentrated its advertisements after 1926 on the newly recorded, but old-fashioned, forms: downhome blues, sermons, and spirituals. Illustrations of dignified quartets or old-time baptisms (fig. 101), however elaborate and well executed, showed black people in traditionally safe activity. By treating downhome blues as a kind of folk music, the industry put the black in his place: back in time and far away in the country, or newly arrived and in wonder at the city. A close look at the history of the advertisements and at the climate of opinion regarding black Americans, along with a knowledge of recording and sales trends (as discussed in chap. 6), will support this hypothesis.

Among white Americans – record industry officials were no exception – there was perhaps more anti-black feeling during the twenties than during any other decade since Reconstruction. The more emotional whites supported the powerfully resurgent Ku Klux Klan, while the intellectuals relied upon scientific support for their racism. The 1924 Immigration Act distinguished even among whites, establishing quotas based on national origins. Blacks were thought inferior, intellectually and morally; anyone questioning this could be shown the eleventh, twelfth, or thirteenth edition of the prestigious *Encyclopaedia Britannica.* The entry "Negro," written by the U.S. Census Bureau's chief statistician, who was also a professor of social science at Cornell University, reads in part:

> Mentally the negro is inferior to the white. The remark of F. Manetta, made after a long study of the negro in America, may be taken as generally true of the whole race: "the negro children were sharp, intelligent, and full of vivacity, but on approaching the adult period a gradual change set in. The intellect seemed to become clouded, animation giving place to a sort of lethargy, briskness yielding to indolence. We must necessarily suppose that the development of negro and white proceeds on different lines. With the latter the volume of the brain grows with the expansion of the brainpan, in the former the growth of the brain is on the contrary arrested by the premature closing of the cranial sutures and the lateral pressure on the frontal bone." This explanation is reasonable . . . but evidence is lacking . . . and the arrest or even deterioration in mental development is no doubt due to the

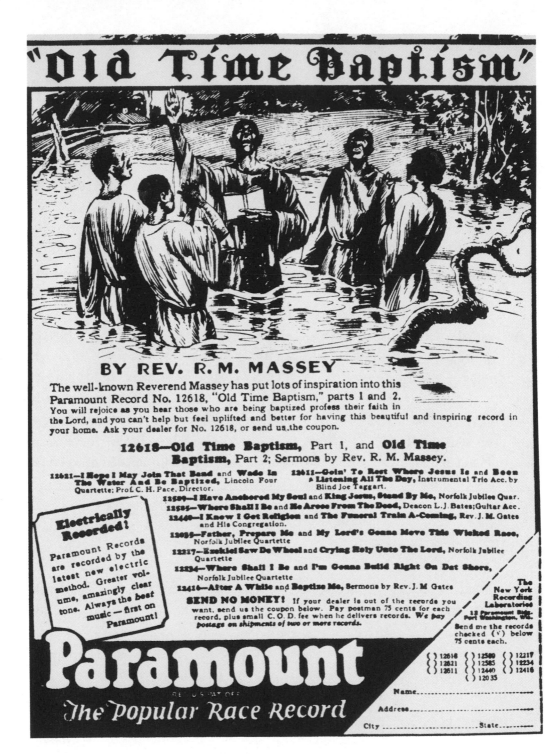

FIGURE 101. *From the* Chicago Defender, *May 12, 1928*

fact that after puberty sexual matters take the first place in the negro's life and thoughts. . . .

The mental constitution of the negro is very similar to that of a child, normally good-natured and cheerful, but subject to sudden fits of emotion and passion during which he is capable of performing acts of singular atrocity.

The basic elements of the plantation stereotype are present in the *Britannica* entry, disguised, dignified, and transformed into objective reality. In the common stereotype – disturbingly easy to construct out of one's head today – the black person was lazy, superstitious, friendly, flamboyant, gullible, cunning (but easily seen through), impressionable, loyal as a dog, and irresponsible. The other side of the stereotype emphasized the savage underneath the smile. Sexually promiscuous, and a casual adulterer, the black man was a menace to white women. As the *Britannica* put it, he was "capable of performing acts of singular atrocity" – perhaps a cannibal.[3] To chart the moral progress of blacks in America, the author of the *Britannica* entry, Walter Francis Wilcox, cited a decline, from 1890 to 1904, in the per capita number of blacks in prison. One might just as well argue that black moral progress is indicated by a decrease in the number of lynchings.

The dual stereotype – carefree on the outside, cannibal underneath – is illustrated in a Columbia Records catalog supplement dated September, 1920 (just before the race record era). The drawing (fig. 102) depicts a happy crew of black dancers and a banjo player, all dressed in farm garb. The insert shows a solemn, bearded Arab outside a tent playing a lyre, which the illustrator mistakenly took to be an ancestor of the *bania*, from which the banjo is commonly thought to have derived. The copy praises the banjo's "barbaric vigor." It places the instrument in the hands of "dark-faced negroes, with shining teeth and eyes, . . . under the stars over Southern leeves [*sic*]" and, originally, in the hands of "ancient nomadic Arabs," who had supposedly given a prototype of the *bania* to Senegambian "savages," who, in turn, presumably brought the banjo to America. Among the banjo records listed are "Nigger Love a Watermelon, Ha! Ha! Ha!" and "Uncle Tom." If this is not an illustration of the black plantation stereotype, I do not know what is.

Visual representations of the black stereotype were, of course, well established and widespread. A drawing by "WLS" entitled *The Levee. – I Done Tole Ye All about Dat, Now"* in the December, 1873, *Scribner's Monthly* (fig. 103) depicts storytelling roustabouts; the shoeless man at the left sports a knife in his belt. The buffoon side of the "coon" stereotpye also received frequent illustration. E. W. Kemble, well known for his drawings of blacks, was singled out in an article on American caricature which appeared in the December, 1889, *Scribner's Magazine*. His *Thompson Street Poker Club* (fig. 104) is one of many drawings showing black people in what were thought to be humorously

Music of the Banjo

THE music of the banjo has a fascination peculiarly its own. There is a barbaric vigor to its ringing tone and drumlike rhythm which carries us away from the staid music room of our home out under the stars over Southern leeves where groups of dark-faced negroes, with shining teeth and eyes, sing plantation melodies to the strumming strings; back to the Senegambian savages with their **bania,** the parent of our American banjo; still further back to ancient nomadic Arabs who brought their stringed instruments to the negroes of Western Africa centuries ago.

In all the developments of the banjo, since the negro first brought it to this country, it has never lost its spell. There are pages of banjo records in the Columbia Catalog, music of all kinds, accompaniment and solo. No instrument records more perfectly. Your Musical Library is only complete when you have selected some of the banjo gems listed.

Some Columbia Banjo Records

I WANT TO GO BACK TO MICHIGAN. Medley Fox-trot. Van Eps' Banjo Orchestra.
SOUP TO NUTS. One-step. Van Eps' Banjo Orchestra. — A1629 / 10-inch / $1.00

OH, BOYS CARRY ME 'LONG. Harry C. Browne.
L'IL LIZA JANE. Harry C. Browne and Peerless Quartette. Banjo and piano accompaniment. — A2622 / 10-inch / $1.00

OLD DAN TUCKER. Harry C. Browne.
NIGGER LOVE A WATERMELON, HA! HA! HA! Harry C. Browne. Banjo and Orchestra accompaniment. — A1999 / 10-inch / $1.00

UNCLE TOM. One-step. Vess Ossman's Banjo Orchestra.
BENEATH A BALCONY. Fox-trot. Vess Ossman's Banjo Orchestra. — A2113 / 10-inch / $1.00

MY HAWAIIAN SUNSHINE. Fox-trot. Vess Ossman's Banjo Orchestra.
YOU'LL ALWAYS BE THE SAME SWEET BABY. Vess Ossman's Banjo Orchestra. — A5928 / 12-inch / $1.25

FIGURE 102. *From a Columbia catalog supplement, September, 1920. Courtesy of the John Edwards Memorial Foundation, UCLA.*

FIGURE 103. The Levee. - "I Done Tole Ye All about Dat, Now." *From* Scribner's Monthly, *December, 1873, p. 134.*

FIGURE 104. The Thompson Street Poker Club - "Whad yo' got?" *From* Scribner's Magazine *6 (1889), 736.*

incorrect imitations of white activities; note, for example, the hat used as a spittoon. Black buffoons and savages appeared frequently in the cover illustrations for sheet music containing minstrel songs. Lest it be thought that illustrators were incapable of drawing dignified pictures of black people, I offer *A Negro Policeman* (fig. 105) from the December, 1873, issue of *Scribner's Monthly*. Illustrators certainly knew the difference between draftsmanship and caricature. But the frequency with which they drew caricatures strengthened the stereotypes in the minds of white Americans, stereotypes which were reinforced by minstrel shows and popular literature. "Negro novelty" record advertisements like the Columbia banjo ad (fig. 102) continued the tradition.

Since the industry wanted black people to purchase records, it felt the stereotypical illustrations might have to be abandoned. Guessing, at first, that these would be offensive, the industry followed the pattern of the opera ads in the earliest race record illustrations, though the latter were not so elaborately drawn. In 1921, a simple photograph or sketch of the singer, an announcement of the song titles, and brief copy (in plain English) praising the singer made up the small, straightforward ad. By this time the industry had abandoned grand sketches of the concert stage for photographs which allowed the reader to see the "human side" of the opera singers.[4] Clearly, the earliest advertisements for black records were meant to be similarly dignified.

But in January, 1922, OKeh announced that its dealers' window displays would henceforth be "based on the idea that the thing people like best is entertainment, and that folks love to laugh." Rejecting the "pretty pictures that don't make sales," they promised to illustrate new black recordings in "cartoon style, because of the proven success of our newspaper advertising, which is done in cartoon style throughout."[5] In some ways this was a natural turn, for white popular music and novelty records had often been illustrated, in advertisements or on sheet music covers, with "comic cartoons, depending on the numbers featured. . . . [When a] popular jazz came to the front, it was embellished in its presentation by extravagant pictures, done in the spirit of the funny sheets."[6]

It is nonetheless unlikely that poor record sales prompted the switch to illustrations which the industry – soon following OKeh's lead – felt were more appropriate to the music. For vaudeville blues, the cartoons caricatured the song's title, while the singer sometimes was illustrated in a photograph; the copy usually was couched in jive talk. The "lonesome mamma" in an OKeh ad from the August 19, 1922, *Chicago Defender* (fig. 106), with her bandanna kerchief, polka-dot dress, squat shape, and tearful blackface countenance is, of course, a representation of the stock stage "mammy." Indeed, the double *m* in *mamma* underscores the resemblance. But the "wailing, moaning saxophone" was not intended to make the listener cry like the lonesome mama; instead, he was supposed to "almost get up and shout" and dance to "the best toe-tickler since 'Muscle Shoals Blues.'" In short, the copy told the reader to take the illustration as a joke. Still, there

FIGURE 105. A Negro Policeman. *From* Scribner's Monthly, *December, 1873.*

FIGURE 106. *From the* Chicago Defender, *August 19, 1922*

are uncertainties worth pointing out, distinctions worth making. The cartoon illustrates the instrumental version of "Lonesome Mamma Blues" by "Markels' Orchestra," not Mamie Smith's vocal alternative. Further division shows up in the description of the singers: Mamie Smith is listed as a "popular colored singer," whereas Lizzie Miles, also a black vocalist, is billed merely as a "contralto with orchestra." (Since Miles was one of the more elocution-conscious vaudeville blues singers, the distinction is perfectly sensible.) Uncertainty over what to call the records is evident. The OKeh tag, soon to become "OKeh Race Records" for the 8000 series, is here simply "OKeh – The Record of Quality," with the qualifier that "the latest OKeh list contains 68 records by race artists."

Early advertising copy came to take on more and more of the vernacular in that section which described the sound of the record illustrated. The ad in the December 1, 1923, *Defender* for Ida Cox's version of "I've Got the Blues for Rampart Street" (fig. 107) describes it as a "moanin' low-down" and promises that the sound will take the listener back to New Orleans. Misspellings of artists' names were not uncommon; thus Tommy Ladnier becomes "Ladiner." On the reverse side of the record Lovie Austin "tickles the ivories" accompanying "those slippery Chattanooga Blues." Ida Cox is given a complimentary drawing in a stage dress, and the illustration depicts the elegance of fast life on Rampart Street.

A July 19, 1924, *Defender* advertisement for Bessie Smith's "Hateful Blues" (fig. 108) illustrates some of the extremes to which copywriters took language in their attempts at humor. "Having a phonograph without these records is like having pork chops without gravy – Yes, indeed!" tops the recent-release list. Smith is given a photo with a crown on her head, befitting her title, "Empress of the Blues." The copy identifies her as the "I" of the song, apparently serious in her hatred; the illustration shows a woman swinging a cleaver as a man scoots away. The listener is invited to laugh and be entertained, through a sequence of unbearable puns such as "Every note is a hate note. No quarter for anybody." There were thoughtful aspects to the copy as well; the black consultants worked hard, supplying such idiomatic phrases as "commence to start now" to reflect black English.

But if the idea simply was entertainment, it also held a deeper meaning. The copywriters were bold in their use of the vernacular. Advertising manuals agreed that slang usually was misplaced in advertisements. One adviser wrote:

> There are no clearly defined separations of the castes among words, any more than there are among people in this country. The difference between the bottom and the top of the social order is wide and clearly evident, but the intermediate stages blend imperceptibly without definite lines of demarcation. At the bottom of the scale is slang, particularly the slang of the underworld, the race track, and the prize ring. Such words as *gat, tout, con, simp, boob, spiel,* and *lobbygow* would hardly be admitted to any kind of advertising copy. Slang words and phrases of a less objectionable sort have been used by a few daring advertisers.[7]

For the significance of this kind of advertising, we may turn to a popular textbook of the 1920s, *Introduction to Advertising,* in its revised 1935 form. By 1935, the authors, responding to the increasing use of the vernacular, had concluded that "slang, when skillfully

FIGURE 107. *From the* Chicago Defender, *December 1, 1923*

FIGURE 108. *From the* Chicago Defender, *July 19, 1924*

Race Record Advertisements 231

employed, adds a touch of clean humor to the copy. . . . there are degrees of slanginess, however, and slang, if used at all, should be of the milder sort, and never so extreme that it might seem offensive or vulgar. It must be entirely appropriate to the article in connection with which it is used; otherwise it becomes a violation of both good taste and good salesmanship."[8] What they meant by "appropriate" can be derived from an earlier directive regarding the writing of advertising copy, where the student is advised that "style should be suited in language and plan of attack to the intelligence, the station in life, and the mental attitude of the readers."[9] Certainly the cartoons in the race record ads were meant to appeal to people in a stage of arrested development – the children so thoroughly described by the *Encyclopaedia Britannica*.

But the issue of vernacular is more complex; its appeal cannot be written off by suggesting that its vigorous humor was unmatched anywhere in the *Defender* except in the children's "Defender Junior" section, containing the comics. As the decade progressed, more vaudeville blues singers were recorded; as sales increased, the advertisements became larger and more elaborate, while the slang grew increasingly insistent. In 1925, for example, Columbia ran twelve full-page displays in the *Defender*. The full-page OKeh ad for Sara Martin and her jug band which appeared in the January 10, 1925, *Defender* (fig. 109) sums up many characteristics of the vaudeville blues advertisements. The design is bold and well balanced, dynamic and forceful; a model layout, it is the equal of the best contemporary advertising design. Unquestionably, the designers considered the constantly changing illustrations a challenge to their ingenuity. The drawings of the singer and her band are complimentary; the band is portrayed not as rubes dressed in work clothes, but as young men in formal musicians' attire, while Martin is elegantly gowned and jeweled. Yet a closer look reveals some potentially conflicting aspects, and the result, in retrospect, is ambiguous. The musicians are not only dressed alike, they look identical – they have the same heads, the same facial features. Even with what may have been the best of intentions, the illustrators were unable to break free from the "blacks look alike" stereotype. If an artist does not draw an individual, it is because he does not perceive one. Moreover, the slick jive talk has a shrill tone, an overeagerness to please, as it mixes urbane vernacular with downhome images:

YES, SIR, Sara Martin has gone and got herself a real, genuine, honest-to-goodness Jug Band. What's a Jug Band? Why, that's some mean moanin' papas blowin' the sweetest molasses coated buzzin' out of a regular jug that you've ever heard. For these papas parade their stuff right over the old home plat every time. And them's the truest true words that were ever sounded. There's no denyin' the harmony that these jugs pour forth. It's got a kick that sure is as powerful as the most powerful corn liquor. Move your doggies right down to your OKeh man's

FIGURE 109. *From the* Chicago Defender, *January 10, 1925*

place right quick and have him wrap up OKeh No. 8176. It's the biggest sample of gloom destroyer that's ever been put on one record. Yes, sir, it's an OKeh.

Take a good look at those boys tootin' the blues. And when they pour all their good nature into those jugs, it sure comes out hot. They're there, that's that. And you'll find every OKeh Record the same. Take your pick. They're all hot.

The shrill note and the zeal to please suggest nervousness, perhaps a need to share a joke with the black reader – and a need for the temporary friendship a shared laugh brings.

Not all titles lent themselves to plantation stereotype cartoons. And those cartoons were ill suited for the increasingly urban-centered lyrics of vaudeville blues songs. That sophisticated city black at whom the jive talk was aimed suddenly appeared threatening. Walking stylishly down the street, appearing to have all the money and women he wanted, he made a mockery of the American dream by reaping and cheapening its reward. The trouble was that he had the prize without seeming to have worked hard for it. The work ethic told the believer to keep plugging, but it did not tell him that his object would remain virtuous and innocent only so long as he chased it. When she is captured, the golden girl becomes a woman. Like his white Jazz Age counterpart, the city black was hated and envied and secretly admired. Of course, the stylish urban black man was as much a stereotype as the plantation darky; perhaps he suited *his* style to the intelligence, the station in life, and the mental attitude of the whites. His was a stereotype that was difficult to live against, and remains so. The white-owned and white-operated record companies had to confront it visually; they could not come to terms with it. Whenever they could not avoid illustrating the sporty black city-dweller, they did one of two things: they caricatured him as an emasculated inhabitant of the imaginary Darktown, or, if he was caught in some dignified activity, they drew white figures in the advertisements.

The generally accepted explanation for the coming of recorded downhome blues is this: the clamor of listeners for "real" blues in the 1920s pushed record companies into recording the older style, and the sales success of Blind Lemon Jefferson's records ensured that the companies would devote their efforts in the latter part of the decade to finding and recording other downhome blues singers, who might even be more successful. Samuel Charters, for instance, wrote:

The slick blues songs and the stylish accompaniments seemed to have less and less relationship to the music still being sung in the South. . . . The audience that was buying blues records was to turn the record companies more and more to the blues of the rural South. . . .

As the companies began to reach a larger and larger rural market, they realized that the most popular blues singers in the South were not the girls who were making endless records of city blues, but local singers, singing the country blues.[10]

Most of today's downhome blues enthusiasts have not questioned this agreeable hypothesis. But record sales, as far as we know them, do not bear it out. Collectors canvassing for race records in the homes of southern blacks find that Bessie Smith's records were as highly regarded as Blind Lemon Jefferson's, that vaudeville blues records are plentiful, and that downhome blues records are rare. Dan Mahony's discographical booklet on the Columbia race series shows that anticipated sales figures for vaudeville blues records remained generally higher, throughout the decade, than the figures for downhome blues records.[11] The hypothesis of a call for downhome blues from record dealers and mail-order customers is partially correct.[12] And it is true that the industry experimented with different kinds of race material and followed up strongly that which sold well. But the theory does not sufficiently account for the activities of the industry and for the enthusiasm with which they pursued the older forms: spirituals, sermons, and downhome blues.

The arrival of downhome blues records is best explained by the congruence, on the one hand, of the industry's desire not to confront the image of the slick city black and, on the other, of the climate of opinion which led, in 1923, to the opening of a market for hillbilly records – that cluster of ideas which locates virtue in a simpler life closer to nature, back in time, on a farm or in the mountains. The music growing out of this folk-like existence must be simple, substantial, untainted. In an oft-repeated speech which caught and shaped the mood of the times, a longing for "normalcy" after World War I, Warren Harding proclaimed in his election campaign of 1920: "What is the greatest thing in life, my countrymen? Happiness. And there is more happiness in the American village than in any other place on the face of the earth."[13] Despite the growing sophistication of the Jazz Age, American voters four years later chose Calvin Coolidge, whose Vermont upbringing and personality "typified the virtues which were celebrated on ceremonial occasions as the unfailing sources of prosperity and accumulation: thrift, prudence, and simplicity."[14] And four years after that, they elected Herbert Hoover by an overwhelming majority over liberal, anti-Prohibition New Yorker Al Smith. The Jazz Age was as dislocating, as unsettling, as the music which gave it its name; a fear and a feeling of moral disintegration, of palpable evil, moved into the consciousness of many adult Americans. Thousands of stories, some printed and illustrated, detailed the horrors of city life, the menacing music that threatened America's youth. At the center of the music, of course, was the newly migrated city black pressing visibly for his place in the promised land. No wonder the climate was right for black-baiting; no wonder the time was right to recall that the simple life of rural virtue had, after all, been responsible for America's greatness. While the Jazz Age was taking the country to hell and damnation, it was time to get off that appropriately titled Black Diamond Express, derail it if possible, and set the nation back on the right track, which presumably meant spreading the gospel of democracy and the virtues of capitalism based on a golden rule somehow inverted to laissez-faire.

In the confusion of values, the ideals of Jeffersonian America were not, of course, new; they had received expression in the nation before it had become one. Indeed, explorers' accounts had begun the myth of the bounty of nature in America, but there had to be a European audience receptive to that idea if colonization – or exploitation – was to take place. At every stage in America's history, the idea that the best possible life is the one close to the rhythms of the natural world has competed with the idea that the finest fruits of man's greatest achievement – civilization – are to be enjoyed in the large cities, where art and technology have not merely replaced nature, but have improved it. Harding's location of the village as a middle landscape, a place between the natural and the artificial worlds where there was happiness because the villager could enjoy the fruits of both nature and civilization, struck the same pastoral note that America's artists, literary and otherwise, have sounded since Captain John Smith described the East Coast as a most marvelous place for a colonial plantation.[15] In times of great stress, when fundamental questions are asked and assumptions challenged, the matter of how and where to live in America, or, recently, whether it was possible to live in America at all, becomes particularly critical. In these times the effects of stress are visible in American institutions as much as in the lives of individuals, their social and scientific thought, and their artistic creations.

One indication of the "folk" vogue was the appearance during the 1923–24 Broadway season of four plays based upon the lives of mountaineers in North Carolina and Kentucky: *Sun-Up* and *The Shame Woman* by Lula Vollmer, *Hell-Bent for Heaven* by Hatcher Hughes, and *This Fine-Pretty World* by Percy MacKaye. It was precisely then that the New York-based OKeh and Columbia companies began to draw upon the pastoral image of rural America to illustrate the newly recorded hillbilly music. The record companies faced similar problems regarding black music and hillbilly music: what to call it, how to advertise it; and they shared a predisposition against the music's worth.

Just as there was a plantation stereotype available for race record illustrations, so a pejorative hillbilly stereotype was on hand to illustrate that music. A vigorous nineteenth-century literary tradition whose roots have been traced to Byrd's 1728 *History of the Dividing Line* made fun of the poor white highlander.[16] Fanny Kemble's recollections of antebellum Georgia included this description of the hill-country folk: "[they are] the most degraded race of human beings claiming an Anglo-Saxon origin that can be found on the face of the earth – filthy, lazy, ignorant, brutal, proud, penniless savages."[17] The visual counterpart of the literary stereotype is apparent in *A Couple of "Crackers"* from the August, 1874, *Scribner's Monthly* (fig. 110). Visual identification of the hillbilly (cracker, clodhopper, turdkicker, etc.) with his fiddle and whiskey is at least as old as *The Arkansas Traveler,* painted between 1845 and 1850 by Edward Washburn.

FIGURE 110. A Couple of "Crackers." *From* Scribner's Monthly, *August, 1874.*

FIGURE 111. *William Sidney Mount (1807–68),* Dancing on the Barn Floor, *1831. 25" × 30"; oil on canvas. Courtesy of the Museums at Stony Brook, Gift of Mr. and Mrs. Ward Melville, 1955.*

But the record companies did not use this pejorative stereotype. Instead, they used a stereotypical image more in keeping with the farm virtues of Jeffersonian America. Among the widely popular genre paintings in the nineteenth century were those depicting barn-dance scenes, often with black fiddlers, sometimes with white ones; the dancers ordinarily were white. Images like William Sidney Mount's 1831 painting *Dancing on the Barn Floor* (fig. 111), not *A Couple of "Crackers,"* became the basis of the companies' hillbilly record illustrations. A 1924 Victor *Olde Time Fiddlin' Tunes* catalog cover (fig. 112) derives clearly from the barn-dance paintings; the rosy cheeks, the outdated clothes, and the pleasant, healthy-looking people were the pure products of the natural environment which produced hillbilly music. Of course, it was not called "hillbilly music" in the advertisements; the companies used labels like "familiar tunes," "hill country tunes," "olde-time music," and "old fashioned southern songs and dances" to evoke the proper emotions from the reader. When the singers were pictured in ads, they were photographed as musicians, not as rubes. Most of the early sketches (e.g., fig. 113) showed that

FIGURE 112. *A 1924 Victor catalog cover. Courtesy of the John Edwards Memorial Foundation, UCLA.*

FIGURE 113. *From the* Talking Machine World, *June 15, 1924. Courtesy of the John Edwards Memorial Foundation, UCLA.*

rural musicians dressed up to come to the city; doubtless this is the way they appeared in the studios. But some of the photographs pictured the musicians in performance poses which conformed to the hillbilly stereotype. A 1924 Columbia advertisement (fig. 114) showed fiddler Gid Tanner in a typical comic expression not much different from the stage poses he had struck years before the coming of hillbilly records (fig. 115). Nonetheless, the barn-dance image prevailed in the catalogs and supplements, as a 1927 Paramount illustration indicates (fig. 116), until it combined with a western image to reflect what became known as country-and-western music in the 1930s. A 1930 Vocalion catalog illustrates the wedding, however temporary, of Wild West and settled agricultural West (fig. 117). But there were no black cowboys in the downhome blues advertisements.

Downhome blues songs and singers were exhibited in their advertisements as old-fashioned; Blind Lemon Jefferson's first advertisement (fig. 99) made that point several times. The lyrics and titles of downhome blues songs enabled the illustrators to place the plantation stereotype more firmly in the drawings. As for the city black, he was invited, by the jive talk, to laugh at his country cousin. The dignity of the singer customarily was preserved in a photo which separated him from the "I" of the song, while the reader and prospective listener was supposed to laugh at the predicament of the character whose troubles he sang about. A few examples will illustrate.

For "No Job Blues" (fig. 118) the singer, Ramblin' Thomas, receives a photograph; the "I" of the song is placed on a chain gang, dreaming of a beautiful country woman putting a mouth-watering chicken on the table. Rather than bemoan the character's predicament, the copy emphasizes the skill of the singer and promises that he "spills the latest joy notes" – hardly a fit accompaniment for a song apparently about a man on a chain gang. For "Barbecue Blues" the singer is rudely caricatured entertaining at a barbecue (fig. 18), while the copy extends the cooking metaphor outrageously. It should be noted that after his debut song became a best seller, Barbecue Bob received more complimentary treatment. "You dogs will just itch and tingle to get going," runs the copy for "Guitar Boogie" (fig. 119), which might have employed an urban street scene for illustration, but shows a porch instead. A classic of the genre is the drawing for Charley Patton's "Down the Dirt Road Blues" (fig. 120), in which a dejected man is seen sitting on a sympathetic mule as they leave his shack. Here the copy finds nothing amusing about the situation. To be sure, the characters are not always dressed in farm garb, as "Gutter Man Blues" (fig. 121) illustrates. Sometimes they are dressed in prison clothes. An exception that proves the rule, Blind Lemon Jefferson did not escape caricature in the drawings. "Lock-Step Blues" (fig. 122) shows him leading a group of prisoners; the copy identifies him as the "I" of the song. In "Black Snake Moan No. 2" (fig. 123) his likeness is caricatured in a bed surrounded by snakes, while an urbane couple of no recognizable color walk arm in arm outside. In "'Lectric Chair Blues" (fig. 124) his like-

FIGURE 114. *From the* Talking Machine World, *June 15, 1924, p. 17. Courtesy of the John Edwards Memorial Foundation, UCLA.*

FIGURE 115. *"Picturesque figures of old fiddlers' convention, Atlanta." From* Musical America, *March 21, 1914, p. 23.* Below, left to right: *Gid Tanner, J. R. Bobo, and Deacon Ludwig of Cobb County, chairman of the convention.* Above: *Gid Tanner (center) with two other contestants.*

ness sits on the bed in his cell, while the copy makes fun of his predicament: "SALTY TEARS – wet tears – big, round tears – all kinds of tears and heart throbs, and you should put yourself in his place to feel just as blue. 'Lectric chair is the next place he's gonna sit down in, and he ain't tired either, so he don't wanta sit down. Don't fail to hear Blind Lemon Jefferson, helped out by his snappy guitar. . . ." This account is quite a contrast to the lyrics of the song, in which the "I" further insulates himself from the listener through the device of a companion who sings most of the lines:

FIGURE 116. *A 1927 Paramount catalog cover. Courtesy of the John Edwards Memorial Foundation, UCLA.*

ARE YOU taking advantage of the opportunity offered you to indicate who and what you would best like to hear on Vocalion Records of Old-Time Tunes? There's a coupon inside, and if you didn't fill it out and turn it in last month, be sure to do so this time. You certainly have some preferences of Vocalion Artists and Old-Time Tunes you would like to hear. Indicate them on the coupon enclosed and Vocalion will try to make the records you would specially like to hear.

FIGURE 117. *A 1930 Vocalion catalog cover. Courtesy of the John Edwards Memorial Foundation, UCLA.*

FIGURE 118. *From the* Chicago Defender, *March 31, 1928*

FIGURE 119. *From the* Chicago Defender, *November 2, 1929*

FIGURE 120. *From the* Chicago Defender, *November 23, 1929*

FIGURE 121. *From the* Chicago Defender, *July 20, 1929*

FIGURE 122. *From the* Chicago Defender, *October 27, 1928*

FIGURE 123. *From the* Chicago Defender, *May 18, 1929*

FIGURE 124. *From the* Chicago Defender, *April 7, 1928*

I want to shake hands with my partner and   ask him how come he's here
I want to shake hand with my partner and   ask him how come he's here
I had a mess with my family   they goin' to send me to the electric chair

I wonder why they electrocute a man after the   one o'clock hour of night
I wonder why they electrocute a man after the   one o'clock hour of night
Because the current is much stronger   then the folkses turn out all the lights

I sat in the electrocutin' room   my arms folded up and crying
I sat in the electrocutin' room my   arms folded up and crying
But my baby had to question whether they gonna   electrocute that man of mine

Well they put me in a coffin to   take me all the way from here
Well they put me in a coffin to   take me all the way from here
I'd rather be in some new world   than to be married in the 'lectric chair

I seen wrecks on the ocean   I seen wrecks on the deep blue sea
I seen wrecks on the ocean   wrecks on the deep blue sea
But my wreck that wrecked my heart when they brought my electrocuted daddy
   to me

Even though Jefferson was never, to my knowledge, on death row, and the speaker clearly is a persona, the song's intent is serious. There are few downhome blues stanzas more grim than the one explaining that the 1:00 A.M. death hour is chosen because more current is available after people have gone to bed. The advertising caricature can only be described as ludicrous.

The illustrators were aware of some of the things they were up to. Songs with double-entendre or otherwise sexually humorous titles usually received an amusing literal representation. The masterful illustration for Blind Blake's "Rumblin' and Ramblin' Boa Constrictor Blues" (fig. 125) shows a large snake untwining itself from a tree in a dark forest and about to strike, in a manner most uncharacteristic of boas, a terrified black woman. As in Jefferson's "Black Snake Moan No. 2," the snake stands for the penis, while the forest is, of course, rich in suggestion. The ad copy remarks on the size of the snake and calls attention to Blake's "trusty" guitar. The illustration for "All I Want Is a Spoonful" (fig. 126) shows a man with a gigantic spoon pursuing three scantily clad young women, while the copy feigns innocence, asking, "What does 'Papa Charlie' mean by that?"

The advertising men probably were unaware of some of the implications, however. As a rule, they backlisted blues and religious records together; their photographs of preachers next to blues singers (fig. 127) could only have hurt the sale of sacred material.

FIGURE 125. *From the* Chicago Defender, *August 25, 1928*

"All I Want Is a Spoonful"

by "Papa" Charlie Jackson

[**12320 — All I Want Is a Spoonful** and **Maxwell Street Blues**, "Papa Charlie" Jackson.]

WHAT does "Papa Charlie" mean by that? You laugh when you hear the words to this new, big Paramount hit. "All I Want is a Spoonful" combines snappy words, nifty tune and some great guitar strumming by "Papa". Don't miss it! At your dealer's, or send us the coupon (below).

12322 — Go Back Where You Stayed Last Night and **Tennessee Blues**, Viola Bartlette, acc. by Lovie Austin's Serenaders.

12317 — Come On, Coot, Do That Thing and **Have Your Chill, I'll Be Here When Your Fever Rises**, "Coot" Grant and "Kid" Wesley Wilson, with Fletcher Henderson's Orchestra.

12313 — Craving Blues, Ethel Waters, acc. by Lovie Austin and Her Serenaders and **Too Sweet for Words**, Lovie Austin's Serenaders.

{ **12318 — Coffin Blues** and **Rambling Blues**, Ida Cox, Organ and Cornet acc. }

12311 — Rough and Tumble Blues and **Memphis Bound Blues**, "Ma" Rainey and Her Georgia Jazz Band.

12307 — Long Distance Blues and **Lonesome Blues**, Ida Cox. acc. by Lovie Austin and Her Serenaders.

Danny Small and Ukelele Mays, new exclusive Paramount artists, stop the show wherever they go. Hear their first record: **12319 — Sweet Georgia Brown** and **Loud Speaking Papa**.

Inspiring Spirituals

12314 — You Must Come In At The Door and **When I Come Out of the Wilderness**, Sunset Four Jubilee Quartette.

12234 — Where Shall I Be and **I'm Gonna Build Right On Dat Shore**, Norfolk Jubilee Quartette.

12301 — Somebody's Always Talking About Me and **Sit Down, Sit Down, I Can't Sit Down**, Norfolk Jubilee Quartette.

Hot-Stepping Dance Tunes

12321 — Milenberg Joys and **Sugar Babe**, Jimmy O'Bryant's Famous Original Washboard Band.

12312 — Everybody Pile and **Charleston Fever**, Jimmy O'Bryant's Famous Original Washboard Band.

12294 — Three J Blues and **Steppin' On The Gas**, Jimmy O'Bryant's Famous Original Washboard Band.

Send No Money! If your dealer hasn't the Paramount Records you want, check the numbers on the coupon and mail to us. Pay postman 75 cents each, plus small C.O.D. fee. We pay postage and insurance on orders for more than one record.

New York Recording Laboratories
12 Paramount Bldg.,
Port Washington, Wis.

Send me the records I've checked ( ). 75 cents each, C.O.D.

( ) 12320   ( ) 12311   ( ) 12301
( ) 12322   ( ) 12307   ( ) 12321
( ) 12317   ( ) 12319   ( ) 12312
( ) 12313   ( ) 12314   ( ) 12294
( ) 12318   ( ) 12234

Name_____

Address_____

City_____

Paramount

The Popular Race Record

FIGURE 126. *From the* Chicago Defender, *December 5, 1925*

FIGURE 127. *A May, 1927, Columbia catalog cover*

In some of the advertisements, such as the "Spoonful" illustration (fig. 126), white faces appeared. These depicted women more often than men. The drawing for "How Long – How Long Blues" (transcr. 14) shows a black man waiting for and dreaming of his white "sweetie" (fig. 16). The copy identifies the man in the drawing with the singer, Leroy Carr, and calls his lover his "good woman." Certainly, the illustrators were unskilled at drawing black likenesses, though they were, of course, proficient at stereotyping. It is possible that this illustrator drew the white girl out of habit. The illustration may have been a joke. It may have projected an unconscious fear, though I cannot verify that from the evidence of race record ads. Convention may explain the Gibson Girl figure weeping over the coffin in "Coffin Blues" (fig. 128), but it does not explain the white figures in the advertisement for "Hometown Skiffle" (fig. 129). The several advertisements in which white faces, or faces of indeterminate color, appear suggest a disturbing conclusion. The illustrators may have drawn whites in those dignified situations where they were conventionally unable to place blacks, and in those urban situations where emasculated Darktown caricatures were clearly out of place. I do not mean to imply that no blacks appeared in dignified poses or urban situations, for some did appear thus; but there was a strong tendency to avoid such illustrations or, if unavoidable, to use white figures in them.

Most downhome blues advertisements emphasized the predicament of the country-bumpkin "I" of the song, attributing his misfortune to his naïveté. The lyrics, of course, usually did no such thing. Sorrow in downhome blues rarely is self-inflicted; instead, it results from circumstance or mistreatment beyond the "I"'s control. However black people responded to the advertisements – whether they were insulted, amused, or both – they certainly bought the records. Meanwhile, the industry, emphasizing that this was real, honest-to-goodness, old-fashioned, country folk music, both kept the black in his place and suggested that that place was a healthy one.

Downhome blues freed the record companies from directly confronting the image of the stylish urban black. Paradoxically, it was this same person the advertisements meant to placate, through jive talk and a shared, joking camaraderie at the expense of the country clown who was thrown in jail or who could not hold on to his woman. Certainly, the advertising was racist – we would expect that. At the same time, the ads reveal the nature of white uncertainties. The companies tried hard to accommodate the record buyers, and they listened to the advice of black consultants on music and advertisements. If it is true that they could not come to terms with the newly visible urban black, would they themselves have preferred to be back in time, on a farm, in the country? Were they projecting their desires, as well as their fears, in the advertisements? If we consider only the record industry personnel, the quick answer is no; most of them were too close to their own humble country origins to feel nostalgia for the poverty of their early years. So, of course, were the blacks; the joke was on the country boy after all.

FIGURE 128. *From the* Chicago Defender, *November 21, 1925*

FIGURE 129. *From the* Chicago Defender, *February 22, 1930*

But there were powerful cultural currents opposing the Jazz Age. The country represented that simpler, more substantial life, that return to normalcy which came to be the mood of a large proportion of white Americans, including those who lived in the cities (and summered in the country) and those who, aided by the automobile and commuter trains, opened up the suburbs. Despite the attractiveness of city life and the indisputable fact that more and more people were migrating there, despite Sinclair Lewis's bestselling novels exposing the emptiness in Harding's happy village, white America celebrated – as the event of the decade – country-nurtured Charles Lindbergh's solo flight over the Atlantic, and located the source of his strength in his Minnesota farm upbringing.[18] The country promised not only the good life, but also the nurture necessary to master the machine (Lindbergh's airplane) that represented the century's greatest challenge: a technology in which means determined ends.

Today, desperately trying to reassert innocence after another unpopular war, one in which our technology played no small part in getting us involved, and a large part in determining our role, white Americans face the insistence of inner-city black Americans and the challenge of both their organized, explicit attack on what they perceive to be rotten in white America and their cultivation of a black counterculture. If, in the 1920s, young white Americans were attracted to opulence and opportunities in the Jazz Age cities despite the lamentations of the older generation, today the situation for a large and growing number of them is reversed. It is they who want to go back to farms they never inhabited, eat food from their organic gardens, and enjoy a simple folk-like existence. In time, perhaps, black folklorists and record companies will come along and discover *their* music, if they have any interest in it.

AFTERWORD

In the spring of 1993, I was invited to deliver a paper at the annual meeting of the Finnish Ethnomusicology Society. The society's president, Erkki Pekkilä, arranged for me to lecture at several Finnish universities as well. I was glad to try reindeer meat in Jyväskylä and interested to see a singer-songwriter from Minnesota perform (in Finnish) at a club in Helsinki. But when I asked my hosts why they had chosen me, I was surprised to hear them mention *Early Downhome Blues*. "That old thing? It's almost twenty-five years old," I said. "Maybe, but it has been very influential on our cognitive ethnomusicology," I was told.[1] "How did you come to write it?" They were referring to the musical analysis in chapters 3 and 4, particularly the idea that musical analysis ought to aim at creating a model of the generative system in the brain responsible for the music being produced. Perhaps, I thought, there is some reason for the book to be back in print. And how *did* I come to write it?

Early Downhome Blues began as my doctoral dissertation in American studies at the University of Minnesota.[2] I researched it during the last half of the 1960s and completed the writing in the summer of 1971. I also had the great good fortune to find a press interested in my topic. At the meeting of the Midwestern Modern Language Association in the winter of 1970, I stood up after Henry Glassie delivered a paper and pointed out a few things I thought he overlooked when he spoke about blues. Afterward, Richard Wentworth, the new director of the University of Illinois Press, came up to me and asked if I was working on a manuscript on blues. When I said I was writing my dissertation on the subject, he told me that his press was beginning a series on music in American life and that he wanted to see the manuscript when it was done. I was flattered, and of course not long after it was completed I sent it to him. Judith McCulloh gave it a careful reading and made several suggestions, and early in 1972 the Press issued me an advance contract, asking me to revise and then resubmit the manuscript. I reorganized it, added a demonstration of the song-producing model in chapter 4, and sent off the final version to the University of Illinois Press in early 1974. Production took longer than usual, and it was published on Halloween, 1977. Two years later, the Press brought it out in paper, and they kept it in print until 1990.

Permit me to backtrack and say something about how I came to write about blues in the first place. My father was an amateur jazz guitarist, and as a teenager in Atlanta I learned to play guitar. At Amherst College, where I majored in American studies, the new world of blues guitar opened up to me. But it was not until 1965 when I began graduate school at the University of Minnesota, again in American studies, that I pursued blues in earnest. Here I listened to the recordings of older downhome blues guitarists Robert Johnson, Charley Patton, and Blind Blake, trying to figure out what they were doing and how to imitate them and then develop a style of my own. At the same time, I listened to the music of the "rediscovered" blues singers such as Mississippi John Hurt, Skip James, and Son House, as well as country blues singers like Fred McDowell, Elizabeth Cotten, and Mance Lipscomb, who, although they did not have recording careers in the 1920s like the others, also picked acoustic guitar with their fingers. Singing the blues was, I thought, beyond me, so when I heard guitarist John Fahey create instrumental compositions from the old blues accompaniments, I decided I wanted to pursue a similar path. And so I did, performing mainly at The Scholar, a coffeehouse in Minneapolis owned and operated by Mike Justen, a local man with an interest in folk music. (I well remember the time in 1966 when Mike asked my opinion of a demo tape sent by a young fellow from St. Cloud who wanted to play at The Scholar. The tape, consisting of original instrumental compositions for guitar, was mesmerizing; it sounded like a younger, faster, and rawer version of Fahey. "What a composer!," I said. "What a guitarist!" It turned out to be Leo Kottke at the very beginning of his career.)

The Scholar had also given Bob Dylan a musical start, and it was a regular venue for Dave Ray, John Koerner, and Tony Glover – all well known in national folk music circles. But I was not searching for fame and fortune in folk music; I simply enjoyed being part of the community of musicians and others who sang and played and congregated there. This community was extremely important to me, not only because I further developed my musical knowledge within it but also because of the friendships it provided. In 1967 some of us began a music school called The Scholar Music Workshop, modeled on Chicago's Old-Town School of Folk Music. We offered classes on folk instruments in six-week terms for around $25. We also published a newsletter that contained a calendar of events at The Scholar as well as reviews of record albums and other bits of information. It was as a part of this musical community that I met Lazy Bill Lucas, the blues singer and pianist to whom I dedicate this book.[3]

Because Bill had been born with a nervous eye disorder that made him legally blind, his parents got a piano and bought him a guitar before he was in his teens so he would have a means of making his way in the world. Gradually the family migrated north from Arkansas through St. Louis to Chicago, where Bill pursued a career as a blues singer, guitarist, and pianist. In the early 1960s he moved to the Twin Cities, forming bands with George "Mojo" Buford, Sonny Boy Rogers, David Hartley, and JoJo Williams. I met him in 1966 when we both played in a concert at the University of Minnesota sponsored by an anti–Vietnam War coalition. (Playing in that same concert was Lewis Hyde, a poet and later the author of *The Gift*,[4] a well-received book on the meaning of art.)

For the next few years, Bill and I played music together informally, mostly at his apartment. As I got to know him and his friends, I learned more and more about blues and the people who sang and played it. Was this fieldwork? I have thought a great deal about that question. For years I felt it was not fieldwork, for I was unself-consciously making friends within a community, not consciously adopting a research strategy. Yet now I am persuaded that it was a kind of fieldwork. Bruce Jackson has written that fieldwork is not ordinary life, emphasizing that it involves ethical responsibilities far more serious than those found in casual relationships with others.[5] But what if we do not enter into relationships casually? I would like to think that there are different kinds of fieldwork, some good, some not so good. Fieldwork that is quick and seemingly efficient can be superficial, even exploitative. Unfortunately, much of our folk music has been collected that way. But fieldwork need not center on collecting; it can involve friendship, as two people who were once infinitely far apart begin the process of coming together to understand one another.[6] Therefore, rather than dismiss fieldwork as inherently colonialist, I prefer to think that it can be as nurturing and sustaining as the agricultural metaphor behind it suggests.

In the late 1960s, three things helped me decide to make early downhome blues my dissertation topic. First, in 1969 Bill asked me to become the rhythm guitarist in his band. I am sure that it was not because I was a good musician – if I was any good as a blues guitarist at all, it was playing the sort of music that is the focus of this book, not the amplified Chicago blues of a later generation that Bill favored – but because I was dependable and showed up for jobs. So I did my best to play rhythm guitar for Bill, and I stayed in his band for two years. We played local clubs, bars, and coffeehouses, and we also had some jobs at colleges, but we never had much success, except for appearances at the Wisconsin Delta Blues Festival and the Ann Arbor Blues Festival. The latter, in 1970, was a very large affair, with an audience of 10,000 who saw and heard more than thirty blues performers and their bands. Freddie King, Albert King, B. B. King, Muddy Waters, Howlin' Wolf, Son House, John Lee Hooker, Ko Ko Taylor, Johnny Winter, Luther Allison, Otis Rush – it was fast company for us.

Second, the University of Minnesota hired an ethnomusicologist, Alan Kagan, to teach in the music department. In a musicology seminar in the spring of 1966, my professor, Johannes Riedel, said, "Jeff, you'll be pleased to know that we've hired an ethnomusicologist for next year." "A what?" I had no idea what ethnomusicology was, but I soon learned. Alan defined it, as most ethnomusicologists did at the time, as the "study of music in culture." If American studies was "the study of American culture, past and present" (as *it* was defined at the time), then it made perfect sense for me to learn ethnomusicology in order to further my studies of American music in culture. And so I took just about every course Alan offered. He was most generous with his time. Self-consciously now, I applied the methods of ethnomusicology to blues. I had subscribed to the British blues research magazine, *Blues Unlimited,* which published interviews with blues musicians, and it now occurred to me that I might interview my friends. Over the next few years, the magazine published my interviews with Bill, Mojo, and JoJo, and the John Edwards Memorial Foundation published the musical autobiography of Leonard "Baby Doo" Caston as he told it to Bill and me in Bill's apartment.[7]

Did this interviewing signify a fall from my prior unself-conscious world of conversation? Although I tried hard to avoid doing the investigative kind of interviews heard on television talk shows or the evening news, the musicians wanted to talk primarily about the facts of their musical careers. This information was important, particularly for the blues magazines, but eventually I found that if I left large but encouraging silences or asked them to "tell me about . . . ," they would represent their lives in stories. Although I did not discover all the names, places, and dates that way, I heard something far more valuable: how they remembered their experiences and how they felt about them. I turned these ideas about spoken autobiographical narrative into an article entitled "The Life Story," published in 1980 in the *Journal of American Folklore.*[8]

Third, in January, 1969, I heard a lecture by Archie Green at the University of Chicago Folk Festival, a major annual event that lasted several days and featured many outstanding traditional artists such as Clark Kessinger, John Jackson, Franklin George, Carl Martin, Ted Bogan, Freddie King, and Bill Monroe. Every year the festival organizers invited someone to give a lecture in conjunction with the musical presentations. Archie at that time was a professor of industrial and labor relations and a folklorist at the University of Illinois at Champaign–Urbana. In his talk he made reference to the wealth of folk music in the blues that had been recorded on 78 rpm recordings in the 1920s, and for a few moments he showed slides of some of the race record advertisements. He treated this material, with which I was intimately familiar, as an object of serious academic study. I was thrilled; it had never crossed my mind that a professor might be truly interested in these things. I wrote to Archie and told him what I hoped to do: present as my doctoral dissertation a comprehensive treatment of downhome blues in the 1920s from an ethnomusicological viewpoint. Not only did he encourage me, but he generously sent me several very early issues of *Blues Unlimited,* saying I would have more use for them than he.

I then began to research blues in the 1920s systematically. For a while I entertained the idea that my dissertation would be a comparative study of recorded downhome blues and hillbilly music during that decade, but after a pleasant January in 1970 doing research on hillbilly music at the John Edwards Memorial Foundation at the University of California at Los Angeles, I realized I had taken on too large a task and decided to set hillbilly music aside. I read every book on blues, and many on jazz, that I could get my hands on. I had already accumulated a sizable personal collection of blues recordings, and I was lucky to find a fellow-enthusiast in St. Paul, Joe Grosz, who generously shared with me his enormous collection of blues reissues – it was his ambition to own a copy of every prewar country blues recording ever made, and he was a long way toward achieving it. And so I was able to listen to several thousand recordings of all the major and most of the minor blues artists. I read the back issues of blues research magazines such as *Blues Unlimited, Blues World,* and the just-begun *Living Blues.* Finally, I interviewed as many of the downhome blues musicians who had performed in the 1920s as I could. Most were dead, but I did get the chance to speak with Booker White, Furry Lewis, Fred McDowell, and, most important, Son House.

Early Downhome Blues emerged, then, when I brought to bear the two academic disciplines of my graduate work – American studies and ethnomusicology – upon my experience and love of blues music. It was one of the first academic studies of blues. From ethnomusicology came the procedures of musical transcription and analysis used in chapters 3 and 4, although I believe that in modifying ordinary analytical procedures and demonstrating that analysis can lead to synthesis and a generative model based on an analogy from Chomskyan linguistics I was doing pioneer work.[9]

Also from ethnomusicology came chapter 2, on the singers' ideas about their music. Alan Merriam had written about what he called "folk evaluation" (the term is originally Paul Bohannon's) in *The Anthropology of Music,* where he developed his influential tripartite model of music in culture: conceptions about music, social behavior in regard to music, and music-sound.[10] I wanted to be certain to include the blues singers' own ideas, and so I interviewed musicians who had sung and played blues in the 1920s and 1930s (most notably Son House) and researched others' interviews in books, periodicals, and record album liner notes.

Chapter 1 was historical, an attempt to review the sociological and anthropological studies of African American life downhome that were written in the 1920s and 1930s while considering blues lyrics as contrafactual social documents that allowed the culture to speak for itself. Its own rules suggested solidarity and cultural integrity, whereas the social scientists, using middle-class standards, saw breakdown. Chapter 6 was again historical, relying mainly on Robert M. W. Dixon and John Godrich's fine book, *Recording the Blues*.[11]

Chapter 5 was, I think, the least successful chapter. I now know why I was so literal in my interpretations of blues lyrics there. I had read John Fahey's master's thesis on the music of Charley Patton, and because I admired Fahey so much as a guitarist, I was persuaded by his adamant rejection of the romantic bias toward blues that characterized most of the writing at the time. In his literal reading of Patton's lyrics, Fahey mocked the idea that Patton was some sort of spokesman for his race, a critic of social conditions and racial discrimination. The lyrics were about love and sex and floods and bootlegging and farming, not about social or racial protest. As I later continued transcribing blues lyrics for an anthology of post–World War II songs, I changed to my current emphasis. In that anthology, and the article from which much of its introduction was drawn, I stressed that freedom from mistreatment was the overarching theme in blues lyrics.[12] The mistreater usually was a lover but sometimes a boss. And although the lyrics, with a few notable exceptions, did not express social or racial protest directly, they referenced racism through the general theme of mistreatment.

Chapters 6 and 7 most exemplified American studies. They were little noticed in the reviews at the time, probably because most readers thought that the record industry and its advertisements were peripheral. But today, within a cultural studies framework, I understand the activities of the record industry both as cultural appropriation and as the constituting of an object – blues.

Rethinking chapter 7 now, I would add two key early images that preceded the race record cartoons, for white anxieties toward black Americans were thoroughly embedded in the pre–Civil War minstrel portrayals of Jim Crow and Zip Coon (figs. 130 and 131). The "Zip Coon" song, with its "Turkey in the Straw" tune, was introduced about 1829 by George Washington Dixon. The Zip Coon character was associated with "malapropisms of speech" and with "a boastful and often violent disposition," according to Rosemary Cullen, a curator at the John Hay Library who has made sheet music illustrations and their meaning her specialty. Although the Jim Crow minstrel charac-

MR T. RICE

as

THE ORIGINAL JIM C

New York Pub. by E. RILEY. N°29 C

FIGURE 130. *"Jim Crow." Published about 1831 by E. Riley, New York. The sheet music illustration shows blackface minstrel performer Thomas Dartmouth Rice in the Jim Crow role that he originated a few years earlier. Courtesy of the Sheet Music Collection, John Hay Library, Brown University.*

FIGURE 131. *"Zip Coon." Sheet music published in 1834 by Endicott and Swett, New York. The tune is the well-known "Turkey in the Straw." Courtesy of the Sheet Music Collection, John Hay Library, Brown University.*

ter is understood as a buffoon whose provenance is the rural southern plantation while Zip Coon is a northern, urban dandy, I see a good deal of dandyism, even if it is mock-dandyism, in the dress of Jim Crow.

It was that dandyism, with its concomitant threatening image, that disappeared from the downhome blues race record advertisements. It was, however, amply present in the late nineteenth-century black sheet music that preceded race records: for example, in the 1885 "coon song," "De Coon dat Had de Razor" (fig. 132). The humorous side of the stereotype appeared in "Coon Hollow Capers" (1899), while the savage side is exemplified in the apelike features of the characters in an 1879 sheet music cover containing three songs by the African American composer James Bland (figs. 133 and 134). (These figures replace the *O Dat Watermillion!* and *Horse Car Sports Going to a Chicken Show* illustrations in the original edition of *Early Downhome Blues.*) A later but no less interesting depiction of the hillbilly with his fiddle and whiskey is shown in figure 135, the cover of an 1863 songster (which replaces *The Arkansas Traveller. Scene in the Back Woods of Arkansas* in the original edition). Here the fiddler is depicted as a ruffian. The record industry, however, did not employ this pejorative in its advertisements of early country music, whereas it continued the pejorative stereotyping of African Americans in the race record advertisements.

Bill Ferris, David Evans, and I each did research on blues while in graduate school in the late 1960s, and much of it eventually was published. Evans and I corresponded with each other at the time. Evans was a reader of my manuscript for the University of Illinois Press and later I was a reader of his for the University of California Press. Portions of Ferris's doctoral dissertation at the University of Pennsylvania became *Blues from the Delta,* largely a description and interpretation of blues house and juke parties that Ferris attended during the 1960s.[13] Evans's dissertation was delayed for several years because his university, UCLA, was not authorized to award a doctoral degree in folklore until the mid-1970s. Nonetheless, his *Big Road Blues* (1982) was a revision of *Tommy Johnson* (1971) and his 1976 dissertation.[14]

In *Studying Popular Music,* Richard Middleton attacks the "folk music" paradigm that Ferris, Evans, and I used to interpret blues. He argues both that downhome blues fails to fit the criteria for folk music and that it is better understood as "a proto-proletarian form" of popular music that represents an African American response to "the beginnings of capitalist agricultural development in the South."[15] Middleton's critique, however, like most neo-Marxian critiques of contemporary folklorists' work, is directed against a conceptualization of folklore and folk music that most American folklorists abandoned around 1970 – the idea that folklore comprises traditional products of largely homogeneous, rural, isolated, folk societies. Few contemporary folklorists accept this

FIGURE 132. *"De Coon Dat Had de Razor." Sheet music published in 1885 by White, Smith & Company, Boston and Chicago. Courtesy of the Sheet Music Collection, John Hay Library, Brown University.*

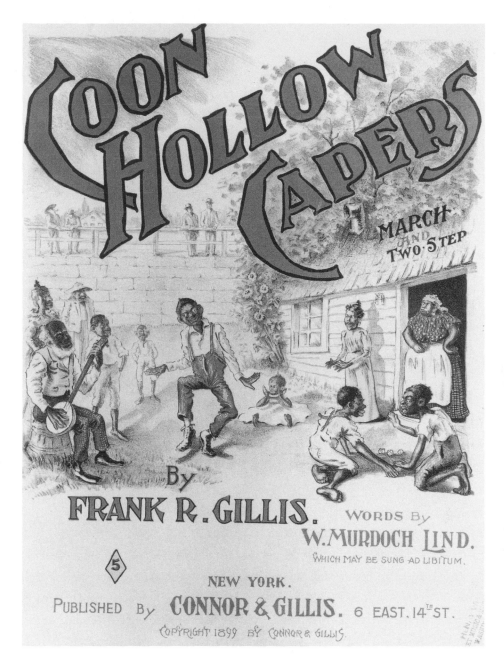

FIGURE 133. "*Coon Hollow Capers.*" *Sheet music published in 1899 by Connor & Gillis, New York. Courtesy of the Sheet Music Collection, John Hay Library, Brown University.*

Words and Music by JAMES BLAND, of Sprague's Georgia Minstrels.

FIGURE 134. *Cover illustration for sheet music containing three songs by James Bland: "Carry Me Back to Old Virginny," "In the Morning by the Bright Light," and "Oh Dem Golden Slippers." Published in 1879 by John F. Perry & Company, Boston. Courtesy of the Sheet Music Collection, John Hay Library, Brown University.*

definition, and certainly I did not have it in mind for, as Middleton points out, I was uneasy with its popular connotations when I wrote in the Preface to *Early Downhome Blues* that "early downhome blues is best regarded as folk music . . . despite the dangers of the implication that if downhome blues is folk music, then downhome black Americans must constitute a folk group." I was aware of those dangers after interpreting the race record advertisements and the social science monographs about black life "downhome" in the 1920s and 1930s. I thought that blues could accurately be viewed as a folk music because it met the criteria of tradition and oral transmission within the modern definition of the folk group. Middleton admits that blues meets such criteria but discounts it because he believes popular music meets the same criteria.[16] Yet although academic folklorists have abandoned the "folk society" concept, among the general public the old definition lingers, and the newer academic definitions that call attention to folklore as expressive culture and artistic communication within small groups, whether rural or urban, homogeneous or heterogeneous, have not yet captured the popular imagination.[17] In the course of his book, Middleton finds fault not only with "folk" concepts of

FIGURE 135. *"Arkansas Traveler's Song Book."* Songster published in 1863 by Dick & Fitz-Gerald, New York. Courtesy of the Harris Collection, John Hay Library, Brown University.

blues but also with ethnomusicology and even with cultural studies. Something of an empiricist and an essentialist, he favors musical analysis.

Of course, musical analysis is not cultural studies – far from it.[18] One of the problems I see in *Early Downhome Blues* is that it exemplifies the music-culture dualism of its time. My view now is that the proper object of our study is people making music rather than music "in" culture or music "as" culture. People "make" music insofar as they constitute it as an object; it follows that musical analyses are "made" also.[19] But when I wrote *Early Downhome Blues*, I regarded music as other ethnomusicologists did – as a part of culture. It could, I thought, be discussed both as a thing in itself (a generative system) and as a manifestation of culture. Now I believe that once musical analysis is conceived as a process separate from cultural analysis, it is impossible to bring the two together, except by metaphor and analogy.

What brings blues squarely into cultural studies today is the new blues revival of the 1990s and two of its consequences: blues tourism the debate over whether blues should be understood primarily as an African American tradition or as a musical genre and style open to all comers. At work here is a cultural politics even more fascinating than the cultural politics of the 1960s blues revival.[20] At stake is nothing less than our understanding of blues, for various subcultural groups are competing in an effort to represent and therefore define or constitute it.

Representing blues as an African American tradition takes place chiefly on cultural rather than musical ground, for nonblacks began singing blues at least as early as the 1910s and have continued to do so since: Sophie Tucker, Al Jolson, Jimmie Rodgers, Bill Monroe, Janis Joplin, Paul Butterfield, the Rolling Stones, Led Zeppelin, Eric Clapton and Cream, Stevie Ray Vaughn, Johnny Winter – to name a few of the more successful. In this sense, blues presents a picture similar to jazz. But African American literary historians Houston Baker and Henry Louis Gates, Jr., as well as folklorist Roger Abrahams, argue – convincingly in my view – that blues embodies an African American approach to the world, one that they call "signifying." Signifying involves wit, irony, indirection, masquerading, appropriating, encoding, and a host of other means toward obtaining one's ends through shrewdness rather than force. The epitome of signification is the trickster – for example, Br'er Rabbit or the Signifying Monkey. Signifying is viewed as a historical as well as a contemporary strategy among African Americans in the face of white hegemony. Blues is but one of its products.

Allied with these scholars who represent blues as an African American tradition is the staff of *Living Blues*, arguably the most important blues magazine. In response to a flurry of letters protesting the magazine's inattention to white blues artists, Paul Garon, one of *Living Blues*'s founding editors, explained: "Only the very specific sociological, cultural, economic, psychological, and political forces faced by working class African

Americans – forces permeated with racism – produced the blues. *Nothing else did!* ... Indeed, while anyone can play or sing the blues, it is the unique engendering nature of black culture that has always been our prime concern. *Only the complex web of racist oppression suffered by blacks at the hands of whites produced the blues, regardless of the many types of suffering with which the blues deals in the manifest content of its songs*" (emphasis in original).[21]

Opposed to this argument are the editors of magazines such as *Guitar Player* and, especially, *Blues Revue Quarterly*. The latter is a magazine born of the 1990s blues revival that features coverage of white as well as black "acoustic and traditional" blues artists. Still, most of the features are on African American artists, and *Blues Revue Quarterly* has published some important research articles on early downhome blues singers like Blind Lemon Jefferson.[22] Editor Bob Vorel defends its policy on the basis of nondiscrimination: "I must honestly tell you that I never put together an issue and think of the 'color balance.' Only after the issue is out do I stop to consider, and I think we've done well so far. Frankly, the day I HAVE to think about the color of the man is the day I wrap it up" (emphasis in original).[23]

Vorel and those who agree with him claim that blues is primarily a musical form that, although developing out of specific social-historical circumstances, is, and ought to be, open to all, and that artists should be appreciated and evaluated solely on the basis of musical merit. In a recent piece for the *New York Times Book Review*, however, Russell Davies wrote: "Jazz today is an idiom existing independently of its black roots and available to all."[24] Is this the logical outcome of Vorel's affirmative action argument? If blues is to be available to all, must it exist "independently of its black roots"? No. Here I side with Garon, who writes that "racism and its pervasive attempts to devalue black culture at its every instance is as overwhelming as ever. ... When the mostly white jury that bestows the Grammy awards singled out white artists to be recipients in both the traditional and modern blues categories, it again became clear that even the anti-racist position of the white performers themselves does little to affect the overall systematic racism of white America."[25] No music exists independently of its roots or its social practice, not even classical music; and by ignoring the history of blues, I believe we practice not only racism but ignorance.

Tourism is another issue affecting blues today that involves cultural and subcultural representation and confrontation. When I wrote *Early Downhome Blues*, there was no organized blues tourist industry, but now there is. What does tourism mean for blues?

A tourist is a traveler looking for recreation, enjoyment, and perhaps education outside his or her ordinary environment. Organized tourism provides tourists with experiences that cater to their desires in exchange for money. Barbara Kirshenblatt-Gimblett and Edward M. Bruner claim that "the consequences of tourism – processes of production and representation of culture for outsiders, interactions between local people and more affluent visitors, and economic and social impacts – offer fertile areas for study."[26] Blues tourism offers an opportunity to examine representations of blues music and culture. We live in an age when most people recognize that tourist representations are in some sense artificial, but as Kirshenblatt-Gimblett and Bruner point out, "All culture is invented, not just tourist attractions, and . . . authenticity is not given in the event but is a social construction. . . . The issue is therefore less one of authenticity and more one of authentication: who has the power to represent whom and to determine which representation is authoritative?"[27] Of course, it is not just the tourist industry that is involved in cultural production; scholars are implicated as well, and this book certainly is an example.

In New Orleans, a jazz tourist industry has been in place for several decades. In the 1980s, a number of blues tourist sites arose on Beale Street in Memphis, many honoring Memphian W. C. Handy, putative father of the blues. One of the more significant developments in blues tourism occurred late in 1992 when Isaac Tigrett's House of Blues restaurant and blues club opened in Harvard Square in Cambridge, Massachusetts. Tigrett, responsible for the multimillion-dollar worldwide chain of Hard Rock Cafés, promised to do for blues what he had done for rock music. His House of Blues is a $3 million representation of a Mississippi Delta juke joint. Never mind that with $3 million you could purchase all of the juke joints in the Delta and transport them whole to Cambridge and have enough money left over to retire. The House of Blues has a $350,000 ceiling with nearly 100 panels of plaster reliefs of blues stars. Harvard University invested $10 million of its endowment in Tigrett's proposed House of Blues chain.[28] Fantasy aspects of this representation aside, its politics became a source of controversy in the spring of 1993 when it was revealed that not a single African American had had any input in planning or building Cambridge's monument to the blues, nor was any African American involved in its management. Who indeed had the power to represent whom? Cambridge's black community leaders protested, and a group of black advisers was hurriedly formed. But the club has not changed significantly since that time, and, as far as I know, Harvard's money is still invested.

A national resurgence of interest in blues took place beginning about 1990 with the publicity surrounding the (second) Columbia reissue of the complete recordings of early downhome blues singer-guitarist Robert Johnson. Until that time, blues tourism was largely an exploratory affair: people who wanted to seek out the music traveled to the clubs in Chicago or Mississippi where it could be found in a black cultural context. But today in Mississippi alone black as well as white tourists attend any of several local festivals devoted entirely to blues, while in Clarksdale a Delta Blues Museum established in 1979 is attached to the Carnegie Library. A 1993 "Delta Blues Map Kit," for sale at the Stackhouse/Delta Record Mart in Clarksdale, identifies about seventy-five tourist sites in the Delta alone. These include the graves of Memphis Minnie, Mississippi John Hurt, and Charley Patton; a variety of important places, such as Dockery Farms, where Charley Patton and Willie Brown lived; numerous clubs and juke joints that feature blues; a guide to local blues festivals; and two competing church sites of Robert Johnson's grave (each with a recently placed tombstone).

The ceremony surrounding the placement of the second Robert Johnson tombstone reveals the money at stake and who some of the players are. Columbia Records paid for a gravestone that was to be placed at the first site, but a rock band got there before Columbia and set up another Johnson tombstone in late February, 1991.[29] When the Columbia tombstone was delivered later, a deacon refused to accept it because one was already in place. Not to lose the momentum of the occasion and its attendant publicity, Columbia placed its Johnson tombstone at the second site – a different church. Most of the people attending the Columbia ceremony were from out of state – record company officials, blues promoters, producers, and media representatives sent to cover the story – and they overwhelmed the small black congregation at the church. One eyewitness told me that during the service a small hound dog entered the church and began howling. Because Robert Johnson had sung about hell-hounds on his trail, this dog was taken as a sign of Johnson's presence, or perhaps Satan's. Moreover, the stone was placed in front of the church and cannot possibly mark the site of Johnson's grave, which remains unknown. Nevertheless, both sites are visited by people from around the globe, and many leave offerings, such as guitar picks.

It was with great anticipation, then, that I read my invitation to a Delta Blues Tour in conjunction with the annual conference of the Society for Ethnomusicology in Oxford, Mississippi, in 1993. I have attended this conference almost every year for the last twenty or so years, but it had never before been held in Mississippi. I signed up for the tour, determined to undergo the tourist experience. Ethnomusicologists were to be bused en masse from Oxford to Clarksdale and the Delta Blues Museum and Stackhouse Records. After some time there, we were to be taken to the Hopson Plantation, a restored cotton plantation somewhat like Dockery's, where we were to eat a catfish and hushpuppy supper in the commissary. We were then to be "turned loose" in Clarksdale to go to whichever of the blues clubs we wished.

My sense of delight mingled with unease as we got onto our tour bus. The temperature had plunged to the freezing mark as an unusual cold wave gripped Mississippi late in October. Would the bus driver point out some of the sites as we passed them, explaining their significance? Fortunately he did not. At Stackhouse Records, most of the tour group pushed into the store ahead of me, and I lingered outside, walking around, looking at the dilapidated houses and boarded-up shops and thinking that the Department of Tourism had not been able to transform the place very much.

Two moments in the tour stand out in my memory. The first was my impression of the Delta Blues Exhibit inside the museum. The museum had a series of rather ordinary exhibits with photographs – some I recognized as my own – of Mississippi music-makers, but the Delta Blues Exhibit managed a wild quality that (no doubt by design) escaped the taming influences of the museum. A wax figure of Muddy Waters, dressed in a suit and seated on a chair on a bare stage, holding a guitar, served as a centerpiece. A plaque read: "Muddy Waters life figure created and donated by Ray and Mary Daub. . . . (Suit donated by his widow Marva Morganfield.)" The figure and its plaque sabotaged the boundary between propriety and bad taste and in so doing challenged the very idea that blues could be represented as a series of objects in a museum. I stared at this effigy for several minutes and then visited the rest of the museum, spotting a "Reference Library" shelf containing a number of books on blues and black culture in Mississippi. I found a copy of *Early Downhome Blues* there and autographed it with my best wishes.

The second memorable moment occurred when a group of perhaps fifty of us descended upon one of the Clarksdale blues clubs. It did not appear as if they had changed anything in anticipation of our visit. The bar served straight gin and tall cans of a single brand of beer. A shelf with clothing strewn over it stood next to the beer cooler. The tables were of the cheapest black Formica, and many of the plastic and tubular steel chairs were missing their backs. Perhaps twenty people were in the club when we entered, and the band was not playing. They soon started up, and we drank and danced for the next hour. A soul band, they were quite good, rendering a modern version of the 1960s Muscle Shoals Stax-Volt sound. What intrigued me about the moment was their first offering: a medley of Righteous Brothers songs. I am not sure how many of the other ethnomusicologists recognized what they were hearing, but the Righteous Brothers were a popular white duo from the 1960s whose music regularly crossed over from the pop charts to the black soul charts. These "blue-eyed soul brothers," as they were affectionately known in black communities, enjoyed airplay on black radio stations. Their records were also purchased and enjoyed in many black households.

At that moment I had to smile. The band was sending us a message, signifying on us. Were we blue-eyed soul brothers and sisters? We were rather a mixed group. Some of us were from foreign lands; some were of Asian, African, Latin, or Native American ancestry; many of us belonged to at least one ethnic group and had married into at least one other. Yet for a night, or at least until the time was up – the bus had to leave, and we all exited on cue – we tourists had assumed a role whose meaning, I felt, the band had a large part in determining. If this was appropriation, it cut both ways. Again, as in the museum, it seemed to me as if the blues was able to break through the stereotypical tourist experience. The incident showed me that the blues music culture still has enough resources to throw us into a realm of signification in which we can ponder who we are and whom we might become – something that tourism at its best enables.

Further Reading

Since 1977, when *Early Downhome Blues* was originally published, research has uncovered additional information on some of the major artists whose songs appear in the book. A brief list of recent works treating early downhome blues follows.

Reference books: Researchers seeking information on specific blues topics or artists will find Mary L. Hart et al., eds., *The Blues: A Bibliographical Guide* (New York: Garland Press, 1989), exhaustive up to about 1985. Sheldon Harris, ed., *Blues Who's Who* (New York: Da Capo, 1981), contains accurate career biographies of nearly 600 blues singers. Robert M. W. Dixon and John Godrich's massive prewar discography, *Blues and Gospel Records, 1902–1943*, 3d ed. (Essex, England: Storyville Publications, 1982), is standard. Kip Lornell, *Virginia's Blues, Country, and Gospel Records, 1902–1943* (Lexington: University of Kentucky Press, 1989), is annotated with artist biographies and a research guide. Because of the current blues revival, many reissued recordings that were available on LP have been reissued yet again on compact disk. The following books recommend CDs, cassettes, and out-of-print LPs. Paul Oliver, ed., *The Blackwell Guide to Recorded Blues*, rev. ed. (Cambridge: Cambridge University Press, 1991), contains an uneven overview of styles and periods, with a guide to recordings. Frank Scott, ed., *The Down Home Guide to the Blues* (Pennington, N.J.: A Capella Books, 1991), is an annotated list of 3,000 blues recordings. In addition, liner notes to recent CD reissues often summarize the latest biographical information on the artists.

Books: Giles Oakley, *The Devil's Music* (New York: Harvest/HBJ, 1976), and Lawrence Cohn, ed., *Nothing but the Blues* (New York: Abbeville Publishing Group, 1993), offer broad historical coverage and many photographs. Regional blues studies include David Evans, *Big Road Blues* (1982; reprint, New York: Da Capo, 1987), a thoughtful scholarly book on an important Mississippi blues tradition; Bruce Bastin, *Red River Blues* (Urbana: University of Illinois Press, 1986), based on the author's field research on prewar blues singers in the southeastern states; Robert Palmer, *Deep Blues* (New York: Penguin, 1982), a popular book on the music of the Mississippi Delta and its migration north to Chicago; and Steve Tracy, *Going to Cincinnati: A History of Blues in the Queen City* (Urbana: University of Illinois Press, 1993). Samuel Charters, *The Bluesmakers* (New York: Da Capo, 1991), is a reprint of two earlier books and contains transcriptions and musical analyses; the biographical information, however, is outdated. Alan Lomax, *The Land Where the Blues Began* (New York: Pantheon, 1993), is a personal memoir from a pioneer fieldworker who collected and promoted folk blues in the 1930s, 1940s, and 1950s. Julio Finn, *The Bluesman* (New York: Interlink, 1992), interprets blues lives and lyrics within the context of African and African diaspora religious traditions, offering a corrective to those blues writers who have ignored or dismissed the connection between blues and vodun. In *Origins of the Popular Style* (Oxford, England: Clarendon Press, 1989), Peter van der Merwe argues that a musical knowledge of blues is central to understanding twentieth-century popular song. Paul Oliver, *Songsters and Saints* (Cambridge: Cambridge University Press, 1984), discusses race records that contained material other than blues – spirituals, gospel music, humor, folk songs, show tunes, and so forth. Among the studies of individual artists, Sandra Lieb, *Mother of the Blues* (Amherst: University of Massachusetts Press, 1981), is an unfailingly intelligent appraisal of Ma Rainey's life and the meaning of her lyrics. Other useful works on individuals include Peter Guralnick, *Searching for Robert Johnson* (New York: Dutton, 1989); Charles Wolfe and Kip Lornell, *The Life and Legend of Leadbelly* (New York: Harper Collins, 1992); Paul Garon and Beth Garon, *Woman with Guitar: Memphis Minnie's Blues* (New York: Da Capo, 1992); and David Evans's biography of Charley Patton in Robert Sacre, ed., *The Voice of the Delta: Charley Patton*, 2nd ed. (Liège, Belgium: Presses Universitaires de Liège, 1987). Houston Baker, *Blues, Ideology, and Afro-American Literature* (Chicago: University of Chicago Press, 1984), and Henry Louis Gates, Jr., *The Signifying Monkey* (New York: Oxford University Press, 1988), place blues at the metaphorical center of African American experience and, therefore, literature.

Magazines: The outstanding English-language blues research magazines today are *Living Blues* (Center for the Study of Southern Culture, University of Mississippi, University, MS 38677); *Juke Blues* (P.O. Box 148, London w9 1dy, England); *Blues & Rhythm: The Gospel Truth* (1 Cliffe Lane, Thornton, Bradford BD13 3DX, England); and *Blues Review Quarterly* (Rt. 2, Box 118, West Union, WV 26456). Only *Blues Review Quarterly* contains musical analysis.

Videos: A stunning concert by the rediscovered Son House is featured in a video entitled *Son House / Bukka White* (Newton, N.J.: Yazoo 500, 1991; Shanachie Recording Company, P.O. Box 284, Newton, NJ 07860).

APPENDIX A
Patterns of Record Purchase and Listening

Recordings do reveal certain performance aspects of early downhome blues music, but they are more than mere documents; as mass culture artifacts the early records must be understood as items that generated their own listening and behavior patterns. How did listeners choose new records to purchase? Where did they buy them? On what occasions did they listen to them? Were the phonograph recordings a substitute for live performances, or did they fill another role? Beginning in the summer of 1970 I made a concerted effort to answer these questions.

Most of the people I spoke with had purchased race records during the 1920s in a store in a town near their home.[1] Floyd Johnson bought them in his hometown of Keokuk, Iowa; Hugh Lewis bought them in his hometown of LaGrange, Missouri; Annie Mae Webb bought them in nearby Tunica, Mississippi, from a store owned by a man named Perry; C. P. Turner, who lived in Bolton, Mississippi, bought records in Jackson; Isabel Green purchased them in her hometown of Lake Providence, Louisiana; Asilee Jones bought them in her hometown of Bonita, Louisiana; Willis Wilcher bought them in his hometown of Attalla, Alabama, or in neighboring Gadsden. J. B. Funches of Utica, Mississippi, and Leola Murphy White (wife of blues singer Booker White), who grew up in Whiteville, Tennessee, purchased them by mail. An informant in Sikeston, Missouri, who would not give his name, reported buying religious race records in his local church.

Asked why they chose the records they did, many replied that the owner of the record store put the new records on his store machine, and what they liked they bought. Beyond that, they were interested in the most recent releases by their favorite artists. They could not remember, or state, what made one record better than another (or I could not find a proper way of eliciting this information). Those who ordered by mail usually ordered the newest releases by their favorite singers. No one recalled having seen newspaper advertisements, but almost everyone remembered the displays that hung in the record stores. Because these advertisements reflected the record companies' perception of the audience, rather than the audience's perception of itself, the response of this admittedly small sample is not discouraging. It may even indicate that the companies were able to sustain the consumer market despite the plantation stereotyping, as long as rural buyers did not see the pejorative images in the newspaper advertisements, though of course they saw some in the store displays. Asked their reaction to the displays, they said they were amused by them.

Records were played on three kinds of occasions. People sat and listened alone at home, or families invited neighbors over to listen or dance to the records, or portable phonographs were taken to outdoor parties to supply music for listening and dancing. The spring-wound motors would play anywhere (fig. 136).

Anyone might listen at home, but this practice was favored by women and young children who, after all, spent more time there. Willis Wilcher said he listened to records for relaxation after working in the fields. Annie Mae Webb listened at home in the afternoon while sewing and mending. She enjoyed downhome blues very much, but thought that the rough Saturday night juke joints were not the proper place for a young girl. Because she had a record player, she could listen to downhome blues whenever she had a spare moment. Leola Murphy White listened alone or with her family at home, during morning or afternoon rests from household chores. She had a strict upbringing, and her parents would not let her go to dances or to shows.

Downhome blues records thus enabled women who did not wish or were not allowed to go dancing to enjoy the music. In those areas where there were local musicians, a woman who did not go to Saturday night parties still could hear live music from serenaders or at picnics and barbecues. But not every section had semiprofessional or professional local musicians to supply weekly entertainment. Floyd Johnson said no blues musicians lived in Keokuk, Iowa; this is not surprising, for black people were not concentrated heavily there in the 1920s. Isabel Green of Lake Providence said there were no local musicians there. That *is* surprising, for Lake Providence is a large town in the Delta. When I learned that Son House had spent some years there as a young man, I asked him about local musicians; he confirmed that there were none. Lazy Bill Lucas said no local musicians lived near the small towns of Advance and Commerce, Missouri, where he grew to manhood in the early 1930s.

Families often invited friends and neighbors to their homes to listen or dance to blues records. Asilee Jones's family used to have people visit at night and listen to records. They did not dance because it was forbidden by the church. Without prompting, she recalled the name of Blind Lemon Jefferson, and a favorite song about the iceman.[2] Despite the church prohibition on dancing, she still had fun listening to blues records. Her family also listened to spiritual and sermon records; they responded to and spoke about the words to each record while it was playing and after it was over. Fred McDowell recalled records by Blind Lemon Jefferson, and one by Charley Patton about the Pea Vine Railroad ("Pea Vine Blues," Paramount 12877): "We had those wind-up victrolas, wasn't no electricity then, y'understand. We would maybe stop by after work at someone's house who had one; this'd be on a week night; and we'd listen there. Wouldn't be no dancing, just a small bunch of us gathered around listening in the shack. Those people who had a victrola really had something, y'understand."[3]

Most of the people with whom I spoke said that blues records provided dance music, either at home or outdoors. Velma Richardson grew up in Morrilton, Arkansas, where some local musicians called themselves the Franklin Band – evidently a semi-professional group. However, quite often her family, or another family with a phonograph, invited people over on weekends around 7:00 P.M. or later for dancing. C. P. Turner recalled that most people in Bolton, Mississippi, had phonographs, and frequently invited others for an evening of dancing. The most popular steps were the waltz, fox-trot, and two-step. None of the people I consulted mentioned square dancing to phonograph records, though often they square danced to live music. Evidently square dancing was so noisy that one could not hear the record, so active that the needle would jump. J. B. Funches, who grew up in Utica, Mississippi, said that he and his young friends danced to records behind the backs of the old people who disapproved of dancing; the most popular dances were the Charleston and the two-step. Bud Rogers, of Benoit, Mississippi, remembered that the shimmy and the two-step were the most popular dances in Malvina, Mississippi, when he was a young man; people there visited each other almost any night of the week to listen and dance to records. Thomas Hale, Sr., and Willis Wilcher were neighbors in Cherokee County, Alabama, near Attalla; Wilcher owned a phonograph and invited people over on weekends to dance.

Spring-wound phonographs were carried outside, too. Hale recalled that every Sunday one of his neighbors regularly took his for a picnic atop a nearby peak. On Easter Sunday, 1926, a man was killed at one of these affairs, and the practice stopped. Though Wilcher disputed the story as apocryphal, Hale said that the man's wife, believing the phonograph was responsible for her husband's death, picked it up and threw it off the mountain. Lazy Bill Lucas remembered that since there were no local musicians in the small towns of Commerce and Advance, Missouri, someone brought a phonograph and many people brought records to Saturday night parties. Dancing and bootlegged whiskey were featured, just as they were at the parties with live entertainment. The phonographs were taken to picnics and barbecues, too.[4] Baby Doo Caston emphasized that people took phonographs everywhere, even in the cities, on the streets and in the parks, where others gathered around to listen. He compared this to the practice of teenagers today, who take transistor radios and cassette recorders to the beach. Many people who did not have phonographs bought records anyway and played them on other people's machines. Son House said that even in the areas where he and Charley Patton and Willie Brown supplied live music, some people carried phonographs to picnics for dancing.[5]

Although phonographs were used in some localities as a substitute for live music at parties, they were used also at smaller gatherings, where people had more control over

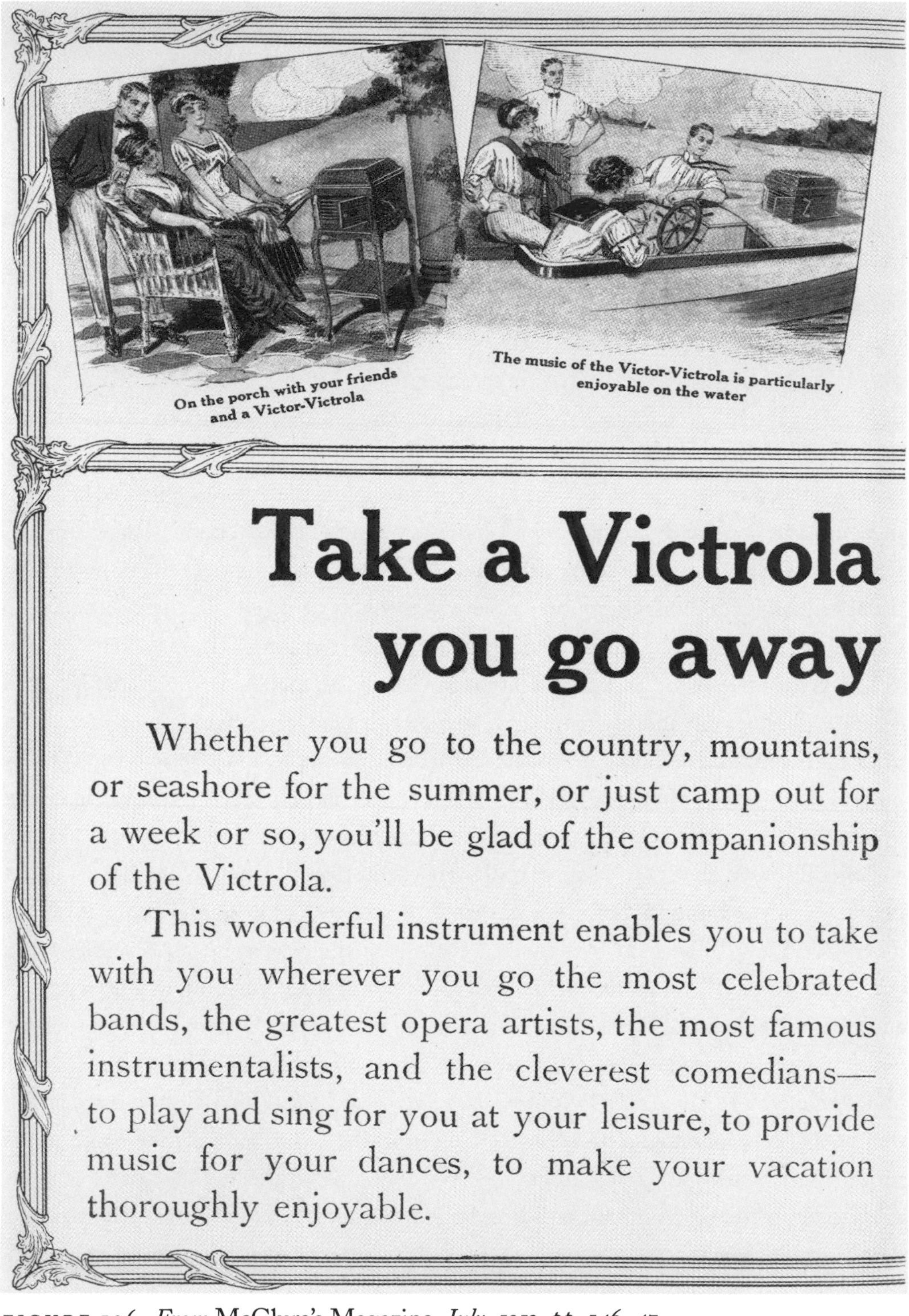

On the porch with your friends and a Victor-Victrola

The music of the Victor-Victrola is particularly enjoyable on the water

Take a Victrola you go away

Whether you go to the country, mountains, or seashore for the summer, or just camp out for a week or so, you'll be glad of the companionship of the Victrola.

This wonderful instrument enables you to take with you wherever you go the most celebrated bands, the greatest opera artists, the most famous instrumentalists, and the cleverest comedians— to play and sing for you at your leisure, to provide music for your dances, to make your vacation thoroughly enjoyable.

FIGURE 136. *From* McClure's Magazine, *July, 1913, pp. 146–47*

An impromptu dance with
a Victor-Victrola

The Victor-Victrola is an important
part of the camping outfit

with you when this summer

And even if you don't go away, a Victrola will entertain you and give you a delightful "vacation" right at home.

You can buy a Victrola for $15, $25, $40, $50, $75, $100, $150, $200.

Any Victor dealer in any city in the world will gladly play your favorite music and demonstrate the Victrola to you.

Victor Talking Machine Co., Camden, N. J., U. S. A.
Berliner Gramophone Co., Montreal, Canadian Distributors

Always use Victor Machines with Victor Records and Victor Needles—*the combination*. There is no other way to get the unequaled Victor tone.

Victor Steel Needles, 5 cents per 100
Victor Fibre Needles, 50 cents per 100 (can be repointed and used eight times)
New Victor Records are on sale at all dealers on the 28th of each month

Victor

"HIS MASTER'S VOICE"
REG. U.S. PAT. OFF.

associated activities. The music was not so loud, the situation less intense. Yet, given a choice, most people preferred live music for dancing. Son House declared, "[Live music] looked like it was more real to [the audience]. They'd rather be lookin' at the individual; well, the fact of the business is you could get more out of it that way than a record. Wouldn't have to be worried about gettin' up, settin' it back, turnin' it round, crankin' the crank, primin' it up, and lettin' the horn down, and have to go buy little old nails to put in the thing."[6] Frequent interruptions to change records focussed the listeners' attention on the mechanics of playing the records, whereas at a live performance a single "song" lasted for a long time – sometimes as much as a half-hour – and people were able to concentrate on the music or the dancing or whatever else was at hand.

In areas where there were no local musicians, race records supplied the only ongoing professional black musical entertainment. Moreover, since they enabled many people who disapproved of the rough Saturday night parties to hear a version of the music under more controlled circumstances, they increased the number of listeners familiar with the music. Race records also introduced singers and songs to an audience that otherwise might never have heard them. A youngster who wanted to be a blues singer could aspire to the fame of a Blind Lemon Jefferson and try to imitate Jefferson's style by listening to his records.

A few people said that because race records were sinful, they never bought them. More frequently, religious-minded black people purchased spiritual and sermon records. Lily Randall of Beulah, Mississippi, sang in her church choir; she used to invite fellow choir members over to listen to spirituals, and they sang them afterwards. Friends who were not in the choir also listened. None of the people with whom I spoke ever said that portable phonographs were used to provide music in churches, however.

Considering the scarcity of money, it is significant that blacks down home chose to purchase phonographs and race records instead of spending their money in other ways. It shows the high value they placed on music and entertainment, and their willingness to undergo greater hardship in other areas in order to provide for it. Surely music was an essential part of their lives.

APPENDIX B
Sermon by the Reverend Emmett Dickinson:
"Is There Harm in Singing the Blues?"

The Reverend Emmett Dickinson and the Three Deacons,
"Is There Harm in Singing the Blues?," Paramount 12925.
Grafton, Wisconsin, January, 1930. No reissue.

[Spoken]
Uh I'm speaking to you from this subject
It's no harm to sing the blues
There's so-called preachers all over this land
Are talking about the man or woman who sings the blues
You don't know the meaning of the blues
The blues is only an outward voice to that inward feeling
And way back yonder
When Adam and Eve was put out of the Garden of Eden
To till the earth
He began to sing a song
I don't know what he sang
But I imagine he sang

[Sung]
I didn't know my burden was so hard
Oh I didn't know my burden was so hard
Oh I done made up my mind
Oh how I had some *preachin'* kind
I didn't know my burden was so hard

[Chanted]
Way back yonder
Uh when Israel crossed the Red Sea
On dry land
And landed on the other side
I'm told that they sang a new song
I don't know what they sang
But I call that the Israelite blues
I imagine they sang

"I just made my escape
And got over yonder"
And way back down ———
When Paul and Silas
Was in the Philippian jail
Paul said "Silas
Uh do you feel like singing"
Silas says "I never felt as much like singing before
In all my life"
I call that the jailhouse blues
They tell me that Silas sing
Or prayed
The old jail reeled and rocked like a drunken man
The chains fell from their hands
The shackles fell from their feet
The old jail doors sprang open
Uh but they done kept on singing those
Jailhouse blues
Way early in the morning
The jailer came
And saw the jail was standing ajar
And he just drew back his sword
To take his own life
Uh but Paul said "Just stay your hand
For we are all here"
I imagine they continued to sing
The jailhouse blues
Way down yonder
Uh when our foreparents was in slavery
They sang George Washington offer his *song*
They sang Abraham Lincoln on his *song*
I call that the slave time blues

NOTES

Preface

1. See chap. 6.

2. Samuel Charters, *The Country Blues*. (Full citations for materials referred to in footnotes may be found in the Bibliography.)

3. Jeff Titon, *From Blues to Pop*, p. 23.

4. See Alan Lomax, "The Evolutionary Taxonomy of Culture," pp. 228–29. Certain features of musical performance which Lomax has identified, such as organization of the singing group, width of melodic intervals, and amount of verbal information in song texts, have been found to correlate well with certain basic social and cultural conditions outlined in George Peter Murdock's *Ethnographic Atlas*, such as range of subsistence activity (gathering, hunting, slash-and-burn horticulture, plow agriculture, etc.), political complexity, class stratification, size and stability of settlement, and severity of sexual mores. Lomax provides a detailed explanation of his system, called "cantometrics," in *Folk Song Style and Culture*. His "Evolutionary Taxonomy of Culture" contains the results of more recent research.

5. I have purposely omitted comparisons between blues and various kinds of music in Africa. It would take another volume to do justice to that subject. The following materials, however, are essential for anyone who wishes to make himself aware of the difficulties involved in tracing blues back to Africa, and the controversies these problems have engendered: Winthrop Sargeant, *Jazz;* Alan Lomax, "The Homogeneity of African-Afro-American Musical Style"; Paul Oliver, *Savannah Syncopators*, "Some Comments," and "Echoes of the Jungle"; Lynn Summers, "African Influence and the Blues"; and David Evans, "Africa and the Blues."

Chapter 1

1. Interviews, Aug. 13 and 20, 1969, Minneapolis, Minn. (Unless noted otherwise, all interviews were conducted by the author.)

2. The lyrics are printed in Shirley, *Book of the Blues*, pp. 64–65. A July 30, 1921, *CD* advertisement noted that Waters's song was the "biggest hit of the season." (Periodical abbreviations are listed in the Bibliography.)

3. *CD*, Nov. 19, 1921.

4. For contemporary analyses see George E. Haynes, "Negro Migration," and Charles S. Johnson, "The Negro Migration."

5. See Reynolds Farley, "The Quality of Demographic Data for Nonwhites."

6. *U.S. Census of Agriculture: 1910*, Vol. 5, p. 925.

7. Hortense Powdermaker, *After Freedom*, p. 80. See also Charles S. Johnson, *Shadow of the Plantation*, pp. 2–3, 16–25 *passim*. Johnson properly brings up the feudal analogy between the antebellum plantation ideal and the English manorial system. That analogy may be more valid still regarding the post-Civil War economics of southern farm tenancy. Indeed, the word *farm* comes from ML *firma* 'a fixed payment' and AS *feorm* 'a payment in food provision,' as in *cyninges feorm*, that which was owed the king. A similar analogy certainly was on Arthur F. Raper's mind when he titled his 1936 monograph on blacks in Macon and Greene counties, Ga., *Preface to Peasantry*.

8. See, e.g., the migration route of Lazy Bill Lucas's family as he recalled it in his autobiography, which is included in the author's notes to Philo LP 1007, *Lazy Bill Lucas*. See also David Evans, *Tommy Johnson*, p. 24, and Johnson, *Shadow*, pp. 25–27.

9. Reissued on Yazoo L-1020, *Charley Patton: Founder of the Delta Blues*. According to David Evans's research, Patton learned to sing and play guitar in 1895; moving to Dockery's plantation in

1897 at the age of fifteen or sixteen, he followed an older musician, Henry Sloan. We do not yet know what sort of "blues" Sloan played, for no one has been able to recall his style, and he did not make any recordings. Nor do we know how much older than Patton he was. By 1912 Patton was the most influential blues singer in the Drew area. Most likely he was able to perform versions of many of the songs he recorded twenty years later. If Patton learned these songs from Sloan, that would make Sloan the probable source of the Delta tradition and the oldest known musician who sang and played downhome blues similar to what was recorded in the 1920s. See Evans, *Tommy Johnson*, pp. 17–26 *passim*.

Here, and in subsequent examples, the larger spaces indicate vocal pauses (caesuras). To compare the rhythm of the lyrics, as they are spaced on the page, with the rhythm of the music, see the transcriptions in chap. 3.

10. I.e., the University of Mississippi.

11. A cotton factor lent capital to growers.

12. Joe Rice Dockery to Stephen Calt, May 6, 1969.

13. Johnson, *Shadow*, p. 16.

14. Federal Writers' Project of the WPA, *Mississippi*, pp. 99–101. See also Robert L. Brandfon, *Cotton Kingdom of the New South*, chaps. 3–5.

15. Johnson, *Shadow*, pp. 105–6.

16. Ibid., pp. 112–13.

17. E. A. Boerger and E. A. Goldenweiser, *A Study of the Tenant Systems of Farming in the Yazoo-Mississippi Delta*, pp. 6–7.

18. Ibid., pp. 3, 7.

19. Powdermaker, *After Freedom*, pp. 81 (quoting 1930 census), 90.

20. Johnson, *Shadow*, p. 105.

21. Raper, *Preface to Peasantry*, p. 21.

22. For an early (1881) account of this annual event, see David C. Barrow, "A Georgia Plantation," p. 835.

23. Jeff Titon, *From Blues to Pop*, pp. 5–6.

24. The word *juke*, which described taverns in the Black Belt long before "juke boxes" came into them, may be derived from Bambara *dzugu* 'wicked' via Gullah *joog* 'disorderly'. See Paul Oliver's liner notes to Blues Classics BC-23, *Juke Joint Blues*. Zora Neale Hurston defined a "jook" as "a fun house. Where they sing, dance, gamble, love,

and compose 'blues' songs incidentally" (*Mules and Men*, p. 82).

25. See Powdermaker, *After Freedom*, pp. 75–110, 223–85 *passim*; Jeff Titon, "Mojo Buford," *BU*, no. 76, p. 13.

26. Johnson, *Shadow*, p. 13.

27. Ibid., pp. 47–90; Powdermaker, *After Freedom*, pp. 143–74.

28. See below, pp. 16–17.

29. Raper, *Preface to Peasantry*, pp. 42–43; Johnson, *Shadow*, pp. 100–102; Dorothy Dickins, *A Nutrition Investigation of Negro Tenants in the Yazoo-Mississippi Delta*, pp. 15–48.

30. Dickins, *Nutrition Investigation*, p. 47.

31. Johnson, *Shadow*, p. 102.

32. Howard Snyder, "Traits of My Plantation Negroes."

33. Ibid., p. 369. Cf. Johnson's account below, pp. 17–18.

34. Interview by Barrett Hansen, John Fahey, and Mark Levine, 1965, Los Angeles, Calif.

35. Interview, May 8, 1971, Minneapolis, Minn.

36. Snyder, "Traits," pp. 371–73.

37. Powdermaker, *After Freedom*, pp. 86–87.

38. Johnson, *Shadow*, p. 124.

39. In the author's notes to Philo LP 1007, *Lazy Bill Lucas*, Lucas is reported as saying that southern Missouri landlords juggled the books to *prevent* tenants from finishing a season in debt, lest they leave. Even in the rich Delta, the labor force was inadequate. Brandfon, e.g., described the "stiff competition" for black labor from other southern enterprises – coton mills, phosphate mines, railroads, cotton oil mills, sawmills, road and levee building – and noted the Delta planters' bitter complaints about "the Negro's reaction to growing indebtedness. He literally walked away from it, shiftlessly drifting from one plantation to another or to new adventures in one of the Delta towns" (*Cotton Kingdom*, pp. 142–43).

40. Powdermaker, *After Freedom*, p. 86.

41. An early notation of the rhyme can be found in Newman I. White, *American Negro Folk-Songs*, p. 383.

42. Powdermaker, *After Freedom*, p. 87. But some families stayed on a single plantation for several years. Cf. Johnson, *Shadow*, p. 25: "Their one outstanding means of asserting freedom is this mobility, although within an extremely narrow range."

43. Plantation owners sought laws to discourage the northern migration and thus conserve the labor force (Johnson, "Negro Migration," p. 314).

44. Powdermaker, *After Freedom*, pp. 60–69.

45. Ibid., p. 61.

46. Powdermaker did not believe this as serious a handicap as I: "Something of the male point of view was revealed through the women, in the men's observable behavior, and by the few men whom it was possible to interview" (ibid., p. xvi). It would, of course, have violated community decorum and made less reliable her interviews with whites had she attempted to interview many black men. See also her *Stranger and Friend*, p. 156.

47. Johnson, *Shadow*, p. 16.

48. Ibid., p. 49.

49. Ibid., p. 64.

50. Ibid., p. 49.

51. Black Americans attend to differences in complexion between light and dark, describing people as, e.g., "high yellow" or "coffee" or "chocolate."

52. Johnson, *Shadow*, pp. 75–79.

53. Ibid., p. 82.

54. Ibid., p. 90.

55. See Richard Wright, foreword to *Blues Fell This Morning*, by Paul Oliver.

56. The basic themes of blues lyrics are taken up in detail in chap. 5.

57. That a predominantly urban black middle class was engaged in this bleaching process did not go unnoticed by contemporary black artists. In "The Negro Artist and the Racial Mountain," Langston Hughes wrote: "One of the most promising of the young Negro poets said to me once, 'I want to be a poet – not a Negro poet,' meaning . . . 'I would like to be white.' . . . But this is the mountain standing in the way of any true Negro art in America – this urge within the race toward whiteness. . . . This young poet's home is, I believe, a fairly typical home of the colored middle class. . . . But, to my mind, it is the duty of the younger Negro artist, if he accepts any duty at all from outsiders, to change through the force of his art that old whispering 'I want to be white,' hidden in the aspirations of his people, to 'Why should I want to be white? I am a Negro – and beautiful!'" (pp. 692–94).

58. Jeff Titon, "Structure and Function in Blues and Black Preaching."

59. Rod Gruver, "The Blues as a Secular Religion."

60. Charles Keil, *Urban Blues*, pp. 72–73.

61. E. Franklin Frazier, *The Negro Church in America*, provides a good brief introduction to the subject.

62. Printed texts of black oral sermons, such as those published by James Weldon Johnson (*God's Trombones*) or otherwise "improved" by collectors for anthologies of black folklore, give a terribly misleading impression. The reader is advised to attend services in a rural black church or, failing that, to hear live recordings of some of the contemporary urban black preachers, such as the Reverend C. L. Franklin on Chess records. Martin Luther King's recorded sermons are not representative.

63. The last section of James Baldwin's *Go Tell It on the Mountain* contains a vivid description of such a conversion experience.

64. Interview, May 8, 1971, Minneapolis, Minn.

65. Frazier, *Negro Church*, p. 45.

66. See Powdermaker, *After Freedom*, pp. 274–85; Johnson, *Shadow*, p. 150; Raper, *Preface to Peasantry*, pp. 359–72.

67. Frazier, *Negro Church*, p. 43.

68. Ibid., p. 34. This is the "clean sheets" doctrine.

69. Johnson, *Shadow*, p. 151. A widening gap is curious, for it argues that Black Belt social behavior was drawing further and further from white middle-class ideals.

70. Sermons on the Prodigal Son were common in the 1920s, judging from commercial recordings: Rev. Calvin P. Dixon, "The Prodigal Son" (Columbia 14057-D); Rev. E. D. Campbell, "I Will Arise and Go to My Father" (Victor 35824); Rev. A. W. Nix, "The Seven R's" (Vocalion 1125); Rev. D. C. Rice, "I Will Arise and Go to My Father" (Vocalion 1231); Rev. C. F. Thornton, "The Prodigal Son" (Columbia 14233-D). A study of black church doctrine based on recorded sermons remains to be written. See Bruce Rosenberg, *The Art of the American Folk Preacher*, for analysis of oral formulas and formulaic composition in black sermons.

71. Raper, *Preface to Peasantry*, pp. 387–402; Johnson, *Shadow*, pp. 180–85.

72. Johnson, *Shadow*, p. 184.

73. Raper, *Preface to Peasantry,* p. 66.

74. Samuel Charters, brochure notes to RBF 5, *An Introduction to Gospel Song.*

75. In 1808 a British traveler in the United States reported hearing a rowing song – the earliest reference to slave worksongs I have run across. See Eileen Southern, *The Music of Black Americans,* p. 177. Frederick Law Olmsted, *Journey in the Seaboard Slave States,* pp. 394–95, reported a field holler he heard in 1853.

76. Black people had entertained white Americans (and each other) since colonial times. Jefferson referred to black musicians playing the African "banjar" in his *Notes on Virginia* (see Gilbert Chase, *America's Music,* p. 262). See also Paul Oliver, *Savannah Syncopators,* pp. 20–25. Tony Russell, in *Blacks, Whites and Blues,* pp. 26 ff., shows that black and white country entertainers in the early twentieth century shared a common repertoire. A "breakdown" is a quick tune usually associated with fiddle or banjo and played primarily for square dancing. Black people sang minstrel songs for their own entertainment as well, substituting, e.g., *preacher* for *nigger.* See below, pp. 187–88.

77. Interview, May 8, 1971, Minneapolis, Minn.

78. Evans, *Tommy Johnson,* pp. 18–19.

79. Interview, Aug. 26, 1970, Attalla, Ala.

80. William Ferris, Jr., *Blues from the Delta,* p. 28. On p. 30 Ferris implies that blues began shortly after the Civil War.

81. Keil, *Urban Blues,* pp. 34–39. In a sermon recorded in 1930, "Is There Harm in Singing the Blues?" (Paramount 12925), the Reverend Emmett Dickinson stated that Jews captive in Egypt must have sung the "Israelite Blues." The full text of this sermon appears in Appendix B.

82. See Rudi Blesh and Harriet Janis, *They All Played Ragtime.*

83. Henry Edward Krehbiel, *Afro-American Folksongs,* is a case in point. For an application of this attitude to blues, see Dorothy Scarborough, *On the Trail of Negro Folk-Songs,* p. 264.

84. John Work, *American Negro Songs and Spirituals,* pp. 32–33.

85. See Abbe Niles, "The Story of the Blues," pp. 18–20, 25–28.

86. W. C. Handy, *Father of the Blues,* p. 147.

87. Howard Odum, "Folk-Song and Folk-Poetry as Found in the Secular Songs of the Southern Negroes," p. 283 and *passim.*

88. Bruce Jackson, in *The Negro and His Folklore in Nineteenth-Century Periodicals,* reprints thirty-two essays; these stanzas appear in several of them (see, e.g., pp. 30–31, 58–59, 70–71, 84–101).

89. Odum, "Folk-Song." Odum did not consistently indicate the number of times a line was repeated to make up a stanza. David Evans has suggested to me that since Odum had not heard the term *blues* he probably was unaware that a new form was emerging (or, more precisely, had emerged) in which AAB stanzas were a defining feature.

90. Handy, *Father,* pp. 148–49. While the 1896 date is approximate (ibid., pp. 33–35), it could not have been later, nor more than a couple of years earlier.

91. Ibid., p. 78.

92. Ibid., p. 79.

93. Ibid., p. 81.

94. Odum, "Folk-Song," pp. 360–61, 396.

95. Ibid., p. 271.

96. Alan Lomax, *Mister Jelly Roll,* pp. 21, 269–71.

97. See Rosenberg, *Art of the American Folk Preacher.*

98. Yannick Bruynoghe, *Big Bill Blues,* pp. 53–59. Odum ("Folk-Song," p. 351) reported an AAA form.

99. Odum prints "Po' Boy Long Way from Home" with this and other stanzas in "Folk-Song," p. 270. He gives some stanzas a three-line AAA form and others a two-line AA form. But in *The Negro and His Songs,* Odum and Guy B. Johnson print the same text and remark that "each stanza consists of a single line repeated several times" (p. 169). Many versions were recorded by commercial singers in the 1920s.

100. The case for east Texas origins remains to be well documented. In New York, Nov. 11, 1972, Alan Lomax told me that his many years of collecting black American folksongs had convinced him that blues originated in Texas; as an afterthought he cited the formulaic line "Well, the blues come to Texas, lopin' like a mule" (see transcr. 31, where it occurs in Blind Lemon Jefferson's "Got the Blues"). It does not appear that any Texas blues singer who recorded in the 1920s was of the same generation as Charley Patton; those who were as old as Patton simply did not sing much that was blues, while those who sang blues were younger. More research needs to be done.

101. Though downhome blues is associated with Black Belt farm culture, it is important to realize that the downhome style developed elsewhere. Logging communities in Mississippi, Louisiana, Arkansas, and Florida were built around sawmills. When the logging camps moved far from the sawmills, the companies often provided a building where the men could drink, gamble, and make love to women imported for the purpose. A piano inside such a joint was not uncommon, for the company machinery could easily haul it about. Itinerant piano players kept many of the camps supplied with better music than the workers themselves could provide. They played dance music – boogie or "fast western" style – and often sang amusing "dirty" lyrics. But not all logging camps had pianos, and even if one did, it might turn out that the best camp or local musician was a guitarist, like "Baby Doo" Caston's cousin Alan Weathersby, who played regularly in logging camp barrelhouses in the sawmill areas around Natchez in the 1920s. Pianos were effective accompanying uptempo blue songs and boogies in whorehouses, gambling joints, and flats regularly set aside for house parties in towns such as Dallas and St. Louis, which became known thereby as piano towns. Other towns, such as Atlanta, Jackson, and Memphis, were better known for solo guitarists and string bands. Good musicians usually were mobile, traveling in and out of the farming areas and into towns and cities. But when downhome blues songs were recorded commercially in the 1920s, the recording companies were partial to singers accompanying themselves on guitars, the chief instrument used in the Black Belt.

102. Evans, *Tommy Johnson*, pp. 19–25.

103. Bob Groom, *Blind Lemon Jefferson*, p. 2.

104. Pete Welding, "Reverend Robert Wilkins," *BU*, no. 51, pp. 14–15.

105. Pete Welding, "Tapescripts," p. 56.

106. Fred McDowell, interview, July 21, 1970, Minneapolis, Minn.

107. Jeff Titon, "All Pretty Wimmens," *BU*, no. 64, p. 13.

108. Interview, May 8, 1971, Minneapolis, Minn.

109. Evans, *Tommy Johnson*, p. 24.

110. Chris Strachwitz, "An Interview with the Staples Family," p. 15.

111. Johnson, *Shadow*, pp. 181–82.

112. Raper, *Preface to Peasantry*, p. 390.

113. Victoria Spivey, "Blind Lemon and I Had a Ball," p. 9.

114. Titon, "All Pretty Wimmens," *BU*, no. 64, p. 13.

115. Interview, May 8, 1971, Minneapolis, Minn.

116. Ibid.

117. John Fahey, *Charley Patton*, pp. 52–55.

Chapter 2

1. W. C. Handy, *Father of the Blues*, p. 16. David Evans has suggested to me that the frequent imitations of environmental noises (horses, trains, bells, etc.) in black folk music provide additional support for Handy's viewpoint. But the issue here is source, not resource.

2. Handy, *Father*, p. x. Handy has borrowed a very old concept, the natural symphony. Cf. Godfrey Goodman's 1616 depiction of the musician as artificer: "The little chirping birds (The Wren, and The Robin) they sing a meane; the Goldfinch, the Nightingall, they joyne in the treble; the Blackebird, the Thrush, they bear the tenour; while the four footed beasts with their bloating and bellowing they sing a bass. . . . Only man, as being a wild and fierce creature, hath no certaine note or tune . . . his instruments are the guts of dead creatures, a token of his crueltie, and the remainder of his riot" (*The Fall of Man*, quoted in John Hollander, *The Untuning of the Sky*, p. 127).

3. Handy, *Father*, p. 13.

4. Pete Welding, "Reverend Robert Wilkins," *BU*, no. 56, p. 12.

5. As reported by his brother, the Reverend LeDell Johnson, in David Evans, *Tommy Johnson*, pp. 22–23. While it is possible that LeDell's vocation shaped this account, I believe it is reliable.

6. Paul Oliver, *Conversation with the Blues*, p. 81.

7. Jeff Titon, "Mojo Buford," *BU*, no. 77, p. 9.

8. William Ferris, Jr., *Blues from the Delta*, p. 47.

9. Jeff Titon, *From Blues to Pop*, p. 9.

10. Welding, "Reverend Robert Wilkins," *BU*, no. 56, p. 12.

11. Pete Welding, "Tapescripts," p. 57.

12. Oliver, *Conversation*, p. 45.

13. Jeff Titon, "All Pretty Wimmens," *BU*, no. 65, p. 14.

14. David Evans, "Babe Stovall," p. 53.

15. David Evans, "The Rev. Rubin Lacy," *BU*, no. 42, p. 5.

16. Jacques Roche, "Henry Stuckey."

17. David Evans reports (*Tommy Johnson*, p. 50) that Tommy Johnson had a reputation for singing short songs. Additional evidence for the great length of party performances is provided by Zora Neale Hurston, who describes one song which lasted for at least thirty-seven stanzas (*Mules and Men*, p. 33).

18. Lester Melrose, "My Life in Recording," p. 61.

19. "Match Box Blues" is used by permission of George H. Buck, Jr., Southland Records, Atlanta, Georgia. Both takes appeared on records bearing the Paramount release number 12474. Master numbers were assigned by the record companies for their files and show the order in which songs were recorded in the studio. Evidently twenty-one intervening takes of perhaps a dozen songs were recorded—and not, apparently, by Jefferson. Even if he did not record the song twice on the same day, he would have heard the playback of his first version just before making the second, so that the song would have been fresh in his mind (playback of previous takes was standard recording studio practice).

20. Transcribed by Bob Groom in *Blind Lemon Jefferson*, p. 7.

21. Walter "Furry" Lewis, interview, Aug. 20, 1970, Memphis, Tenn. Multiple takes of Johnson's 1936 and 1937 recordings are reissued on Columbia CL 1654 and C 30034, *Robert Johnson: King of the Delta Blues Singers, Vols. 1 and 2*.

22. Ed Morrow, "Skip James Talking," *BU*, no. 22, p. 4. David Evans's notes to Testament T-2222, *It Must Have Been the Devil*, point out that most of James's music was traditional, not original.

23. Oliver, *Conversation*, pp. 105–6. The speaker is Henry Townsend.

24. Evans, "Rev. Rubin Lacy," *BU*, no. 44, p. 7.

25. Oliver, *Conversation*, pp. 101–2.

26. Ibid., p. 114.

27. Welding, "Tapescripts," p. 55.

28. E.g., Paul Garon, in *The Devil's Son-in-Law*, reconstructs Peetie Wheatstraw's life and personality upon the assumption that they were expressed directly in his songs. Paul Oliver states in *The Story of the Blues* that "blues singers nearly always sing about themselves" (p. 30).

29. Disagreeing with me, Rod Gruver argues that blues songs are best perceived as dramatic monologues. See his "Blues as Dramatic Monologues"; for my reply, see "Autobiography and Blues Texts"; for his rejoinder, see "The Autobiographical Theory Re-Examined."

30. Evans, "Rev. Rubin Lacy," *BU*, no. 44, p. 7.

31. See David Evans, "Afro-American One-Stringed Instruments."

32. Al Wilson, *Son House*, p. 11.

33. Interview, Aug. 9, 1970, Ann Arbor, Mich.

34. Oliver, *Story of the Blues*, p. 27.

35. See Tony Russell, "OTM Transcription."

36. For "Vastopol," see Robert Fleder's liner notes to County 523, *Old-Time Mountain Guitar*.

37. Mike Stewart, Stephen Calt, Nick Perls, and David Evans, in liner notes for Yazoo records' reissue series, have developed the fullest case for regional guitar styles.

38. "Fred McDowell Talks to Pete Welding," p. 9.

39. Evans, "Rev. Rubin Lacy," *BU*, no. 42, p. 5.

40. Interview, May 8, 1971, Minneapolis, Minn.

41. This subject needs more research. It has not been pursued because recent blues scholarship has tended to specialize in either downhome or vaudeville blues. A promising topic for investigation is the appearance of vaudeville blues lyrics in downhome blues songs.

42. For a discussion of the black "artistic metropolis" see p. 199.

43. Ronald C. Foreman, Jr., "Jazz and Race Records, 1920–1932," p. 157.

44. Perry Bradford, *Born with the Blues*, p. 15.

45. Oliver, *Conversation*, pp. 133–34.

46. Wilson, *Son House*, p. 12.

47. John Fahey, *Charley Patton*, p. 18.

48. Interview, May 8, 1971, Minneapolis, Minn.

49. Evans, "Rev. Rubin Lacy," *BU*, no. 44, p. 7.

50. Interview by Barret Hansen et al.

51. Interview, May 8, 1971, Minneapolis, Minn.; Samuel Charters, *The Poetry of the Blues*, p. 20.

52. Interview, May 8, 1971, Minneapolis, Minn. See the two takes of Tommy Johnson's "Lonesome Blues" (transcrs. 12 and 13).

53. Interview, Aug. 20, 1970, Memphis, Tenn.

54. Ibid.

55. Interview, ca. Feb. 15, 1970, Minneapolis, Minn.

56. Interview, May 8, 1971, Minneapolis, Minn.

57. Ibid.

58. Charters, *Poetry*, p. 16.

59. Interview, Aug. 20, 1970, Memphis, Tenn.

60. Interview, ca. Feb. 15, 1970, Minneapolis, Minn.

61. Son House, interview, May 8, 1971, Minneapolis, Minn.

62. Titon, *Blues to Pop*, p. 7.

63. Interview, Aug. 9, 1970, Ann Arbor, Mich.

64. Interview, June 16, 1973, Lexington, Mass.

65. Interview, ca. Jan. 30, 1970, Chicago, Ill.

66. Titon, *Blues to Pop*, pp. 12–13.

67. Interview, ca. Nov. 20, 1967, Northland, Minn.

68. Interview, ca. Jan. 30, 1970, Chicago, Ill.

69. Tony Russell, "Key to the Bushes."

70. Lewis made the predominantly white audience laugh at these songs and jokes when he performed them at the Beloit, Wisconsin, Delta Blues Festival, March 27–28, 1970. Some laughed with him, others at him.

71. Mack McCormick, "Mance Lipscomb."

72. Bob Groom, "Big Bill Broonzy," p. 9.

73. Fahey, *Charley Patton*, pp. 18, 21, 26, 31; Pete Welding, "Howlin' Wolf," p. 4; Fred McDowell, interview, July 21, 1970, Minneapolis, Minn.

74. Fahey, *Charley Patton*, p. 21; David Evans, "Roosevelt Holts."

75. David Evans, "Babe Stovall," p. 55.

76. Son House confirmed that if he felt a particular person would be affected by his lyrics, he would look directly at that person (interview, Aug. 9, 1970, Ann Arbor, Mich.).

77. Alan Lomax, "Folk Song Style," p. 930.

78. Alan Lomax, *Folk Song Style and Culture*, pp. 194–203.

79. Alan P. Merriam, *The Anthropology of Music*, pp. 123–30.

80. Titon, *Blues to Pop*, p. 4.

81. Fahey, *Charley Patton*, p. 28.

82. Interview, May 8, 1971, Minneapolis, Minn.

83. [Nick Perls], "Scenes."

84. Fahey, *Charley Patton*, p. 29. Stanzas which show direct social or racial protest are rare in Patton's lyrics (as in recorded downhome blues generally), but, contrary to Fahey's assertion, they do exist. Consider these stanzas from "High Sheriff Blues":

Let me tell you folkses   how he treated me
Let me tell you folkses   how he treated me
And he put me in a cell lord   it was dark as it
    could be

Lay there late one evenin'   Mr. Purvis was
    standin' round
It was late one evenin'   Mr. Purvis was standin'
    round
Mr. Purvis told Mr. Webb to let poor Charley
    down

I was in trouble   ain't no use to scream and . . .
When I was in prison   it ain't no use to
    screamin' and cry'n'
Mr. Purvis in his mansion   he just pay no mind

Chapter 3

1. Interview, July 23, 1970, Minneapolis, Minn.

2. I have not included "ragtime" songs, popular songs and show tunes, spirituals, Anglo-American and Anglo-American-derived folksongs, pieces without lyrics, or blues songs by jazz or vaudeville singers accompanied by jazz bands or stride piano players (except as noted) in the representative sample, simply because they are not downhome blues songs. The so-called ragtime songs come closest, for they were performed regularly at downhome parties. These bear greater resemblance to Tin Pan Alley ragtime than to the rags of Scott Joplin or James Scott. They exhibit these prominent characteristics: two- or four-line stanzas often including nonsense syllables (e.g., "beedle-um-bum") as double-entendre euphemisms; quick tempos; rapid chord changes in an accompaniment which relies more on harmonic support than on melodic counterpoint; harmonic support frequently using the ii^7 and vi^7 chords, harmonies seldom used in downhome blues songs of the 1920s; melodies which were constructed chromatically or which were "gapped" versions of the Ionian mode, emphasizing the major seventh as a leading tone. A typical ragtime song, such as Georgia Tom's "Pigmeat Blues" (Gennett 7008) or Barbecue Bob's "Easy Rider Don't Deny My Name" (Columbia 14257-D), relied on repetition of the chord progression I-vi^7-ii^7-V^7, the V^7 supplying the major seventh of the scale. On commercial recordings, ragtime songs increased in popularity toward the end of the decade, as jazz singers and downhome singers alike took them up.

3. It is interesting to hear how the reissuers have come increasingly to tolerate high-frequency noises. The earliest reissues, on Origin Jazz Library, sound as if the highs were sharply fil-

tered above 5000 cycles; the latest reissues leave in much more. I have nevertheless found that certain preamplifiers made in the early 1950s with equalization for 78s improve not only the 78s but also the reissues. Since there is little demand for these monophonic, tube-type relics, they can be had inexpensively – if they can be located. The MacIntosh Record Compensator and the Marantz Audio Consolette are superb. Some of the most expensive preamplifiers being built today also incorporate variable equalization circuits.

4. Because of speed variations in recording and playback equipment, one cannot be certain of the absolute pitch of the tonal centers.

5. Such discographical information may be found in the standard reference, John Godrich and Robert M. W. Dixon, *Blues and Gospel Records, 1902–1942*.

6. Addresses of the reissuing companies will be found in the Bibliography. I tried to use easily available records, so that anyone who wishes can check my transcriptions.

7. For another way of rendering temporal utterances spatially, see Charles Olson's essay "Projective Verse," which discusses the relation of breath to line. I have used this alternate layout in other published blues transcriptions.

8. "Stranger Blues" by Rosie Mae Moore. Copyright 1929 by Peer International Corporation. Copyright renewed Peer International Corporation. Used by permission.

9. "Jacksonville Blues." Lyric and music by Spencer Williams. © Copyright 1928 by Edwin H. Morris & Company, Inc. Renewed and assigned to Edwin H. Morris & Company, Inc. Used by permission.

10. "Early Morning Blues" is used by permission of George H. Buck, Jr., Southland Records, Atlanta, Georgia.

11. "Mama 'T'ain't Long fo' Day" by Willie McTell. Copyright 1928 by Peer International Corporation. Copyright renewed Peer International Corporation. Used by permission.

12. "Poor Man's Blues." Words and music by Bessie Smith. © 1930 Empress Music Inc. © Renewal effective 1958 Empress Music Inc. Used by permission.

13. "Me and My Gin." Words and music by J. C. Johnson. © Copyright 1928 by J. C. Johnson. © renewed 1955 by J. C. Johnson. Reproduced by special

permission. All rights reserved.

14. "Minglewood Blues" by Noah Lewis. Copyright 1929 by Peer International Corporation. Copyright renewed Peer International Corporation. Used by permission.

15. "Writin' Paper Blues" by Willie McTell. Copyright 1928 by Peer International Corporation. Copyright renewed Peer International Corporation. Used by permission.

16. "Mistreatin' Mamma" by Furry Lewis. Copyright 1929 by Peer International Corporation. Copyright renewed Peer International Corporation. Used by permission.

17. "K.C. Moan" by Tewee Blackman. Copyright 1929 by Peer International Corporation. Copyright renewed Peer International Corporation. Used by permission.

18. "James Alley Blues" by Robert Brown. Copyright 1927 by Peer International Corporation. Copyright renewed Peer International Corporation. Used by permission.

Chapter 4

1. Interview, Mar. 19, 1971, Minneapolis, Minn.

2. For the discussion of models I am, of course, indebted to the pioneering work of Noam Chomsky in linguistics. For a good introduction to Chomsky's work, see his *Language and Mind*. My proposals appeared in my dissertation, "Ethnomusicology of Downhome Blues Phonograph Records, 1926–1930," but there I could not demonstrate their song-producing properties. I am also grateful to my friend and colleague Dan Dennett for his invaluable suggestions in this area.

3. Of course other blues stanza forms suggest different models.

4. Exceptions are "Fo' Day Blues" (transcr. 38), "Sunshine Special" (transcr. 30), "Barbecue Blues" (transcr. 26), "Roll and Tumble Blues" (transcr. 37), "My Black Mama," part 1 (transcr. 34), "Minglewood Blues" (transcr. 36), "It Won't Be Long" (transcr. 39), "Got the Blues" (transcr. 31), "Long Lonesome Blues" (transcr. 32), and songs which do not display the three-line stanza form.

5. [o] as in *bone*, [a] as in the first syllable of *mama*, [ɔ] as in *bought*. [o] was less common because of the rounding of the lips.

6. [θ] as in *thing*, [ð] as in *this*.

7. Foot stomping was considered such an in-

tegral part of some performances that a second microphone – the first was used for the voice – sometimes was placed midway between the guitar and the singer's feet. See p. 215.

8. David Evans, liner notes to Yazoo L-1007, *Jackson Blues, 1928–1938*.

9. A most interesting example of the kind of confusion which duple and triple rhythmic alternation can engender may be heard at the end of Leroy Carr's 1934 "Hurry Down Sunshine" (Vocalion 12741; reissued on Columbia c 30496).

10. Winthrop Sargeant, *Jazz*, pp. 62–63, in chap. 4, "Elementary Rhythmic Formulas." For a general discussion of polymeter and polyrhythm in Afro-American music, see Richard Alan Waterman, "African Influence on the Music of the Americas."

11. Jeff Titon, review of *Charley Patton*, by John Fahey, and "Ethnomusicology."

12. Regrettably, they do not agree on what the "blue note" is or how it is used. Some think it is one pitch, others a group of pitches; still others believe it is a slur. Some locate it as a "flatted" third or seventh which replaces the major interval; others include both the "flatted" (sometimes distinguished from "minor") and the major interval. See, e.g., John Work, *American Negro Songs and Spirituals*, p. 34; Harold Courlander, *Negro Folk Music, U.S.A.*, p. 18; Samuel Charters, *The Bluesmen*, pp. 13, 30; John Fahey, *Charley Patton*, p. 42. The best overall discussion appears in Sargeant's *Jazz*, pp. 161–65. Sargeant hears the blue note as a slurring tone – not surprising, because he was listening to instrumental jazz. Had he listened in more detail to vocal blues songs, he might have decided that the "blue third" occurred not only as a single slur, but also in a variable sequence of pitch gradations which corresponded individually to each newly sung syllable, with slurs between the gradations. Rather than use the term *blue notes*, I prefer to point to complexes – pitch sequences around the third, fifth, seventh, and tenth of the downhome blues mode – and to say that the complexes are used in specific but characteristically idiosyncratic ways. These complexes, with the exception of the fifth, contain at least three degrees of the scale: the major, the minor, and a distinct pitch approximately halfway between them, sometimes closer to one, sometimes to the other, depending on its position in the phrase and the pitch that precedes it.

13. Fahey, *Charley Patton*, p. 34.

14. I did not tally the third line of "Roll and Tumble Blues" (transcr. 37), displaced, as it was, an octave upward; nor did I count the songs which did not conform to the three-line stanza pattern.

15. In *Charley Patton*, John Fahey proposed this definition of tune family: "For our purposes a 'tune family' means a group of melodies with a similar sequence of stressed pitches, with similar or identical pivotal pitch sequences (or pitches). Metrical differences are disregarded, as well as harmonic or chordal differences in the instrumental accompaniment" (p. 52). As Judith McCulloh observed in a June, 1972, letter to me, Fahey's use of *pivotal* is ambiguous; it may mean "important" or refer to a melodic pendulum point. But the blues songs which I regard as sharing "similar melodies" fulfill Fahey's "tune family" criteria regardless. The question must be, *so what* if the tunes are related? Samuel Bayard defined tune family as "a group of melodies showing basic interrelation by means of constant melodic correspondence, and presumably owing their mutual likeness to descent from a single air that has assumed multiple forms through variation, imitation, and assimilation" ("Prolegomena to a Study of the Principal Melodic Families of British-American Folk Song," p. 97). The difficulties of this historic-geographic approach in tracing the origin, transmission, and diffusion of blues tunes are considerable (cf. Bertrand Bronson, "Two Reviews," p. 142). A more fruitful alternative uses the *fact* of related tunes to derive a productive system. Not only does this yield a tool powerful enough to make up new songs, it may also provide insight into creative processes in the human mind. Moreover, the models may be tested, verified, refined, and improved, on the basis of relatively easily available data, whereas the search for origins and transmission routes must remain based on insufficient data (in most cases) and ingenious guesswork.

16. As for the stressed syllables (refer to the transcription in chap. 3), Patton emphasizes the opening *what* of phrases a, c, and e, and the opening *he* of phrases b and d by a combination of dynamics (coming after a rest) and syncopation. The *he* receives added emphasis as the highest pitch of a sequence and as entry into the E′ complex. A combination of syncopative and durational emphasis is placed on *crow* and *day* in phrases b and d, and on

noth- and *say* in phrase f. *Won't* in phrase f receives durational, syncopative, and pitch emphasis. Pitch emphasis also is placed on *roos-* in phrases a and c, and on *man* in e. But there is a curious syncopative and durational emphasis on the article *a* in phrase a, c, and e.

17. Other variations remain unaccounted for; they might be mistakes, whimsical improvisation, or insignificant differences. For example, *-ma* in figure 79 is held for a slightly shorter duration than *-ma* in figure 81. The amount of movement within the E′ complex varies from not much (fig. 78) to considerable (figs. 77 and 80), but the movement itself is fairly consistent. In the first full measure, the third part of the first-beat triplet is always E♭′. Except in figures 78 and 82, the second beat, also a triplet, has a quarter-note E′ followed by an eighth-note E♭′. The third and fourth beats vary slightly.

18. William S. Burroughs, *The Wild Boys* (New York: Grove Press, 1971), p. 11.

19. The following structure would also emphasize *swings* satisfactorily and accommodate *-p'ran-* as well:

Es-p'ran - za swings

20. The triplet rhythm is not a constraint of blues family II. Were it a constraint of the skeletal tune for "Lonesome Blues" — a likely possibility — the tune in figure 86 could easily be reset to conform to the triplet rhythm.

Chapter 5

1. Albert B. Lord, *The Singer of Tales*, p. 4.
2. Ibid., p. 37.
3. Ibid., p. 36.
4. Lord's emphasis on the creative aspect of the singer's use of formulas indicates his belief that the Serbo-Croatian singers generated lyrics.
5. "Pony Blues" (transcr. 1), st. 1, l. 3.
6. "Lonesome Blues" (transcr. 12), st. 6, l. 3, and ibid. (transcr. 13), st. 6, l. 3.
7. "Mama 'T'ain't Long fo' Day" (transcr. 25), st. 2, ll. 1–2.
8. "Got the Blues, Can't Be Satisfied" (transcr. 10), st. 1, ll. 1–2.
9. "Prison Bound Blues" (transcr. 15), st. 1, l. 1.
10. "Lonesome Home Blues" (transcr. 18), st. 4, l. 1.
11. "Pony Blues" (transcr. 1), st. 5, l. 3.
12. "Lonesome Home Blues" (transcr. 18), st. 2, ll. 1–2.
13. "Long Lonesome Blues" (transcr. 32), st. 7.
14. "Barbecue Blues" (transcr. 26), st. 1, ll. 1–2.
15. "Fo' Day Blues" (transcr. 38), st. 1, ll. 1–3.
16. "Mama 'T'ain't Long fo' Day" (transcr. 25), st. 1, l. 1.
17. "Early Morning Blues" (transcr. 8), st. 1, l. 1.
18. "Lonesome Blues" (transcr. 12), st. 4.
19. Michael Taft, "'I Woke Up This Morning.'" I am grateful to Taft for a copy of his unpublished paper.
20. "Barbecue Blues" (transcr. 26), st. 3, l. 1.
21. "Lonesome Blues" (transcr. 12), st. 1, l. 1, st. 6, ll. 1–2, and ibid. (transcr. 13), st. 1, l. 1, st. 6, l. 2.
22. Harold Courlander, *Negro Folk Music, U.S.A.*, p. 136.
23. Spoken during a performance at the 1969 Ann Arbor Blues Festival, Ann Arbor, Mich.
24. While a larger sample might reveal a different order of importance, no new commonly expressed ideas and attitudes should emerge. Of course, I may have overlooked some in this sample.
25. "Banty Rooster Blues" (transcr. 2), st. 1.
26. "Got the Blues, Can't Be Satisfied" (transcr. 10), st. 3.
27. "Number Three Blues" (transcr. 11), st. 1.
28. "How Long – How Long Blues" (transcr. 14), sts. 1–2.
29. "Bumble Bee" (transcr. 16), st. 1.
30. "Barbecue Blues" (transcr. 26), st. 1.
31. "Mistreatin' Mamma" (transcr. 43), st. 1.
32. "Pony Blues" (transcr. 1), st. 6.
33. "Fo' Day Blues" (transcr. 38), st. 7.
34. "Mama 'T'ain't Long fo' Day" (transcr. 25), st. 4.
35. "It Won't Be Long" (transcr. 39), st. 7.
36. "Lonesome Blues" (transcr. 12), sts. 1, 6.
37. "Early Morning Blues" (transcr. 8), sts. 3–4.
38. "James Alley Blues" (transcr. 47), st. 8.
39. "44 Blues" (transcr. 33), st. 1.
40. "Got the Blues, Can't Be Satisfied" (transcr. 10), st. 5.
41. Charles Keil, *Urban Blues*, pp. 71–73. In the category "urban blues" Keil includes a mixture of styles; those of B. B. King, Bobby Bland, and James Brown (ca. 1964) are lumped together. The

category represents urban black music rather than blues, however, since James Brown has rarely used the blues form. By "city blues" Keil seems to have in mind primarily the Chicago-based Chess blues singers, such as Muddy Waters and Howlin' Wolf. But there were many blues singers in other cities, North and South, with roots as solidly down home as those of Wolf and Waters, whose songs were not so boastful; and there were those urban shouters of the 1940s and 1950s, such as Eddie "Cleanhead" Vinson, whose songs most assuredly were boastful. While Keil's categories seem too broadly based to suggest a common blues style, that broadness does enable him to discuss patterns which appeared, generally, in black American music of the 1960s, and to relate them most convincingly to black American culture in the northern and western cities.

42. "Jacksonville Blues" (transcr. 5), sts. 3–4.

43. "Biddle Street Blues" (transcr. 42), st. 4.

44. "Prison Bound Blues" (transcr. 15), st. 4. Jail is a significant theme in the sample under consideration. See also "The Jail House Blues" (transcr. 19), "Dupree Blues" (transcr. 6), and "Dying Pickpocket Blues" (transcr. 44).

45. "One Time Blues" (transcr. 9), st. 2.

46. "Mistreatin' Mamma" (transcr. 43), st. 5.

47. "Whiskey Moan Blues" (transcr. 22), st. 1.

48. "Dead Drunk Blues" (transcr. 3), sts. 1, 4.

49. Ibid., st. 3.

50. "Got the Blues, Can't Be Satisfied" (transcr. 10), st. 2.

51. "Writin' Paper Blues" (transcr. 40), st. 5.

52. "Bootlegging Blues" (transcr. 45), sts. 4–6.

53. Ibid., sts. 7–8.

54. "M. and O. Blues" (transcr. 17), st. 1.

55. "Fo' Day Blues" (transcr. 38), st. 4.

56. "Lonesome Home Blues" (transcr. 18), st. 3.

57. Roger Abrahams, *Positively Black*, p. 109. Of course, these are not the only responses of black men to urban life.

58. Keil, *Urban Blues*, p. 73.

59. S. I. Hayakawa, "Popular Songs vs. the Facts of Life," p. 393.

60. Ibid., p. 394.

61. Very few blues songs attain national popularity through record sales or radio play today; of the small number of records which do, most are as carefully designed and engineered as disco songs. These blues singers do not patch their songs together; the songs are composed around one central idea. Sometimes that idea is that the man and woman should solve their problems together, but the main thrust of the lyrics remains a description of the alleged mistreatment.

62. Tony Russell, *Blacks, Whites and Blues*, p. 18.

63. William F. Allen, Charles P. Ware, and Lucy M. Garrison, *Slave Songs of the United States*, p. 89.

64. William Ferris, Jr., "Racial Repertoires among Blues Performers." A balanced discussion of protest themes in blues lyrics can be found in Samuel Charters, *The Poetry of the Blues*, pp. 98–110.

65. The text is given by Moses Asch and Alan Lomax in *The Leadbelly Songbook*, p. 24.

66. Richard Wright, foreword to *Blues Fell This Morning*, by Paul Oliver, p. 9.

67. Paul Oliver, *Screening the Blues*, p. 258.

68. Eric Klinger, *Structure and Functions of Fantasy*, pp. 326ff.

69. James Baldwin, Buddah 2004, *The Struggle*.

Chapter 6

1. Quoted in Roland C. Gelatt, *The Fabulous Phonograph*, p. 147. Sousa's essay, "The Menace of Mechanical Music," appeared in 1906.

2. E.g., Victor V-1, "Actual Song of the Canary Bird," recorded at Reich's Aviary, Bremen; Columbia A2832, "Bird Calls with Story." In Victor 18915, "Victor Records for Health Exercises," prepared under the supervision of Prof. Charles H. Collins of the Collins Institute for Physical Culture, Philadelphia, the announcer explained the exercises and then counted them off while an orchestra played inspirational background music.

3. In *On the Trail of Negro Folk-Songs*, Dorothy Scarborough wrote: "I hope that I may sometime spend a sabbatical year loitering down through the South on the trail of more Negro folk-songs, before the material vanishes forever killed by the Victrola, the radio, the lure of cheap printed music" (pp. 281–82).

4. Gelatt, *Fabulous Phonograph*, p. 46.

5. Ibid., pp. 50–51.

6. Ibid., pp. 54–55.

7. Ibid., p. 142.

8. Ibid.

9. Ibid., pp. 188–90. See also Marshall Stearns

and Jean Stearns, *Jazz Dance*, pp. 95–98, for information on the dances of the decade.

10. Gelatt, *Fabulous Phonograph*, p. 208.

11. Ronald C. Foreman, Jr., "Jazz and Race Records, 1920–1932," pp. 34–38.

12. Ibid., pp. 16–21.

13. See St. Clair Drake and Horace R. Cayton, *Black Metropolis*, Vol. 1, pp. 77–83.

14. See Edmund David Cronon, *Black Moses*, pp. 133–56.

15. Ibid., p. 135.

16. W. C. Handy, *Father of the Blues*, chap. 10 ("Blue Diamonds in the Rough Polished and Mounted").

17. See Chadwick Hansen, "Social Influences on Jazz Style," for an examination of the genteel standards imposed on black jazz musicians in the 1920s.

18. Perry Bradford, *Born with the Blues*, pp. 13, 114.

19. See David Evans, "An Interview with H. C. Speir," p. 118.

20. Bradford, *Born with the Blues*, p. 14.

21. Ibid., pp. 121–25.

22. Ibid., p. 115.

23. Gelatt, *Fabulous Phonograph*, pp. 210–11.

24. Robert M. W. Dixon and John Godrich, *Recording the Blues*, p. 42.

25. For an account of the extensive radio activity in the hillbilly music field during the 1920s, see Bill C. Malone, *Country Music, U.S.A.*, pp. 33–78 *passim*. There is no comparable account of radio activity in the race field. There may have been no such organized activity during the twenties, though there have been some reports of blues singers broadcasting. Paul Oliver notes (*Conversation with the Blues*, p. 141) that Lonnie Johnson and Putney Dandridge sang blues over Chicago radio station WATM for four months (fifteen minutes a day, twice a week) in 1929. Robert Wilkins told Dick Spottswood ("Rev. Robert Wilkins," p. 5) that he played once for an hour on a Memphis radio program late in 1928 or early 1929. Bessie Smith sang over the radio in some of the towns she visited on tour. Further research is needed on the subject.

26. Dixon and Godrich, *Recording the Blues*, p. 104.

27. Odum and Johnson's estimate (in *Negro Workaday Songs*, p. 34) was based on the sales of only three record companies.

28. Brian Rust, *The Victor Master Book, Vol. 2: 1925–1935*. The number of songs listed is greater than the number of songs issued. Approximately 80 percent of the race titles which Victor recorded in 1928 were issued. In categories other than race, the percentage was higher, except in hillbilly, where it was approximately the same. However, Victor had a higher percentage of unissued race material than most other companies. The extent of the race and hillbilly catalog in 1927–29 is astonishing when one considers the small number of potential buyers and their financial condition. That they did, in fact, purchase these records in large quantities may indicate the value they placed on music.

29. Quoted in Harry Smith, brochure notes to Folkways FA 2951, *American Folk Music*, inside front cover. Peer's remarks first appeared in *Collier's Magazine*, Apr. 30, 1938.

30. Foreman, "Jazz and Race Records," pp. 92–94. Even casual reading of the *Defender* during the period just after World War I will show how widespread the phrase "the Race" was.

31. Ibid., p. 133.

32. See Archie Green, "Hillbilly Music."

33. A March 17, 1923, OKeh advertisement in the *Defender* informed readers of the addresses of dealers in St. Louis, Chicago, Detroit, Cleveland, Atlanta, Knoxville, Pittsburgh, New York, Milwaukee, Indianapolis, Lexington, Wellsville (Ohio), and Huntington (W. Va.). An April 14, 1923, Paramount advertisement in the *Defender* identified dealer locations in Chicago, Cleveland, Buffalo, Cincinnati, Louisville, Birmingham, Montgomery, Atlanta, Dallas, St. Louis, Philadelphia, Pittsburgh, Oklahoma City, Des Moines, Los Angeles, Little Rock, Kansas City, Memphis, Vicksburg, Dayton, Indianapolis, New York, New Orleans, St. Paul, Evansville, Massillon (Ohio), Ensley (Ala.), Lexington, Jackson (Miss.), and Meridian. Collectors have attempted to trace leftover stock from these dealers.

34. In his brochure notes to RBF 1, *The Country Blues*, Samuel Charters writes that "often local distributors, like the Hauk company in Memphis, arranged for Victor records to press small quantities of blues performances by local favorites and the initial pressing, usually 5000 copies, was sold within a small area." That is a high figure for an initial pressing of a locally distributed record, but it was a break-even figure for the record com-

panies; initial pressings on nationally distributed records were not much higher. Local distribution explains why record collectors who canvass homes for downhome blues records in the South find singers' records most frequently in those areas where they performed locally. One would not expect to find the missing Charley Patton records in North Carolina, for example. But some downhome blues singers enjoyed national distribution for their records; Blind Lemon Jefferson and Jim Jackson were two who became well known to black listeners throughout the United States.

35. Foreman, "Jazz and Race Records," pp. 60–62. Langston's column appeared Mar. 6, 1921.

36. *Talking Machine World* 17 (Dec., 1921), 78.

37. Paul Oliver, *Bessie Smith*, p. 14.

38. Quoted in Oliver, *Conversation*, pp. 131–33. "Moonshine Blues" was a hit record in the spring and summer of 1924. See also Chris Albertson, *Bessie*, p. 101, for another description of Rainey's birth-entrance from the giant stage phonograph. While the importance of the record medium is clear, the symbolism suggests more than was intended.

39. Albertson, *Bessie*, p. 66.

40. Oliver, *Bessie Smith*, p. 6.

41. Dan Mahony's *Columbia 13/14000-D Series* gives figures for the initial pressing orders on Columbia's race records in the 1920s. The statistics show an overall decline in numbers, but no shift from vaudeville to downhome blues. Complete sales figures are, regrettably, unavailable.

42. This subject is treated at length in chap. 7.

43. Dixon and Godrich, *Recording the Blues*, p. 40.

44. *CD*, Mar. 17, 1923.

45. Bill C. Malone's standard history, *Country Music, U.S.A.*, contains a reasonably detailed account of the events surrounding Carson's recording as well as the early commercial period of radio and phonograph record hillbilly music.

46. There is some question about where Bogan's recordings were made. In *Blues and Gospel Records, 1902–1942*, John Godrich and Robert M. W. Dixon place four Bogan titles in New York in early June, 1923, the month Peer supposedly recorded her in Atlanta. They also indicate that in mid-June, 1923, she made another record for OKeh, this time in Chicago. Evidently, Peer went from Atlanta to Chicago (see Foreman, "Jazz and Race Records,

1920–1932," pp. 151–54) and could have recorded her there. Archie Green ("Hillbilly Music," p. 208) believes that Bogan was recorded in Atlanta, and Dixon and Godrich, in a later work (*Recording the Blues*, p. 27), appear to agree, suggesting that "Pawn Shop Blues" was recorded in Atlanta instead of Chicago. In any event, her records must not have sold well, for she was not given the chance to make another until 1927. Field scouts continued to look for blues singers in southern cities, but until 1926 they were interested almost exclusively in female vaudeville blues singers.

47. The earliest downhome blues *record* I have heard is Daddy Stovepipe's "Sundown Blues" and "Stove Pipe Blues" (Gennett 5459), recorded on May 10, 1924, three months before Jackson made his "Papa's Lawdy Lawdy Blues" (Paramount 12219). A month earlier, Ed Andrews sang "Barrel House Blues" (OKeh 8137), accompanying himself on guitar; this may be an earlier downhome blues record than Daddy Stovepipe's – but I have not heard it. In 1923, Sylvester Weaver recorded some guitar solos for OKeh which are immediately identifiable as skillful instrumentals in a downhome style. But in the search for that first, historic record, I think it unwise to abandon the criterion of blues *singing;* the method of oral composition, the shape of the phrase and line, and the subject matter of the texts are all essential components of the blues song.

48. David Evans, "The Rev. Rubin Lacy," *BU*, no. 42, p. 5; Dixon and Godrich, *Recording the Blues*, p. 34.

49. Paramount master numbers place the date of the recording in late December, 1925, or early January, 1926. But the record (Paramount 12386) was not released until three of Jefferson's blues records were issued.

50. Alex Moore, "Letter from Dallas," p. 4. Although Moore's memory regarding Specialty records, organized in the late 1940s, and Decca, which began U.S. operations in 1934, is faulty, his impression of a swarm of eager scouts seems justified. His naming Blind Lemon and Lonnie Johnson, both blues recording "stars" of the 1920s, fixes the date properly.

51. For further information on these field recording trips, see Godrich and Dixon, *Blues and Gospel Records*, pp. 11–29, and their *Recording the Blues*, pp. 41–63.

52. Dixon and Godrich, *Recording the Blues,* p. 64. Also see n. 41.

53. "Jazz and Race Records," p. 175.

54. Arthur Raper, *Preface to Peasantry,* p. 6.

55. Foreman, "Jazz and Race Records," pp. 160–61.

56. When Ralph Peer's initial announcement of his 1927 trip to Bristol, Tennessee, failed to draw a sufficient turnout, Peer wrote an article for the local newspaper in which he called attention to hillbilly singer Ernest Stoneman's $3600 Victor income the previous year. It "worked like dynamite," Peer recalled, "and the very next day we were deluged with long-distance telephone calls from the surrounding mountain region" (Charles K. Wolfe, "Ralph Peer at Work," p. 12). Among the singers Peer recorded in Bristol were the Carter Family and Jimmie Rodgers.

57. Pete Welding, "An Interview with Carl Martin."

58. George Mitchell, "I'm Peg Leg Howell," p. 7. David Evans has suggested to me that "Brown" might have been Howell's misunderstanding of "Brockman."

59. Oliver, *Conversation,* p. 116. See transcr. 33.

60. Gayle Dean Wardlow, "Legends of the Lost," pp. 27–28.

61. Ibid., p. 25.

62. Evans, "Interview," p. 119.

63. Oliver, *Conversation,* p. 116.

64. John Fahey, *Charley Patton,* p. 26.

65. Foreman, "Jazz and Race Records," p. 158.

66. Ibid. The instrument sounds to me like a plucked zither with a few dozen strings and no frets. Similarities in the names *dulceola* and *dulcimer* are obvious; possibly the instrument was a hammered dulcimer.

67. Ledger deposited at the John Edwards Memorial Foundation, UCLA.

68. Evans, "Interview," p. 119.

69. Foreman, "Jazz and Race Records," p. 159.

70. Mitchell, "I'm Peg Leg Howell," p. 7.

71. David Evans, "Booker White," *BU,* no. 36, p. 12.

72. Interview by John Fahey, Barret Hansen, and Mark Levine, Los Angeles, Calif., May, 1965; Al Wilson, *Son House,* p. 4.

73. Fahey, *Charley Patton,* p. 8.

74. See Pat Cather, "Birmingham Blues," p. 6.

75. Rounder Collective, "The Life of Blind Alfred Reed," p. 115. Reed recalled that the Victor representative urged him to stay near his New York hotel so that he would not get lost.

76. Chris Albertson, *Bessie,* pp. 44–46.

77. Speir told Wardlow ("Legends of the Lost," p. 28) that ordinarily he offered an artist a choice between "$50 a side or either 10% of the royalties of the sell of issued titles." It is not clear to what the 10 percent refers. If the royalties were 2 cents per record, the artist's share on a title that sold 5,000 copies would have been only ten dollars.

78. Interview by Fahey, Hansen, and Levine, Los Angeles, Calif., May, 1965.

79. Fahey, *Charley Patton,* p. 25.

80. Godrich and Dixon, *Blues and Gospel Records,* p. 355.

81. Fahey, *Charley Patton,* p. 25.

82. Ibid., p. 13.

83. Oliver, *Conversation,* p. 19.

84. Yannick Bruynoghe, *Big Bill Blues,* p. 47.

85. Norm Cohen, "'I'm a Record Man,'" p. 19.

86. Interview, May 8, 1971, Minneapolis, Minn.

87. For a good essay on sexual metaphor and obscenity in blues lyrics, see Paul Oliver, "The Blues Blues," in *Screening the Blues,* pp. 164–261.

88. Evans, "Interview," p. 120. Speir was referring to this line as it appeared in Kokomo Arnold's "Milk Cow Blues" (Decca 7026), recorded in 1934. The line was a common formula.

Chapter 7

1. A partial list of chapter headings from George Burton Hotchkiss's 1924 textbook, *Advertising Copy,* reveals the psychological approach of the burgeoning advertising industry in those days: "The Mind of the Reader," "Marginal Streams of Thought," "Subconscious Ideas," "The Rarity of Buying Ideas," "Finding a Point of Contact," and "Putting the Message among the Reader's Interests." "We may try to awaken the subconscious instincts and emotions," wrote Hotchkiss, "and relate our message to these" (p. 43).

2. Ronald C. Foreman, Jr., "Jazz and Race Records, 1920–1932," pp. 220, 260.

3. In this context, the jokes about the Christian missionary and the African cannibals are worth attention. The missionary, who may be taken to represent Western culture, finds himself in the cannibal pot; unlike Brer Rabbit, his wits fail to trick

his captors, and he is devoured. Do these jokes express a real fear in symbolic fashion?

4. S. G. Marden, "Phonograph Books Have New Motif," p. 14.

5. "OKeh Window Display Service," *Talking Machine World* 18 (Jan., 1922), 48 (quoted in Foreman, "Jazz and Race Records," p. 216).

6. Marden, "Phonograph Books," p. 14.

7. Hotchkiss, *Advertising Copy*, p. 238. A "lobbygow" is an errand-boy.

8. Arthur Judson Brewster and Herbert Hall Palmer, *Introduction to Advertising*, pp. 109–10.

9. Ibid., p. 106.

10. Samuel Charters, *The Country Blues*, pp. 46, 48.

11. Dan Mahony, *The Columbia 13/14000-D Series*. See also chap. 6, n. 41.

12. Charters, *Country Blues*, pp. 46–48; Robert M. W. Dixon and John Godrich, *Recording the Blues*, pp. 22–23, 26–27.

13. Quoted in Charles A. Beard and Mary R. Beard, *The Rise of American Civilization*, p. 676.

14. Charles A. Beard and Mary R. Beard, *America at Midpassage*, p. 5.

15. See Leo Marx, *The Machine in the Garden*, for an analysis of American pastoral, particularly in the nineteenth century, and the response of American writers to industrialization.

16. See Shields McIlwaine, *The Southern Poor-White*.

17. Quoted in Archie Green, "Hillbilly Music," p. 206, which is concerned with the word *hillbilly* and its linkage in print to the word *music*. I am indebted to Green for many observations on hillbilly record advertisements; his "Commercial Music Graphics" series in the *JEMF Quarterly* is a sustained attempt to probe the iconography and iconology of hillbilly record advertisements, handbills, song folios, and the like.

18. John William Ward, "The Meaning of Lindbergh's Flight," is the classic analysis.

Afterword

1. Musical perception and cognition is an important branch of contemporary Finnish music scholarship. See, for example, Juoko Laaksamo and Jukka Louhivuori, eds., *Proceedings of the First International Conference on Cognitive Musicology* (Jyväskylä, Finland: University of Jyväskylä

Department of Music, 1993).

2. Jeff Todd Titon, "Ethnomusicology of Downhome Blues Phonograph Records, 1926–1930" (Ph.D. diss., University of Minnesota, 1971), available from University Microfilms, Ann Arbor, Michigan.

3. For more on Lazy Bill Lucas, see Jeff Todd Titon, ed., *Worlds of Music*, 2nd ed. (New York: Schirmer Books, 1992), pp. 125–36, and the brochure notes to *Lazy Bill Lucas*, 12" LP recording (North Ferrisburg, Vt.: Philo 1007, 1974).

4. Lewis Hyde, *The Gift* (New York: Random House, 1983).

5. Bruce Jackson, *Fieldwork* (Urbana: University of Illinois Press, 1987), p. 279.

6. Dennis Tedlock, *The Spoken Word and the Work of Interpretation* (Philadelphia: University of Pennsylvania Press, 1983), p. 323.

7. "Calling All Cows: Lazy Bill Lucas," *Blues Unlimited*, no. 60 (Mar., 1969), pp. 10–11; no. 61 (Apr., 1969), pp. 9–10; no. 62 (May, 1969), pp. 11–12; no. 63 (June, 1969), pp. 9–10; "All Pretty Wimmens: The Story of Jo Jo Williams," *Blues Unlimited*, no. 64 (July, 1969), pp. 13–14; no. 65 (Sept., 1969), pp. 13–14; "Mojo Buford," *Blues Unlimited*, no. 76 (Oct., 1970), pp. 13–14; no. 77 (Nov., 1970), pp. 9–10; no. 78 (Dec., 1970), pp. 14–15; *From Blues to Pop: The Autobiography of Leonard "Baby Doo" Caston*, John Edwards Memorial Foundation Special Series, no. 4 (Los Angeles: University of California at Los Angeles, 1974).

8. Jeff Todd Titon, "The Life Story," *Journal of American Folklore* 93 (1980), 276–92.

9. I realized later that others were doing similar work at about the same time. See, for example, John Blacking, *How Musical Is Man* (Seattle: University of Washington Press, 1973), and F. Lerdahl and R. Jackendoff, *A Generative Theory of Tonal Music* (Cambridge: MIT Press, 1983). In recent years, the computer has made it possible for this work to continue in a far more efficient way.

10. Alan Merriam, *The Anthropology of Music* (Evanston, Ill.: Northwestern University Press, 1964).

11. Robert M. W. Dixon and John Godrich, *Recording the Blues* (London: Studio Vista, 1970).

12. Jeff Todd Titon, "Thematic Pattern in Downhome Blues Lyrics: The Evidence on Commercial Recordings since World War II," *Journal of American Folklore* 90 (1977), 316–30; Jeff Todd

Titon, ed., *Downhome Blues Lyrics: An Anthology from the Post-World War II Era,* Twayne Music Series (Boston: G. K. Hall, 1981; 2nd ed., Urbana: University of Illinois Press, 1990).

13. William Ferris, Jr., "Black Folklore from the Mississippi Delta" (Ph.D. diss., University of Pennsylvania, 1969), and *Blues from the Delta* (London: Studio Vista, 1970; rev. ed., New York: Anchor Press, 1978).

14. David Evans, "The Blues of Tommy Johnson: A Study of a Tradition" (master's thesis, University of California at Los Angeles, 1967); *Tommy Johnson* (London: Studio Vista, 1971); "Tradition and Creativity in the Folk Blues" (Ph.D. diss., University of California at Los Angeles, 1976); and *Big Road Blues* (Berkeley: University of California Press, 1982). Evans has continued to make important contributions to early downhome blues, including biographical and critical works on Blind Willie McTell and Charley Patton.

15. Richard Middleton, *Studying Popular Music* (Buckingham, England: Open University Press, 1990), p. 145.

16. Ibid., p. 143.

17. Although I have defended folklorists' right to consider blues to be a folk music, particularly in the preface to *Downhome Blues Lyrics,* I am aware that it creates problems outside the academic world. But perhaps I am overestimating folklorists' influence. After all, when most North Americans hear the term "folk music," they think of the music played by a singer-songwriter with an acoustic guitar.

18. Richard Middleton critiques cultural studies because it fails to analyze the music itself. Because I believe that people make music, I think there is no such thing as "the music itself."

19. See Titon, *Worlds of Music,* p. xxi.

20. *Early Downhome Blues* was a product of that revival because I took part in it as a musician, promoter, record producer, newspaper columnist, and music teacher as well as a scholar. In "Reconstructing the Blues: Reflections on the 1960s Blues Revival," in *Transforming Tradition: Folk Music Revivals Examined,* ed. Neil Rosenberg (Urbana: University of Illinois Press, 1993), pp. 220–40, I discuss the cultural politics of that era and my participation in them.

21. Paul Garon, "Speak My Mind," *Living Blues,* no. 109 (May–June, 1993), p. 53.

22. Vinny Cortese, "Blind Lemon's Blues," *Blues Revue Quarterly,* no. 19 (Summer, 1993), pp. 26–33.

23. *Blues Revue Quarterly,* no. 10 (Fall, 1993), p. 7.

24. Russell Davies, review of *Jazz: The American Theme Song, New York Times Book Review,* Nov. 21, 1993, p. 31.

25. Garon, "Speak My Mind."

26. Barbara Kirshenblatt-Gimblett and Edward M. Bruner, "Tourism," in *Folkore, Cultural Performances, and Popular Entertainments,* ed. Richard Bauman (New York: Oxford University Press, 1992), p. 300.

27. Ibid., pp. 303–4.

28. Dana Wechsler Linden, "Spread the Blues," *Forbes Magazine,* Sept. 13, 1993, p. 90.

29. The name of the rock band was the Tombstones, thereby adding another kind of symbolic appropriation to the event.

Appendix A

1. The persons, places, and dates of these interviews are listed in the Bibliography. If a person was interviewed more than once, the specific date involved is indicated in the notes.

2. Several blues songs, of which Bo Carter's "All Around Man" (Bluebird B6295) is representative, featured humorous situations with a real or pretended iceman who promised to keep the lady of the house cool and to make love to her until her husband came home.

3. Interview, July 23, 1970, Minneapolis, Minn.

4. Interview, July 7, 1970, Minneapolis, Minn.

5. Interview, May 8, 1971, Minneapolis, Minn.

6. Ibid.

BIBLIOGRAPHY

For a brief listing of more recent works treating early downhome blues, see pp. 279–80.

Interviews

Except for the 1965 interview with Eddie "Son" House, these interviews were conducted by the author.

Bogan, Ted. Chicago, Ill., ca. Jan. 31, 1970.

Buford, George "Mojo." Minneapolis, Minn., Dec. 29, 1970, and Jan. 25, 1971. A tape recording of the interview is in the possession of the author.

Caston, Leonard "Baby Doo." Minneapolis, Minn., May 25, 1971. A tape recording of the interview is in the possession of the author.

Davis, Rev. Gary. Northland, Minn., ca. Nov. 20, 1967.

Funches, J. B. Eudora, Ark., Aug. 22, 1970.

Green, Isabel. Lake Providence, La., Aug. 21, 1970.

Groves, Mrs. Thomas. Doddsville, Miss., Aug. 24, 1970.

Hale, Thomas, Jr. Attalla, Ala., Aug. 26, 1970.

Hale, Thomas, Sr. Attalla, Ala., Aug. 26, 1970.

House, Eddie "Son." Los Angeles, Calif., May, 1965. Interviewed by John Fahey, Barret Hansen, and Mark Levine. A tape recording of the interview is on deposit at the John Edwards Memorial Foundation, UCLA.

———. Beloit, Wis., Mar. 28, 1970.

———. Ann Arbor, Mich., Aug. 9, 1970.

———. Minneapolis, Minn., May 8, 1971. A tape recording of the interview is in the possession of the author.

Johnson, Floyd. Keokuk, Iowa, Aug. 18, 1970.

Jones, Asilee. Eudora, Ark., Aug. 22, 1970.

Lewis, Hugh. Keokuk, Iowa, Aug. 18, 1970.

Lewis, Walter "Furry." Memphis, Tenn., Aug. 20, 1970.

Lucas, William "Lazy Bill." Minneapolis, Minn., Aug. 13, 1968. A tape recording of the interview is on deposit at the John Edwards Memorial Foundation, UCLA.

———. Minneapolis, Minn., Apr. 29, 1969.

———. Minneapolis, Minn., July 7, 1970.

———. Minneapolis, Minn., Mar. 19, 1971.

McDowell, Fred. Minneapolis, Minn., July 21 and 23, 1970.

McGhee, Brownie. Chicago, Ill., ca. Jan. 30, 1970.

Martin, Carl. Chicago, Ill., ca. Jan. 31, 1970.

———. Lexington, Mass., June 16, 1973.

Randall, Lily. Beulah, Miss., Aug. 23, 1970.

Richardson, Velma. Sikeston, Mo., Aug. 19, 1970.

Rogers, Bud. Benoit, Miss., Aug. 23, 1970.

Rogers, Sam. Cleveland, Miss., Aug. 24, 1970.

Turner, C. P. Sondheimer, La., Aug. 21, 1970.

Walker, Carrie. New Madrid, Mo., Aug. 19, 1970.

Webb, Annie Mae. Memphis, Tenn., Aug. 20, 1970.

Webb, George. Memphis, Tenn., Aug. 20, 1970.

White, Leola Murphy. Memphis, Tenn., Aug. 20, 1970.

Wilcher, Willis. Attalla, Ala., Aug. 26, 1970.

Wilkins, Rev. Robert. Minneapolis, Minn., ca. Feb. 15, 1970.

Williams, John. Lake Providence, La., Aug. 21, 1970.

Williams, Joseph "Jo Jo." Minneapolis, Minn., Aug. 20, 1968. A tape recording of the interview is on deposit at the John Edwards Memorial Foundation, UCLA.

Williams, Robert Pete. Minneapolis, Minn., ca. Feb. 15, 1970.

Recordings

The standard discography for downhome (and vaudeville) blues records recorded before World War II is John Godrich and Robert M. W. Dixon's *Blues and Gospel Records, 1902–1942*, 2nd ed. (London: Storyville Publications, 1969). It is presently out of print. A third edition is in preparation.

Although the original 78 rpm downhome blues phonograph records from the 1920s are now rare, some may still be found by canvassing. A majority have been reissued on long-playing record albums by the following companies:

> Biograph Records, P.O. Box 109, Canaan, N.Y. 12029
>
> Origin Jazz Library, P.O. Box 863, Berkeley, Calif. 94701
>
> RBF Records, 701 Seventh Ave., New York, N.Y. 10036
>
> Roots Records, P.O. Box 17, 2345 Brunn am Gebirge, Austria
>
> Yazoo Records, 245 Waverly Place, New York, N.Y. 10014

Inquiries to these companies requesting a catalog and the name of the nearest supply house will receive prompt attention. Mail-order houses advertise in the two leading blues research periodicals, *Blue Unlimited* (8 Brandram Road, Lewisham, London, SE13 5EA, England) and *Living Blues* (P.O. Box 11303, Chicago, Ill. 60611). It should also be noted that the Archive of Folk Song (Library of Congress, Washington, D.C. 20540) includes the most recent addresses of these and other companies on its "List of Some American Record Companies Specializing in Folk Music."

Periodicals Consulted

BU   *Blues Unlimited.* No. 4 (Aug., 1963)– No. 100 (Apr., 1973). 36 Belmont Park, Lewisham, London SE13 5DB, England.

BW   *Blues World.* No. 6 (Jan., 1966)–No. 44 (Autumn, 1972). Now defunct.

CD   *Chicago Defender.* Apr. 2, 1921–Nov. 15, 1930.

JEMFN *JEMF Newsletter.* 1, pt. 1 [no. 1] (Oct., 1965)–4, pt. 4 [no. 12] (Dec., 1968). Continued by the *JEMFQ.*

JEMFQ *JEMF Quarterly.* 5, pt. 1 [no. 13] (Spring, 1969)–9, pt. 1 [no. 29] (Spring, 1973). John Edwards Memorial Foundation, Folklore and Mythology Center, University of California, Los Angeles, Calif. 90024.

LB   *Living Blues.* No. 1 (Spring, 1970)–No. 12 (Spring, 1973). 2615 N. Wilton Ave., Chicago, Ill. 60614.

OTM *Old Time Music.* No. 1 (Summer, 1971)– No. 8 (Spring, 1973). 33 Brunswick Gardens, London W8 4AW, England.

Books and Articles

Abrahams, Roger D. *Positively Black.* Englewood Cliffs, N.J.: Prentice-Hall, 1970.

Agriculture Yearbook 1923. Washington, D.C.: U.S. Department of Agriculture, 1924.

Albertson, Chris. *Bessie.* New York: Stein and Day, 1972.

———. Liner notes to Columbia G 30450, *Empty Bed Blues.* 2 12" LPs.

Allen, William F., Charles P. Ware, and Lucy M. Garrison. *Slave Songs of the United States.* 1867. Reprinted, Freeport, N.Y.: Books for Libraries, 1971.

Asch, Moses, and Alan Lomax, eds. *The Leadbelly Songbook.* New York: Oak Publications, 1962.

Baldwin, James. *Go Tell It on the Mountain.* 1953. Reprinted, New York: Dell Publishing Co., 1970.

———. *The Struggle.* Buddah 2004. 12" LP.

Barrow, David C. "A Georgia Plantation." *Scribner's Monthly* 21 (Apr., 1881), 830–36.

Bastin, Bruce. *Crying for the Carolines.* London: Studio Vista, 1971.

———, and Pete Lowry. "Blues from the Southeast." *BU,* no. 67 (Nov., 1969), pp. 4–6; no. 68 (Dec., 1969), pp. 7–8; no. 69 (Jan., 1970), pp. 8– 9; no. 70 (Feb.–Mar., 1970), pp. 7–8; no. 71 (Apr., 1970), pp. 7–8; no. 72 (May, 1970), pp. 4– 6; no. 73 (June, 1970), pp. 4–5; no. 77 (Nov., 1970), pp. 14–15; no. 78 (Dec., 1970), p. 11; no. 79 (Jan., 1971), p. 13; no. 80 (Feb.–Mar., 1971), p. 15; no. 81 (Apr., 1971), p. 14.

Bayard, Samuel. "Prolegomena to a Study of the Principal Melodic Families of British-American Folk Song." *Journal of American Folklore* 63 (Jan.–Mar., 1950), 1–44. Reprinted in *Readings in Ethnomusicology,* edited by David McAllester, pp. 65–109. New York: Johnson Reprint Corp., 1971.

Beard, Charles A., and Mary R. Beard. *America at Midpassage.* New York: Macmillan Co., 1939.

———. *The Rise of American Civilization.* 1927. Reprinted, New York: Macmillan Co., 1930.

Blesh, Rudi, and Harriet Janis. *They All Played Ragtime,* 2nd ed. New York: Oak Publications, 1966.

Boerger, E. A., and E. A. Goldenweiser. *A Study of the Tenant Systems of Farming in the Yazoo-*

Mississippi Delta. U.S. Department of Agriculture Bulletin No. 337. Washington, D.C., 1916.

Bradford, Perry. *Born with the Blues.* New York: Oak Publications, 1965.

Brandfon, Robert L. *Cotton Kingdom of the New South: A History of the Yazoo Mississippi Delta from Reconstruction to the Twentieth Century.* Cambridge, Mass.: Harvard University Press, 1967.

Brewster, Arthur Judson, and Herbert Hall Palmer. *Introduction to Advertising,* 2nd ed. New York: McGraw-Hill, 1935.

Bronson, Bertrand H. "Two Reviews: Frank Brown and North Carolina Folklore." *Virginia Quarterly* 29 (Winter, 1953), 146–52, and 34 (Summer, 1958), 474–80. Reprinted in Bronson, *The Ballad as Song,* pp. 211–23. Berkeley and Los Angeles: University of California Press, 1969.

Bruynoghe, Yannick. *Big Bill Blues: Big Bill Broonzy's Story as Told to Yannick Bruynoghe.* 1955. Reprinted, New York: Oak Publications, 1964.

Calt, Stephen. Brochure notes to Origin Jazz Library OJL-14, *Alabama Country.* 12" LP.

Cather, Pat. "Birmingham Blues: The Story of Jaybird Coleman." *Music Memories* [Birmingham, Ala.] (Sept., 1962). Reprinted in *Back Woods Blues,* compiled by Simon Napier, pp. 5–7. Bexhill-on-Sea, Sussex: Blues Unlimited, 1968.

Charley Patton. Blues World Booklet No. 2. Cheshire: Blues World, 1969.

Charters, Samuel. *The Bluesmen: The Story and the Music of the Men Who Made the Blues.* New York: Oak Publications, 1967.

———. *The Country Blues.* New York: Holt, Rinehart, and Winston, 1959.

———. *The Poetry of the Blues.* New York: Oak Publications, 1963.

———. Brochure notes to RBF 1, *The Country Blues.* 12" LP.

———. Brochure notes to RBF 5, *An Introduction to Gospel Song.* 12" LP.

———. Brochure notes to RBF 15, *The Atlanta Blues.* 12" LP.

Chase, Gilbert. *America's Music: From the Pilgrims to the Present,* rev. 2nd ed. New York: McGraw-Hill, 1966.

Chomsky, Noam. *Cartesian Linguistics.* New York: Harper & Row, 1966.

———. *Language and Mind,* enl. ed. New York: Harcourt Brace Jovanovich, 1972.

Cohen, Norm. "'I'm a Record Man': Uncle Art Satherley Reminisces." *JEMFQ* 8 (Spring, 1972), 18–21.

Courlander, Harold. *Negro Folk Music, U.S.A.* 1963. Reprinted, New York: Columbia University Press, 1970.

Cronon, Edmund David. *Black Moses: The Story of Marcus Garvey and the Universal Negro Improvement Association.* Madison: University of Wisconsin Press, 1968.

Dickins, Dorothy. *A Nutrition Investigation of Negro Tenants in the Yazoo-Mississippi Delta.* Mississippi Agricultural Experiment Station Bulletin No. 254. A. & M. College, Miss., Aug., 1928.

Dixon, Robert M. W., and John Godrich. *Recording the Blues.* London: Studio Vista, 1970.

Drake, St. Clair, and Horace R. Cayton. *Black Metropolis: A Study of Negro Life in a Northern City,* Vol. 1. 1945. Reprinted, New York: Harper & Row, 1962.

Epstein, Jerome. Liner notes to Yazoo L-1010, *Buddy Boy Hawkins and His Buddies.* 12" LP.

Evans, David. "Africa and the Blues." *LB,* no. 10 (Autumn, 1972), pp. 27–29.

———. "Afro-American One-Stringed Instruments." *Western Folklore* 29 (Oct., 1970), 229–45.

———. "Babe Stovall." In *Back Woods Blues,* compiled by Simon Napier, pp. 50–55. Bexhill-on-Sea, Sussex: Blues Unlimited, 1968.

———. "Blues on Dockery's Plantation, 1895 to 1967." *BU,* no. 49 (Jan., 1968), pp. 3–4; no. 50 (Feb., 1968), pp. 14–15.

———. "Booker White." *BU,* no. 36 (Sept., 1966), pp. 11–12; no. 37 (Oct., 1966), pp. 7–9; no. 38 (Nov., 1966), pp. 6–7; no. 39 (Dec., 1966), p. 13.

———. "Charley Patton's Life and Music." In *Charley Patton,* Blues World Booklet No. 2, pp. 3–7. Cheshire: Blues World, 1969.

———. "An Interview with H. C. Speir." *JEMFQ* 8 (Autumn, 1972), 117–21.

———. "The Rev. Rubin Lacy." *BU,* no. 40 (Jan., 1967), pp. 3–4; no. 41 (Feb., 1967), pp. 8–9; no. 42 (Mar.–Apr., 1967), pp. 5–6; no. 43 (May, 1967), pp. 13–14; no. 44 (June–July, 1967), p. 7.

———. "Roosevelt Holts." *BW,* no. 15 (July, 1967), p. 4.

————. *Tommy Johnson*. London: Studio Vista, 1971.

————. Liner notes to Origin Jazz Library OJL-17, *The Mississippi Blues, No. 3*. 12" LP.

————. Liner notes to Testament T-2222, *It Must Have Been the Devil*. 12" LP.

————. Liner notes to Yazoo L-1007, *Jackson Blues, 1928–1938*. 12" LP.

Fahey, John. *Charley Patton*. London: Studio Vista, 1970.

Farley, Reynolds. "The Quality of Demographic Data for Nonwhites." *Demography* 5 (1968), 1–10.

Federal Writers' Project of the Works Progress Administration. *Mississippi*. American Guide Series. 1938. Reprinted, New York: Hastings House, 1949.

Ferris, William, Jr. *Blues from the Delta*. London: Studio Vista, 1971.

————. "Racial Repertoires among Blues Performers." *Ethnomusicology* 14 (Sept., 1970), 439–49.

Fleder, Robert. Liner notes to County 523, *Old-Time Mountain Guitar*. 12" LP.

Foreman, Ronald C., Jr. "Jazz and Race Records, 1920–1932." Ph.D. diss., University of Illinois, 1968.

Foster, George M. "What Is Folk Culture?" *American Anthropologist* 55 (Apr.–June, 1953), 159–73.

Frazier, E. Franklin. *The Negro Church in America*. 1964. Reprinted, New York: Schocken Books, 1966.

"Fred McDowell Talks to Pete Welding." In *Back Woods Blues*, compiled by Simon Napier, pp. 8–9. Bexhill-on-Sea, Sussex: Blues Unlimited, 1968.

Garon, Paul. *The Devil's Son-in-Law: The Story of Peetie Wheatstraw and His Songs*. London: Studio Vista, 1971.

Gelatt, Roland C. *The Fabulous Phonograph*. Philadelphia: J. B. Lippincott, 1955.

Godrich, John, and Robert M. W. Dixon. *Blues and Gospel Records, 1902–1942*, 2nd ed. London: Storyville Publications, 1969.

Green, Archie. "Commercial Music Graphics: One." *JEMFQ* 2 (June, 1967), 48–53. Continuing series.

————. "Hillbilly Music: Source and Symbol." *Journal of American Folklore* 78 (July–Sept., 1965), 204–28.

Groom, Bob. "Big Bill Broonzy." *BW*, no. 33 (Aug., 1970), pp. 7–9.

————. *Blind Lemon Jefferson*. Blues World Booklet No. 3. Cheshire: Blues World, 1970.

————. "The Georgia Blues, Part 7." *BW*, no. 17 (Nov., 1967), p. 3.

————. "The Legacy of Blind Lemon." *BW*, no. 18 (Jan., 1968), pp. 14–16; no. 21 (Oct., 1968), pp. 30–32; no. 23 (Apr., 1969), pp. 5–7; no. 24 (July, 1969), pp. 9–10; no. 25 (Oct., 1969), pp. 9–10; no. 27 (Feb., 1970), pp. 13–14; no. 28 (Mar., 1970), pp. 8–9; no. 29 (Apr., 1970), pp. 8–9; no. 30 (May, 1970), pp. 13–14; no. 35 (Oct., 1970), pp. 19–20.

Gruver, Rod. "The Autobiographical Theory Re-Examined." *JEMFQ* 6 (Autumn, 1970), 129–32.

————. "The Blues as a Secular Religion." *BW*, no. 29 (Apr., 1970), pp. 3–6; no. 30 (May, 1970), pp. 4–7; no. 31 (June, 1970), pp. 5–7; no. 32 (July, 1970), pp. 7–9.

————. "The Blues as Dramatic Monologues." *JEMFQ* 6 (Spring, 1970), 28–31.

————. "A Closer Look at the Blues." *BW*, no. 26 (Jan., 1970), pp. 4–10.

————. "The Funny Blues: Cryin' Just to Keep from Laughin'." *BW*, no. 33 (Aug., 1970), pp. 19–20; no. 34 (Sept., 1970), pp. 19–21; no. 35 (Oct., 1970), pp. 20–21.

Guralnick, Peter. *Feel Like Going Home: Portraits in Blues and Rock 'n' Roll*. New York: Outerbridge & Dienstfrey, 1971.

Handy, W. C. *Father of the Blues: An Autobiography by W. C. Handy*, edited by Arna Bontemps. 1941. Reprinted, New York: Collier Books, 1970.

————, ed. *Blues: An Anthology*. 1926. Rev. ed. as *A Treasury of the Blues*. 1949. Revised by Jerry Silverman as *Blues: An Anthology*. New York: Macmillan Co., 1972.

Hansen, Chadwick. "Social Influences on Jazz Style." *American Quarterly* 12 (Winter, 1960), 493–507.

Hayakawa, S. I. "Popular Songs vs. the Facts of Life." *Etc.* 12 (Winter, 1955), 83–95. Reprinted in *Mass Culture*, edited by Bernard Rosenberg and David Manning White, pp. 393–403. New York: Free Press, 1964.

Haynes, George E. "Negro Migration: Its Effect on Family and Community Life in the North."

Opportunity 2 (Sept., 1924), 271–74; 2 (Oct., 1924), 303–6.

Higgins, Humphrey. Liner notes to Yazoo L-1006, *The Blues of Alabama.* 12" LP.

Hollander, John. *The Untuning of the Sky.* 1961. Reprinted, New York: W. W. Norton, 1970.

Hotchkiss, George Burton. *Advertising Copy.* New York: Harper & Brothers, 1924.

Hughes, Langston. "The Negro Artist and the Racial Mountain." *Nation,* June 16, 1926, pp. 692–94.

Hurston, Zora Neale. *Mules and Men.* 1935. Reprinted, New York: Harper & Row, Perennial Library, 1970.

Jackson, Bruce, ed. *The Negro and His Folklore in Nineteenth-Century Periodicals.* Austin: University of Texas Press, 1967.

Johnson, Charles S. *Growing Up in the Black Belt: Negro Youth in the Rural South.* 1941. Reprinted, New York: Schocken Books, 1967.

———. "The Negro Migration: An Economic Interpretation." *Modern Quarterly* 2 (1924–25), 314–26.

———. *Shadow of the Plantation.* 1934. Reprinted, Chicago: University of Chicago Press, 1966.

Johnson, James Weldon. *God's Trombones: Seven Negro Sermons in Verse.* 1927. Reprinted, New York: Viking Press, 1969.

Jones, LeRoi [Imamu Amiri Baraka]. *Blues People.* New York: William Morrow, 1963.

Keil, Charles. *Urban Blues.* Chicago: University of Chicago Press, 1966.

Klinger, Eric. *Structure and Functions of Fantasy.* New York: John Wiley & Sons, 1971.

Krehbiel, Henry Edward. *Afro-American Folksongs.* New York: G. Schirmer, 1914.

The Latest Blues by Columbia Race Stars. New York: Columbia Phonograph Co., May, 1927.

Laws, G. Malcolm, Jr. *Native American Balladry,* rev. ed. Philadelphia: American Folklore Society, 1964.

Leadbitter, Mike, "My Girlish Days." *BU,* no. 78 (Dec., 1970), pp. 8–9.

Lomax, Alan. "The Evolutionary Taxonomy of Culture." *Science,* July 21, 1972, pp. 228–39.

———. "Folk Song Style." *American Anthropologist* 61 (Dec., 1959), 927–54.

———. *Folk Song Style and Culture.* Washington: American Association for the Advancement of Science, 1968.

———. "The Homogeneity of African-Afro-American Musical Style." In *Afro-American Anthropology,* edited by Norman E. Whitten and John Szwed, pp. 181–201. New York: Free Press, 1970.

———. *Mister Jelly Roll.* 1950. 2nd ed. Berkeley and Los Angeles: University of California Press, 1973.

———. "Song Structure and Social Structure." *Ethnology* 1 (Oct., 1962), 425–51.

Lord, Albert B. *The Singer of Tales.* 1960. Reprinted, New York: Atheneum Publishers, 1965.

Lowry, Pete. "Some Cold Rainy Day." *BU,* no. 103 (Aug.–Sept., 1973), p. 15.

McCormick, Mack. "Mance Lipscomb: Texas Sharecropper and Songster." In *American Folk Music Occasional,* No. 1, edited by Chris Strachwitz, pp. 61–73. Berkeley: Chris Strachwitz, 1964.

McIlwaine, Shields. *The Southern Poor-White: From Lubberland to Tobacco Road.* Norman: University of Oklahoma Press, 1939.

Mahony, Dan. *The Columbia 13/14000-D Series: A Numerical Listing,* 2nd ed. Stanhope, N.J.: Walter C. Allen, 1966.

Malone, Bill C. *Country Music, U.S.A.: A Fifty-Year History.* Austin: University of Texas Press, 1968.

Marden, S. G. "Phonograph Books Have New Motif." *Printers Ink Monthly* 1 (Apr. 20, 1920).

Marx, Leo. *The Machine in the Garden: Technology and the Pastoral Ideal in America.* New York: Oxford University Press, 1964.

Melrose, Lester. "My Life in Recording." In *American Folk Music Occasional* [No. 2], edited by Chris Strachwitz and Pete Welding, pp. 59–61. New York: Oak Publications, 1970.

Merriam, Alan P. *The Anthropology of Music.* Evanston, Ill.: Northwestern University Press, 1964.

Metfessel, Milton. *Phonophotography in Folk Music.* Chapel Hill: University of North Carolina Press, 1928.

Mitchell, George. "I'm Peg Leg Howell." *BU,* no. 10 (Mar., 1964), p. 7.

———. Liner notes to Testament T-2204, *The Legendary Peg Leg Howell.* 12" LP.

Moore, Alex. "Letter from Dallas." *BW,* no. 6 (Jan., 1966), pp. 3–5.

Morrow, Ed. "Skip James Talkin'." *BU*, no. 22 (May, 1965), pp. 3–4; no. 23 (June, 1965), p. 11; no. 28 (Dec., 1965), pp. 17–18; no. 29 (Jan., 1966), p. 19.

Mossel, Eric. "Every Day I Heard the Blues." *BW*, no. 8 (May, 1966), pp. 11–18.

Murdock, George Peter. *Ethnographic Atlas.* Pittsburgh: University of Pittsburgh Press, 1967.

Napier, Simon. "Cryin' Mama, Mama, Mama. . . ." *BU*, no. 30 (Feb., 1966), pp. 14–15.

Nettl, Bruno. *Theory and Method in Ethnomusicology.* New York: Free Press, 1964.

Niles, Abbe. Introduction to *Blues: An Anthology,* edited by W. C. Handy. 1926. Reprinted as "The Blues" in *Frontiers of Jazz,* edited by Ralph de Toledano. 1947. Revised as "The Story of the Blues," foreword to *A Treasury of the Blues,* edited by W. C. Handy. New York: Charles Boni, 1949.

Noblett, Richard. "American Folk Blues Festival 1968." *BW*, no. 23 (Apr., 1969), p. 10.

Odum, Howard. "Folk-Song and Folk-Poetry as Found in the Secular Songs of the Southern Negroes." *Journal of American Folklore* 24 (July–Sept., 1911), 255–94; 24 (Oct.–Dec., 1911), 351–96.

———, and Guy B. Johnson. *The Negro and His Songs.* 1925. Reprinted, Hatboro, Pa.: Folklore Associates, 1964.

———. *Negro Workaday Songs.* Chapel Hill: University of North Carolina Press, 1926.

Oliver, Paul. *Bessie Smith.* 1959. Reprinted, New York: A. S. Barnes, 1961.

———. *Blues Fell This Morning.* 1960. Reprinted as *The Meaning of the Blues.* New York: Collier Books, 1963.

———. *Conversation with the Blues.* London: Cassell, 1965.

———. "Echoes of the Jungle." *LB*, no. 13 (Summer, 1973), pp. 29–32.

———. *Savannah Syncopators: African Retentions in the Blues.* London: Studio Vista, 1970.

———. *Screening the Blues: Aspects of the Blues Tradition.* London: Cassell, 1968.

———. "Some Comments: African Influence and the Blues." *LB*, no. 8 (Spring, 1972), pp. 13–17.

———. *The Story of the Blues.* 1969. Reprinted, New York: Chilton Books, 1974.

———. Liner notes to *Juke Joint Blues.* Blues Classics BC-23. 12" LP.

Olmsted, Frederick Law. *Journey in the Seaboard Slave States.* New York: Dix and Edwards, 1856.

Olson, Charles. "Projective Verse." *Poetry New York,* No. 3 (1950). Reprinted in *Charles Olson: Selected Writings,* edited by Robert Creeley, pp. 15–26. New York: New Directions, 1966.

Olsson, Bengt. "Ed Bell." *LB*, no. 11 (Winter, 1972–73), p. 31.

———. *Memphis Blues and Jug Bands.* London: Studio Vista, 1970.

The Paramount Book of Blues. Port Washington, Wis.: New York Recording Laboratories, 1927.

Paulson, Gary. "J. R. Fulbright Interviewed." *BU*, no. 51 (Mar., 1968), pp. 6–9.

[Perls, Nick.] "Scenes." *Village Voice,* May 8, 1969, p. 27.

Powdermaker, Hortense. *After Freedom: A Cultural Study in the Deep South.* 1939. Reprinted, New York: Atheneum Publishers, 1968.

———. *Stranger and Friend: The Way of an Anthropologist.* New York: W. W. Norton, 1966.

Raper, Arthur F. *Preface to Peasantry: A Tale of Two Black Belt Counties.* 1936. Reprinted, New York: Atheneum Publishers, 1968.

Redfield, Robert. "The Folk Society." *American Journal of Sociology* 52 (Jan., 1947), 293–308.

Roche, Jacques [Stephen Calt]. "Henry Stuckey: An Obituary." *78 Quarterly* 1, no. 2 (1968).

Rosenberg, Bruce. *The Art of the American Folk Preacher.* New York: Oxford University Press, 1970.

Rounder Collective. "The Life of Blind Alfred Reed." *JEMFQ* 7 (Autumn, 1971), 113–15.

Russell, Tony. *Blacks, Whites and Blues.* London: Studio Vista, 1970.

———. "Key to the Bushes." *BU*, no. 67 (Nov., 1969), p. 19.

———. "OTM Transcription: Spanish Fandango." *OTM*, no. 6 (Autumn, 1972), p. 12.

Rust, Brian. *The Victor Master Book, Vol. 2: 1925–1935.* Hatch End, Middlesex: By the author, 1969.

Sackheim, Eric, and Jonathan Shahn. *The Blues Line: A Collection of Blues Lyrics.* New York: Grossman Publishers, 1969.

Sargeant, Winthrop. *Jazz: Hot and Hybrid.* 1938. Revised and reprinted as *Jazz: A History.* New York: McGraw-Hill, 1964.

Scarborough, Dorothy. *On the Trail of Negro Folk-*

Songs. Cambridge, Mass.: Harvard University Press, 1925.

Scheidt, Duncan. Liner notes to Columbia CL-1799, *Blues before Sunrise*. 12" LP. Reissued as Columbia C 30496, with abridged liner notes.

Shirley, Kay, ed. *The Book of the Blues*. New York: MCA Music, 1963.

Smith, Harry. Brochure notes to Folkways FA 2951, *American Folk Music, Vol. 1: Ballads*. 2 12" LPs.

Snyder, Howard. "Traits of My Plantation Negroes." *Century Magazine* 102 (July, 1921), 367–76.

Southern Eileen. *The Music of Black Americans: A History*. New York: W. W. Norton, 1971.

Spivey, Victoria. "Blind Lemon and I Had a Ball." *Record Research*, no. 76 (May, 1966), p. 9.

Spottswood, Richard K. "Rev. Robert Wilkins." *BU*, no. 13 (July, 1964), p. 5.

Stearns, Marshall, and Jean Stearns. *Jazz Dance: The Story of American Vernacular Dance*. New York: Macmillan Co., 1968.

Stewart, Mike, and Stephen Calt. Liner notes to Yazoo L-1036, *Leroy Carr and Scrapper Blackwell*. 12" LP.

Stewart-Baxter, Derrick. *Ma Rainey and the Classic Blues Singers*. London: Studio Vista, 1970.

Strachwitz, Chris. "An Interview with the Staples Family." In *American Folk Music Occasional*, No. 1, edited by Chris Strachwitz, pp. 13–17. Berkeley: Chris Strachwitz, 1964.

Summers, Lynn S. "African Influence and the Blues: An Interview with Richard A. Waterman." *LB*, no. 6 (Autumn, 1971), pp. 30–36.

Taft, Michael. "'I Woke Up This Morning': A Transformational-Generative Approach to the Formulaic Structure of Blues Lyrics." Paper presented at the 1972 Annual Meeting of the American Folklore Society, Austin, Tex., Nov. 16, 1972.

Titon, Jeff. "All Pretty Wimmens: The Story of Jo Jo Williams." *BU*, no. 64 (July, 1969), pp. 13–14; no. 65 (Sept., 1969), pp. 13–14.

———. "Autobiography and Blues Texts." *JEMFQ* 6 (Summer, 1970), 79–82.

———. "'Calling All Cows': Lazy Bill Lucas." *BU*, no. 60 (Mar., 1969), pp. 10–11; no. 61 (Apr., 1969), pp. 9–10; no. 62 (May, 1969), pp. 11–12; no. 63 (June, 1969), pp. 9–10.

———. "Ethnomusicology of Downhome Blues Phonograph Records, 1926–1930." Ph.D. diss., University of Minnesota, 1971.

———. *From Blues to Pop: The Autobiography of Leonard "Baby Doo" Caston*. JEMF Special Series, No. 4. Los Angeles: John Edwards Memorial Foundation, 1974.

———. "Mojo Buford." *BU*, no. 76 (Oct., 1970), pp. 13–14; no. 77 (Nov., 1970), pp. 9–10; no. 78 (Dec., 1970), pp. 14–15.

———. "Structure and Function in Blues and Black Preaching." Paper delivered at Franconia College, Franconia, N.H., Oct. 20, 1972.

———. Review of *Charley Patton*, by John Fahey. *JEMFQ* 7 (Winter, 1971), 192–95.

———. Review of *Blow My Blues Away*, by George Mitchell. *BW*, no. 42 (Spring, 1972), p. 15.

———. Review of *Tommy Johnson*, by David Evans. *JEMFQ* 8 (Autumn, 1972), 168–70.

———. Liner notes to Philo LP 1007, *Lazy Bill Lucas*. 12" LP.

Travers, Tony. "Lyric Transcript No. 17." *BW*, no. 34 (Sept., 1970), p. 21.

U.S. Census of Agriculture: 1910. Vol. 5. Washington, D.C.: U.S. Bureau of the Census 1911.

Ward, John William. "The Meaning of Lindbergh's Flight." *American Quarterly* 10 (Spring, 1958), 3–16.

Wardlow, Gayle Dean. "Legends of the Lost: The Story of Henry Speir." In *Back Woods Blues*, compiled by Simon Napier, pp. 25–28. Bexhill-on-Sea, Sussex: Blues Unlimited, 1968.

Waterman, Richard Alan. "African Influence on the Music of the Americas." In *Acculturation in the Americas*, edited by Sol Tax, pp. 207–18. Chicago: University of Chicago Press, 1952.

Welding, Pete. "David 'Honeyboy' Edwards." *BU*, no. 54 (June, 1968), pp. 3–12.

———. "Henry Townsend." *BU*, no. 57 (Nov., 1968), pp. 11–12.

———. "Howlin' Wolf." *BU*, no. 59 (Jan., 1969), pp. 4–5.

———. "An Interview with Carl Martin." *78 Quarterly* 1, no. 2 (1968).

———. "Reverend Robert Wilkins: An Interview." *BU*, no. 51 (Mar., 1968), pp. 14–15; no. 52 (Apr., 1968), pp. 3–4; no. 53 (May, 1968), pp. 5–7; no. 54 (June, 1968), p. 14; no. 55 (July, 1968), pp. 11–12; no. 56 (Sept., 1968), pp. 12–13.

————. "Tapescripts: Interview with Rev. Robert Wilkins." *JEMFN* 2 (1967), 54–60.

Whelan, Pete. Brochure notes to Origin Jazz Library OJL-10, *Crying Sam Collins and His Git-Fiddle.* 12" LP.

White, Newman I. *American Negro Folk-Songs.* 1928. Reprinted, Hatboro, Pa.: Folklore Associates, 1965.

Wilson, Al. *Son House.* Collectors Classics, [booklet] 14. Bexhill-on-Sea, Sussex: Blues Unlimited, 1966.

Wolfe, Charles K. "Ralph Peer at Work." *OTM,* no. 5 (Summer, 1972), pp. 10–15.

Work, John W., ed. *American Negro Songs and Spirituals.* New York: Crown Publishers, 1940.

Wright, Richard. Foreword to *Blues Fell This Morning,* by Paul Oliver. London: Cassell, 1960.

Yates, Bob. "Sluefoot or Barefoot." *BW,* no. 7 (Mar., 1966), pp. 18–21.

zur Heide, Karl Gert. *Deep South Piano.* London: Studio Vista, 1970.

————. "Memphis Piano." *BU,* no. 69 (Jan., 1970), pp. 14–15, 18–19.

INDEX

Pruitt, Milas, 99
Pruitt, Miles, 99

Race records: as industry category, xv, 201, 232
Racism, 221, 223, 236, 275; and advertisements, 221, 232, 257
Ragtime songs, 23, 61, 74, 146, 147; defined, 295 (n. 2)
Rainey, Gertrude "Ma," xvii, 23, 43, 44, 60, 99–100, 202–4, 205, 280
Rainey, William "Pa," 100
Range: of voice, 47; used by Bessie Smith, 107; of downhome blues songs, 152–54
Record companies: attitudes of, toward blacks, xvi–xvii; Blind Lemon Jefferson considered model singer by, 59–60, 207, 210; finances of, 200, 210–11; scouting and field trips by, 207, 210–13; criteria of, for recording downhome blues singers, 213; treatment of downhome blues singers by, 213–17; atmosphere in studios of, 215–16. See also Advertisements; Blues records; Records
Records: influence of, on blues style, 38–39, 43, 48, 211; pre-1920 black music on, 196; black middle-class attitudes toward, 196, 198–99. See also Blues records
Reed, Blind Alfred, 214
Rhodes, Walter, 66
Rhyme. See Lyrics
Rhythmic organization, 144–52
Rockwell, T. G., 214
Rodgers, Jimmie, 302 (n. 56)
Rogers, Sonny Boy, 263
Roles of musicians, 53–55
"Roll and Tumble Blues" (transcr. 37), 121–22, 165, 296 (chap. 4, n. 4), 297 (n. 14)
"Rollin' and Tumblin'," 122
Rose, Bayless, 60, 71–72
"Rumblin' and Ramblin' Boa Constrictor Blues," 253–54

"Saddle My Pony," 65
"St. Louis Blues," xviii, 23–24
Satherley, Art, 216
Scale, 152–54
Sermons, 18, 25, 32, 205, 286–88
"She Rolls It Slow," 109
Shuffle Along, xvii
"The Siege of Sebastopol," 42
Signifying, 274

Skeletal tune: defined, 167; stress points in, 167–74; influence of, on lyric formulas, 176–77
"Slidin' Delta," 166
Sloan, Henry, 24, 290 (n. 9)
Smith, Bessie, xvii, 44, 51, 60, 104–7, 157, 165–66, 200, 202, 203, 211, 214, 229, 231, 235, 300 (n. 25)
Smith, Floyd, 48
Smith, Mamie, xvii, 199–200, 202, 228
Smith, Thunder, 102
"Somebody's Been Talkin'," 166
Song-producing model: demonstration of, 170–74
Songsters, 52
Sousa, John Philip, 194–95
"Southbound Blues," 89
"Spanish Fandango," 42
Spaulding, Henry, 128–29, 183
Spier, H. C., 212–13, 217
Spivey, Victoria, 28, 39
Square dances, 22
"Staggering Blues," 74
Stanzas: AAB, 22–25, 141–43; foundation, 33–34
Staples, Roebuck, 28
Stoneman, Ernest, 302 (n. 56)
Stovall, Babe, 33, 52
"Stove Pipe Blues," 301 (n. 47)
"Stranger Blues" (transcr. 4), 67–68, 165
"Sundown Blues," 301 (n. 47)
Sunnyland Slim. *See* Luandrew, Albert
"Sunshine Special" (transcr. 30), 109–11, 296 (chap. 4, n. 4)
Sykes, Roosevelt, 114–16, 157, 212, 213
Syncopation, 145–46, 151, 152. *See also* Polyrhythm

Talent scouts, 212–13
Tampa Red. *See* Whittaker, Hudson
"T.B. Blues," 39
"Teddy Bear Blues," 38
Temple, Johnny, 65
Tempo, 151
"That Will Be Alright" (transcr. 29), 60, 107–9, 143
Thomas, George W., 66
Thomas, Willard "Ramblin'," 42, 241, 246
Thompson, Ashley, 120
"Thought I Heard That K.C. Whistle Blow," 25
"Tom Rushen Blues," 71
Tourism: and blues, 275–78
Townsend, Henry, 97
Transcription: methods, 61–62; supplementary symbols, 62
Tune family, 297 (n. 15). *See also* Blues families

Tunes: constraints of, on texts, 168–70. *See also* Skeletal tune
Tunings: guitar, 42
"2:19 Blues," 25, 71

Urban blues, 182, 298–99 (n. 41)

"Vastapol," 42
Vaudeville blues, 23–24; distinguished from downhome blues, xv–xviii; influence of, on downhome singers, 43–46, 67, 107, 157; early recording history of, 199–200, 202–5
Vinson, Eddie "Cleanhead," 299 (n. 41)
Vocal quality: of vaudeville blues singers, xvii; of downhome blues singers, 47, 52, 143–44; of Bessie Smith, 204; of Ma Rainey, 204. *See also* Diction

Walker, Frank, 212, 213–14
Walker, Willie, 70–71
Wallace, Sippie, 67
Waters, Ethel, xvii, 4, 44

Weathersby, Alan, 53–54
Weaver, Sylvester, 301 (n. 47)
Welsh, Nolan "Barrel House Welch," 131
Wheatstraw, Peetie, 294 (n. 28)
"Whiskey Moan Blues" (transcr. 22), 96–97, 164
White, Booker T., 41, 214, 265, 280
Whittaker, Hudson (Tampa Red), 210, 211
Wilkins, Reverend Robert, 27, 32–33, 39, 46, 300 (n. 25)
Williams, Big Joe, 65, 97
Williams, George, 74
Williams, Joe (trombonist), 104, 106
Williams, Jo Jo, 3, 28, 33, 263, 264
Williams, Mayo, 221
Williams, Robert Pete, 41, 46
Williamson, John Lee "Sonny Boy," 109, 122, 211
Wilson, Edith, xvii
Worksongs, 21, 25, 136
"Writin' Paper Blues" (transcr. 40), 126, 151, 165
Wynn, Al, 204

"Yellow Girl Blues" (transcr. 48), 135–36, 165, 167